Culinary Nationalism in Asia

Also available from Bloomsbury

The Emergence of National Food, edited by Atsuko Ichijo,
Venetia Johannes, and Ronald Ranta
Making Taste Public, edited by Carole Counihan and Susanne Hojlund
Taste, Politics, and Identities in Mexican Food, edited by Steffan Igor Ayora-Diaz

Culinary Nationalism in Asia

Edited by Michelle T. King

BLOOMSBURY ACADEMIC
LONDON • NEW YORK • OXFORD • NEW DELHI • SYDNEY

BLOOMSBURY ACADEMIC
Bloomsbury Publishing Plc
50 Bedford Square, London, WC1B 3DP, UK
1385 Broadway, New York, NY 10018, USA
29 Earlsfort Terrace, Dublin 2, Ireland

BLOOMSBURY, BLOOMSBURY ACADEMIC and the Diana logo are trademarks of
Bloomsbury Publishing Plc

First published in Great Britain 2019
This paperback edition published in 2022

Cover design by Tjaša Krivec
Cover images: Food Maps of China, Japan and India
(© Kiwi and Eagle LLC / www.henryhargreaves.com)

A catalogue record for this book is available from the British Library.

Library of Congress Cataloging-in-Publication Data
Names: King, Michelle Tien, editor.
Title: Culinary nationalism in Asia / Michelle T. King (History, University of North Carolina
at Chapel Hill), editor.
Description: London, UK ; New York, NY : Bloomsbury Academic, 2019. |
Includes bibliographical references and index.
Identifiers: LCCN 2019002808 | ISBN 9781350078673 (hardback) |
ISBN 9781350078680 (ePDF) | ISBN 9781350078697 (ePUB)
Subjects: LCSH: Food habits–Asia. | Food–Asia. | Asians–Ethnic identity. | Cooking, Asian.
Classification: LCC GT2853.A78 C85 2019 | DDC 394.1/2095–dc23
LC record available at https://lccn.loc.gov/2019002808

ISBN: HB: 978-1-3500-7867-3
         PB: 978-1-3502-3686-8
       ePDF: 978-1-3500-7868-0
       ePub: 978-1-3500-7869-7

Typeset by RefineCatch Limited, Bungay, Suffolk

To find out more about our authors and books visit www.bloomsbury.com
and sign up for our newsletters.

Contents

Part Three Global Contexts

Figures

Maps

Foreword: Food in the Making and Unmaking of Asian Nationalisms

Krishnendu Ray
New York University

In Food Studies we know much about the North Atlantic and the Mediterranean worlds, and their settler colonial outposts, but relatively little about food cultures in other locations. This collection attempts to correct that imbalance by drawing us into the Pacific and the Indian Ocean worlds, and the spaces in between, by digging into sources in Mandarin, Japanese, Korean, Hindi, and of course English. To that vastly different spatial episteme, the editor Michelle T. King and a number of authors bring a distinctively different temporal frame that extends the analysis to before and after Euro-American hegemony. In the process, they give us the tools to critically interrogate the coming East Asian domination in capital and cultural accumulation.

The book's central organizing principle is the narration of the relationship between taste, territory, and power. It provides insights in at least four directions. First, that what humans eat, and how they cook and process their food, depends on where they are, where they have moved from, and where they want to move to, spatially and socially. It is about geography and history and as much about social location as aspiration. Second, what social groups eat, value, and despise partly depends on what their neighbors, superiors, and inferiors eat, value, and despise. Sometimes they borrow from each other, sometimes they refuse to do that for religious, racial, class, national, or ethnic reasons. Third, what people eat and consider materially and symbolically important is brimming with memories—good and ugly—and riddled with forgetfulness. Groups and individuals are good at memorializing much of their long-developed practices, often embodied with their palates and hands, but they are also good at faking genealogies and ignoring what is in front of their faces. Remembering is always laced with forgetting. Fourth, people's eating and drinking practices—and all the talking, writing, and image-making about them—are shaped by small-scale institutions of home-building and community-making, and large-scale institutions such as nations, schools, militaries, mass media, and corporations. Each chapter in this collection adjusts the temporal and scalar frame to highlight an aspect of cooking and consumption that might not have been visible when regarded from another level or different time period. The book as a whole is a lovely example of what comes into view and what vanishes when we change the time-space of our analysis.

Almost every chapter is analytically comparative forcing the reader to attend to processes of nation-making rather than assume a standard national cuisine. Every cuisine is merely the claim of some people, from some region, which highlights their own food, while erasing, marginalizing, and misrepresenting culinary cultures of the margins and minorities. Certain kinds of nationalist historical claims are riddled with amnesia of the state of affairs in other time periods. A good example of such a critique is Eric Rath's chapter, which severely undermines the conflation of rurality with contemporary Japanese national cuisine—*washoku* or *Nihon ryōri*—so piously peddled by chefs, restaurant critics, and ideologues East and West. He posits other models of urban and cosmopolitan culinary standards that were superseded when *washoku* was inscribed in the Representative List of the Intangible Culinary Heritage of Humanity by UNESCO in 2013. Here, East and West colluded to produce an exotic, rural, and settled Orient. Instead, Rath concludes: "The fact that today the category of 'cuisine' is so closely defined according to national boundaries provides all the more reason to return to the ideas of Murai Gensai, who imagined creating an international cuisine that would be elegant, healthy, and would bring people of different nationalities together to collaborate as cooks and as eaters." That is a lesson worth learning in this age of revanchist nationalism.

The most virulent form of food-based ethno-nationalism is on display in contemporary India, where Muslims and Dalits (lower castes and outcastes) are lynched for mere rumors of beef consumption. Michaël Bruckert shows how that might be both an expression of a deep-rooted value system in which good taste is immediately transformed into the moral proposition (you are what you eat) and the result of recent political mobilization by Hindu nationalists. That is the dark side of routinely turning questions of palatal aesthetics (what you love to eat) into ethics (what you ought to eat)—the very thing that food movements are trying to achieve in the West, which Western progressives should find troubling. In India, the dangerous consequences of such quarrels are the further marginalization of people on the territorial and social margins: Dalits and Muslims who are butchers, leather-workers, fisher-folks; tribals from the plateaus and the forests, distant from the plains; Christians from the northeastern mountains; and Hindus far from the heartland who *do* eat meat. Rachel Berger underlines the trouble with a Hindu nation imagined exclusively as of the middle class in her analysis of cookbooks and commercial advertisements. It is a class fed by a normative servant-wife complex of cookery and caregiving, whereby the servant is written out, the housewife elevated and imprisoned as the new anchor of domestic modernity, and the food advanced as some authentically indigenous substance, that imparts a moral trajectory for the production of virulent Hindu boys.

Michelle E. Bloom focuses on the inverse process in her chapter on films by the Malaysian-Taiwanese auteur Tsai Ming-liang, which resists both the culinary and the national in his slow-moving long-shots that hinge on hungers, rather than the pleasures of consumption. Food is in this instance a means to repel a distinctive identity. Analogously, Daniel E. Bender shows how a cuisine can be produced without a country, as in Trader Vic's make-believe Polynesian food that married pineapples and papayas to Continental dishes and Chinese-American standards. He links the birth of the "Polynesian" fantasy among Americans to the postwar geopolitics of army bases and tourist resorts that made distinctions between "mainland" and "island" as a form of political-ecological classification of race, nation, and territory, "submerging Pacific cultures and sovereignties in a sea of rum and soy sauce."

With Jean Duruz's chapter on *laksa* we travel away from no identity, or fake imperial identity, to the Asian-ness of Adelaide and Sydney, places nominally outside of Asia. In the process, she re-engages with bell hooks and Lisa Heldke's critique of appropriation of gastroethnicity as "spice, seasoning that can liven up the dull dish that is mainstream white culture" (hooks 1992, as quoted in Heldke 2003, 9). Against them Duruz underlines the transformation of the exotic into the ordinary, enlivening new ambiguities of belonging. She leads us to a more compelling and timely question: can food ever be a source of cultural empathy by way of everyday commensality and yet also escape the clutches of official multiculturalism?

The Chinese conventionally classify the "four great" cuisines as Canton, Sichuan, Huaiyang (or Jiangsu), and northern (or Shandong), which pulls together numerous temporalities and trajectories. For instance, what we know today as Sichuan cuisine did not take shape until the late seventeenth century, and Cantonese cuisine did not acquire high status until the early twentieth century with the simultaneous Sinification and Westernization of parts of southern China. The Taiwanese historian Lu Yaodong notes that Chinese regional cuisines did not acquire their identity "until the purveyors of different cuisines came into contact with one other" and sought to "differentiate the qualities and flavors of their variety of cooking from others" (quoted in Swislocki 2009, 11). In the chapter on Fu Pei-Mei's three-volume Chinese cookbook, Michelle T. King analyzes the conundrum of Chinese culinary nationalism, which has to account for the foods and techniques of at least two nations, each constituted by myriad regions and many diasporas, in one uncontested national palate. The strength of this chapter lies in the use of one well-known Taiwanese author's cookbooks to unsettle the easy assumptions of a fully integrated Chinese cuisine. The claims and the processes of nation-making and nation-breaking are all we have. It clarifies why this book is titled *Culinary Nationalism in Asia*, and not "Asian National Cuisines," by highlighting the vast chasm between the two.

Katarzyna J. Cwiertka takes a scalpel to how national propaganda is used to add value to something as mundane as *kimchi*-making, sowing the insidious effects of nation-branding through public diplomacy. The state-based and market-based efforts to claim *kimchi* for one nation, with the help of the UNESCO Intangible Cultural Heritage (ICH), regularly embroil the Republic of Korea and the Democratic People's Republic of Korea in contesting claims to pickled cabbage styles, folk songs, and other such ubiquitous cultural products as exclusive national patrimony contained by the 38th parallel. The southern Republic's original ICH claim is tarnished by the fact that its per capita *kimchi* consumption has been declining and its *kimchi* production has become increasingly industrialized, with almost a thousand food-processing companies involved in its manufacture. The year 2013, when *kimchi* was inscribed with ICH status, is exactly when, Cwiertka notes, the value of factory-made *kimchi* surpassed the value of home-made *kimchi*. In fact, the national contest over *kimchi* was triggered by its increasing consumption, and hence visibility, in Japan. The nation may sometimes be invented in other national spaces. Furthermore, she shows how the pre-history of industrialized *kimchi* production in South Korea was related to feeding South Korean military personnel in the Vietnam War who were fighting on behalf of the United States (comprising two-thirds of the Free World Military Forces). So the *kimchi* story is entangled with the history of American imperialism in East Asia, an uncomfortable and hidden truth of South Korean nationalism, and its unproblematic diasporic celebration.

Gaik Cheng Khoo raises thoughtful methodological questions in her sensorially rich chapter on Malaysian food—a section spiked with lobster *laksa*, Cantonese *mantou* with foie gras, and toasted chapati with goat yogurt and curried mussels— interrogating the tensions *within* the national between Malay, Indian, Chinese, Eurasian, and Peranakan. She overlays new forces of Islamization, *bumiputera* nativism, and a new global hierarchy of taste (the idiom of professionalized chefs) to the relationship between the inward-looking national project and the outward looking cosmopolitan one. Querying the nature of the connection between home-cooking, street food, and haute cuisine, she asks: which one represents the nation the best and for whom? Khoo, and a number of other authors, raise crucial questions about the dynamic between tradition and innovation in the making of a national cuisine and the consequences of the quest to nail down an elusive, changing artifact into an archetype.

Several authors implicitly argue for provincializing the French and Italian models as a way of studying national cuisine. They hint at a critique of modernity, where theory always comes from the metropole rather than from the postcolonial provinces, which are seen merely as adding color and empirical fact. That is an argument elaborated most consistently by Chen Kuan-hsing in *Asia as Method* (2010). Illustratively, Satoko Kakihara's work on the unusual figure of the female *sake*-maker Natsuko, in the eponymous manga, is an acute interrogation of a new patriarchal theory developed under the sign of nationalism in Japan and first conceived by Partha Chatterjee in the context of Indian nationalism (1989). In the process of interrogating comparative Asian materials as a method, informed by Asian perspectives on the politics and poetics of taste, we are urged to develop theories that can be generated both in Eastern and non-Eastern contexts. Similarly, James L. Watson's closing thoughts on the history of two invented national traditions, Thanksgiving in the United States and the *puhn-choi* one-pot community banquet in Hong Kong, nicely encapsulate the fecund theoretical possibilities of discarding the national envelope of two modern rituals to bare their interiors to analytical incision.

Throughout the book we are led to the heroic task of recovering local modes of connoisseurship from elite notions of good taste that dominate the literature on national culinary cultures. We learn that good taste can flow up and across the class ladder too. Domination still happens, which was Pierre Bourdieu's (1984) perpetual concern, but it happens in conditions not of its own making. Most importantly, this volume clearly demonstrates that the basic tools of cultural history and demography have become so nationalized that they are repressing the centrality of connections between neighboring regions and muting the important relationships across spatial levels of city, province, nation, region, and global network. This book is an instance where below-the-nation spatialization of taste connects to transnational scales above it. It urges us to consider other possibilities, where the nation-state is only one relatively recent crystallization of spatial politics and poetics. For example, Tatsuya Mitsuda's chapter attends to the process of constructing a vegetarian nationalism in Japan in contrast to meaty Meiji Occidentalism. It engages the reader in deep scientific contestations around the uses of animal protein that connects the Japanese discussion to one raging in Germany, Denmark, China, and the United States. As a result, one can safely conclude that the discussion on vegetarianism in Japan between 1880 and 1938 had very little to do with the Buddhist tradition and a lot more to do with the conventions of socialism and modern scientific nutrition. Such an analysis is offered with refreshing acuity, drawing us away from the tendency to explain too much of Japanese culture by way of uninterrogated boxes marked Shintoism or Buddhism.

This collection warns us of excessively strong claims to originality—where did a dish originate, who invented noodles, which nation can take credit for the tandoor, etc.—that litter culinary lore. Most claims of origin are uncertain because the textual record is inadequate and when available provides only second order claims to novelty. In general, exaggerated claims of originality about any everyday food or tool or technique are at best successful marketing gimmicks. Culinary products and processes are often competitively consecrated by a city or a state, as is the case with many *terroir* products and elements of Intangible Cultural Heritage, and who stakes the claim is usually a question of power and primacy made by noisy bureaucratic processes, by forces of the state, or by powers of the marketplace, all of which silence the real, invisible, and anonymous originators who can only be accounted for in the culinary commons. Wherever there are claims to primacy there is probably some propaganda. Thus, along with a suspicion of origins, this book vivifies culture as a destination— where people get to, where they want to go, what they reach for.

We also learn that cities are central to national cultural imaginations. Shanghai's honey nectar peach became the carrier of acute nostalgia for the nation during the Republican period (1912–49) when civil war tore apart the Chinese body politic, as outlined by Mark Swislocki in *Culinary Nostalgia: Regional Food Culture and the Urban Experience in Shanghai* (2009). James Farrer takes us back to Shanghai to reappraise its role in the twenty-first century as a global gastronomic destination via the Michelin Guide. He shows how cosmopolitanism and culinary nationalism are two faces of the same process as locations become incorporated into the world of celebrity chefs, journalists, commentators, and evaluators. We will surely hear a lot more about Shanghai in this century.

There is one persistent problem in Asian historiography reflected in this book: its uneven development between areas and languages. Asia is, of course, a very big place with hundreds of watersheds, hence food-sheds, and linguistic and culinary zones. That unevenness is a product of accidents of colonization and postcolonial organization of power; the geography of development and underdevelopment; patterns of capital and cultural accumulation; and the linguistic capacity of local and transnational researchers. As a result, we have an overdevelopment of work in Japanese, some work in the linguistic zones of Mandarin Chinese, Korean, Hindi, Tamil, and Farsi, and massive underdevelopment in the rest, such as Central Asia and West Asia. My hope is that more work in many more Asian languages will fill out our conceptions of cooking and eating, and further allow us to specify the relationship between taste, territory, and power. That will give us a better handle on the range of provincial and metropolitan realities and generate more robust theories that do not confuse the vernaculars of metropolitan provinces with universal histories of food in the world.

Finally, this volume provides a clear example of how palatal taste can be fruitfully interrogated as an embodied archive of long-term patterns of interaction between the local and global at various tiers. It shows us how taste can also reveal the limits of the ubiquitous presumptions of national cultures. But first it forces us to unthink eighteenth-century Western formulations that have trivialized literal taste. Here authors recover corporeal sensory experience to contest the idea of national cultures by telling us distinct stories at varying spatiotemporal levels of analysis.

Acknowledgments

Thanks to Stephanie Jolly for all her hard work in copy-editing this piece for grammar, word usage, and readability. It would have been riddled with errors and much weaker without her thorough editing.

References

Bourdieu, Pierre. 1984. *Distinction*, Cambridge, MA: Harvard University Press.

Chatterjee, Partha. 1989. "Colonialism, Nationalism, and Colonialized Women: The Contest in India." *American Ethnologist* 16, no. 4: 622–33.

Chen, Kuan-hsing. 2010. *Asia as Method: Towards Deimperialization*. Durham, NC: Duke University Press.

Heldke, Lisa. 2003. *Exotic Appetites: Ruminations of a Food Adventurer*. New York: Routledge.

hooks, bell. 1992. "Eating the Other." In *Black Looks: Race and Representation*, edited by bell hooks, 21–39. Boston, MA: South End Press.

Swislocki, Mark. 2009. *Culinary Nostalgia: Regional Food Culture and the Urban Experience in Shanghai*. Stanford, CA: Stanford University Press.

Acknowledgments

This edited volume originated with papers presented at the "Culinary Nationalism in Asia" conference, hosted by the Department of History, University of North Carolina at Chapel Hill from March 30 to April 1, 2017 (www.culnatasia.web.unc.edu). The major sponsorship of the conference came in the form of a Comparative Perspectives on Chinese Culture and Society Conference Grant from the American Council of Learned Societies, funded by the Chiang Ching-kuo Foundation for International Scholarly Exchange. The same grant also provided a generous publication subvention for this volume.

Additional financial and administrative support for the conference was provided by the following agencies at the University of North Carolina at Chapel Hill: Carolina Asia Center, Global Research Institute, Food for All Steering Committee, College of Arts and Sciences, Department of History, Institute for Arts and Humanities, and the University Library. External financial support for the conference also came in the form of an Association for Asian Studies China and Inner Asia Council Small Grant.

I am indebted to each of these funding agencies for making this conference and subsequent edited volume possible through their generous financial support. I would also like to thank the Institute for Historical Studies at the University of Texas at Austin, which provided me with a residential fellowship in 2016–17, giving me precious time to plan the conference and simultaneously revise the paper included in this volume.

Beyond the immediate contributors to this volume, I would also like to thank all of the other conference presenters and moderators for providing such stimulating papers and comments: Stephanie Assmann, Inger Brodey, Ian Cheney, Yu-jen Chen, Sidney Cheung, Peter Coclanis, Priscilla Parkhurst Ferguson, Emma Flatt, Jia-chen Fu, Sana Ho, Seung-joon Lee, Jayeeta Sharma, Benjamin Siegel, Nancy Stalker, Pin-tsang Tseng, Michael Tsin, and Rubie Watson. The spirit and vigor of their intellectual contributions are contained in this volume, even though circumstances precluded the inclusion of every individual conference paper.

Colleagues at UNC Chapel Hill were crucial in helping to secure financial support for the conference, including Morgan Pitelka, Peter Coclanis, Marcie Cohen-Ferris, Jonathan Hartlyn, Fitzhugh Brundage, Mark Katz, and Hsi-chu Bolick. The hard work of the following UNC graduate and undergraduate students, many of whom were volunteers, ensured that all of the logistical arrangements went without a single hitch: Beth Hasseler, Donny Santacaterina, Xiaowei Wu, Lauren Trushin, Leslie Ga Qi Cao, Olivia Holder, Zardas Lee, Sian Li, Maya Little, Jennifer Na, Justin Wu, and Jacky Zheng. The UNC History Department administrative team also gave their all: Joyce Loftin, Michael Williams, Adam Kent, and Sharon Anderson. Thank you to all for making the conference operations a great success.

Dan Bender, Seung-joon Lee, Jean Duruz, Rachel Berger, Emma Flatt, Flora Cassen, and Sarah Shields gave generous feedback on shaping the introduction. Three anonymous peer reviewers for Bloomsbury Academic were extremely helpful in reworking the introduction and the organization of the volume as a whole. Gabriel Moss designed the maps. Finally, the editorial assistance of Daniele Lauro has helped to bring this volume to fruition. My sincere thanks to all for sharing their expertise, time, and input.

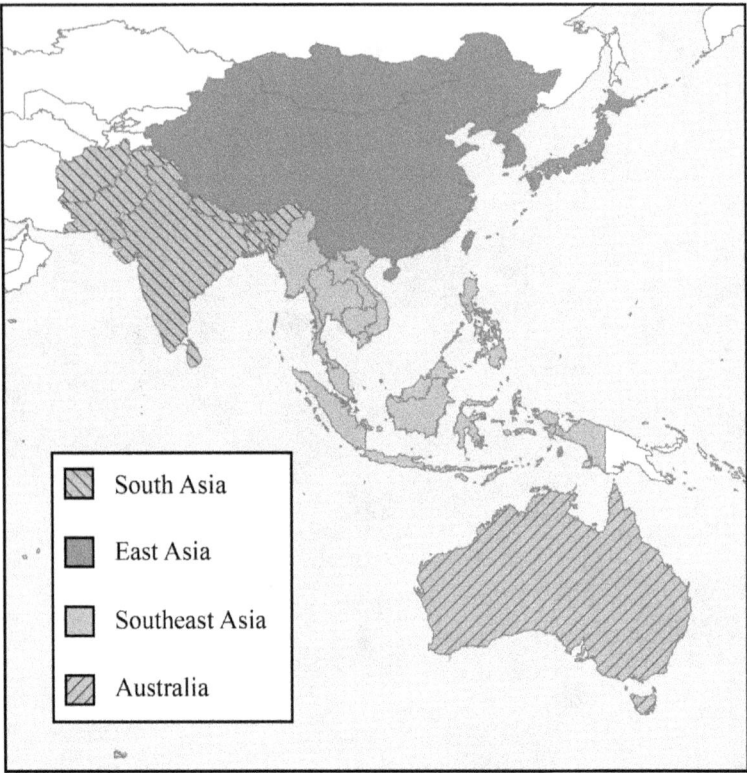

Map 1 World map featuring East Asia, South Asia, and Southeast Asia. Drawn by Gabriel Moss.

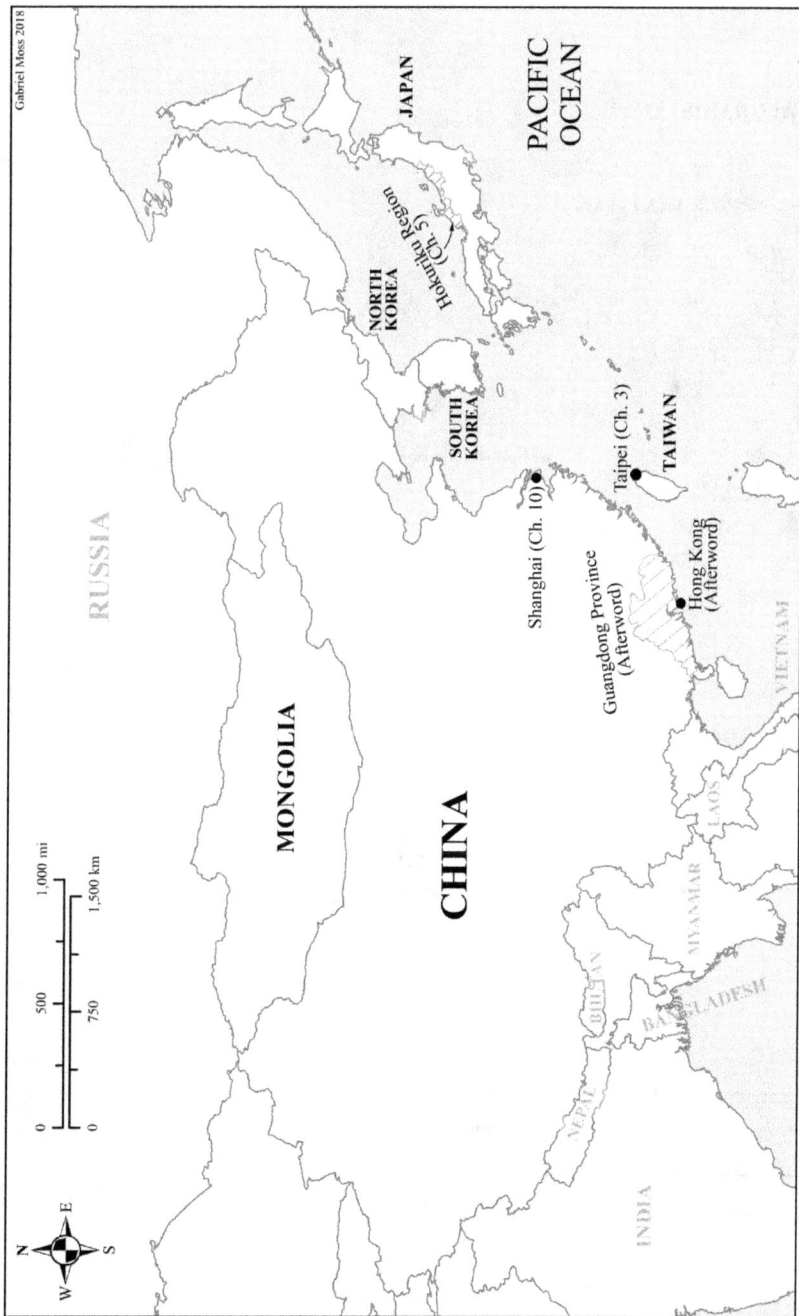

Map 2 Regional map of East Asia. Drawn by Gabriel Moss.

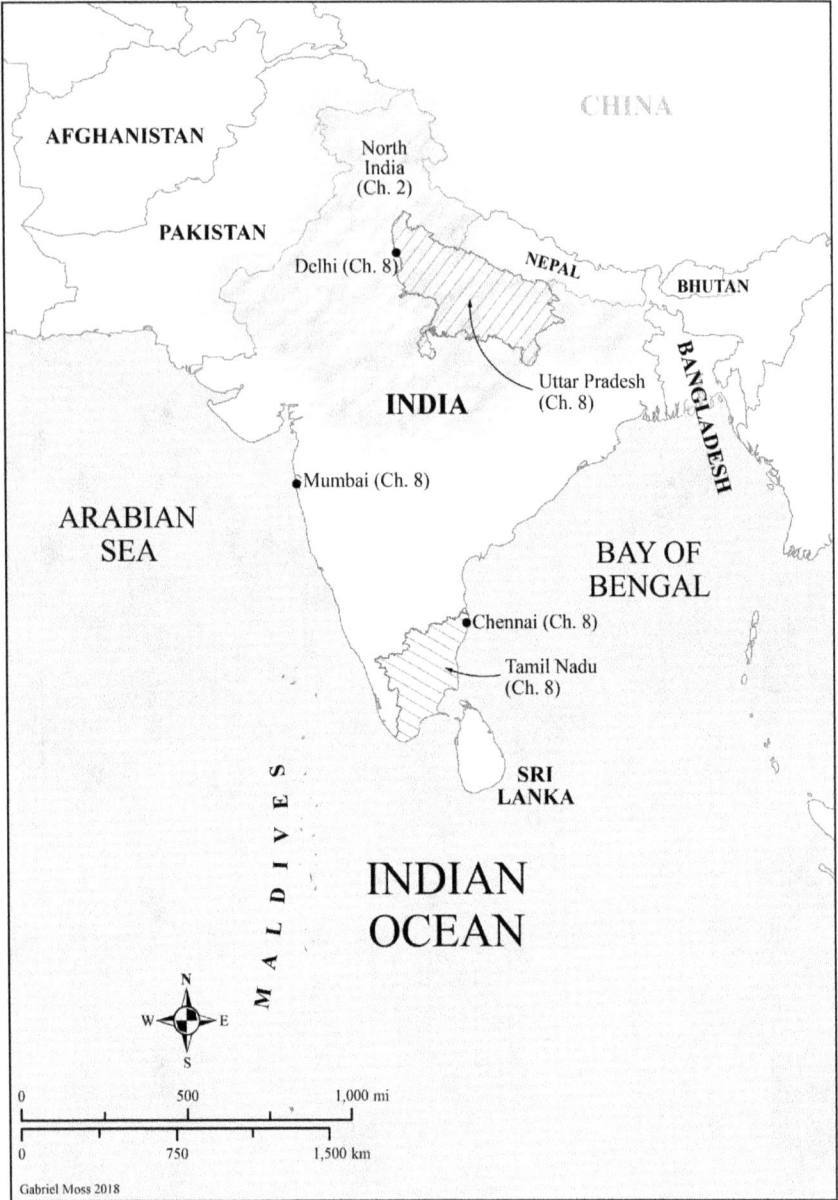

Map 3 Regional map of South Asia. Drawn by Gabriel Moss.

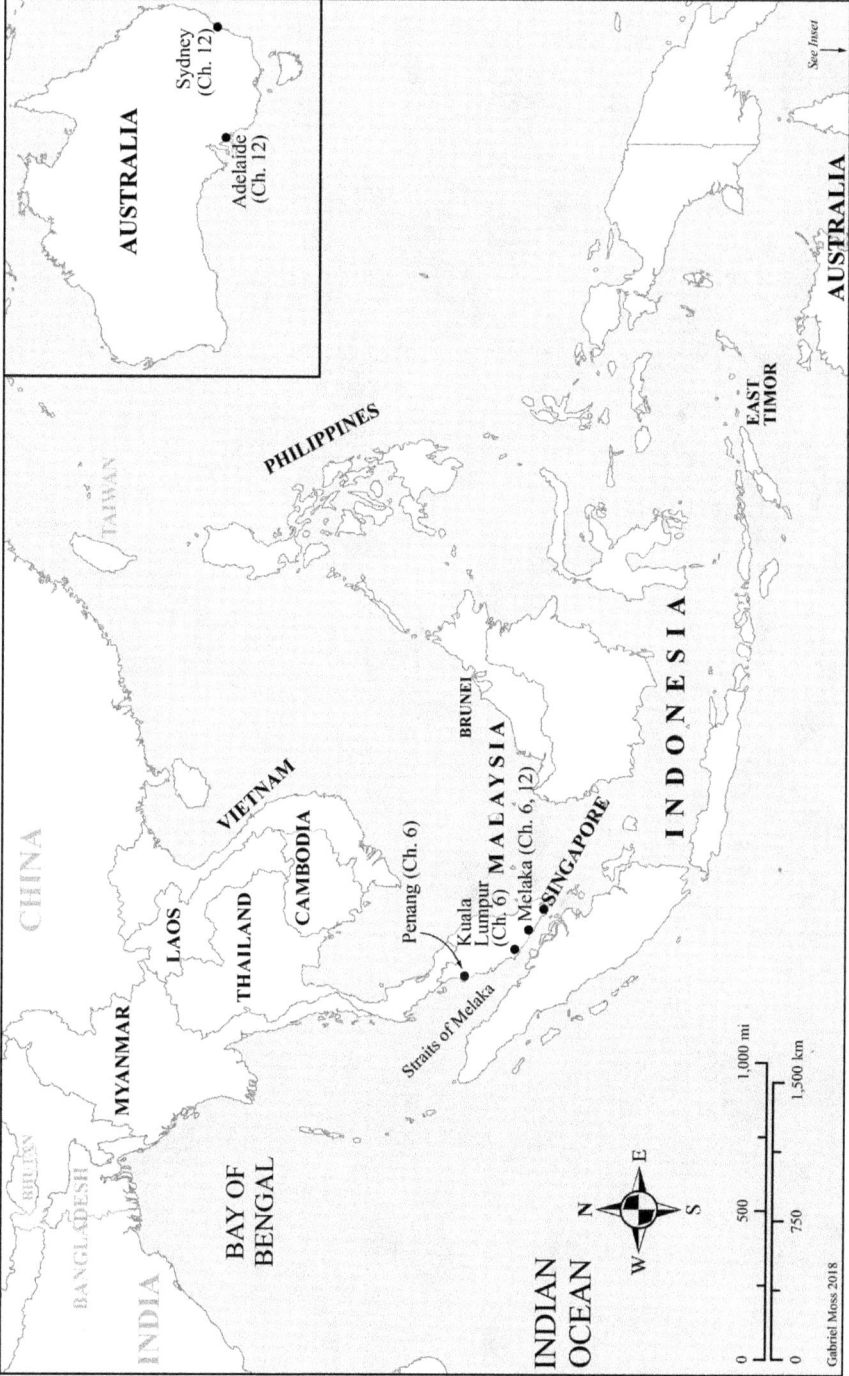

Map 4 Regional map of Southeast Asia. Drawn by Gabriel Moss.

Introduction: Culinary Nationalism in Asia

Michelle T. King
University of North Carolina at Chapel Hill

Introduction

Cuisine and nation intersect all over the world, but nowhere, arguably, with as much depth and intensity as in Asia. The central aim of this book is to explore the manifold nature of this connection between cuisine and nation, in a wide variety of Asian pasts and presents, by bringing together the critical work of scholars from an expansive range of disciplinary perspectives, including history, sociology, anthropology, food studies, geography, Asian studies, literary, and media and cultural studies. The impetus in this volume is to interrogate how culinary practices have been involved in the definition, preservation, transformation, dismantling, and even imagining of Asian national identities. What is being cooked up is not individual dishes or even necessarily particular cuisines but, rather, the nation itself.

In many ways, food and cuisine seem to align perfectly with studies of nationalism. Cuisines have been an integral component of emerging or existing national identities the world over, from Mexico (Pilcher 1998) and the United States (Gabaccia 1998) to Peru (Wilson 2011) and Argentina (Pite 2013); from Equatorial Guinea (Cusack 2004) to Greece (Dalby and Dalby 2017), Turkey (Yenal 2010), Palestine/Israel (Gvion 2012; Raviv 2015); from Russia (Caldwell 2002) to France (Ferguson 2004), Germany (Heinzelmann 2014), Italy (Helstosky 2004; Parasecoli 2014), and Spain (Anderson 2013). Similarly, specific dishes have been feted as iconic representations of the nation, whether at the elevated level of French champagne (Guy 2004) and foie gras (DeSoucey 2016) or the humbler fare of Scottish haggis (Tyrrell, Hill, and Kirkby 2007) and Canadian donuts (Penfold 2008).

At the same time, however, food, cuisine, and taste easily elude and defy rigid national boundaries, through their inherent portability and adaptability at both ends of the spatial spectrum. Krishnendu Ray, along with other scholars, has urged us to move beyond the circumscribed boundaries of national cuisines in order to "rescue taste from the nation" (Leong-Salobir, Ray, and Rohel 2016). Ray's work (K. Ray 2015) seeks to open up our understanding of the circulation of food, taste, labor, and bodies within the Indian Ocean littoral. At the other end of the scale, Sidney Mintz has questioned the very existence of national cuisine, calling it "a holistic artifice based on

the foods of people who live inside some political system, such as France or Spain"
(Mintz 1996, 104). Instead, Mintz insists on attending to the actual eating habits of
much smaller and culinarily cohesive social groups.

Rather than weakening the claims of national identity on food studies, such critiques
actually underscore the way in which the analytical flexibility of cuisine positions it to
offer a fresh perspective on the study of nationalism in general: food may indeed
reinforce essentialized notions of national identity, yet also simultaneously contest
these ideas through the assertion of heterogeneous difference. A recent flap over the
comments of two Caucasian judges on the reality television cooking program,
MasterChef UK, bears out this observation. Australian judge John Torode and English
judge Gregg Wallace dismissed the Malaysian-born contestant Zaleha Kadir Olpin
from the program in April 2018, claiming that her chicken rendang, made to accompany
the iconic rice dish nasi lemak, needed a "crispy skin." Critics around the world
immediately took to social media to ridicule the idea of a "crispy skin" on a slow-
cooked chicken rendang, drawing support from Indonesians, Singaporeans, and
Malaysians alike. Within Malaysia, the event united political rivals—then Malaysian
prime minister, Najib Razak, felt compelled to tweet back at the judges, as did his
nemesis, the former and succeeding prime minister, Mahathir Mohamad, who quipped,
"Maybe you are confusing rendang chicken with KFC" (*Straits Times* 2018). In
Indonesia, another blogger suggested that political antagonisms between Indonesia
and Malaysia—both of which have laid claim to rendang—could be set aside in the
face of a common cause: "There isn't much that could unite the two countries, until
someone else attacks our rendang" (Wargadiredja 2018). The semantic flexibility of
"our" rendang, which contracts or expands to suit audience, context, and situation,
illustrates perfectly how food can serve national identities on multiple levels.

It seems, then, that a different approach to cuisine and nation is required, one that
calls into question the artificial boundaries of national cuisines but recognizes the
significance of these boundaries in everyday understandings of foodways and culinary
practice. When food studies are confined to national borders it is difficult to discern
any broader patterns that might bring together cases of culinary nationalism as they
appear around the world. How can we address and investigate culinary nationalism
as a social phenomenon, and make critical sense of its dynamics of power? Is
there anything that distinguishes culinary nationalism as it takes shape in the Middle
East (Tapper and Zubaida 2000), Africa (Cusack 2000, 2003), Europe (Goldstein
and Merkle 2005), the Caribbean (Beushausen et al. 2014), or other parts of the
Americas?[1] What other groupings, besides regional or continental ones, might make
sense in characterizing patterns of modern culinary nationalism? Can Asian culinary
nationalism serve as a useful comparative framework for thinking through the
process in other non-Western regions, given resonant experiences with colonialism,
imperialism, revolution, decolonization, the Cold War, and global capitalism?

By foregrounding such questions, this book also aims to reconfigure the existing
model of food studies, which more often than not places the historical formation of
European/Western cuisine in general, and French cuisine in particular, at the center of
the plate. If cases of culinary nationalism around the world are properly situated within
their broader regional and historical contexts, with the recognition that modernity has

taken shape in many forms, in many places, and at different moments, then it will quickly become apparent no single location can stand as the unique birthplace of "modern" cuisine (cf. Trubek 2000; Collingham 2017; Ferguson 2004, 2014).

Within this volume, the emphasis is placed on *culinary nationalism*, as opposed to *national cuisine*.[2] Why and what is the difference? The former suggests a dynamic process of creation and contestation, while the latter calls to mind a specific and static product, the exact definition of which assumes exaggerated critical importance. At its most fundamental level, the concept of *national cuisine* promotes the limited perspective of what can be called "menu thinking," as opposed to the more expansive and bountiful "meal thinking" of *culinary nationalism*. "Menu thinking" tends to get caught up in specious debates about exactly which dishes do or do not, can or cannot, should or should not qualify as representing a given nation on its notional national menu. In its most commonplace form, those enamored of national cuisine display an inordinate preoccupation with concepts of "authenticity," "tradition," and "origins," which they wield to blunt effect. The quintessential example of this type of menu thinking are the so-called "hummus wars," waged over which Middle Eastern country gets to claim hummus as its own (Ariel 2012).

"Meal thinking," by comparison, encourages the deeper examination of much broader historical and social contexts that frame an entire meal. How did any given meal come to be? What natural environments, human trade flows, and intellectual arguments made it possible? Who was involved in the production of the ingredients and the corresponding acts of cooking, serving, selling, buying, and eating? Where, when, and how was it consumed, and what about the aftermath of the meal? How was it judged, and why are the stakes of such evaluations so high? And, most importantly for our purposes, how are national and other identities at stake throughout all of these processes? The answers to these questions may not conform to national boundaries or histories, but there is often a strong desire on the parts of governments, industries, food writers, and ordinary citizens alike to behave as if they do or should. That desire represents culinary nationalism and drives the intellectual motor of this book.

To describe culinary nationalism as a dynamic process of formation requires identifying historical trajectories, social patterns, and behaviors shared across many sites. Arjun Appadurai best modeled this approach to the role of food in shaping national identities with his seminal 1988 article, "How to Make a National Cuisine: Cookbooks in Contemporary India." In spite of foregrounding the term "national cuisine" in the article's title, the incisive power of Appadurai's analysis derives from his relentless focus on the active process of "how to make" rather than on the precise outlines of the Indian national cuisine that ostensibly resulted.[3] Appadurai highlights the social role of English-language cookbooks written by and for urban, middle-class Indian women from the 1960s to the 1980s, suggesting that the cookbooks were a means through which a consciousness of Indian food as a "national cuisine" could be systematically articulated. While Appadurai emphasized the social actions of individual housewives, subsequent scholars have focused on the involvement of government institutions and agencies at the international, national, and local levels. Michaela DeSoucey (2010, 2016) characterizes the official branding of national food products within the European Union as "gastronationalism," while Atsuko Ichijo and Ronald

Ranta (2016) present a useful framework for studying contemporary political efforts to bolster national culinary identities by grassroots, state-led, and international actors in their study of *Food, National Identity and Nationalism*.

The present volume builds upon the insights of these earlier works but expands and insists upon the greater conceptual potential of "culinary nationalism" in several ways.[4] First, it is essential to enlarge the spatial scope of culinary nationalism beyond the study of any individual country (cf. Rogers 2003; Ferguson 2004; Raviv 2015), in order to build a better sense of its operational dynamics as it has taken hold in a range of geographies and cultures. Second, it is critical to extend the temporal range of culinary nationalism beyond present-day examples, so as to attend to its shifting loci of power and modes of expression across different stages of national and economic development. Finally, the purposeful designation of "culinary nationalism" as the central organizing rubric of this book moves the discussion away from never-ending debates about "national cuisine"—as the pages of this book will make clear, even in the absence of any agreement about the existence or form of any given national cuisine, examples of culinary nationalism abound. In this book, "culinary" indicates a selected focus on the acts of cooking and consumption; by and large this volume does not address agricultural policy, food supply, or food security, distinct topics that require their own set of comparative perspectives (Chern, Carter, and Shei 2000; Asian Development Bank 2013; Ewing-Chow and Slade 2016).

Defining "Asian" culinary nationalism

Invoking the geographical space of "Asia" and the conceptual space of "Asian" culinary nationalism requires some interrogation, as neither term should be taken as self-evident. Martin Lewis and Kären Wigen (1997) have noted that the geographical designation of "Asia" originated in ancient Greece and was always already framed as the counterpoint to the geographical designation of "Europe." This implicit dichotomy, originally denoting two sides of the Dardanelles and Bosporus Straits, was preserved even as the territories indicated by each label dramatically expanded. From the advent of European colonial expansion overseas in the sixteenth century to American Cold War misadventures abroad in the twentieth century, the geography of "Asia" morphed to encompass everything between the Japanese archipelago in the east to the Anatolian peninsula in the west. The vast expanse and diversity of "Asia" render it a "super-continent," rather than a continent, argue Lewis and Wigen, yet the notion of an assumed comparability between "Asia" and "Europe" still remains with us.

These insights of historical geography are significant for delimiting the scope of the present volume. Conceptually speaking, just as the geographic concept of "Asia" is historically contingent, so too is any notion of "Asian" cuisine. There is no single characteristic or list of attributes that binds together the vast array of regional cuisines on the supercontinent, and to insist upon such a list would be to mistake geographic contiguity for deeper cultural and historic coherence. Therefore, the present volume includes examples of culinary nationalism from East Asia, South Asia, and Southeast Asia (Map 1) but does not include examples from Central Asia, Southwest Asia (the

Middle East), or North Asia (Russia). This is not because these latter three regions cannot offer up their own vivid examples of culinary nationalism, but rather because insisting on their incorporation for the sake of a presumed "Asian" culinary coherence would stretch any analysis to unacceptable thinness. These regions and their culinary nationalisms deserve fuller contextualization in their own dedicated volumes, potentially linking them to other spaces: the culinary practices of Southwest Asia, for example, may well hold more in common with those of North Africa, and any consideration of modern foodways in Central Asia would have to account for the impact of more than seventy years of Soviet control.

At the same time, East Asia, South Asia, and Southeast Asia do share a variety of culinary characteristics and historical trajectories that draw them closer together. While no single ingredient, culinary technique, or flavor profile is found everywhere, many are shared across multiple sites. Rice and wheat appear widely as primary staples within these predominantly agricultural (as opposed to pastoral) cultures, for example, as do certain spices, ingredients, or preserved foods, such as ginger, tea, soy sauce, tofu, sesame, fish sauce, tamarind, lemongrass, chilis, coconut milk, cilantro, black pepper, or cloves. Historically, many of these ingredients were spread or shared throughout the Indian Ocean littoral by a robust spice and commodities trade that already dated from the premodern period (Keay 2007). As ingredients and tastes mingled, so too did the humans who carried them. In later centuries, European colonialism was superimposed upon these native networks of Asian trade, adding yet another layer to culinary interactions.

East Asia (Map 2), South Asia (Map 3), and Southeast Asia (Map 4)—each of which alone is comparable to the whole of Europe in terms of population, geographic range, and culinary diversity[5]—also share a number of other contemporary social characteristics that have shaped their culinary worlds in resonant ways. Chinese, Japanese, Korean, Indian, Thai, and Vietnamese cuisines, in particular, have successfully conquered global tastes, becoming ever more integral parts of cosmopolitan eating habits around the world. At a minimum, this success has been built upon the growing clout of their developing economies, enabling massive transfers of both financial and human capital beyond Asia to the rest of the world. Robust diasporic communities from all corners of East, South, and Southeast Asia have carried their native foodways with them, continually adapting the dishes and eating practices of their homelands to new, local ingredients and tastes (Wu and Cheung 2002; Ray 2004; Tan 2011; Ray and Srinivas 2012; Ku, Manalansan, and Mannur 2014; Padoongpatt 2017).

However, despite an explicit focus on East, South, and Southeast Asia, this book is also *not* structured as a comprehensive catalog of culinary nationalisms from *every* country in each region. This may disappoint some readers looking for in-depth discussions of specific Asian national cuisines not represented here (e.g., Vietnamese, Indonesian, Filipino, Thai, Pakistani, etc.), yet equally deserving of mention. The original intent of this volume, however, was never to present a United Nations roll call of all Asian national cuisines.[6] While such an approach might satisfy some sense of culinary equality, national cuisine by national cuisine, it misdirects reader attention in several ways. For one thing, it reifies national borders and coherent national culinary histories, rather than opening up the contradictory and contested internal dynamics of cuisines to closer examination.[7] For another, it suggests a blind parity among all Asian nations and cuisines, rather than acknowledging real differences in terms of historical legacies of imperialism and colonialism, contemporary economic and political clout, and global diasporic dispersal. Rather than ignoring these imbalances (which to a large degree are reflected by the relative depth of scholarship associated with specific Asian cuisines, particularly Japanese[8]), it is more helpful to confront these disparities head-on and ask what conditions have allowed certain Asian cuisines to amass global followings and attract scholarly attention, while others remain less well-known.

Ultimately, the central idea animating this volume has been to attempt to build a working model of *culinary nationalism as a dynamic process* in Asia, by identifying some initial themes or patterns against which other specific national cases might eventually be compared. In the pages that follow, these shared patterns of culinary nationalism have been divided into three sections: "Historical Legacies," "Internal Boundaries," and "Global Contexts." Rather than interpreting the omissions of the present volume as a deliberate exclusion from the commensal table, the inevitable limits of geographic coverage should be considered as an open invitation to all Asianists, to bring their own national dish to the party and liven the discussion. For all intents and purposes, any serious intellectual project adopting "Asia as method" cannot be the labor of a single scholar, working alone.[9] Instead it requires the collaborative effort of many Asianists, whose expertise is usually circumscribed by formidable linguistic barriers.

Historical legacies

Richly detailed surveys of premodern Asian food traditions from an earlier generation of historians and anthropologists have long served as touchstones for the entire field of food studies. Notable highlights include K. C. Chang's edited volume, *Food in Chinese Culture: Anthropological and Historical Perspectives* (1977), a comprehensive survey of food production and consumption during each of China's major dynastic periods, examined within broader religious, ritual, medicinal, and social contexts.[10] The encyclopedic work of K. T. Achaya, *Indian Food: A Historical Companion* (1994), is also indispensable, covering significant influences in premodern Indian food traditions in roughly chronological fashion, including religious taboos, regional differences, and the use of food as medicine and in royal courts.[11] Because Chang and Achaya offer useful overviews of otherwise vast and complex food traditions, both have achieved iconic status within historical and food studies circles and continue to be widely cited to this day.

These extensive canons of premodern Asian culinary texts are both a blessing and a curse. No one can deny the development of extraordinarily rich food cultures and philosophies in premodern China or India, but the enormous weight of these traditions threatens to displace critical attention to subsequent culinary developments during modern times. To offer but one example, Paul Freedman's edited volume, *Food: The History of Taste* (2007), devotes some early chapters to imperial Chinese gastronomy as well as medieval Islamic cuisine, but thereafter, the story unfolds almost exclusively in Europe, through its Middle Ages, Renaissance, and up through its nineteenth, twentieth, and twenty-first centuries. Other ostensibly global works on food history follow similar patterns, ultimately always arriving in the contemporary United States (e.g., Freedman,

Chaplin, and Albala 2014). It is as if, having given the highly developed gastronomic cultures of premodern Asia their due, culinary development in Asia is arrested, while its modern transformation is always described as taking place elsewhere—namely Europe and the United States. This volume seeks to make this unarticulated but essentially Eurocentric approach to global culinary history less and less tenable.

At the same time, the titles of Chang's and Achaya's influential volumes minimize the fact that there was no such thing as "Chinese" or "Indian" cuisine in the premodern eras they discuss: these cuisines of the past emerge as unified entities under their own book covers only by casting backward from the perspective of the modern nation-state. Earlier native terms used to describe food and cuisine were circumscribed by ethnicity, language, region, humoral theory, or other categories. Sanskrit texts focused on the ritual use of food, particularly its purity or pollution, while Tamil literature described food in "regional and occupational terms" (Achaya 1994, 32–3, 43–4). Early Ayurvedic texts focused almost exclusively on the various humoral properties of food (Achaya 1994, 77–87; Sen 2015, 117–36), as did Chinese medical texts (Anderson 1988, 229–43) and later Unani ones (Alavi 2008, 234–5). Later Chinese writers, such as the eighteenth-century gastronome Yuan Mei (1716–97), occasionally spoke in ethnic terms of "Han" foods as opposed to, say, "Manchu" ones, but never referred to "Chinese" foods (Yuan 2016). In early modern Japan, elites put the category of the culinary to a dizzying array of uses, including as creative fantasy, but there was no articulation of cuisine as "Japanese" (Rath 2010).

How, then, did these expansive premodern Asian culinary traditions evolve, resulting in the highly capitalized, global culinary moment in which we now find ourselves? What has been the significance of Asian national culinary identities before, during, and after such transitions?

One thing that all of these histories of modern Asian national culinary identities *do* share in common is their intractable relationship with "Western cuisine." This is the actual term most commonly used in East Asian languages (Ch. 西餐 *xican*, Jp. 洋食 *yōshoku*, Kor. 양식 *yangsig*), collapsing any distinctions among British, American, French, German, Russian, or other Western foods. Modern-day Hindi speakers, too, have adopted the blanket term "continental" for European/Western cuisines. Encounters with Euro-American powers, as they made colonial and imperial incursions into Asian territories, keenly sharpened the notion of cuisine as a marker of Asian difference in the late nineteenth and early twentieth centuries. Military might was directly connected to culinary influence: indeed, one strand of Asian nationalist thinking was fixated on the need to use scientific methods to emulate Western nutritional standards (and by extension, Western diets) in order to build stronger Indian, Japanese, and Chinese bodies capable of fighting back against foreign dominance (Sengupta 2010; Majima 2002; Fu 2018).

Notably, however, Asian culinary veneration of Europe and America was a highly segmented and ultimately limited affair: unlike Creole elites in Mexico or Argentina (Pilcher 1998; Pite 2013), for example, who "clung to European culture" (Pilcher 2017, 75), most Asians, even elites, never fully embraced European foodways or entertained notions of replacing their native eating habits. Meiji-era (1868–1912) leaders in Japan came the closest to flirting with this model, putting on fully French menus for state diplomatic dinners, but the penetration of Western cuisine outside of elite circles into the rest of Japanese society was much more constrained (Cwiertka 2006; Rath 2016). In China, culinary nationalists such as essayist and bon vivant Lin Yutang (1895–1976) proudly celebrated Chinese cuisine as the one arena in which the Chinese could school the West, if only the latter would realize it. After a century of foreign incursions into China and in the midst of domestic uncertainty, Lin wrote in 1935,

> In the cooking of ordinary things like vegetables and chickens, the Chinese have a rich store to hand to the West, when the West is ready and humble enough to learn it. This seems unlikely until China has built a few good gun-boats and can punch the West in the jaw, when it will be admitted that we are unquestionably better cooks as a nation.
>
> Lin 1935, 341

Yet a third potential mode of culinary hybridity emerged in colonial societies, where popular dishes incorporated native and European ingredients, changing the tables and tastes of colonizers and colonized alike. Kedgeree (curried rice with fish and eggs) and mulligatawny soup (curried soup), for example, returned with colonial officers of the British Raj to the metropole (Collingham 2007), while *bánh mì* (a baguette sandwich, often with cold cuts or pâté) and *cà phê đá* (iced coffee) became everyday habits in Vietnam (Lien 2016).

The chapters in the first section of this book, "Historical Legacies," lay out significant stages in the development of culinary nationalism in modern Asia—from colonialism and imperialism to national awakenings, and from Cold War enmities to global capitalism. Each region of Asia, of course, confronted and experienced colonialism and imperialism in its own way, ranging from direct rule under Portuguese, Spanish, Dutch, British, French, and American powers, to indirect rule or semi-colonial status via unequal treaties, to attenuated forms of independence. While the late nineteenth- and early twentieth-century scramble for colonial possessions forms the substrate from which later nationalist movements developed in Asia, the focus in this book is not on the influence of European foodways in Asia, nor on interactions between European colonists and their native servants (cf. Leong-Salobir 2011). Here, the focus is on emerging Asian national perspectives on cuisine.

For countries in East Asia, in particular, European iterations of imperialism have had a much less profound impact on foodways than the subsequent dominance of Japan, which held Taiwan, Korea, and portions of mainland China as colonial possessions from the late nineteenth and early twentieth centuries to the end of the Second World War.[12] Through his investigation "Japanese vegetarianism," Tatsuya Mitsuda (Chapter 1) highlights the unique status of Japan as a nation jostling for position among European powers while simultaneously harboring imperial ambitions over its immediate Asian neighbors. Modern vegetarianism in Japan developed out of the very same Meiji context of muscular militarism that promoted meat as a way to strengthen Japanese bodies and as a necessary component of national modernization. Numerous scientific experts attributed Japan's victories over Russia in the Russo-Japanese War (1904–5) directly to the stamina afforded Japanese troops through their largely plant-based diets.

Nationalist aspirations across Asia often included shaping the modern, middle-class family as a fundamental cornerstone of the nation, resulting in new visions of domesticity. Rachel Berger (Chapter 2) takes up the project of conceptualizing a history of food and domesticity in early twentieth-century North India, through an exploration of conversations about cooking, health, reproduction, and consumption that took place in Hindi cookbooks, wellness guides, and food advertising from the 1920s to the 1940s.[13] All of these texts revolved around the critical role of the housewife within the nuclear family, making manifest women's contributions to nation work as household managers (with no mention of the actual work done by domestic servants), family caregivers, reproductive mothers, and primary domestic consumers.

Cold War culinary tensions in Asia are revealed in Michelle King's chapter (Chapter 3) on Taiwan's foremost cookbook author and television personality, Fu Pei-mei (1931–2004), best known to international audiences for her three-volume, bilingual Chinese–English cookbook series on regional Chinese cuisines.[14] Fu's cookbooks became ubiquitous reference books for middle-class housewives in Taiwan, but they also moved beyond the domestic sphere, due to their publication (1969–79) during the same Cold War decade that spanned the shift of diplomatic recognition by the international community away from the Republic of China on Taiwan to the People's Republic of China (PRC) on the mainland.

Finally, Katarzyna Cwiertka (Chapter 4) explores culinary nationalism as expressed in today's global capitalist moment, explaining the significance of South Korea's successful 2013 bid to have *kimjang* 김장, or traditional home pickling methods to turn cabbage into *kimchi* 김치, declared an Intangible Cultural Heritage by UNESCO.[15] What the inscription of *kimjang* as an isolated food practice on the ICH list does not capture, Cwiertka argues, is the historic involvement of the commercial *kimchi* industry, which developed after 1965 in response to the South Korean government's desire to supply Korean troops serving in the Vietnam War (1955–75) with canned *kimchi* rations. Today, the South Korean commercial *kimchi* industry has had to find new overseas markets in countries such as Japan, while at the same time vigorously defending itself domestically against cheaper, purportedly lower quality Chinese imports.

Internal boundaries

Although culinary nationalism by definition implies drawing and defending boundaries between nations, it also involves making distinctions *within* nations, between all manner of perceived identity groups or statuses. Who is invited to sit at the national table, and where are different groups told to sit? Moreover, who is allowed to draw up the seating chart in the first place? Marking internal culinary divisions may involve invoking overt, state-sanctioned categories of gender, ethnicity, religion, or more malleable definitions of class. These internal culinary distinctions may intersect and even contradict one another, but they remain potent and meaningful symbols to many in Asia. The 2004 inaugural state banquet in Taiwan under the Democratic Progressive Party (DPP), for example, reified an internal four-fold division of Hoklo, Hakka, mainland Chinese, and Taiwanese aboriginals by including specific dishes from each group. Even though the first three groups are ethnically all Han Chinese, there are strong political reasons to regard these identities as distinct (Chen 2011). In Thailand, meanwhile, ethnic distinctions overlap with class judgments, as Central Thai disparage the culinary preferences of poorer, marginal northeastern Thai-Lao for sticky rice and fermented fish (Lefferts 2005). Expressions of culinary nationalism also thrive on distinctions between all kinds of other, professional status categories, including scientists and human subjects, advertising executives and consumers, politicians and publics, chefs and customers, or culinary gourmets and everyday eaters.

Yet internal boundaries of culinary nationalism do more than distinguish between different status groups. One of the most powerful of internal boundaries is temporal, separating imagined, often nostalgic, "traditional" culinary pasts from contemporary, "modern" foodstuffs and eating practices. Lurking underneath such temporal judgments of cuisine is the nebulous yet pervasive concept of culinary "authenticity," which often selectively imagines and celebrates a rosy vision of the "natural" foodways of the unspecified past, as opposed to the overly processed, industrialized foodways of the present (Laudan 2001). When visions of authenticity are mixed with strains of culinary nationalism, the results can vary tremendously, from innocuous boasting about the origins of specific dishes to violent confrontations between opposing groups.

The four chapters in the section on "Internal Boundaries" examine several often overlapping sites of distinction that deserve particular attention, including divisions of gender, time, class, and religion. Satoko Kakihara (Chapter 5) examines the contradictions of tradition and innovation through recent changes in Japanese *sake* industry, which has sought to expand its domestic appeal to women as both consumers and producers. Kakihara analyzes the depiction of a fictional female *sake* brewer in Oze Akira's manga series, *Natsuko's Sake* (1988–91). By assigning Natsuko the role of upholding traditions of purity and perfection—both within the *sake* and within herself—the narrative reinforces myths about the quintessentially Japanese quality of *sake* and traditional gender and class roles, even as it seems to be upending them.

The effort to blaze paths to new culinary futures often seems to necessitate a nostalgic return to imagined culinary pasts. Gaik Cheng Khoo (Chapter 6) introduces the work of a group of young, contemporary Malaysian chefs, who are defining the concept of "modern Malaysian" cuisine through their innovative creations.[16] One chef in particular, Darren Teoh, aims to move beyond the traditional divisions of Malaysian cuisine into its constituent ethnic components. Instead, Teoh proposes to utilize indigenous ingredients found only or widely in Malaysia, such as *rambai* (a tropical fruit), or *belacan* (shrimp paste). However, Teoh sees no contradiction in using modernist molecular gastronomic techniques and platings to reinterpret these "Malaysian" ur-ingredients.

The divisions of internal boundaries do more than produce new production and consumption patterns. They can also prevent different groups from finding a seat at the national commensal table. Michelle Bloom (Chapter 7) examines the experience of hunger as a stateless, rootless, and emotional experience through two films from the Malaysian-Chinese born Taiwanese director, Tsai Ming-liang. In Tsai's "slow cinema" films, food loses any of its identifiably culinary or celebrated nationalistic qualities.

Instead it serves as the locus of basic, carnal desire, whether for bodily sustenance or sexual intimacy, or as a material connection with the dead in the form of Buddhist offerings.

The ultimate example of a fraught culinary nationalism based on internal boundaries may be found in Michaël Bruckert's (Chapter 8) analysis of the politicization of meat consumption in contemporary India, where right-wing Hindu nationalists have legislated against meat eating by creating "vegetarian-only" zones, and agitated crowds have violently attacked low-caste Hindus, working-class Muslims, and Christians accused of non-sanctioned meat eating. Although meat, including beef, has always been eaten on the subcontinent since the Vedic period (first millennium BCE), the current politics of Hindu nationalism have sanitized this history of animal consumption, attempting to remove it entirely from the national table.

Global contexts

Whereas in centuries past, culinary influence was an outgrowth of military might, today it accompanies economic power and flows of capital and labor. Questions about the relationship between Asia and the West remain relevant in contemporary Asia, where restaurants and entire nations vie for the international recognition bestowed by outside (largely Western) entities, such as the Michelin guide, the World's 50 Best Restaurants List, or UNESCO. But this type of social and economic influence now flows in many directions: restaurants and luxury markets outside of Asia are also actively competing for the economic patronage of the wealthiest of Asian tourists, attesting to the confidence of the emerging economies and elite consumers of China and India, as well as the long-established spending power of Japanese consumers. Culinary influence now radiates in many directions, outward from Asia (particularly Japan, but increasingly, other parts of Asia) to the rest of the world (Farrer 2015).

Anthropologists and sociologists have already made much headway in illuminating the global dimensions of Asian foodways, including the emergence of multinational food corporations and high-end fine dining in Asia, as well as the dispersal of Asian foods, tastes, and people around the world. James Watson's groundbreaking edited volume (1997) on the rise of McDonald's in East Asia represents an early example of this globalized approach. The collection underscored how the multinational corporation imposed its functional standards while attempting to cater to local tastes. Meanwhile, urban residents in Hong Kong, Taipei, Seoul, Tokyo, and Beijing repurposed these corporate spaces and acts of consumption to fit their own local needs. More recent works have moved from Asia out toward the rest of the world, investigating the globalization of Chinese food (Wu and Tan 2001; Wu and Cheung 2002; Tan 2011) and South Asian food (Ray and Srinivas 2012), as well as cross-cultural engagement and transnational networks in Asian food production and consumption (Kim 2015; Farrer 2015). Other studies have focused more on ethnographic descriptions of local Asian encounters with the global in food production, restaurants, and cooking (Cheung and Tan 2007; Cwiertka and Walraven 2002). What all of these studies share in common is the idea that "the relationship of Asians to various cuisines [including their own] is not as simple as that suggested by the nostalgic image of Asian people savoring time-honored local dishes" (Farrer 2015, 2).

Yet global connections do not merely dissolve national loyalties, nor is this phenomenon of globalization reflected only in the contemporary moment. Eric Rath (Chapter 9) introduces the surprising culinary vision of the early twentieth-century Japanese writer, Murai Gensai (1863–1927), through his serialized culinary novel, *Kuidōraku* (1903) (translated as "Pleasures of Eating" or "Gourmandism"). Murai was committed to a vision of modern Japanese cuisine that was decidedly scientific and internationalist, openly borrowing Western recipes, kitchen implements, and nutritional guidelines.

More commonly, though, Asian culinary nationalists have framed foreign culinary influences and practices as competition. James Farrer (Chapter 10) examines the transnational culinary context surrounding elite chefs in Shanghai, upon the release of the first Michelin dining guide to the city in 2016. On the one hand, local Chinese food writers complained that the Michelin judges had no idea how to evaluate Shanghainese cuisine, and therefore missed an astounding number of deserving local restaurants. On the other hand, local chefs (both locally based Westerners and native Chinese) were keen to chase their own stars and elevate their restaurants into recognized, international fine-dining destinations—by acceding to the standards of décor, service, and presentation demanded by (again, Western) culinary cognoscenti.

More broadly speaking, the idea of "Asia" and what constitutes "Asian" cuisines becomes more of an issue the farther one travels outside of East, South, and Southeast Asia. Daniel Bender (Chapter 11) focuses on the postwar creation and rising popularity of the Trader Vic's chain restaurants, whose owner created a suggestive culinary dreamworld of indulgent permissiveness, expressly catering to the fantasies of American tourists as they fanned across the globe at the height of the Cold War. The never-ending Polynesian party at Trader Vic's—fueled by a mix of pineapple-infused Chinese-American dishes and rum cocktails, and served by a visibly East Asian waitstaff—dispensed with any real reckoning with actual histories of colonialism, labor, cuisine, or the extension of the American empire in the South Pacific.

Finally, Jean Duruz (Chapter 12) offers a consideration of Asian culinary communities that extend beyond and outside nation, building instead upon memory, experience, and taste. The chapter is part of her continued journey on the "laksa trail," which began with her study of the first "Asian" restaurants in Adelaide to introduce Australians to *laksa*, a spicy noodle soup emblematic of the Peranakan traditions of Malaysia and Singapore, in the early 1980s (Duruz 2007, 2011). Duruz moves from Australia's modest *laksa* past, built on the economic and cultural contributions of individual Southeast Asian migrants, to its mature *laksa* present, where the dish has become a ubiquitous anchor on urban foodscapes.

Future frontiers

To close the volume, James Watson's Afterword spans several periods and many themes of culinary nationalism, including changing visions of authenticity, nostalgia, and gender and class boundaries, and the effects of global economic development on culinary identities. Seen through the rich perspective of his fifty-year career as an anthropologist of the social lives of Cantonese villagers in the New Territories of Hong Kong, Watson examines the changing status of *puhn-choi* 盆菜, or "common pot" cuisine, a mode of communal dining in which villagers gather together to eat directly from large, wooden basins of food to celebrate weddings, births, or festivals. Watson's earliest observation of these village feasts came in 1969, when Hong Kong was firmly held as a British colony and served as one of the few points of access for foreign scholars interested in Chinese societies. At the time, villagers celebrated this shared eating as a way to struggle together through hard times, while urban residents disparaged *puhn-choi* as an unhygienic, rural custom. Fast forward to 1997, when local and PRC officials prepared to celebrate Hong Kong's return to the PRC, after more than 150 years as a British colony. A sanitized, upmarket version of *puhn-choi* was now featured as a unique and special marker of Hong Kong's *regional* culinary identity.

The vivid example of *puhn-choi* suggests many questions regarding culinary regionalism and its interaction with culinary nationalism in Asia, questions that can serve to animate productive future directions of Asian food studies research. How exactly do regional culinary identities compare or compete with one another, and how do these regional aggregates interact to comprise distinctive national culinary identities? Does culinary regionalism operate in opposition to culinary nationalism, or are they motivated by the same impulses? How have regional culinary identities changed or developed over time? Questions of regional culinary identities are particularly relevant for China and India, where sheer diversity prevents any single regional cuisine from dominating the national table (Swislocki 2009; Lee 2011; Wank 2015; Sengupta 2010; U. Ray 2015; Sharma 2011; Madsen and Gardella 2012), yet finer-grained regional analyses from all corners of Asia will sharpen our understanding of the interplay between culinary nationalism and culinary regionalism.

Taken together, the chapters of this book suggest the outlines of a modern culinary Asia that straddles its premodern civilizations and slippery global futures, all the while defying easy categorization. Fa-ti Fan gracefully brings together this simmering stockpot of ideas in his essay on the possibilities and pitfalls of "Asia as method":

> Asia is not a simple geographic, political, and historical object. It is both a discursive construct and a political reality; it is both a historical agent and a nimble subject position. It is a space, a zone, a site, a nodal point of power relations, and a reservoir of political resources. It is also a method, a fulcrum, a strategy and a toolkit—yet none of these metamorphoses makes it less real. The multiplicity, ambiguity, and elusiveness of "Asia" is, methodologically speaking, an asset.
>
> Fan 2016, 363

To the start of Fan's rich list of descriptors we might profitably add, "Asia is not a simple culinary object." Indeed, the purpose of this book is not to stand as the last word on the subject of culinary nationalism in Asia, but rather as an open invitation to the table.

Notes

1   Pilcher (2017) offers a promising example of regional culinary analysis, comparing processes of "cuisine and nation-building" in France, Latin America, and Asia (specifically China, Japan, and Thailand).

2   For an overview of existing scholarship and the theoretical limitations of "National Cuisines," see Smith (2012).

3   Some dispute Appadurai's assessment of the very existence of an Indian national cuisine. See Panjabi (1995); Nandy (2003, 2004).

4   Ferguson (2010) features the term "culinary nationalism" and offers a range of examples, from early twentieth-century French cookbooks to contemporary international cooking competitions to recent Korean food films, but stops short of providing a comprehensive definition of the term.

5   In terms of area, China (3.71 million mi^2) is almost the same size as Europe (3.93 million mi^2); India (1.27 million mi^2) is more than five times the size of France (248,573 mi^2). China's population (1.39 billion as of 2017) equals the populations of North America, South America, Western Europe, Australia, and New Zealand put together, while India's population (1.34 billion as of 2017) trails not far behind.

6   Cf. Goldstein and Merkle's edited volume (2005) on European national cuisines includes forty essays arranged alphabetically by country, from Armenia to the United Kingdom. The overall effect exaggerates nations as constitutive units of culinary significance. Smith (2012) addresses the uneven assumptions of the individual essays.

7   Cuisine serves as a potent site of expression and identity for ethnic Muslim Uyghurs both inside and outside of China's Xinjiang Province, for example. See Cesàro (2007).

8   Research on modern Japanese cuisine (Bestor 2004; Cwiertka 2006; Kushner 2012; Surak 2012; Solt 2014; Rath 2016) is the most robust compared to all other Asian national culinary identities.

9   The concept of "Asia as method" is taken from the recent work of Chen Kuan-hsing (2010), who has called upon Asianist scholars located both inside and outside of Asia to break free of dominant East–West binaries as well as the intellectual legacies of colonialism, imperialism, and the Cold War, through a much deeper consideration of comparative perspectives *within* Asia. See also Duara (2010) and Wang (2011).

10 On premodern Chinese foodways, see also Anderson (1988), Sterckx (2011), Bray (1984), Huang (2000). On early modern Japan, see Rath (2010).

11 On premodern Indian foodways, see also Khare (1976, 1992), Sen (2015).

12 The impact of Japanese imperialism has been felt in food studies as well: Shinoda Osamu (1899–1978), the pioneering researcher of East Asian foodways first developed his interest in Chinese food while serving in the Japanese army in North China during the Second World War (Cwiertka and Chen 2012).

13 For helpful overviews of Indian food scholarship, see Ray (2012), Sengupta (2014), and Berger (2018).

14 On Cold War culinary effects in Thailand, Korea, Singapore, and Vietnam, see Greeley (2009), Cwiertka (2012), Chua (2016), and Lien (2016).

15 For more on kimchi as the national dish of Korea, see Han (2000, 2011) and Cho (2006).

16 For more on foodways and national identities in Malaysia and Singapore, see Tarulevicz (2013), Duruz and Khoo (2014), and Kong and Sinha (2016).

References

Achaya, K. T. 1994. *Indian Food: A Historical Companion*. Delhi: Oxford University Press.

Alavi, Seema. 2008. *Islam and Healing: Loss and Recovery of an Indo-Muslim Medical Tradition, 1600–1900*. Palgrave Macmillan.

Anderson, E. N. 1988. *The Food of China*. New Haven, CT: Yale University Press.

Anderson, Lara. 2013. *Cooking Up the Nation: Spanish Culinary Texts and Culinary Nationalization in the Late Nineteenth and Early Twentieth Centuries*. Martlesham: Boydell & Brewer.

Appadurai, Arjun. 1988. "How to Make a National Cuisine: Cookbooks in Contemporary India." *Comparative Studies in Society and History* 30, no. 1: 3–24.

Ariel, Ari. 2012. "The Hummus Wars." *Gastronomica* 12, no. 1: 34–42.

Asian Development Bank. 2013. *Food Security in Asia and the Pacific*. Manila: Asian Development Bank.

Berger, Rachel. 2018. "Alimentary Affairs: Historicizing Food in Modern India." *History Compass* 16 (2): e12438. https://doi.org/10.1111/hic3.12438.

Bestor, Theodore C. 2004. *Tsukiji: The Fish Market at the Center of the World*. Berkeley: University of California Press.

Beushausen, Wiebke, Anne Brüske, Ana-Sofia Commichau, Patrick Helber, and Sinah Kloß, eds. 2014. *Caribbean Food Cultures: Culinary Practices and Consumption in the Caribbean and Its Diasporas*. London: Transcript-Verlag.

Bray, Francesca. 1984. "Agriculture." Part 2 of *Biology and Biological Technology*, Vol. 6 of *Science and Civilisation in China*, edited by Joseph Needham. Cambridge: Cambridge University Press.

Caldwell, Melissa. 2002. "The Taste of Nationalism: Food Politics in Postsocialist Moscow." *Ethnos: Journal of Anthropology* 67, no. 3: 295–319.

Cesàro, M. Cristina. 2007. "*Polo, Läghmän, So Säy*: Situating Uyghur Food Between Central Asia and China." In *Situating the Uyghurs Between China and Central Asia*, edited by Ildikó Bellér-Hann, M. Cristina Cesàro, Rachel Harris, and Joanne Smith Finley, 185–202. London: Ashgate.

Chang, K. C., ed. 1977. *Food in Chinese Culture: Anthropological and Historical Perspectives*. New Haven, CT: Yale University Press.

Chen, Kuan-hsing. 2010. *Asia As Method: Toward Deimperialization*. Durham, NC: Duke University Press.

Chen, Yujen. 2011. "Ethnic Politics in the Framing of National Cuisine: State Banquets and the Proliferation of Ethnic Cuisine in Taiwan." *Food, Culture & Society* 14, no. 3: 315–33.

Chern, Wen S., Colin A. Carter, and Shun-Yi Shei, eds. 2000. *Food Security in Asia: Economics and Policies*. Cheltenham: Edward Elgar.

Cheung, Sidney, and Tan Chee-beng, eds. 2007. *Food and Foodways in Asia: Resource, Tradition, and Cooking*. New York: Routledge.

Cho Hong Sik. 2006. "Food and Nationalism: Kimchi and Korean National Identity." *The Korean Journal of International Studies* 46, no. 5: 207–29.

Chua Beng Huat. 2016. "Taking the Street Out of Street Food." In *Food, Foodways and Foodscapes: Culture, Community and Consumption in Post-Colonial Singapore*, edited by Lily Kong and Vineeta Sinha, 23–40. Singapore: World Scientific.

Collingham, Lizzie. 2007. *Curry: A Tale of Cooks and Conquerors*. New York: Oxford University Press.

Collingham, Lizzie. 2017. *The Taste of Empire: How Britain's Quest for Food Shaped the Modern World*. New York: Basic Books.

Cusack, Igor. 2000. "African Cuisines: Recipes for Nation-Building?" *Journal of African Cultural Studies* 13, no. 2: 207–25.

Cusack, Igor. 2003. "Pots, Pens and 'Eating out the Body': Cuisine and the Gendering of African Nations." *Nations and Nationalism* 9, no. 2: 277–96.

Cusack, Igor. 2004. "Equatorial Guinea's National Cuisine Is Simple and Tasty: Cuisine and the Making of National Culture." *Arizona Journal of Hispanic Cultural Studies* 8: 131–48.

Cwiertka, Katarzyna J. 2006. *Modern Japanese Cuisine: Food, Power and National Identity.* London: Reaktion.

Cwiertka, Katarzyna J. 2012. *Cuisine, Colonialism, and Cold War: Food in Twentieth-Century Korea.* London: Reaktion.

Cwiertka, Katarzyna and Yujen Chen. 2012. "The Shadow of Shinoda Osamu: Food Research in East Asia." In *Writing Food History: A Global Perspective,* edited by Kyri Claflin and Peter Scholliers, 181–96. London: Berg.

Cwiertka, Katarzyna, and Boudewijn Walraven, eds. 2002. *Asian Food: The Global and the Local.* Honolulu: University of Hawai'i Press.

Dalby, Andrew, and Rachel Dalby. 2017. *Gifts of the Gods: A History of Food in Greece.* London: Reaktion Books.

DeSoucey, Michaela. 2010. "Gastronationalism: Food Traditions and Authenticity Politics in the European Union." *American Sociological Review* 75, no. 3: 432–55.

DeSoucey, Michaela. 2016. *Contested Tastes: Foie Gras and the Politics of Food.* Princeton: Princeton University Press.

Duara, Prasenjit. 2010. "Asia Redux: Conceptualizing a Region for Our Times." *Journal of Asian Studies* 69, no. 4: 963–83.

Duruz, Jean. 2007. "From Malacca to Adelaide . . . : Fragments Towards a Biography of Cooking, Yearning and Laksa." In *Food and Foodways in Asia: Resource, Tradition and Cooking,* edited by Sidney C. H. Cheung and Chee-Beng Tan, 183–200. New York: Routledge.

Duruz, Jean. 2011. "Tastes of Hybrid Belonging: Following the Laksa Trail in Katong, Singapore." *Continuum* 25, no. 5: 605–18.

Duruz, Jean, and Gaik Cheng Khoo. 2014. *Eating Together: Food, Space and Identity in Malaysia and Singapore.* New York: Rowman and Littlefield.

Ewing-Chow, Michael, and Melanie Vilarasau Slade, eds. 2016. *International Trade and Food Security: Exploring Collective Food Security in Asia.* Cheltenham: Edward Elgar.

Fan, Fa-ti. 2016. "Modernity, Region, and Technoscience: One Small Cheer for Asia as Method." *Cultural Sociology* 10, no. 3: 352–68.

Farrer, James, ed. 2015. *Globalization and Asian Cuisines: Transnational Networks and Contact Zones.* New York: Palgrave Macmillan.

Ferguson, Priscilla Parkhurst. 2004. *Accounting for Taste: The Triumph of French Cuisine.* Chicago: The University of Chicago Press.

Ferguson, Priscilla Parkhurst. 2010. "Culinary Nationalism." *Gastronomica* 10, no. 1: 102–9.

Ferguson, Priscilla Parkhurst. 2014. "The French Invention of Modern Cuisine." In *Food in Time and Place: The American Historical Association Companion to Food History,* edited by Paul Freedman, Joyce E. Chaplin, and Ken Albala, 233–52. Berkeley: University of California Press.

Freedman, Paul, ed. 2007. *Food: The History of Taste.* Berkeley: University of California Press.

Freedman, Paul, Joyce E. Chaplin, and Ken Albala, eds. 2014. *Food in Time and Place: The American Historical Association Companion to Food History.* Berkeley: University of California Press.

Fu, Jia-chen. 2018. *The Other Milk: Reinventing Soy in Republican China*. Seattle: University of Washington Press.

Gabaccia, Donna. 1998. *We Are What We Eat: Ethnic Food and the Making of Americans*. Cambridge, MA: Harvard University Press.

Goldstein, Darra, and Kathrin Merkle, eds. 2005. *Culinary Cultures of Europe: Identity, Diversity and Dialogue*. Strasbourg, France: Council of Europe.

Greeley, Alexandra. 2009. "Finding Pad Thai." *Gastronomica* 9, no. 1: 78–82.

Guy, Kolleen M. 2004. *When Champagne Became French: Wine and the Making of a National Identity*. Baltimore, MD: Johns Hopkins University Press.

Gvion, Liora. 2012. *Beyond Hummus and Falafel: Social and Political Aspects of Palestinian Food in Israel*. Berkeley: University of California Press.

Han Kyung-Koo. 2000. "Some Foods Are Good to Think: Kimchi and the Epitomization of National Character." *Korean Social Science Journal* 27, no. 1: 221–36.

Han Kyung-Koo. 2011. "The Kimchi War in Globalizing East Asia: Consuming Class, Gender, Health and National Identity." In *Consuming Korean Tradition in Early and Late Modernity: Commodification, Tourism and Performance*, edited by Laurel Kendall, 149–66. Honolulu: University of Hawai'i Press.

Heinzelmann, Ursula. 2014. *Beyond Bratwurst: A History of Food in Germany*. London: Reaktion Books.

Helstosky, Carol. 2004. *Garlic and Oil: Food and Politics in Italy*. Oxford: Oxford University Press.

Huang, H. T. 2000. "Fermentations and Food Science." Part 6 of *Biology and Biological Technology*, Vol. 6 of *Science and Civilisation in China*, edited by Joseph Needham. Cambridge: Cambridge University Press.

Ichijo, Atsuko, and Ronald Ranta. 2016. *Food, National Identity and Nationalism: From Everyday to Global Politics*. New York: Palgrave Macmillan.

Keay, John. 2007. *The Spice Route: A History*. Berkeley: University of California Press.

Khare, R. S. 1976. *The Hindu Hearth and Home*. Durham, NC: Carolina Academic Press.

Khare, R. S., ed. 1992. *The Eternal Food: Gastronomic Ideas and Experiences of Hindus and Buddhists*. Albany: State University of New York Press.

Kim, Kwang Ok, ed. 2015. *Re-Orienting Cuisine: East Asian Foodways in the Twenty-First Century*. New York: Berghahn Books.

Kong, Lily, and Vineeta Sinha, eds. 2016. *Food, Foodways and Foodscapes: Culture, Community and Consumption in Post-Colonial Singapore*. Singapore: World Scientific.

Ku, Robert Ji-Song, Martin F. Manalansan IV, and Anita Mannur, eds. 2014. *Eating Asian America: A Food Studies Reader*. New York: New York University Press.

Kushner, Barak. 2012. *Slurp! A Social and Culinary History of Ramen—Japan's Favorite Noodle Soup*. Folkestone: Global Oriental.

Laudan, Rachel. 2001. "A Plea for Culinary Modernism: Why We Should Love New, Fast, Processed Food." *Gastronomica* 1, no. 1: 36–44.

Lee, Seung-joon. 2011. *Gourmets in the Land of Famine: The Culture and Politics of Rice in Modern Canton*. Stanford, CA: Stanford University Press.

Lefferts, Leedom. 2005. "Sticky Rice, Fermented Fish, and the Course of a Kingdom: The Politics of Food in Northeast Thailand." *Asian Studies Review* 29, no. 3: 247–58.

Leong-Salobir, Cecilia. 2011. *Food Culture in Colonial Asia: A Taste of Empire*. New York: Routledge.

Leong-Salobir, Cecilia, Krishnendu Ray, and Jaclyn Rohel, eds. 2016. "Rescuing Taste from the Nation: Oceans, Borders, and Culinary Flows." Special issue. *Gastronomica* 16, no. 1.

Lewis, Martin W., and Kären E. Wigen. 1997. *The Myth of Continents: A Critique of Metageography*. Stanford, CA: Stanford University Press.

Lien, Vu-hong. 2016. *Rice and Baguette: A History of Food in Vietnam*. London: Reaktion Books.

Lin Yutang. 1935. *My Country and My People*. New York: Reynal & Hitchcock.

Madsen, Stig Toft, and Geoffrey Gardella. 2012. "Udupi Hotels: Entrepreneurship, Reform and Revival." In *Curried Cultures: Globalization, Food, and South Asia*, edited by Krishnendu Ray and Tulasi Srinivas, 91–109. Berkeley: University of California Press.

Majima, Ayu. 2002. "Eating Meat, Seeking Modernity: Food and Imperialism in Late Nineteenth and Early Twentieth Century Japan." *ICU Comparative Culture* 34: 95–119.

Mintz, Sidney. 1996. "Cuisine: High, Low and Not at All." In *Tasting Food, Tasting Freedom: Excursions into Eating, Culture, and the Past*, 92–105. Boston, MA: Beacon Press.

Nandy, Ashis. 2003. "Ethnic Cuisine: The Significant 'Other.'" *India International Centre Quarterly* 29, no. 3/4: 246–51.

Nandy, Ashis. 2004. "The Changing Popular Culture of Indian Food: Preliminary Notes." *South Asia Research* 24, no. 1: 9–19.

Padoongpatt, Mark. 2017. *Flavor of Empire: Food and the Making of Thai America*. Berkeley: University of California Press.

Panjabi, Camellia. 1995. "The Non-Emergence of the Regional Foods of India." In *Disappearing Foods: Studies in Food and Dishes at Risk, Proceedings of the Oxford Symposium on Food and Cookery, 1994*, edited by Harlan Walker, 144–9. London: Prospect Books.

Parasecoli, Fabio. 2014. *Al Dente: A History of Food in Italy*. London: Reaktion Books.

Penfold, Steve. 2008. *The Donut: A Canadian History*. Toronto: University of Toronto Press.

Pilcher, Jeffrey. 1998. *¡Que vivan los tamales! Food and the Making of Mexican Identity*. Albuquerque: University of New Mexico Press.

Pilcher, Jeffrey. 2017. "Cuisine and Nation Building." In *Food in World History*, 2nd ed., 72–9. New York: Routledge.

Pite, Rebekah E. 2013. *Creating a Common Table in Twentieth-Century Argentina: Doña Petrona, Women and Food*. Chapel Hill: The University of North Carolina Press.

Rath, Eric C. 2010. *Food and Fantasy in Early Modern Japan*. Berkeley: University of California Press.

Rath, Eric C. 2016. *Japan's Cuisines: Food, Place and Identity*. London: Reaktion Books.

Raviv, Yael. 2015. *Falafel Nation: Cuisine and the Making of National Identity in Israel*. Lincoln: University of Nebraska Press.

Ray, Krishnendu. 2004. *The Migrant's Table: Meals and Memories in Bengali-American Households*. Philadelphia, PA: Temple University Press.

Ray, Krishnendu. 2012. "New Directions of Research on Indian Food." In *Writing Food History: A Global Perspective*, edited by Kyri Claflin and Peter Scholliers, 165–80. London: Berg.

Ray, Krishnendu. 2015. "Culinary Spaces and National Cuisines: The Pleasures of an Indian Ocean Cuisine?" In *The Globalization of Asia Cuisines: Transnational Networks and Culinary Contact Zones*, edited by James Farrer, 23–35. New York: Palgrave Macmillan.

Ray, Krishnendu, and Tulasi Srinivas, eds. 2012. *Curried Cultures: Globalization, Food and South Asia*. Berkeley: University of California Press.

Ray, Utsa. 2015. *Culinary Culture in Colonial India: A Cosmopolitan Platter and the Middle-Class*. Cambridge: Cambridge University Press.

Rogers, Ben. 2003. *Beef and Liberty: Roast Beef, John Bull and the English Nation*. New York: Vintage.

Sen, Colleen Taylor. 2015. *Feasts and Fasts: A History of Food in India*. London: Reaktion Books.

Sengupta, Jayanta. 2010. "Nation on a Platter: The Culture and Politics of Food and Cuisine in Colonial Bengal." *Modern Asian Studies* 44, no. 1: 81–98.

Sengupta, Jayanta. 2014. "India." In *Food in Time and Place: The American Historical Association Companion to Food History*, edited by Paul Freedman, Joyce E. Chaplin, and Ken Albala, 68–94. Berkeley: University of California Press.

Sharma, Jayeeta. 2011. *Empire's Garden: Assam and the Making of India*. Durham, NC: Duke University Press Books.

Smith, Alison K. 2012. "National Cuisines." In *The Oxford Handbook of Food History*, edited by Jeffrey Pilcher, 444–60. Oxford: Oxford University Press.

Solt, George. 2014. *The Untold History of Ramen: How Political Crisis in Japan Spawned a Global Food Craze*. Berkeley: University of California Press.

Sterckx, Roel. 2011. *Food, Sacrifice and Sagehood in Early China*. Cambridge: Cambridge University Press.

Straits Times. 2018. "PM Najib and Mahathir Agree on One Thing at Least: Don't Mess with Malaysia's Rendang!" April 4, 2018. https://www.straitstimes.com/asia/se-asia/pm-najib-and-mahathir-agree-on-one-thing-at-least-dont-mess-with-malaysias-rendang.

Surak, Kristin. 2012. *Making Tea, Making Japan: Cultural Nationalism in Practice*. Stanford, CA: Stanford University Press.

Swislocki, Mark. 2009. *Culinary Nostalgia: Regional Food Culture and the Urban Experience in Shanghai*. Stanford, CA: Stanford University Press.

Tan Chee-Beng, ed. 2011. *Chinese Food and Foodways in Southeast Asia and Beyond*. Singapore: NUS Press.

Tapper, Richard, and Sami Zubaida, eds. 2001. *A Taste of Thyme: Culinary Cultures of the Middle East*. New York: Tauris Parke Paperbacks.

Tarulevicz, Nicole. 2013. *Eating Her Curries and Kway: A Cultural History of Food in Singapore*. Chicago: University of Illinois Press.

Trubek, Amy B. 2000. *Haute Cuisine: How the French Invented the Culinary Profession*. Philadelphia: University of Pennsylvania Press.

Tyrrell, Alex, Patricia Hill, and Diane Kirkby. 2007. "Feasting on National Identity: Whisky, Haggis and the Celebration of Scottishness in the Nineteenth Century." In *Dining on Turtles: Food Feasts and Drinking in History*, edited by Diane Kirkby and Tanja Luckins, 46–63. New York: Palgrave Macmillan.

Wang Hui. 2011. *The Politics of Imagining Asia*, edited by Theodore Huters. Cambridge, MA: Harvard University Press.

Wank, David L. 2015. "Knife-Shaved Noodles Go Global: Provincial Culinary Politics and the Improbable Rise of a Minor Chinese Cuisine." In *Globalization and Asian Cuisines: Transnational Networks and Contact Zones*, edited by James Farrer, 187–208. New York: Palgrave Macmillan.

Wargadiredja, Arzia Tivany. 2018. " 'Crispy Rendang' Mess Shows Indonesians and Malaysians That Differences are Only Skin-Deep." *Vice*, April 4, 2018. https://www.vice.com/en_id/article/zmgz88/crispy-rendang-mess-shows-indonesians-and-malaysians-that-differences-are-only-skin-deep.

Watson, James L., ed. 1997. *Golden Arches East: McDonald's in East Asia*. Stanford, CA: Stanford University Press.

Wilson, Rachel. 2011. "Cocina Peruana Para El Mundo: Gastrodiplomacy, the Culinary National Brand, and the Context of National Cuisine in Peru." *Exchange: The Journal of Public Diplomacy* 2, no. 1: 13–20.

Wu, David, and Sidney Cheung, eds. 2002. *The Globalization of Chinese Food*. Honolulu: University of Hawai'i Press.

Wu, David Y. H., and Tan Chee-beng, eds. 2001. *Changing Chinese Foodways in Asia*. Hong Kong: The Chinese University Press.

Yenal, Zafer. 2010. "The Myth of Turkish Cuisine: National Appropriation of Local Food Cultures." In *Europa im Nahen Osten, der Nahe Osten in Europa*, edited by Angelika Neuwirth and Günter Stock, 271–83. Berlin: Akademie Verlag.

Yuan Mei. 2016. *Yuan Mei's Manual of Gastronomy: Recipes from the Garden of Contentment*. Edited by Jeffrey Riegel and E. N. Anderson. Translated by Sean Chen. Great Barrington, MA: Berkshire Publishing Group.

Part One

Historical Legacies

1

"Vegetarian" Nationalism: Critiques of Meat Eating for Japanese Bodies, 1880–1938

Tatsuya Mitsuda
Keio University

Vegetarianism in Japan

Many Western vegetarians express feelings of frustration at the lack of meat-free options in Japan, with vegans finding it almost impossible to eat out in a country where the meals are saturated with animal-derived ingredients and the natives appear to have few moral qualms about serving and consuming animal flesh.[1] "Being a vegan in Japan is extremely tough," one traveler is quoted as saying. "It is probably the most difficult place I have ever been to try and eat a vegan diet" (quoted in Bulliet 2005, 210). One long-suffering American resident also reported having encountered "very few" Japanese vegetarians and even fewer restaurants with a "proper" understanding of the contents of a vegetarian or vegan meal (Bunker 2016, 213).

Such dismay can turn to bafflement for Westerners upon learning that the Japanese used to be predominantly "vegetarian": for centuries the country forbade the slaughter and consumption of domesticated animals until the Meiji era (1868–1912). Game and fish had continued to be eaten but made up a small proportion of the overall diet. As in other parts of the world, religion, in this case Buddhism, is said to have played a role in Japan's development of a taboo surrounding the killing of such animals as cattle. However, the ruling elites realized, following visits to the United States and Europe in the 1860s and 1870s, that advanced nations tended to eat a lot of meat and dairy, and for this reason the state made concerted efforts to promote the consumption of ingredients derived from livestock, in particular beef and milk. Since then, it has appeared that Japan has given up on its predominantly "vegetarian" ways.

Scholars of Japanese food history have made very little mention of "vegetarianism," with the current literature leaving the impression that people in the modern era showed no significant interest in either its principles or its practices. One major reason for this oversight—which the chapter seeks to rectify—has been the overt focus on the rise of meat eating as an integral part of the country's modernization process. Ever since Emperor Meiji (1852–1912) was presented by the state as a regular consumer of beef and mutton, the dominant narrative has been to chart the almost inexorable rise of foods derived from animals. Leading intellectuals of the late nineteenth century, such as Fukuzawa Yukichi (1834–1901), contributed to this narrative by equating the larger physique of Westerners with their meat-based diet. Experts also proclaimed that animal-derived foods were nutritionally superior because meat and dairy contained greater amounts of protein than the typical indigenous fare that relied mainly on plant-based sources of energy. Pointing to Western nutritional science, they argued that meat was not only "essential to growth, health and strength," but that it was also a "significant source of intellectual and moral capacity" (Cwiertka 2006, 33). Consuming meat was thus often part of becoming civilized, enlightened, and modern, thereby helping the nation to become stronger and more capable of rubbing shoulders with the advanced West. The establishment of countless eateries serving beef stew (*gyūnabe*) helped popularize the taste for meat to such an extent that Harada Nobuo, the leading historian on this subject, has estimated that the country had become a nation of unapologetic meat eaters by the 1880s (Harada 1993, 238).

Existing research has thus tended to reproduce the powerful discourse of meat eating without questioning its force. It has assumed that debates about the desirability of a meat-based society—with a few objections by Buddhists in the 1870s—had already been won in the late nineteenth century. It has implied that the foundation for the boom in the consumption of meat and dairy after the Second World War had already been laid in the Meiji era. And it has struggled to account for the sluggish uptake of meat eating during the Taisho (1912–26) and the early Showa (1926–45) periods.[2] Focusing on the lively debates on "vegetarianism" that took place between 1900 and 1938, this chapter provides a corrective to this meat-affirming narrative. It argues that there were significant and sustained scientific doubts expressed about the merits of a meat-based society; it shows how these debates sparked ideas about the superiority of the Japanese diet, the uniqueness of the Japanese stomach, the richness of indigenous vegetarian meals, and the sophistication of Japanese culinary techniques; it demonstrates how the construction of this "vegetarian nationalism" meant that Japan could boast that it had little to learn from the West on how it should prepare its vegetarian dishes; and it illustrates the striking similarities and differences between Japan and China, as the latter witnessed an ultimately unsuccessful, state-led attempt to advance "vegetarian nationalism" around the same period. While socialists attempted to introduce Western-style vegetarianism to Japan, this chapter shows how its fortunes proved fateful as the government clamped down on the left-wing movement, resulting in a very different understanding of "vegetarianism" to the Western variant.

Toward a meat-based society?

One of the first intellectual heavyweights responsible for equating meat with modernity was Fukuzawa Yukichi. During his trips to the United States and Europe, the founder of Keio University was struck by the amount of meat Westerners consumed. In the pamphlet, "On Meat Eating" (*Nikushoku no setsu*), published in 1870, Fukuzawa specifically criticized Japan's traditional diet that had for centuries privileged the consumption of grains and plants. In his view, this explained why his countrymen were in poor health and weak (Fukuzawa 1963). He took aim at the taboo that considered the act of eating meat and drinking milk as barbaric, pointing to the hypocrisy of those who ate whale. Despite the popular perception that meat was polluting, Fukuzawa argued that the very fish that people ate could be found feeding on corpses and excrement in the seas and rivers in which they were caught. In contrast, the meat derived from cattle and sheep—because they were herbivores—could be considered much cleaner. He explained that beef and dairy could provide a great deal of nourishment, and since they constituted the basic ingredients in the Western diet, he encouraged his countrymen to embrace them. His argument, which was based on the Western science of nutrition, became a major point of reference in future debates about the relative merits of meat-based and plant-based diets. It also laid the foundations of a meat–vegetable dichotomy and contributed to the popular and erroneous impression that all Westerners were voracious meat eaters.

Many intellectuals subsequently joined the chorus espousing the merits of meat eating. Pointing to the healthy and intelligent-looking Westerners living in the treaty port of Yokohama, Yokokawa Shūto despaired that Japanese bodies looked small and ugly by comparison (Majima 2012, 115–16). Miura Michiyoshi, a physician, agreed: "[e]xcept for the most barbarian race, the Japanese has the smallest and worst physique in the world" (Majima 2012, 115). By the 1880s, as the number of medical experts trained in the West increased, the intellectual promotion of meat and dairy gathered pace. Efforts were made to show that meat eating had long been a custom in Japan, as exemplified by the consumption of wild game. Ōsawa Kenji, a physiologist, went as far as to pronounce that "meat-eating should be understood as a resurgence of ancient Japan" (Majima 2012, 117).

Many of the arguments were also couched in imperialistic terms. Intellectuals pointed to British might in India, where a race of 3,500 meat eaters lorded over 250 million plant-eating Indians (Majima 2012, 118). In the case of China, its defeat in the Opium Wars (1839–42 and 1856–60) was explained by the fact that the Chinese only ate pork and chicken, not beef. To become like the powerful British, and to avoid the fate of the weak Chinese, it was thus imperative to become beef eaters. Echoing these views, the Meiji government reformed legislation that had previously forbade the killing of domesticated animals, promoted the consumption of meat, encouraged the importation of foreign livestock to develop stockbreeding, and introduced canned meat—first in the navy, and then the army (Cwiertka 2006, 18; Majima 2012, 122–3; Miyazaki 1987, 33).

Much of this official backing helped, it appears, to sweep aside any lingering religious reservations about the consumption of meat. One example of this occurred in Tsuruga Prefecture, located on the western seaboard and a region famous for being home to a sizeable number of devout Buddhists. Following the establishment of a butcher's shop in 1872, the inhabitants protested at the harmful effects the consumption of meat inflicted on body and soul and took offense at how this practice offended the gods. Undoubtedly aware of a recent attempt by five Buddhist monks to forcibly enter the Imperial Palace in protest of the emperor's promotion of meat, the local government quickly stepped in to remind the inhabitants of the region that beef consumption improved people's health and criticized how these unfounded superstitions served to hold back the country's path toward civilization and enlightenment (Okada 2012, 57). In the official government view, Buddhist qualms were considered secondary to the more pressing task of modernizing the nation. As such, objections to the eating of flesh based on religious grounds virtually disappeared by the end of the century. Unlike in present-day India, where religious vegetarianism carries major political clout thanks to its promotion by the ruling Bharatiya Janata Party, a similar political movement based on Buddhist thinking failed to emerge in Japan.[3]

While religious arguments against meat eating were ignored, scientific ones received more attention in the 1880s. In fact, in contrast to China, which witnessed a conscious attempt to depart from Buddhist vegetarianism in favor of scientific vegetarianism as late as the early twentieth century, Japanese medical publications saw no need to refer to religion (Leung forthcoming). One of the first people to express doubts, if not specifically about a meat-based diet then about the Western diet more generally, was the army surgeon Mori Rintarō (1862–1922). Celebrated more today for his work as a novelist writing under the pen name Mori Ōgai than as the head of the Medical Division of the Army Ministry, Mori belonged to the generation of medical men sent to train in Germany who returned to spearhead the concept of "hygienic modernity," first in Japan and subsequently throughout its formal and informal empire (Rogaski 2004, 136–59, 254–84). Most of the scientific and Western accounts upon which Japanese supporters of a Western diet based their claims viewed protein as the most important nutrient (Thoms 2015, 146–7). This explains why meat, which contained the substance in abundance, was considered healthier than vegetables, which were believed to have less protein and to be harder to digest. At the beginning of the 1880s, the physiological consensus was thus that a largely vegetarian diet was insufficient to maintain health, and the "weak" Japanese body was commonly used as an example (Kellner and Mori 1889, 102).

Mori, as well as numerous other Japanese scientists who had spent time studying in Germany during the period, were skeptical. As Corinna Treitel has recently shown, Kumagawa Muneo (1858–1918), a contemporary, became the first to openly challenge the protein-centric nutritional standard that the physiologist Carl von Voit (1831–1908) had laid down (Treitel 2017, 102). Making himself the research subject, Kumagawa demonstrated that not only were "mixed" (i.e., containing fish) and purely "vegetarian" Japanese diets "perfectly nutritious," but that they also compared favorably to the European diet consisting of beef and pork (Kumagawa 1889, 370–2). Returning from his own stint in Germany between 1884 and 1888, Mori took the same line. He launched a scathing attack on Kaneshiro Takaki (1849–1920), his counterpart in the navy, for peddling the myth that the indigenous diet was deficient, and he showed that the average army diet consisting of rice, fish, tofu, and miso more than adequately met the standards of nutrition that Voit advocated (Bay 2012, 59). In a series of experiments in which the daily food intake of army soldiers was analyzed, Mori discovered that soldiers consumed, on average, 110.84 grams of protein, 22.91 grams of fat, and 524.86 grams of starch, which compared remarkably well to the 105–118 grams of protein, 56 grams of fat, and 500 grams of starch demanded by Voit (Bay 2012, 60). It was thus shown that protein could be derived from a combination of grains, plants, and fish.

Mori did not just stop there. He went on to reject the Eurocentrism of the nutritional standard, arguing that dietary recommendations failed to apply to Japanese bodies, which were five-sixths the size of the average European. Convinced that calories were more important than protein, Mori, together with Kumagawa, went further in demonstrating that a high-carbohydrate and low-protein diet could be just as healthy as a Western diet that boasted similar amounts of calories because "the value of the diet does not depend on the amount of protein, but on the fixed amount of energy" (Bay 2012, 61). Based on his experiments, Mori thus cast doubt on the widespread notion that linked the recommended diet to the progress of civilization itself, claiming instead that the Japanese body, albeit smaller in size, matched the Western body in terms of muscle and strength, and suggested that there was no need to Westernize the indigenous diet (Bay 2012, 59).

Even though Mori's intervention centered on the problem of beriberi—a disease caused by the lack of vitamin B—and focused on soldiers, the wider implications for assessments of meat and vegetables and applications to broader society were apparent: his efforts helped undermine the central premise on which meat's healthfulness had been based and promoted. Mori himself felt that the meat–vegetable dichotomy was an unhelpful one. Both the Western and the Japanese diets were similar: staples were grain-based (bread or rice) and side dishes contained animal-derived foods (meat or fish) and vegetables, and he strongly felt that it was wrong to label foods as bad or good—it was more a matter of combining as many foods as possible to create the right nutritional balance (Imai 2002, 20). For Mori, foods were mere vessels to access the more important chemical components contained within them—the guises that they took were thus a red herring.

A more specific attack on the supposed superiority of a meat-based diet was launched by the German physician and anthropologist, Erwin Baelz (1849–1913). Starting in 1876, he taught at the Medical College of Tokyo Imperial University for close to twenty-seven years, and is seen as one of the founding figures of Western medicine in the country. In 1901, Baelz published his thoughts on the vegetarian diet the Japanese masses followed in the pages of a German medical journal (Baelz 1901b). He explained to his European readers that it was the scientific norm to believe that the Japanese diet lacked the necessary amount of protein and fat. However, like Mori, Baelz was not convinced that Voit's dietary standard—which presupposed a larger European body—should be applied to the diminutive Japanese, whose industriousness was all too apparent in his day-to-day encounters with them.

Baelz suspected that the largely plant-based diet that powered Japanese workers could be shown to have advantages, and to test this hypothesis he invited two rickshaw drivers to participate in an experiment. Both of the drivers upon whom he called were similar in age, height, and experience. For the first round of experiments, both were weighed and fed the same low-protein and high-carbohydrate meal. For the following three weeks, both were asked to carry 80 kilograms of weight over a distance of 40 kilometers each day. As a result, the weight of one of the drivers increased a little while that of the other driver stayed the same. For the second round of experiments the diet of the same drivers was changed. They were fed meals that included beef, raising the amount of protein at the expense of the carbohydrates. Both drivers expressed initial delight at the opportunity to devour what had evidently become a delicacy. However, after just three days, both drivers complained of fatigue, pleading with Baelz to immediately stop his experiment. He complied and reported that, after several weeks, the drivers were back to their former, impressive selves. Supplementing his study with an anecdote about how a single rickshaw driver could cover the 110-kilometer journey from Tokyo to Nikko almost as quickly as six separate horses, he concluded that "a meat diet provides large amounts of energy for the moment and for a short time, while the advantage of a near vegetarian diet lies in stamina" (Baelz 1901b, 692).

Published in German at the turn of the century, Baelz's opinion on the Japanese vegetarian diet also reached a domestic audience of Japanese scientists in 1901 (Baelz 1901a). His work became accessible to the wider public several years later and was elevated to folkloric status in the 1920s and 1930s. One of the first to seize on his pronouncement was a dietetic manual edited by *Hygiene News* (*Eisei Shinpō*), a newspaper that focused on spreading information about proper hygiene. Responding to the question of whether the Japanese, in their quest to be as healthy as Westerners, should imitate the lifestyle of Europeans and Americans, the editors cast doubt on the widespread notion that the Japanese body lacked protein and other necessary nutrients (*Eisei Shinpō* 1906, 24). Pointing to Baelz, who had earlier shown that rickshaw drivers were strong and energetic, the manual boasted to its readers that the West was now coming around to a reassessment of the Japanese diet.

By the early twentieth century, Western scientists had become increasingly doubtful of the validity of the protein-centered standard. In the United States, Russell Chittenden (1856–1943), a highly regarded professor of physiological chemistry at Yale University, took on the nutritional establishment. He conducted a series of experiments involving Yale athletes, army volunteers, and laboratory members. He demonstrated that people could live on significantly less than the amount of protein nutritional science conventionally recommended (Chittenden 1905). He also showed that low-protein diets could be healthier because the body did not have to deal with the disposal of such protein breakdown products as uric acid (Carpenter 1994, 112).

In Europe, the fight against the protein doctrine was taken up most forcibly by Danish nutritionist Mikkel Hindhede (1862–1945). Characterized as a "fanatic agitator" and "an agrarian anti-modernist," Hindhede conducted a series of experiments in which he showed that humans could live on as little as 25 grams of vegetable protein per day (Overgaard 2001, 204). Pointing to the superior health of small farmers in his native region of West Jutland, Hindhede constructed, in the words of the historian Sven Skafte Overgaard, "a food pyramid that dismissed meat and protein in favour of calories, wholegrain, bread and potatoes" (Overgaard 2001, 204). Most strikingly, Hindhede managed to show how wartime rationing had actually helped Danes to become healthier. Due to the fact that 80 percent of pigs had been slaughtered to make way for the production of grains, the domestic population had made do by consuming more porridge, brown bread, and potatoes. Consumption of meat, pork, butter, margarine, and white bread had had to be significantly reduced. Pointing to a causal relationship between the strict diet Danes followed and the lowest mortality rate the country had ever experienced, Hindhede hailed the First World War as the healthiest period in the history of European health.

The works of Chittenden and Hindhede were significant to the Japanese context. They were referred to intermittently in dietetic publications, and their conclusions were interpreted as endorsements of the Japanese diet. Most Japanese, *Eisei Shinpō* explained, followed a near-vegetarian diet. Foods such as fish, meat, eggs, and chicken were the preserve of the wealthy, which remained a small proportion of the population. As Hindhede had, the publication suggested a return to a simpler, more rural way of living, which remained a possibility because meat had not yet made major inroads. By the early twentieth century, confidence in the merits of the indigenous diet had thus grown: the likes of Mori and Baelz helped deflate the myth that had grown around the eating of meat.

Socialism and the vegetarian ideal

While Baelz helped spearhead a scientific reappraisal of the indigenous vegetarian diet, socialists became interested in vegetarianism for distinctly different reasons. Back in 1888, the publisher Aoki Teizo (1858–89) had been the first to introduce Western vegetarianism to Japan, bringing out a pamphlet bearing the title "Discussions About Simple Foods" (*soshoku* 素食) that essentially summarized the chief arguments of the Vegetarian Society of England (Aoki 1888). The term *soshoku* derived from the ancient Chinese term *sushi* (素食), but apart from the word itself, the booklet belied very little Chinese influence (Leung, forthcoming) and the publication itself seems not to have made much of an impact. In the early twentieth century, however, socialists went further than merely introducing the principles and rules that Aoki had outlined: they reported on actual events and debates abroad as lived experiences and considered whether Japan should follow suit. They also called the practice *saishokushugi* 菜食主義—the now accepted translation of the English word, vegetarianism.

Nobody embodied this change in outlook more than Kōtoku Shūsui (1870–1911), who wrote about his encounter with vegetarianism in the United States in *Katei Zasshi*, a short-lived magazine whose aim was to implement socialist values through reform of the home (Kōtoku 1906, 15–17). Prior to his travels abroad, Kōtoku had been arrested for publishing the first Japanese translation, together with Sakai Toshihiko (1871–1933), of the Communist Manifesto in the socialist newspaper *Heimin Shinbun*. Radicalized during his internment by the ideas of the Russian anarchist Peter Kropotkin (1842–1921), Kōtoku traveled to California and Chicago shortly after his release. Members of the American Left and Russian dissidents whom he met influenced the foundation of his own Socialist Revolutionary Party.

During his time in the United States, Kōtoku was impressed by female socialists who had converted to vegetarianism. He reflected on his encounter with a Chicago housewife who had suffered from a weak physique and stomach-related illnesses. Since renouncing meat 15 years previously, however, she had not needed to return to the doctor once. His earlier impression that vegetarians lacked energy was obliterated by the boundless energy that "Mrs. Merrill" exuded. She opened a school in her home and taught classes from 9:00 a.m. to 10:00 p.m., all the while carrying out her household chores and going shopping in between classes without the help of a maid (Kōtoku

1906, 15). This encounter prompted Kōtoku to try out vegetarianism himself when he fell ill. He happily reported that after he stopped eating meat his condition vastly improved. From his direct experience, Kōtoku thus observed that meat-related products were difficult to digest, decayed easily, emitted toxins, and produced disease. "Unless one has a strong stomach," he concluded, "meat must be considered very dangerous" (Kōtoku 1906, 17). His conclusions were also informed by the view that meat merchants, as capitalists, had only their profits in mind: butchers showed little concern about flogging diseased meat to unsuspecting customers. Renouncing meat was thus also about breaking ties with the market economy that had helped create this exploitation.

While it remains unclear whether Kōtoku became a committed vegetarian, a close acquaintance of his, Kaneko Kiichi (1876–1909), an active socialist living in the United States, showed the way forward (Kaneko 1906). More than his counterparts back in Japan, Kaneko took to heart the need to begin with socialism in the home, believing that reform started with changing the hierarchical relationship between husband and wife. For Kaneko, marriage was nothing less than a union of two equals, and upon marrying the American feminist Josephine Conger (b. 1874), he converted to vegetarianism as a consummation of this very principle (Kitamura 2007, 123). Even before their decision to become vegetarians, the couple was moved to buy less meat following the disclosures made by Upton Sinclair in his non-fiction novel, *The Jungle* (1906), which caused a massive public outcry in the United States for exposing the exploitative, unsanitary, and inhumane practices of the meatpacking industry in Chicago.

More directly, the Kaneko-Congers were moved to act following a conversation with a female teacher, who, although harshly critical of the uncivilized practices involved in meat production, could not bring herself to abstain from meat for "even a single day" (Kaneko 1906, 12). Railing against her hypocrisy for "just talking the talk," the Kaneko-Congers resolved to become vegetarians themselves. In accordance with the vegetarianism of the day, the couple continued to eat eggs and dairy, but gradually turned the rest of their diet into one consisting of rice, bread, fruits, and vegetables. After just two weeks, Kaneko reported, they were able to go completely without meat. An unexpected surprise was a palpable improvement in their health. They also decided that they could go without eating three times a day, and reduced their diet to two meals with no adverse effects. Reflecting on his conversion, Kaneko waxed lyrical: "I am a believer that, if society were to follow as I did a vegetarian diet and pursued two meals a day, that they would be able to bid farewell to all sorts of illnesses, making it possible for people to lead a healthy and pure life" (Kaneko 1906, 15). For the Kaneko-Congers, conversion to vegetarianism was about more than just improving their health: becoming vegetarian and limiting meals to twice a day was a form of protest against the elaborate arrangement by which food was prepared in wealthy households. Critical of the excessive practice in which an army of servants, cooks, butlers, and maids would be employed to prepare meals for just two or three people, vegetarianism offered a way to end what they viewed as being tantamount to slavery.

In contrast to Kōtoku and Kaneko, Sakai Toshihiko, a major writer and figure in the socialist movement in Japan, added a moral argument to his pronouncement on why the eating of meat had to be rejected (Sakai 1904). In his passionate account describing his conversion to vegetarianism, Sakai saw the possibility for society and families to become "kinder" through the humane treatment of animals (Sakai 1906). As a child, Sakai had felt guilty when he joined his friends in beating a chicken with wooden swords, but given the general climate in which meat eating was being promoted, he could not bring himself to speak out: "You cannot become strong without eating well. Whether it be pigs or cows, the discourse is that eating meat is a must" (Sakai 1906, 18). Following his decision to become a member of the Society for the Prevention of Cruelty to Animals, however, Sakai became convinced that this wrong had to be put right.

Such a humanitarian outlook was closely aligned with his socialist views: his call to renounce meat symbolized a larger concern with the development of capitalism, which he could not separate from the rise of a meat-based society. He pointed out how advocates of competition, Social Darwinists, and winners in life looked at how nature appeared to favor the survival of the fittest, exploiting this biological fact to justify the kind of behavior that created vast gaps between the rich and the poor (Sakai 1906, 19). Common to them all was that capitalism involved the same species kicking, beating, and even killing one another. Socialism was about creating a society in which humans did not go after one another's throats. Why should interspecies relationships be any different? Socialism also needed to make efforts to hold in check the same mechanisms that allowed the kicking, killing, and beating of animals for the purposes of producing meat.

Three main criticisms emerged from the moral debate that Sakai helped instigate (Sakai 1905). First, critics struggled to fathom why animals should be included in the struggle for a socialist society: humans themselves were still far from attaining equality or reining in the excesses of capitalism. Why should concerns about animals be placed on an equal footing? Pushing the argument Sakai made to its logical conclusion, skeptics also wondered whether vegetables would also need moral consideration, because plants could be seen to be alive as well. In response, Sakai accepted that the eventual inclusion of all animals was best left for the future, but remained adamant that "as our sympathies develop, the principle should be extended from higher animals to low animals and then eventually to plants" (Sakai 1905).

Second, critics pointed to the contradictions inherent in vegetarianism. Referring to the guidelines of the Vegetarian Society of England, they expressed surprise that animal-derived foods such as eggs and dairy were allowed. "What is the difference," they asked, "between eating eggs and eating chicken, or between drinking milk and eating beef?" (Sakai 1905). In his defense, Sakai tried to show how a vegetarian diet was healthy. He also made use of the argument that monkeys—as humankind's closest relatives—do not eat meat. He also stressed that the development of a meat-based society contributed to increased violence, intimating that rising instances of aggression inflicted on animals strongly correlated with that perpetrated on humans. Refraining from the consumption of meat, he argued, would result in more peaceful people.

Finally, critics expressed doubts about the impact of this dietary advice on the working class—the very people whose plight the socialist movement aimed to alleviate. In the view of the physician Ōishi Rokutei (better known as Seinosuke) (1867–1911), the scientific consensus was that a vegan diet—which Sakai seems to have been ultimately advocating—was insufficient to maintain health (Sakai 1905). This was why, he explained, Western vegetarians supplemented their diet with milk, eggs, butter, and cheese so as to absorb enough nutrients. For Ōishi, the dangers of romanticizing a diet based on vegetables was that it helped glorify the existing diet of the working class, who had to make do with cheap, imported "Nanjing rice" and "pickled leaves" (Sakai 1905). There was no better way, he castigated Sakai, of keeping the working class hapless, impoverished, and downtrodden than to recommend from on high a vegetarian diet.

Most of the socialist debate into vegetarianism took place between 1905 and 1906, a heady period which witnessed the establishment of the first Socialist Party in the country; it also bore witness to Kōtoku's controversial decision to take direct action in toppling the government. Due to increased state interference, the party was forced to dissolve in 1907 and *Heimin Shinbun* had to close in the same year. In 1909, Kaneko, suffering from tuberculosis, returned from the United States and died shortly afterward; *Katei Zasshi*, which had served as the main forum of debate, also folded in 1909. Both Kōtoku and Ōishi—viewed by the police as ringleaders in an attempt to assassinate the emperor—were arrested in 1910 for high treason and sentenced to death a year later. Sakai was spared the same fate as he had already been interned on charges relating to a different incident; but socialism as a political force was severely weakened, and the vegetarian ideals the movement espoused lost their power, along with the moral and humanitarian arguments that had been put forward. While it is impossible to know whether vegetarianism would have flourished in Japan had these figures lived on, their deaths certainly spelled the end of a vegetarianism that attempted to replicate the Western example.

The rise of vegetarian nationalism

What emerged instead was a more ominous reappraisal of the indigenous diet that resulted in the construction of a very different type of "vegetarianism." Numerous wars were among the factors responsible for this shift. In particular, the Russo–Japanese War (1904–5) and the First World War (1914–18) helped furnish, so it seemed, the hard evidence that had been lacking in the results derived from the clinical trials conducted by the likes of Baelz, Kumagawa, and Mori. Following a Japanese victory in the Battle of Liaoyang (1904), the first major land battle of the Russo–Japanese War, the newspaper *Yomiuri Shinbun* was quick to report on Baelz's view that Japanese success could be attributed to the vegetarian diets on which the Japanese soldiers had been raised (*Yomiuri Shinbun* 1904, 1). A few years after the conclusion of hostilities, Kamimura Kensuke, a physician, surmised that the war had shown how Japanese soldiers, at least with regard to work and walking, could be regarded as superior to the Russians. He referred extensively to Baelz's experiments involving rickshaw drivers as evidence that proved that Japanese working men, because they followed a natural vegetarian diet, were indefatigable (Kamimura 1918). News about the First World War—during which the health of European soldiers was found not to deteriorate from a reduction of meat in their rations—served to further bolster the view that the nutritional importance of meat was an exaggeration (Ishigami 1919, 113; Shimizu 1924, 175).

The extent to which the Russo–Japanese War shook the belief of intellectuals in the power of meat can be gleaned from the diaries of the literary scholar Uchigasaki Sakusaburō (1877–1947), who encountered an active vegetarian movement while studying at Oxford between 1908 and 1911. He tried his best to explain why the English were turning their backs on meat. He contended that this dietary blip hardly undid the progress that had been made over the centuries and warned his Japanese compatriots not to follow suit (Uchigasaki 1911, 89). As a country that still had a lot of catching up to do, the promotion of "vegetarianism"—at least at this stage of history—was tantamount to developmental suicide in his view. Uchigasaki was adamant that his nation's unexpected victory in the Russo–Japanese War had nothing to do with the indigenous "vegetarian" diet (Uchigasaki 1911, 90). Rather than turn back the clock to a "vegetarian" diet, Uchigasaki argued that it was important to continue to consume more meat. He recommended that the overall proportion of meat in the Japanese diet should be elevated to at least half. He also urged other Asian countries to follow suit. In his time as a student at Oxford, he took to task an Indian student who strongly believed in the benefits of a vegetarian diet. As long as Indians followed a plant-based diet, he warned, the country would never manage to become independent. Meat was for the colonizers, he quipped, while vegetables were for the colonized (Uchigasaki 1911, 92).

Despite Uchigasaki's protestations, dietetic publications continued to confirm the benefits of the near-vegetarian Japanese diet, in particular by showing how Japanese men possessed stamina in abundance. Building on the work of Baelz, Sawamura Makoto (1865–1931), the most prolific writer on nutrition during this period, reassured his readers that while the Western body might look impressive, the Japanese had little to fear: not only were they just as strong, but they also had greater staying power (Sawamura 1919, 323–6). He referred to such carnivores as lions and tigers whose ferocity as hunters was severely compromised by their pitifully low levels of endurance. Plant-eating prey, he suggested, managed to survive lengthy attacks because they had more stamina. More to the point, he argued that plant-eating mammals such as cows and horses had little trouble working all day. By way of analogy, he argued that because the Japanese were plant eaters as well, they were less vulnerable to the fatigue that afflicted meat eaters who needed to waste energy breaking down the proteins contained in meat to produce uric acid. Since uric acid is not produced by the consumption of vegetables, the Japanese could also endure long hours of hard work.

Connected to this argument was a belief in the peculiarity of the Japanese stomach that had a long pedigree: it was expressed by the likes of the influential neo-Confucian scholar Kaibara Ekken (1630–1714), who wrote that the Japanese gut had more problems digesting meat than Korean or Chinese stomachs (Kaibara 2015, 160). Biomedicine—without referring to traditional dietetics—helped modernize the argument. In 1916, Yamada Kōho wrote that the Japanese gut was better able to break down dietary fiber, a feat that Western intestines failed to match (Yamada 1916, 99–100). In contrast, the Japanese struggled to produce as much gastric acid as Westerners were able to when digesting meat—a reflection, he argued, of the very different diets the two groups traditionally followed. What also helped, Satō Hisashi chimed in, was that the Japanese stomach was not only bigger than that of a Westerner, but its efficacy was also bolstered by the consumption of side dishes like tofu, *natto* (fermented soy beans), and miso, all of which improved levels of digestion (Satō 1921, 133–4). He showed that, in terms of digestion, the Japanese body was ideally suited to breaking down plant-derived foods. He demonstrated that the Japanese stomach digested as much as 91 percent of all foods ingested. Based on these results, Satō refuted the widely held Western view that vegetables themselves were hard to digest. By selecting the correct accompaniments, levels of digestion could be improved.

One upshot of this scientific turnaround in the assessment of a vegetarian diet was to elevate, more than ever before, the impression that Japanese foods were superior. The roots of this realization can be traced as far back as to the socialist debate over how a vegetarian diet could be implemented. In the view of Ōishi Rokutei, a physician who had qualified in the United States, the problem with following the Western vegetarian diet was the cost: the kinds of cereals, fruits, and vegetables that Western practitioners made use of were too expensive (Ōishi 1906). Eggs, olive oil, and milk were also hard to come by in Japan. Moreover, replicating the culinary techniques of the West was difficult. Based on these difficulties, Ōishi advocated the consumption of more domestic vegetarian meals that would be affordable, varied, and fit better into the country's food culture.

More significantly, Ōishi suggested that Japanese culinary tradition was better at producing a more complete vegetarian package. In their enthusiasm to render meals more appetizing, Western vegetarians had to compromise: a variety of sauces had to be poured over the vegetables and cereals in order to make the dishes tastier. They were also heavily dependent on butter and cream. In contrast, the Japanese had soy sauce. Favorites such as *nimono* (simmered dish), soup stock, grilled fish, and pickled side dishes all went well with the condiment, which, produced as it is from fermented soybeans, contained ample amounts of protein, thereby rendering the Japanese vegetarian meal more nutritious (Ōishi 1906, 35). Even though Ōishi welcomed the introduction of Western foods such as fried potatoes, croquettes, beans, and vegetable soup in the repertoire of the meals the Japanese could afford to prepare, his call for people to look to their own culinary heritage for inspiration set an important precedent.

Confidence in the ingredients used in Japanese cuisine soon extended to commentaries on the natural conditions in which plant-derived ingredients had come into being. In his dietetic manual, Ishigami Rokunosuke forged a strong link between food and land (Ishigami 1919). He noted how, in comparison with Western countries, the Japanese diet reflected more strongly the influence of soil and climate. Each region, he claimed, was different. He remarked that eating locally produced foods corresponded with the laws of nature. There was a reason why the gods had blessed the land with certain foods. Consequently, Ishigami proposed that the most "natural" Japanese foods consisted of the five grains, vegetables, fish, and game. He allowed for regional variations—it was inevitable that inhabitants on the coasts and the mountains would have different diets—but insisted that plant-derived meals remain central, maintaining that meat should only be served as a side dish and that its proportion in the overall diet should remain small (Ishigami 1919, 109).

By the mid-1930s, the various strands that linked history, ingredients, side dishes, culinary techniques, and nature had become the basis upon which a nationalistic view of the domestic diet was expressed. In 1932, *Yomiuri Shinbun* reported on the trip

Egawa Tsuneo (d. −1964), a high-ranking army officer, made to Europe (Egawa 1932a, 1932b). Like many before him, Egawa expressed surprise at the extent to which the vegetarian movement was making inroads on the continent. Struck by the connection the popular Western discourse drew between excessive levels of meat consumption and various diseases, he warned that Japan, while still free of the diseases linked with a meat-based society, could also tread a similar path if it rushed too quickly to become like the West. Yet Egawa remained optimistic; Japan could already hark back to a long history in which a plethora of vegetables—alongside seafood—had been put to use to foster the kind of mature "vegetarian culture" (菜食文化 *saishokubunka*) that would prevent his country from being afflicted by Western diseases.

One major difference between Europe and Japan, as Egawa perceived it, was that Europe simply did not have a rich and sophisticated vegetarian culture to fall back on. The meals recently developed by European vegetarians tasted "revolting," while Japanese culinary techniques, which he described as "the best in the world," had managed to render vegetarian meals more exquisite (Egawa 1932b). Many of his ideas, which erroneously assumed that Europe was a meat-centered civilization, were far from accurate. Nor could his definition of "vegetarian" be considered correct, especially when measured against Western standards. Rather, the significance of his opinions lies less in their accuracy and more in the fact that Egawa did not feel the need to imitate the West in vegetarian matters—the Japanese, he said, could be proud of the fact that Japan had a more advanced vegetarian culture. By maintaining links with this heritage, he implied that there was no need to organize a movement: it was part of who the Japanese were all along.

Such a view was echoed by Kimura Kaneaki, a nutritionist who published an article discussing vegetarianism in *Dai Ajia* (*Greater Asia*), a journal that embraced a pan-Asiatic ideal and sought to eliminate European imperial influences from the region (Kimura 1936). Espousing a negative view of the Westernization of the Japanese diet, he repeated the main mantras about the adverse impact a meat-based diet could have on health, warning urban inhabitants in particular of the risks. Meat was difficult to digest, fatigued the body, contained toxins, and lacked vitamins and minerals, he explained (Kimura 1936, 70). In contrast, vegetables were free of toxins, were easier to digest, increased stamina, rejuvenated the cells, and helped purify blood, all of which resulted in healthy bowels and lively nerves (Kimura 1936, 71–2).

Referring to the twenty years of Western interest in the Japanese diet that had come before, Kimura proclaimed that European scientists now considered the Japanese vegetarian diet to be "perfect" (Kimura 1936, 73). Research conducted by "German and French scientists into the stamina, energy, and strength of East Asians and Japanese," he explained, demonstrated a strong connection between food and climate, or 風土 *fūdo*, an expression that went beyond mere changes in weather conditions to encapsulate a cultural and spiritual condition (Kimura 1936, 72). No other country, Kimura went on to state, was blessed with as much nature, or boasted as many types of vegetarian meals, or possessed such sophisticated culinary techniques (Kimura 1936, 73). In Kimura's view, the recent Western turn toward vegetarianism vindicated what the Japanese had been practicing for millennia. Concluding that Japan had little to learn from the West, including from its particular brand of vegetarianism, Kimura recommended a vegetable-centered diet, supplemented by small amounts of disease-free fresh meat.

Conclusions

In her recent work on the history of vegetarianism in China, Angela Leung (forthcoming) has observed how the country initially embraced vegetarianism in the early twentieth century, only to turn against it in the late 1920s. She has described how the vegetarianism espoused by the literati departed from traditional dietetic notions of *sushi* to embrace a Western nutritional reframing that focused on the toxins in the meat of sick animals. Benefiting from the scientific doubt cast on the health benefits of eating meat, Leung has demonstrated how socialists and political figures promoted a vegetarian diet that elevated the supposed superiority of Chinese cuisine as part of their nation-building efforts. Such a movement resulted in the foundation of a vegetarian society, a culinary research institute tasked with improving vegetarian meals, the opening of eateries and restaurants (especially in urban and cosmopolitan areas), and students pressuring Peking University to set up a vegetarian canteen in which ingredients such as soy milk and bean curd took pride of place. By the late 1920s, however, nationalist enthusiasm for a vegetarian diet, Leung argues, decreased as it became clear that the weakness of China lay in the backward, vegetarian diet of the peasantry. For China to compete internationally, this deficiency had to be reformed through industrialization, and thereby set back the fortunes of vegetarianism for decades.

When compared to the Chinese experience, the Japanese encounter with vegetarianism bears witness to history in reverse. Unlike China, which began the early twentieth century by lauding vegetarianism as an alternative path to modernity, Japan began promoting meat eating as the only way to the future from as early as the 1870s. In both cases, the influence of the Western science of nutrition was paramount. However, whereas the Japanese encountered a meat-centric international protein discourse in the 1870s, the Chinese experienced a decidedly different nutritional discourse in the early twentieth century, not least because Japanese researchers had by this time helped cast doubt on the nutritional merits of animal-derived foods. As the twentieth century wore on, and Japan gained confidence as an imperial power, the "vegetarianism" that emerged came to symbolize the superior health of the Japanese body, the sophistication of the country's food culture, and the uniqueness of the nature and climate in which its vegetables were cultivated. Similar to how it was used in China, although under decidedly different circumstances, Western nutritional language was employed in Japan to paper over traditional dietetic notions, and indigenous culinary techniques were lauded to show that the country's own vegetarian meals were tastier and more sophisticated than those eaten in the West. Given the nationalistic nature of Japanese vegetarianism, however, neither vegetarianism nor the vegetarian diet came to mean the same or include the same ingredients as it did in the West: fish, game, and even the meat of domesticated animals—as long as they were not central to the dish— could be included in the meal because they were seen as part of the historic, natural, and indigenous diet.

What is equally remarkable is how, in both China and Japan, political influences swayed the fortunes of vegetarianism. In both countries, socialists and anarchists were heavily involved in the promotion of vegetarianism. In contrast to China, which witnessed the emergence of eateries and societies, Japanese socialist interest in vegetarianism did not go beyond the promise it held as an anti-capitalist ideology, not least because the main promoters had little opportunity to develop its principles. Crucial to the fortunes of vegetarianism, it thus appears, was the involvement of the state. While in China vegetarianism was promoted by state officials, this was not the case in Japan. Government suspicion of the socialist movement in Japan would not have likely endeared vegetarianism to officials, and the state continued to encourage the production and consumption of meat, with Korea and China becoming major suppliers of cheap meat as the empire expanded into East Asia (Nakazato 1990; Noma 2001).

Such a sustained interest in vegetarianism and the vegetarian diet during the period under review also complicates the predominant narrative of meat's ascent in pre-war Japan. It helps to explain in part the sluggish take up of meat in the Taisho and early Showa periods. What this chapter also reclaims is a past that has hitherto remained hidden in contemporary discussions of vegetarianism in Japan. No longer can Buddhist traditions continue to be touted as the sole example of vegetarian Japan—it must now take into consideration the socialist and the scientific "vegetarianism" espoused in the early twentieth century. Ultimately, vegetarianism as a concept appears weakly or poorly understood in Japan, at least partly because its tenets were influenced by a nationalism that saw its own historic and natural "vegetarian" diet—which saw no contradiction in including fish or game—as superior to that of the West.

Acknowledgments

I would like to extend my thanks to Michelle King, Angela Leung, and Katsura Sako for their incisive comments on earlier drafts of this chapter.

Notes

1   This chapter defines "vegetarian" as a practice that makes a conscious effort to eat as much vegetables, fruits, grains, and nuts as possible. The practice of "veganism" will be defined by efforts to exclude animal products altogether from the diet. To avoid confusion between Western and Japanese "vegetarianism," quotation marks will be used when referring to the latter.
2   See the works by Cwiertka (2006), Majima (2012), and Miyazaki (1987) for the powerful discourse on meat. The point about the sluggish uptake of meat eating has been made recently by Smil and Kobayashi (2012, 49) and Rath (2016, 160). Majima (2012) has also made the point that meat eating did not reach the masses in the period in question.
3   See Chapter 8 in this volume, by Michaël Bruckert, for the Indian situation.

References

青木貞三 Aoki Teizo. 1888. 素食論 *Soshokuron* [*Discussions About Simple Foods*]. Tokyo: Yajima Ryōkichi.

Baelz, Erwin. 1901a. "植物食ノ多衆栄養ト其堪能平均トニ就キテ Shokubutsu shoku no tashū eiyō to sono tannō heikin to ni tsukite" ["On the Vegetable Foods in the Common Diet and Its Average Levels of Endurance"]. 中外医事新報 *Chūgai Iji Shinpō* 516: 1247–8.

Baelz, Erwin. 1901b. "Über vegetarische Massenernährung und über das Leistungsgewicht" ["About the vegetarian mass diet and the power to weight ratio"]. *Berliner klinische Wochenschrift* 38, no. 26: 689–93.

Bay, Alexander R. 2012. *Beriberi in Modern Japan: The Making of a National Disease.* Rochester, NY: University of Rochester Press.

Bulliet, Richard. 2005. *Hunters, Herders, and Hamburgers: The Past and Future of Human-Animal Relationships.* New York: Columbia University Press.

Bunker, Douglas. 2016. *A Survival Guide for the Vegetarian in Japan.* Yokohama: Pace Pace Publishing.

Carpenter, Kenneth. 1994. *Protein and Energy: A Study of Changing Ideas in Nutrition.* Cambridge: Cambridge University Press.

Chittenden, Russell H. 1905. *Physiological Economy in Nutrition, with Special Reference to the Minimal Protein Requirement of the Healthy Man: An Experimental Study.* London: F. A. Stokes.

Cwiertka, Katarzyna J. 2006. *Modern Japanese Cuisine: Food, Power and National Identity.* London: Reaktion Books.

江川恒雄 Egawa Tsuneo. 1932a. 菜食に帰れ（一）•日本の野菜料理は世界一 "Saishoku ni kaere 1. Nihon no yasai ryōri wa sekai ichi" ["Go Back to the Vegetarian Diet 1. Japan's Vegetable Meals Are the Best in the World"]. 読売新聞 *Yomiuri Shinbun*, April 26, morning edition: 4.

江川恒雄 Egawa Tsuneo. 1932b. 菜食に帰れ（四）•日本の野菜料理は世界一 "Saishoku ni kaere 4. Nihon no yasai ryōri wa sekai ichi" ["Go Back to the Vegetarian Diet 4. Japan's Vegetable Meals Are the Best in the World"]. 読売新聞 *Yomiuri Shinbun*, April 29, morning edition: 4.

衛生新報 *Eisei Shinpō*, ed. 1906. 養生篇： 実用問答 *Yōjōhen: Jitsuyōmondō* [*Essays on Self-care: Practical Questions and Answers*]. Tokyo: Maruyamasha.

福澤諭吉 Fukuzawa Yukichi. [1870] 1963. "肉食之説 Nikushoku no setsu" ["On Meat Eating"]. In 福澤諭吉全集 *Fukuzawa Yukichi Zenshū*, edited by 慶應義塾 Keio Gijuku, 38–41, Vol. 20. Tokyo: Iwanami Shoten.

原田信男 Harada Nobuo. 1993. 歴史の中の米と肉 *Rekishi no Naka no Kome to Niku* [*Rice and Meat in History*]. Tokyo: Heibonsha.

今井佐恵子 Imai Saeko. 2002. "森鴎外と福澤諭吉の食生活論 Mori Ōgai to Fukuzawa Yukichi no shokuseikatsuron" ["Mori Ōgai and Fukuzawa Yukichi's Essays on Dietary Habits"]. *Kyōto Tanki Daigaku Ronshū* 30, no. 1: 17–24.

石上録之助 Ishigami Rokunosuke. 1919. 六十三大家生活法：比較研究 *Rokujyūsan taika seikatsuhō: hikakukenkyū* [*Ways of Living for 63 Distinguished Families: A Comparative Study*]. Tokyo: Chūseidō.

貝原益軒 Kaibara Ekken. [1712] 2015. 養生訓 *Yōjōkun* [*Rules for Keeping Healthy*]. Tokyo: Chichi Shuppan.

神村兼亮 Kamimura Kensuke. 1918. "車夫に実験せる肉食と菜食 Shafu ni jikken seru nikushoku to saishoku" ["Experiment of Meat Diet and Vegetable Diet on a Rickshaw Man"]. 食養雑誌 *Shokuyō Zasshi* 128, no. 6: 19–21.

金子喜一 Kaneko Kiichi. 1906. "予が實行せる菜食主義 Yo ga jikkō seru saishoku shugi" ["Vegetarianism Which I Perform"]. 家庭雑誌 *Katei Zasshi* 4, no. 9: 12–15.

Kellner, O. J., and Y. Mori. 1889 "Untersuchungen über die Ernährung der Japaner" ["Investigations into the Diet of the Japanese"]. *Zeitschrift für Biologie* 25: 102–22.

木村矩晟 Kimura Kaneaki. 1936. "肉食と菜食 Nikushoku to saishoku" ["Meat Diet and Vegetarian Diet"]. 大亜細亜 *Dai Ajia* 4, no. 3: 69–73.

北村巌 Kitamura Iwao. 2007. 金子喜一とその時代 *Kaneko Kiichi to Sono Jidai* [*Kaneko Kiichi and His Times*]. Sapporo: Hakurōsha.

幸徳秋水 Kōtoku Shūsui. 1906. "菜食主義 Saishoku shugi" ["Vegetarianism"]. 家庭雑誌 *Katei Zasshi* 4, no. 6: 15–17.

Kumagawa, Muneo. 1889. "Vergleichende Untersuchungen über die Ernährung mit gemischter und rein vegetabilischer Kost mit Berücksichtigung des Eiweissbedarfs" ["Comparative Investigations into the Diet Consisting of Mixed and Purely Vegetarian Fare from the Perspective of Protein Needs"]. *Virchows Archiv* 116: 370–2.

Leung, Angela Ki Che. Forthcoming. "To Build or Transform Vegetarian China? Two Republican Projects." In *Moral Foods: The Construction of Nutrition and Health in Modern Asia*, edited by Angela Ki Che Leung and Melissa L. Caldwell. Honolulu: University of Hawai'i Press.

Majima, Ayu. 2012. "Eating Meat, Seeking Modernity: Food and Imperialism in Late Nineteenth and Early Twentieth Century Japan." In *Critical Readings on Food in East Asia*, edited by Katarzyna J. Cwiertka, 107–33, Vol. 1. Leiden: Brill.

宮崎昭 Miyazaki Akira. 1987. 食卓を変えた肉食 *Shokutaku wo kaeta nikushoku* [*The Dinner Table Changed by Meat Eating*]. Tokyo: Nihon Keizai Hyōron Sha.

中里亜夫 Nakazato Tsuguo. 1990. "明治・大正期における朝鮮牛輸入（移入）・取引の展開 Meiji-Taishō ki ni okeru chōsengyū yunyū (inyū) torihiki no tenkai" ["The Import (and Introduction) of Korean Cattle in the Meiji and Taishō Periods and the Expansion of the Trade"]. 歴史地理学紀要 *Rekishi Chirigaku Kiyō* 32: 129–59.

野間万里子 Noma Mariko. 2011. "日露戦争を契機とする牛価高騰と食肉供給の多様化 Nichiro sensō wo keiki to suru gyūka kōtō to shokuniku kyōkyū no tayōka" ["Sudden Rise in Cattle Price and Diversification of Meat Supply, After the Russo-Japanese War"]. 農林業問題研究 *Nōringyō Mondai Kenkyū* 47, no. 1: 60–5.

大石禄亭 Ōishi Rokutei. 1906. "菜食實行法 Saishoku jikkōhō" ["Methods for Implementing a Vegetarian Nutrition"]. 家庭雑誌 *Katei Zasshi* 4, no. 8: 33–5.

岡田哲 Okada Tetsu. 2012. 明治洋食時始め　とんかつの誕生 *Meiji Yōshoku Koto Hajime. Tonkatsu no tanjō* [*The Beginning of Western Foods in the Meiji Period: The Birth of Tonkatsu*]. Tokyo: Kōdansha.

Overgaard, Sven Skafte. 2001. "Mikkel Hindhede and the Science and Rhetoric of Food Rationing in Denmark 1917–1918." In *Food and War in Twentieth Century Europe*, edited by Ina Zweiniger-Bargielowska, Rachel Duffett, and Alain Drouard, 201–16. London: Routledge.

Rath, Eric C. 2016. *Japan's Cuisines: Food, Place and Identity*. London: Reaktion Books.

Rogaski, Ruth. 2004. *Hygienic Modernity. Meanings of Health and Disease in Treaty-Port China*. Berkeley: University of California Press.

堺利彦 Sakai Toshihiko. 1904. "菜食主義 Saishoku shugi" ["Vegetarianism"]. 平民新聞 *Heimin Shinbun* 56: 3.

堺利彦 Sakai Toshihiko. 1905. "菜食主義について Saishoku shugi ni tsuite" ["On Vegetarianism"]. 直言 *Chokugen* 2, no. 10: 6.

堺利彦 Sakai Toshihiko. 1906. "菜食主義に就て Saishoku shugi ni tsuite" ["On Vegetarianism"]. 家庭雑誌 *Katei Zasshi* 4, no. 6: 18–19.

佐藤寿 Satō Hisashi. 1921. 学説実験若返り健康法 *Gakusetsu jikken wakagaeri kenkōhō* [*Healthy Ways by Which You Can Get Younger: Experimental Theory*]. Tokyo: Nihon shoin.

沢村真 Sawamura Makoto. 1919. 農村教育と生活問題 *Nōson kyōiku to seikatsu mondai* [*Rural Education and Daily Life Problems*]. Tokyo: Shizendō.

清水秀夫 Shimizu Hideo. 1924. 実用衛生講話続 *Jitsuyō eisei kōwa zoku* [*Lectures On Practical Hygiene, Continued*]. Tokyo: Tomikura.

Sinclair, Upton. 1906. *The Jungle*. New York: Jungle Publishing Co.

Smil, Vaclav, and Kazuhiko Kobayashi. 2012. *Japan's Dietary Transition and Its Impacts*. Cambridge, MA: MIT Press.

Thoms, Ulrike. 2015. "Vegetarianism, Meat, and Life Reform in Early Twentieth-Century Germany and Their Fate in the 'Third Reich.'" In *Meat, Medicine and Human Health in the Twentieth Century*, edited by David Cantor, Christian Bonah, and Matthias Dörries, 145–57. New York: Routledge.

Treitel, Corinna. 2017. *Eating Nature in Modern Germany: Food, Agriculture and Environment, c. 1870 to 2000*. Cambridge: Cambridge University Press.

内ヶ崎作三郎 Uchigasaki Sakusaburō. 1911. 英国より祖国へ *Eikoku yori sokoku e* [*From Britain to the Motherland*]. Tokyo: Hokubunkan.

山田耕甫 Yamada Kōho. 1916. 安易生活と食物の活用 *An'i seikatsu to shokumotsu no katsuyō* [*A Life of Ease and the Practical Use of Food*]. Tokyo: Bunyūdo.

読売新聞 *Yomiuri Shinbun*. 1904. "日本兵が強いのは菜食に因ると言う Nihon hei ga tsuyoi no wa saishoku ni yoru to iu" ["They Say that Japanese Soldiers Are Strong Because of Their Vegetarian Diet"]. September 11, morning edition: 1.

2

Food, Gender, and Domesticity in Nationalist North India: Between Digestion and Desire[1]

Rachel Berger
Concordia University

The expanse of Indian food history, both methodologically and conceptually, has worked to set up food culture within sites of encounter: food becomes an ontology of the subcontinent, represented through the grains, plants, and herbs of its lands, matched in turn by an epistemological focus on flavor, aromas, texture, and presentation. Food in India, however, has a history—one that collides, confirms, refutes, and departs from the imperial rendering of it in significant ways. Perhaps more importantly, broader movements in the Indian engagement with imperial modernity identify food as a pertinent topic, relying on notions of the essential, the indigenous, and the ahistorical in ways similar to those employed by cosmopolitan imperial actors. From Gandhian abstention to Tagore's dyspeptic nationalists, the acts of eating, of cooking, and of ingesting are continually called upon to articulate the tensions of the late colonial/high nationalist period (Alter 2000).[2] This is a backdrop for a new history of food in India. While agricultural or economic historians contribute to the rethinking of food substances themselves, a study of the social and cultural resignifying of food provides insight into the ways in which it came to serve as a discursive axle upon which negotiations of modernity turned (Ray 2015; Sengupta 2010; Amrith 2008). These moments provide insight into the use of food to delineate the historical, but also take steps to historicize the representation of food according to the political demands made of it.

The deployment of food in these moments destabilizes and reintroduces understandings of home, nation, and consumption as experienced in mid-twentieth-century North India (Map 3). Taken together, what emerges is the way in which the reordering of the domestic space of the kitchen—and the activities that happened within it—became central to the political project of constructing an image of the nation: at a time when women were being sidelined from formal politics, the domestic sphere was acquiring and shaping a new one of its own. This chapter will examine the way in which the discursive deployment of food as a greater anchor of the historical, the political, the economic, and the cultural helped to shape debates about the Indian nation. These moments are situated in late colonial/high nationalist North Indian history, articulated through the circulation of ideas within the Hindi public sphere, and in dialogue with larger imperial and transnational conversations on the subjects at hand. As such, food is more substantially linked to the transformative social processes of the day: food demands a space for storage and preparation; it has an economic value, both in terms of its purchase and the costs associated with its preparation; it conforms or refutes an understanding of health and wellness, and of pleasure and abstinence, that pull it into the realm of the moral.

This genealogy of food charts three instances in which food was deployed as analytic to comment upon or transform the social condition and maps out the transition to and eventually from the period of high nationalism in India. Beginning in the early twentieth century, food emerged as a category of analysis and discussion amid broader movements to rationalize and modernize middle-class domestic space and was "scientified" according to the logic of home economics and the new concern over family health. By the 1920s, as the politics of the home transitioned into a more sophisticated politics of the nation, the substantive nature of food products became an indigenous response to the imposition of foreign and synthetic technologies and techniques of birth control, used to articulate desire and to monitor reproductive health. Finally, in the 1930s and 1940s, as new food technologies were developed and introduced, food advertising became the site for a break away from the rigidity of these messages, and yet still relied upon the intersection of the family, its physical and moral constitution, and the health of the nation to make way for innovative modes of consuming food.

Food preparation: Cookbooks and labor in the Indian kitchen

The question of food in Indian modernity was most dramatically transformed by the political and cultural processes that began to politicize the domestic space and its practices within the broader political spectrum, especially surrounding the role of Indian women within both politics and the home. The late nineteenth century has come to symbolize, in the Indian context, the pinnacle moment of a century of reform centered on the female body and the subject of femininity. Gayatri Chakravorty Spivak connects this process to a decade of imperial control, in which "white men saved brown women from brown men" through the consistent focus on the need for the reform of women's lives within "traditional" Indian patriarchy (Sengupta 2010). Partha Chatterjee, in turn, argues that this discursive interchange organized around the plight and state of the Indian female subject allowed Indian men to articulate a nationalist politics, organized around the reform of their women. This was a politics that they could discard and relegate to the home when a more formal, public, and political organization was formulated with the advent of the Indian National Congress in 1885 (Chatterjee 1989). This dismissal of the women's question from the realm of formal politics has occluded the dynamic transformation that resulted from the recentering of gender politics in the domestic space.

Mary Hancock and others have highlighted the role of empire in attempting to structure the Indian home according to the rational, liberal tenets of the modern household (Hancock 2001). Focusing on the advent of new realms of "scientific" education made popular in the field of home science, the state and various imperial charitable organizations introduced domestic guides to household upkeep, and the formal teaching of home economics in new schools for women (Hancock 2001, 873). More recently, historians working in vernacular languages in regional contexts have begun to piece together a set of Indian responses to this trend, sketching a coherent arc (characterized by a diverse set of experiences) that gives voice to Indian female-authored acquiescence and resistance to the imperial norms of domesticity imposed upon them—as well as the series of reforms discussed by Indian nationalists. The large body of writing on the household, which exploded from the late 1890s through the 1910s, provides a much more complex, nuanced, and diverse set of interventions, refutations, commentaries upon and ambivalences to this process, made public in cheap textual material aimed at—and often authored by—women (Gupta 2002; Orsini 2002).[3]

The idea of "home," however, was itself an imagined ideal. While Chatterjee and others have relied upon it as a counter to the "public" space of the nation, the new space of informal nation-building was itself undergoing a huge transformation. Rather than resolving the role of women in both imperialism and nationalist protest, what resulted was a radical reworking of the role of the domestic sphere, therein positing "home" as a central ideology of Indian modernity (Burton 1997). The task of containing an indigenous authenticity, replete with the feminine energy of the spiritual East, had to respond also to the modernist leanings of the newly formalized and politicized tenets of national thought. The notion of dichotomous spheres, where men could be modern in public and traditional in private, was itself an imagined state: rather than offering reprieve from public space, the home, instead, was transformed to meet the demands made of it by public politics. The physical and moral constitution of the family was at the center of this transformation. Where nineteenth-century debates had taken up marriage and education as the targets of gender reform, the twentieth century ushered in the idea of the middle-class nuclear family as a nationalist ideal—gone was the larger context of the joint family, the complexities of kinship ties, and the addition of laborers who amassed around large households. Instead, the focus lay on the housewife, her progeny, and the contested space over which she reigned.

The pragmatics of negotiating this new space of the nuclear family are seldom held up as objects of study and are instead cast as the subject of more intricate explorations of discourse *around* the home. This is where the history of food and its related affects and activities can offer an intervention: instructions on selecting, cleaning, preparing, and serving food products carries a variety of assumptions, of details and of revelations about the set-up of the household that are merely hinted at in these other explorations of "home" and "nation." The space of the kitchen, the designation of the cook, and the substantive focus on particularities of the food at hand offer insight into the lived experience of social transformation. Rather than seeing food preparation and consumption as a product of discourse, initiated as a conscious transformation by agentive housewives keen on adhering to the new social order, the change in food culture can be seen as a transformative—and also ambivalent—component of a broader project to articulate, identify, and delineate the Nationalist ideals of middle-class life.

The impetus for social change around food consumption took the form of the cookbook, a largely twentieth-century commodity aimed at the newly reading women of the emerging Indian middle class. The idea of the cookbook was not an entirely new one, especially among more affluent families; ledgers of meals cooked, food bought, and instructions for its preparation had been a standard practice among large households for centuries. This practice, however, was the product of a much broader set of social and labor relations—domestic laborers who managed the household kept ledgers relating to food costs, and records of meals were kept among the broader context of family lore. The cookbook reconfigured a notion of household labor by raising questions about the distribution of labor in the household and the constitution of "women's work." What was the relationship between the reader and the process of food preparation and distribution in the household? Missing from most guides was a discussion of which members of the household completed aspects of food preparation, a time-consuming activity for most recipes.

The most glaring difference between the traditional culture of cooking and the instructions set out in printed form was the absence of any mention of the role of the domestic servant, an omission that ignored the lived domestic experience of most of the women in a position to both purchase and read a cookbook. Food and its preparation has traditionally had great significance in Indian culture, as in most areas of the world, and the delineation of hierarchy and status in a household was often represented—and perhaps even reinforced—by the preparation of food. At the same time, because of the anxiety about pollution that was of particular concern to Brahmans, as well as those attempting to attain "Brahmanic" status in society, it was not uncommon to employ a Brahman cook or to keep domestic helpers of "outcaste" status away from the kitchen duties.[4] At the same time, a menstruating woman was considered to be impure, and, in some households, relieved of her kitchen duties if another family member or domestic servant could replace her.[5] The recipes as they appeared in the cookbook ignored all of these processes and put forth instead an uncomplicated ideal of food preparation that was far removed from the lived experience of cooking and eating in middle-class households. This representation of the Indian household that posited the housewife as primary laborer was itself a move toward envisioning a new kind of domestic space.

The tenacity of this transformational ideal is easily readable in the format of the cookbooks made popular during this time, which tended to be straightforward and simplistic. They generally contained an index of recipes, with each one laid out in similar ways: list of ingredients, cooking instructions and, sometimes, a note or two on the expected results or the benefits of the dish to the family. While some cookbooks were published by individuals, others were published by women's groups, sometimes to raise funds for a particular cause. For instance, a cookbook compiled by J. A. Sharma in 1933 had ties with regional and religious groups: Though it was published by Chand, one of the most popular women's magazines, *Pāk-Vijñāna* (*Science of Cooking*) was commissioned by the Adarsh-Parivar ("Ideal Family"), a women's group affiliated with the newly founded Hindi Sahitya Samellan ("the Hindi Academy"), which encouraged the promotion of printed materials in Hindi, and had close ties with the Arya Samaj religious movement (J. Sharma 1933). Included on the list of contributors were prominent ranis and maharanis (queens and princesses within the aristocracies of Indian princely states and other landholdings), securing its role as one of the many books sold by women involved with charity work featuring recipes from individuals celebrated in other fields (J. Sharma 1933, 3).

Manirama Sharma, a specialist author of cookbooks who published three different books several years apart, provides an interesting entry point to this genre. His first was a simple cookbook, but in the second, *Pāk-Chandrīkā* (*A Volume Related to Culinary Education*) though recipes remained the focus, the first part of the book, entitled "On the Subject of the initial preparation of food" was concerned with things like "the necessity of food," "the most important task of the housewife," and the "signs that it is time to make certain sauces" (Sharma 1926, 3–4). The author also discussed the importance of food to the development of a healthy body, warning that it is a daily project to make—and keep—oneself healthy (Sharma 1926, 1–2). He related this to the broader health of the nation, stating that the aim of the book is to create "healthier people of the land."

The most prominent cookbook writer of this period was Yashoda Devi, a descendant of Ayurvedic practitioners who invoked the science of Ayurvedic medicine when putting together domestic science guides. While Sharma's book and others like it dealt primarily with food, and touched briefly on its larger significance, Yashoda Devi's work had at its root the idea that food and health were intimately connected, and that a discussion about one necessarily touched upon the idea of the other. She addressed women's health in her cookbooks, promoting a holistic approach to the specific health-care issues that threatened her female readers. Yashoda Devi began her book with an explanation of food and what it does to the body, discussing everything from the correct time to eat, to the quality of different oils, to food-related causes of illness (Devi 1915, 1–2). At the same time, the book was region-specific, and she took great pains to explain the particulars of the agriculture of North India, including the varieties of fruits and vegetables in each season, along with instructions on what to eat in different sorts of temperature: the rainy season, for instance, consists of many entries, and the varieties of mango in the summer get their own entry (Devi 1915, 2–3). She also included a section on flowers and their use in cooking, as well as different methods of making vegetable curry with them. She also dedicated chapters to discerning the quality of onions and other root vegetables, spices, beans, and oil. In so doing, she introduced a logic behind food that wove together questions of embodiment, economy, and environment, synthesizing eating, cooking, and caring as stalwarts of efficient modern living. Yashoda Devi, in turn, referred to her cookbooks as *Pakshastras*, literally the "written scriptures of nutrition," echoing a Sanskritic turn of phrase that gave historic gravitas to her writings as textually authoritative, and backed by the sense of "timeless wisdom" allotted to classical texts of the Hindu tradition. Her invocation of the "ancient" put the anxieties of her readers to rest by smoothing over the aggressive methods of modernization, and by presenting them in a familiarized form.

While the cookbook shed new light for modern housewives on the relationship between food, the body, and the maintenance of health, its most disruptive contribution lay in the way in which it reconceptualized the labor traditions around food preparation, distribution, and consumption. The food presented was simply purchased and prepared, generally familiar to the reader, representing staples of a diet already entrenched by region, class, and common practice. Its symbolism, however, was entirely new: rather than relying upon someone else to make a decision about the daily practices around food consumption, the middle-class housewife was encouraged to imagine food as the key to her and her family's successful transition to modernity. The relegation of women back into the realm of the household, and the consequent politicization of the domestic sphere as crucial to the nation, worked to solidify the home—and, more specifically, the kitchen—as the center of indigenous Indian life. The recasting of the labor involved in food preparation and distribution, now undertaken solely by the housewife, worked to reimagine labor relations in the household, undoing the effects of caste, class, and religion that had previously dominated.

Food consumption: Gendering food production, sexualizing reproduction

The initial boom in cookbook and recipe publishing gave way in the 1920s and 1930s to a more profound commentary on food and its embodied effects that revealed the gendering of food consumption, and the importance of sexuality to understandings of what food could do in the body. These conversations took on the broader discourses of sexuality and reproduction, which were interlinked and dominant themes of North Indian popular discourse. As such, food was cast as important to the performance of sexuality, and to the national pledge to create a strong, vibrant, and superior Hindu nation. By the 1920s, the relationship between women and the household, and the role of food within it, had been successfully transformed into a rhetorical "truth"—and discursive context—for discussions of modernity and intimacy. In the 1910s, housewives had to be taught to take up their "proper" role in the kitchen to wield some control over the household. By 1930, however, the focus shifted to more literal questions about the physical constitution of the nation, moving away from the kitchen to the contested space of the marital bed. As Nationalist India began to draw communal and communitarian boundaries around the national community, often privileging religious, ethnic, or caste community over the racial make-up of the nation in empire, the question of what made a proto-citizen/colonized subject truly Indian reared its head.[6] At the same time, a particular strand of Indian eugenics that valued the strong and superior citizen sought to make extinct the socially marginal, economically unproductive, and physically "weak" members. Buttressed by the growing importance of global debates about these issues, the question of the authentic Indian resonated along nationalist lines, but also transnational ones. Food, especially in its most basic, substantive form, took center stage in the popular discussions, not as a cooked commodity as it had done earlier, but as an organic, ahistorical, and authentically indigenous substance, invoked in constructions of desiring the nation, but also in the discussions of its appropriate regeneration.

The question of population had been an important one in India from the mid-nineteenth century on. Early attempts to define, categorize, and calculate the many "peoples" of South Asia had resulted in the refinement of an India-wide census from the

1860s onward, made manifest through a wide variety of practices set on collecting information about Indians, their affiliations, and their practices.[7] As the population debate began to shift transnationally from a concern about the local into a conceptualization of the global, India's place amid humanity, as both colony and independent entity, began to take on new significance. Early British eugenicist discourse posited a variety of Indian characteristics that helped define the role of Britons within empire, where brownness gave shape and substance to debates about race and degeneration. In later Anglo-American debates about birth control, India's Hindu (read: non-Catholic) and teeming masses made it a prime site for the experiments of birth control advocates Margaret Sanger and Marie Stopes (Ahluwalia 2007).

It is in this context of a heightened concern about the constitution of the nation and the pragmatics of its regeneration that the language of science and the question of indigeneity were reframed. Moving away from the specificity of cookbooks and other earlier domestic guides that aimed to regulate the home front, the new turn in women's writing tended to address larger questions of the nation. The interesting turn is that the language of national importance, made evident in the scientific rhetoric used to describe social and economic problems of overpopulation, facilitated a foray into the world of sexuality never before allowed to circulate in polite society. For instance, one author had this advice to offer her audience:

> After bathing with sandalwood, applying *haldi* (turmeric) to the body, putting on perfume and having eaten strengthening substance, and wearing clothes of saffron and perfume of musk deer and camphor, or what's available at the time, and having eaten *paan* (betel nut), a healthy man who has extreme desire for producing a son and is happy in the love of his dear wife, should go to his wife when his desire is strong. He should adorn his wife with jewels; there should be the desire in both to have intercourse to produce a son.
>
> Sen 1929

While the actual curative value of these substances for this purpose is specious at best, the prescriptive language, written in a guide to health, and coupled with the distinctly indigenous nature of the ingredients, lent these instructions scientific authority. The mention of the desire to produce a son justified a foray into the more illicit acts implied in the encounter. Finally, the mention of a saffron shirt, widely recognized within the Hindu tradition as an auspicious color, situated desire within a distinctly communal context. Science, in this instance, responded to the social demands made of it. This set of instructions and others like it focused on the stimulation of the senses, and relied upon a variety of organic, indigenous, and substantive ingredients that reinforced the discussions of the Indian authentic that were circulating more broadly in the public sphere.

Desire, however, was only one facet of this conversation, and was made a relevant discussion for public consumption when it was situated within its broader context: the regeneration of the Indian nation. Sexual desire was only made respectable within the context of the pragmatics of the sexual act, which amounted to conceiving, carrying, and birthing a male citizen of the nation. The writing on sex and sexuality was almost always framed within the reproductive processes and their outcomes. In fact, some of the debates about the illicit nature of several different texts that addressed homosexuality framed the homoerotic act as depraved because it considered desire primarily as the fulfillment of pleasure, rather than the perfunctory function of reproductive necessity. Most notable is the 1927 text *Chaklit* (Chocolate), which articulated homoerotic themes of desire among teenage boys through their desire for indulgent food, hiding and revealing their desire from each other (Sharma 2009).

The reliance on indigeneity, both substantive and imaginary, however, carries through. Food came into fruition as a prime mode of signifying the authentic indigeneity of the entire enterprise, building on the idea of appropriate Indian bodies conceiving of appropriately Indian babies. Indigenous food substances and food practices became central tenets of the birth control, population control, and reproductive health guides—often making operational the politics of the authors involved and signifying a uniquely Indian experience of maternity that determined the experience, progress, and health of regeneration. For instance, Yashoda Devi, in her *Dampati Ārogyatā Jivanṣāstra* (Guide for a Healthy Married Life), detailed the development of the fetus in each month in a section called the "Cures for Illness in the Womb" (Devi 1924). In the section, she described the various herbs and plants that should be imbibed in each month to ensure the health and development of the child. The birthing process is not ignored, but is discussed in medical terms, explaining the way in which the baby turns in the womb, and descends through the vagina. In another passage, one of the signs of pregnancy was revealed as a desire for certain foods, with a prediction of gender linked to the grammatical gender of the food craved (Devi 1924, 237).

Other guides instructed mothers on the uses of their bodies for child-rearing after birth, and how to make judgments about the health of their children. Guides entitled *Śiṣu Pālan* (Caring for Children) and *Hindu Mata* (Hindu Mother) were among the most popular publications of the day, sold cheaply but published in huge print runs (Gurunncharay 1926; S. Sharma 1933). A very popular 1918 guide called *Dūdh-Chikitsā* (The Curative Aspects of Milk) written by Ramnarayan Sharma, explained the benefits of milk to ensure a child's healthy development—but also to ensure the mother's recovery. The book begins with the author's reference to the work of a *videshi mahila* (a foreign woman) called Edith Wheeler Wilcox, who claimed that a lack of milk in children led to "*hardayase sambandh raknevale rogonko,*" which the author translated himself in parentheses as "organic heart trouble," while drinking milk could also rid a body of cancer (Sharma 1918, 1).

However, in the next line, the author tempers this foreign knowledge of the body with the reiteration of the appropriateness of native medical regimes for native bodies, claiming that "a body will be free of illness if a plain diet is followed, according to the *panchjanevale*, the Ayurvedic five-way path, and if spicy foods like *mirch masala* (chili-based spice mixture) that have a sharp edge are avoided" (Sharma 1918, 2). In *Dūdh-Chikitsā*, we see the coming together of a variety of themes that framed the discussion of female-centered medical discussions around the preparation of food. First and foremost, the author situates his discussion of female reproduction within the context of the nation, using the health of the national child to speak about the potential ill health of the mother. Second, health edicts that were foreign in nature were made appropriate through their incorporation into a wider specter of health care based around the consumption and preparation of inherently indigenous substances.

Throughout these conversations about conception, reproduction, and the regeneration of the nation, the careful and incisive use of Indian food substances in their natural forms served to underline the Indian stake in a transnational debate. Ultimately, food was employed as both an aid to the stimulation of desire, and also as the means to facilitate the transformation of desire into the fulfillment of the Nationalistic reproductive imperative. The competing discourses of international eugenics and global (over)population introduced a range of models for thinking through the constitution of the Indian nation. The nation was then interpreted by different groups along sectarian, religious, ethnic, regional, and linguistic lines, and reformulated by each to compete with each other, but also to stake a place in the world of nations and states. The negotiation of an inherent claim to authentic indigeneity was central to popular conversations about the reproduction and regeneration of the nation, and food emerged as a pragmatic stalwart of the Indian authentic: food was tied to the land, it was represented as timeless and without history, used as both determinant and marker of health, and entirely produced in its most substantive form outside of the realm of global politics or global capital. Though not a direct focus of debate—as it had been in the first days of the cookbook, and as it would be in the new era of food advertising—it remained an uncontested and inherently authentic anchor of Indian identity in an era when the Indian nation was both coming into being, and coming into question.

Food distribution: Making new foods for the masses

The subsequent turn in this genealogical reading of the evolution of food and its discourse explores its commodification in different forms. Taking as given the reformation of the space and morality of the household, this next manifestation of food culture built upon the easy consumption of "modern" ideas about food in order to sell new food products to the Indian middle class. This final section will therefore explore the visual and textual cues used by food advertisers to link food consumption with the already-developed understandings of the importance of food to the body, but will also shed light on the ways in which new food products and technologies were introduced to the Hindu middle class.

The history of advertising in India is strongly linked to the further solidification of class identity among the Indian bourgeoisie in the interwar period, along with the evolution of branding and the introduction of brand-name ready-made goods developed, in part, to serve them (Haynes et al. 2010; Daechsel 2006; Mazzarella 2003).[8] The interwar period witnessed an explosion in advertising: in the 1920s, advertising consisted of a series of graphic-free, printed ads that occasionally marked the pages of newspapers and the back page of popular books; in the 1940s, advertising took up most of the page of local and national newspapers (with articles structured visually by the space allotted to the ad). The style of advertisements had changed as well with the advent of graphics, photographs, and catchy slogans dominating the field from the early 1930s on, often conceptualized by an advertising firm or by the marketing department of brand-name companies (Haynes et al. 2010, 188–9). The struggle to market ready-made goods, to both serve the perceived "needs" of the population and to stimulate the steady growth of consumption, was in essence a struggle to overcome the lure of the easily accessible and affordable presence of the bazaar.

While the lure of luxurious or limited goods could adopt an affect of the unattainable—for instance, a printed sari, a pair of new shoes, or a collection of holiday cards—products that aimed to replace goods easily conjured or created by bazaar purchases remained a harder sell (McGowan 2010).[9] This was particularly prescient with regard to food products, considering the ways in which food had become a site of resistance to other modes of modernization, Westernization, and the encroaching global that organic, wholly substantive, and authentically indigenous food substances had helped to stave off. The introduction, branding, and marketing of prepared food products that already circulated widely in unbranded forms posed a particularly vexing problem to advertisers, as consumers had to be taught to purchase—at a mark-up—the ready-made goods (curry pastes, tea bags, and packaged spice mixes, for example) that they were used to preparing for themselves. Food needed to be marketed in such a way as to convince the consumer to negotiate his or her relationship to its preparation.

The Dalda spice company's January 1943 ad for canned *vanaspati ghee* (clarified butter) to be added to *sabzi* (vegetable) dishes, which appeared in *Madhuri*, provides an interesting example of the genre. The advertisement bears pictures of fresh fruit and vegetables laid out on a very basic-looking *thali*, a traditional Indian plate. Somewhat obfuscated by the image of fresh produce is a cookbook that bears the name of the company, and features a tin of the ghee; a tiny image of a woman, her tiny arms spread over the large corner of the book, strives to open its pages. Atop this image is a slogan in large, bold print reading "It will build strength." Also featured across the text of the advertisement is the figure of a woman in a sari, clearly the mother figure, looking down at a group of boys running toward her; placed across from her is a man, legs spread, hands firmly on hips, and chin facing upward. Clearly he is meant to be the father, and the instigator of the family's shift in consumption. Lower down the page, the toothy grin of a boy is featured, with a cartoon bubble in which he informs the reader that "father says that this will invigorate me." The slogan of the company, found at the bottom of the advertisement, placed next to the company's name, reads "for invigoration."

Tea posed another interesting question for advertisers. Though tea had played a role in daily Indian life for a couple of centuries by this point, the mass consumption of tea is an inherently modern phenomenon. The infusion of herbs in water is an ancient practice, but the infusion of leaves resembling *Camellia sinensis* (the most common tea leaf), taken from the Indian Sanjeevani plant, did not become a popular practice until the mid-nineteenth century. The British attempted to cultivate tea from the 1860s on, resulting in the development of colonial tea plantations in the damp and elevated hills of various pockets of the subcontinent—including, for example, Darjeeling, Ootacamund, the Nilgiris, the lower Himalayan foothills, and Munar in Kerala—as a way to curb the need to import tea from China (Collingham 2006, 190–1).[10]

Despite rough beginnings, South Asian (both from India and Ceylon) tea accounted for almost 90 percent of the tea consumed in the British Empire by the turn of the twentieth century.

Already a British leisure activity, running the gambit from genteel high tea and tea parties to the tea breaks (and suppers) of the working classes, the expansion of British tea production also called for the identification of new markets, and colonial contexts provided just that. Indians were taught to make tea a part of their everyday activities through a rigorous series of tea-drinking campaigns, beginning in the late nineteenth century, which often targeted key upper-caste/class families in regional districts, with the aim of having the trend trickle down. At the same time, a *chai* break was readily incorporated into the culture of work among the laboring classes, with the hope that laborers would incorporate the practice into their home life. Tea also became a staple of migratory and travel and experiences, sold on train platforms, while cries of "*chai garam! garam chai!*" (tea that's hot! hot tea!) became an accepted part of the travel encounter (Collingham 2006, 196).

This is where the Bharat Chai company enters the picture: not as the means to introducing a new product, but rather interested in reclaiming an older one, staking their own claim as an Indian producer of Indian tea. The challenge facing Bharat Chai was to sway the Indian masses away from their affinity for tea as a British commodity, and to appreciate it as an Indian one instead. A popular ad for Bharat Chai (Indian tea), proclaimed that tea was "A Good Habit to Exert," but rather than employing a visual aid that privileged the genteel or practical aspects of drinking tea, the ad used a photograph of a young mother feeding her toddler tea. Rather than using a teacup, the girl was learning to drink tea poured into a saucer—a common practice for cooling down hot tea and other hot substances in the subcontinent. Both mother and child are wearing tikka marks (noting their Hindu identity) and are adorned in simple but elegant jewelry, marking them as members of the middle class, and therefore reflecting the appropriate consumers of the substance and appropriate advocates for the practice. The intimate depiction of the act of feeding and being fed, in which both figures are smiling happily, lends to the framing of this activity as natural, comforting, and safe.

A more complicated category of food product development and advertising was posed around the question of baby formula. This product was most disruptive to the natural order of things in South Asia as it posed a quandary for those babies imbibing it: it presented the literal substitution of the mother's own product, breast milk, with a fundamentally foreign substance, hailing from Western discourses of health practice, and also located outside of the body. The construction of this product in the public sphere most closely follows some of the logic of these other conversations about reproduction and regeneration discussed earlier: that bodies needed to be controlled, that the health of the child is paramount to the health of the nation, that modern scientific rationales for health must replace "outdated" practices.

The constitution of the Vitamilk ads reinforced the ideal of the family, with an interesting twist. Where other ads depicted figures racialized as Indian and often ethnicized as Hindu, the milk ads—including Vitamilk, Ovaltine, and milk substitutes for older children—tended to depict children as deracialized objects: The tikka marks, "Indian" features (most often visualized through black hair), and South Asian clothing and accessories were replaced by naked, chubby, curly-haired babies, whose gender was generally ambiguous and whose hair was outlined but never filled in. In essence, the cleverly crafted racial neutrality of the child—constructed through simple lines, invoking hair rather than depicting it overtly, and absenting color rather than filling it in—could serve as the default child of the world. The racial politics at play in this construction of the child subject is obvious: the absence of race, ethnicity, and gender results in the construction of a "neutral" global child, whose parents (and whose state) are less invested in the politics of identity than in the demands of health, and thus erases the concerns of nationalism, anti/imperialism, and interwar internationalism in the everyday experiences of consumption. In fact, the attempts to identify one's child with the Other, to literally adopt the claim that childhood is not mediated by the citizen/subject dichotomy of interwar politics, makes evident the importance of these larger questions in the minds of nations caught up in thinking beyond the parameters of contemporary politics—and thinking forward, instead, to a differently balanced political future.

This strategy reveals the uncontested tenacity of these themes, which were secure enough in the realm of the social imaginary that they could be relied upon to introduce new behaviors into daily life. Ultimately, food advertising was made readable and relevant by the earlier cementing of food as a marker, a determinant, and a protector of health and wellness in the family, and, subsequently, the nation. That it turned this argument on its head, using the health of the nation to introduce new food technologies, further intertwined the steady relationship between the body, its needs, and its place in the nation. However, this was simply a continuation of the working of food and nationalism that had come to be well established. The evolution of the tie between food, gender, and the nation traces the growing sophistication of the argument about what it meant to be a modern Indian poised to inhabit an independent state, and provides insight about how this argument itself evolved over the course of the High Nationalist period.

In the 1910s and 1920s, as the growing fervor for a collective nationalist movement was being established, the private world of the home became the purview of political focus; as such, the cooked meal was relied upon heavily to secure the image of the new household within its older orientation and function. In the 1930s, as debates about the family became more sophisticatedly tied to the future of the nation, food became more simplified, both literally and discursively, representing the unchanging, organic substance that so thoroughly symbolized the Indian authentic; this matched the growing scientification of these debates about National regeneration, where food became a part of how the nation might literally grow. By the 1940s, as the political work of running the state fell more to elected officials, the discourse of indigeneity was rendered more complex and less ideological, more geared for commerce than for consciousness-raising; consequently, the tenacity of the ideals of family, health, reproduction, and regeneration could be mobilized by industry to secure the introduction of new ready-made food technologies, like baby formula and processed goods, to the Hindu middle class. Food, in essence, provided a historical reference point for new debates about the nation, meaningfully linking modernity to the Indian past, and projecting the possibility of new futures for the independent nation.

Notes

1　A slightly different version of this chapter was first printed in Berger (2013), under a different title. It has been reprinted here with permission.
2　Gandhian abstention is well-documented throughout the various analyses of his life and times, and figures prominently in Alter (2000).
3　The nature and expanse of women's writing has been thoroughly explored in Gupta's (2002) groundbreaking work on issues of sexuality and the obscene in Hindi literature. Orsini (2002) provides insight into the broader context, circulation, and reception of women's writing in Hindi in Chapter 4.
4　See Malamoud (1996, Chapter 2) on textual and sociological perspective on food and society in ancient India. See Khare (1976) on the more contemporary systems of managing food in the Indian society, especially from the point of view of class and caste distinctions.
5　See Leslie (1996) on the prohibitions relating to menstruation in Hinduism.
6　The notion of the communal is particularly prescient in the modern Indian context, where it refers specifically to a community-based identity constructed along lines of religion and caste. The term "communalism" comes not from community, but rather from "tension between (religious) communities," and is often characterized by the potential for—or eruptions of—violence done in its name (Pandey 2006, 9).
7　A now classic take on the role of the census in the determination of Indian identity can be found in Appadurai (1993).
8　The historiography of advertising specifically and consumption more generally is only beginning to develop in the South Asian context, and is more concerned with themes of globalization, communalism, and caste/class in the postcolonial period. As yet, there has been no attempt to compile or analyze data that might shed light on the constitution of the field of advertising, from either quantitative or qualitative perspectives. Various scholars have made inroads into determining patterns of advertising, as well as major themes taken up by, and often constituting different varieties of, advertisements.
9　McGowan (2010) has identified these and other objects of desire for middle-class housewives in Western India and has posited them as desired goods rather than those deemed to fit into a rational household budget.
10　Collingham (2006) also notes that tea was the prime commodity imported from China between 1811 and 1819, but was an unreliable commodity, as tea was grown on private, family-owned plantations and so its availability was haphazard.

References

Ahluwalia, Sanjam. 2007. *Reproductive Restraints: Birth Control in India, 1877–1947.* Urbana-Champaign: University of Illinois Press.
Alter, Joseph S. 2000. *Gandhi's Body: Sex, Diet, and the Politics of Nationalism.* Philadelphia: University of Pennsylvania Press.
Amrith, Sunil S. 2008. "Food and Welfare in India, c. 1900–1950." *Comparative Studies in Society and History* 50, no. 4: 1010–35.
Appadurai, Arjun. 1993. "Numbers in the Colonial Imagination." In *Orientalism and the Postcolonial Predicament: Perspectives on South Asia*, edited by Carol A. Breckenridge and Peter van de Veer, 314–40. Philadelphia: University of Pennsylvania Press.

Berger, Rachel. 2013. "Between Digestion and Desire: Genealogies of Food in Nationalist North India." *Modern Asian Studies* 47, no. 5: 1622–43.

Burton, Antoinette. 1997. "House/Daughter/Nation: Interiority, Architecture, and Historical Imagination in Janaki Majumdar's 'Family History.'" *The Journal of Asian Studies* 56, no. 4: 921–46.

Chatterjee, Partha. 1989. "The Nationalist Resolution of the Women's Question." In *Recasting Women: Essays in Colonial History*, edited by Kumkum Sangari and Sudesh Vaid, 233–53. Delhi: Kali for Women Press.

Collingham, Lizzie. 2006. *Curry: A Tale of Cooks and Conquerors*. Oxford: Oxford University Press.

Daechsel, Markus. 2006. *The Politics of Self-Expression: The Urdu Middle-Class Milieu in Mid-Twentieth Century India and Pakistan*. Abingdon: Routledge.

देवी यशोदा Devi, Yashoda. 1915. गृहणी कृत्वय शास्त्र *Gṛihiṇī kṛtvya ṣāstṛā [A Guide to Duties of a Female Householder]*. Allahabad: Sriram Sharma ne Banita Hitaushi Press Prayag mei.

देवी यशोदा Devi, Yashoda. 1924. "पुत्र के लक्षण *Putṛ ke Lakshaṇ*" ["How to Know if It's a Boy / Signs of a Boy / Symptoms if It's a Boy / It's a Boy"]. In यशोदा, देवी Y. Devi, दम्पति आरोगयता जीवनशास्त्र अर्थात रतिशास्त्र संततिशास्त्र *Dampati Ārogyatā Jivanṣāstra Athārth Ratīṣāstra wSantantītṣāstra*.

Gupta, Charu. 2002. *Sexuality, Obscenity, Community: Women, Muslims, and the Hindu Public in Colonial India*. Delhi: Permanent Black.

गुरुणाचार्य Gurunncharay. 1926. हिन्दू माता अर्थात हिन्दू शिशु स्वास्थय रक्षा (हिन्दू स्त्रीयों के लिये शिशु सवास्थय और शिशु सम्बन्धी पुस्तक) *Hindū Mātā Athārth Hindū ṣiṣu Svāsthya Rakshā (Hindū strīyon ke liye ṣiṣu Svāsthya aur ṣiṣu Saṃbandhī Pustak) [Health Care of Hindu Mothers and Infants (A Book on Health Care of Hindu Women and Infants)]*.

Hancock, M. 2001. "Home Science and the Nationalization of Domesticity in Colonial India." *Modern Asian Studies* 35, no. 4: 871–903.

Haynes, Douglas E., Abigail McGowen, Thirthankar Roy, and Haruka Yanagisawa, eds. 2010. *Towards a History of Consumption in South Asia*. Oxford: Oxford University Press.

Khare, Ravindra. S. 1976. *Culture and Reality: Essays on the Hindu System of Managing Foods*. Simla: Indian Institute of Advanced Study.

Leslie, Julia. 1996. "Menstruation Myths." In *Myth and Mythmaking: Continuous Evolution in Indian Tradition*, edited by Julia Leslie, 87–105. London: Curzon.

Malamoud, Charles. 1996. *Cooking the World: Ritual and Thought in Ancient India*. Translated by David White. New York: Oxford University Press.

Mazzarella, William. 2003. *Shoveling Smoke: Advertising and Globalization in Contemporary India*. Durham, NC: Duke University Press.

McGowan, Abigail. 2010. "Consuming Families: Negotiating Women's Shopping in Early Twentieth-Century Western India." In *Towards a History of Consumption in South Asia*, edited by Douglas E. Haynes, Abigail McGowen, Thirthankar Roy, and Haruka Yanagisawa, 155–84. Oxford: Oxford University Press.

Orsini, Francesca. 2002. *The Hindi Public Sphere, 1920–1940: Language and Literature in the Age of Nationalism*. Delhi: Oxford University Press.

Pandey, Gyanendra. 2006. *The Construction of Communalism in Colonial North India*. Delhi: Oxford University Press.

Ray, Utsa. 2015. *Culinary Culture in Colonial India*. Cambridge: Cambridge University Press.

गणनाथ सेन Sen, Gananath. 1929. "दम्पति मिलना *Dampati Mīlanā*" ["Coming Together to Create Life"]. In प्रत्यक्ष शारीरम *Pratyaksha ṣāriram*, edited by गणनाथ सेन Gananath Sen. Dehradun.

Sengupta, Jayanta. 2010. "Nation on a Platter: The Culture and Politics of Food and Cuisine in Colonial Bengal." *Modern Asian Studies* 44, no. 1: 81–98.

शर्मा, जे.ए. Sharma, J. A. 1933. पाक-वजिनान *Pāk-Vijñāna* [*Science of Cooking*]. Benares: Chand Publications.

शर्मा, मनिराम Sharma Manirama. 1926. पाक-चन्द्रिका: पाक-शिशा सम्बन्धी वृहत ग्रन्थ *Pāk-Chandrīkā: Pāk-Śiśā Sambandhi Vṛhat Granth* [*Pāk-Chandrīkā: A Volume Related to Culinary Education*]. Allahabad: Chand Publications.

Sharma, Pandey Bechan "Ugra." 2009. *Chocolate and Other Writings on Male Homoeroticism.* Translated by Ruth Vanita. Durham, NC: Duke University Press.

पं. रामनारायण शर्मा Sharma, Pt. Ramnarayan. 1918. दूध-चिकित्सा *Dūdh-Chikitsā* [*The Curative Aspects of Milk*]. Bombay.

शर्मा, श्री नर्मदेशवर Sharma, Srinarmdeshvar. 1933. शिशु पालन *Śiśu Pālan* [*Caring for Children*]. Banaras.

3

A Cookbook in Search of a Country:
Fu Pei-mei and the Conundrum of
Chinese Culinary Nationalism

Michelle T. King

University of North Carolina at Chapel Hill

The banquets Richard Nixon attended at the Great Hall of the People in Beijing during his historic trip to the People's Republic of China (PRC) in 1972 were culinary and diplomatic performances writ large, both for the immediate participants as well as for millions of television viewers around the world. As a signal moment of gastrodiplomacy (see Cwiertka, Chapter 4 in this volume), the banquets were overt displays of culinary nationalism.[1] But the culinary version of nationalism is no different from other forms in the way that "erasures, repressions and hence symbolic violence [are] committed in the name of nationhood" (Yenal 2010, 274). The gleaming success of the Great Hall banquets, for example, was built upon the turbulent earlier history of the Chinese Civil War, in which the Communist Party under the leadership of Mao Zedong emerged victorious on the Chinese Mainland in 1949, while supporters of Nationalist Party, under the leadership of Chiang Kai-shek, retreated to the island of Taiwan, the last territorial remnant of the Republic of China (ROC). After the Nixon détente, the United States would eventually recognize the PRC as the legitimate government of China in 1979 and break diplomatic relations with Taiwan.

Traces of this political rupture emerged in the most unlikely of places, the food pages of the *New York Times*. American readers wishing to recreate at home some of the dishes from the Nixon farewell banquet could consult two recipes printed there, one for sweet-and-sour fish and another for a sweet dessert soup made from walnuts (*New York Times* 1972).[2] The walnut soup recipe was adapted from *Pei Mei's Chinese Cookbook* (1969) and appeared to be innocuous enough in itself, calling for simple ingredients such as shelled walnuts, peanut oil, sugar, salt, and cornstarch. Yet for those familiar with the cookbook or its author, the inclusion of the recipe represents the height of irony, perfectly encapsulating the conundrum of Chinese culinary nationalism for those in Taiwan, in the immediate postwar decades and continuing until today.

Fu Pei-mei 傅培梅 (1931–2004) was Taiwan's best-known cooking celebrity, appearing on instructional cooking programs on Taiwan Television for forty years, from the launch of the medium there in 1962. Along with dozens of other cookbooks, she authored a best-selling, bilingual, three-volume cookbook series on Chinese cuisine, *Pei Mei's Chinese Cookbooks* (培梅食譜 *Peimei shipu*) (1969–79), the first of which supplied the walnut dessert soup recipe appearing in the *New York Times*. Fu herself had fled Mainland China for Taiwan as a teenager in the aftermath of the Chinese Civil War, along with some million other migrants loyal to Chiang Kai-shek's Nationalist Party. She eventually resettled in Taiwan's capital, Taipei (Map 2). During the whole of her professional career, she consciously took up the mantle of "culinary ambassador" (美食大使 *meishi dashi*), promoting Taiwan as a bastion of authentic Chinese cuisine. To have one of her recipes appear in an article on the Nixon banquets in Beijing, events which heralded the subsequent decline of Taiwan's status on the international political stage, seems cruel irony indeed.

Written in the long shadow of the Communist Party's victory on the Chinese Mainland and the Nationalist Party's retreat to Taiwan in 1949, Fu Pei-mei's cookbooks could never be just value-neutral presentations of Chinese cuisine, for any discussion of "Chinese" cuisine begged the ultimate question of what this cultural and political identity should now consist of. The fact that the *New York Times* could so easily ignore Fu's political identity as a ROC citizen hints at the inextricable tension between cultural and national definitions of Chinese cuisine. On the one hand, the reference to Fu's walnut soup recipe underscored her success in representing what she claimed were "authentic and correct" Chinese cooking methods to broader, international audiences of the time—a success that framed Chinese cuisine as a cultural product. On the other hand, this very same success obscured Fu's vigorous efforts to advance the ROC's culinary superiority as a partisan cause—a failure that framed Chinese cuisine as a national product. For foreign audiences, these subtle distinctions made little sense: Chinese food was Chinese food, and Fu had written a "Chinese" cookbook, not a Republic of China cookbook.

With regard to culinary nationalism, Priscilla Parkhurst Ferguson has observed that "cookbooks tie food to place, and they do so whether or not we put the recipe in the oven and on the table" (Ferguson 2010, 102). Other scholars have written extensively about the role of cookbooks in creating national culinary identities in India, Mexico, France, Argentina, and Spain (Appadurai 1988; Pilcher 1998; Ferguson 2004; Pite 2013; Anderson 2013). But what about a cookbook such as Fu Pei-mei's, which encompasses a turbulent political past and throws into question the very culinary geography it purports to represent? What makes Fu Pei-mei's best-known work, in other words, a cookbook in search of a country? There is no doubt, as the following paragraphs will demonstrate, that Chinese culinary nationalism manifested itself in Fu Pei-mei's cookbooks and overseas cooking demonstrations. Yet unlike the national culinary identities of other countries, the case of China and Chinese cuisine offers an illuminating counterpoint because its geopolitical and culinary borders do not overlap so neatly. The historic split between the PRC and ROC is but one factor in complicating the example of Chinese culinary nationalism; another factor are the great numbers of Chinese diasporas scattered around the world, who have ensured that any understanding of "Chinese" cuisine can never be constrained solely within national boundaries (*Chinese Restaurants* 2005).

This chapter presents the conundrum of Chinese culinary nationalism from the vantage point of the Republic of China, as seen through the pages Fu Pei-mei's cookbook, juxtaposing her textual presentation with her personal efforts as a female culinary ambassador. What was Fu's vision of China as a culinary nation? How did it differ, if at all, from earlier versions of culinary China? How might it compare with visions of culinary Taiwan today? One crucial question her cookbooks and overseas cooking demonstrations raise is the question of audience: for whom and for what purposes did Fu create her vision of Chinese cuisine? As we shall see, Fu's cookbooks were crafted as bilingual Chinese–English texts, allowing her to reach both domestic and foreign audiences, yet the message for these audiences was not necessarily the same.[3] Fu attempted to promote the ROC's diplomatic agenda of international recognition during numerous cooking demonstrations abroad, but her message was received quite differently by domestic and foreign audiences. Ultimately, Fu's attempt to serve as a culinary ambassador for Chinese cuisine writ large (presenting Chinese cuisine as a cultural construct) overshadowed her efforts to promote the specific interests of the Republic of China (presenting Chinese cuisine as a national construct).

Cold War context

Fu's comprehensive vision of Chinese food as seen through her cookbooks is particularly compelling because it spanned the shift of diplomatic recognition by the global community away from the government of the ROC on Taiwan, in favor of the government of the PRC on the Chinese Mainland. The three volumes of *Pei Mei's Chinese Cookbook* were published in 1969, 1974, and 1979 respectively. The confident tone and celebratory claims about Chinese cookery in her first volume mirrored the status of the ROC at the height of its international influence. At that moment, Fu had no difficulty laying claim to a common Chinese historical and political lineage stressing the importance of food, stretching back from Sun Yat-sen (1866–1925), forefather of modern China, all the way to the philosophers of the Spring and Autumn Period (*c.* 771–476 BCE).

Two short years later, in 1971, ROC representatives were ousted from the United Nations in favor of PRC representatives, beginning a rapid shift of allegiance within the international community. In the second volume of her series, Fu still pointed to Sun's guiding political manifesto, the Three People's Principles, but now referred to Taiwan's political and material success more explicitly: "Today, those citizens living in Taiwan, the Republic of China's model province of the Three People's Principles, are living in a peaceful, affluent, and happy environment as a result of the rapid development of the economy and the progress of society toward prosperity" (Ch) (Fu 1974, 2).

By the time of the publication of the third and final volume of her best-selling series, Taiwan's political stature was greatly diminished: this was the same year in which the United States switched its diplomatic recognition to the PRC. Fu retreated from referencing Taiwan's political claims, and instead described her country in cultural terms alone, as a paradise of Chinese cuisine in miniature, writing, "At present, it is only in Taiwan that the pleasure of eating authentic Chinese food from all parts of China can be experienced . . . In Taiwan, there are people from every part of China, and thus there are restaurants representing each province" (E) (Fu 1979, 3).

Like many others of her generation, Fu promoted the idea that Taiwan alone had preserved authentic Chinese culinary traditions. This perspective was part and parcel of the Nationalist Party's broader claim that traditional Chinese culture flourished only on Taiwan, while it had been destroyed on the Chinese Mainland after the Communist takeover. Popular perception, too, insisted that Chiang Kai-shek had brought with him to Taiwan some of the best Chinese chefs, in addition to the treasures of the imperial art collection and the reserves of the central bank. With regard to the maintenance of traditional Chinese foodways, there was at least some merit in Nationalist claims: in the same decades that Fu built up her career, Mainland China was roiled by the tumultuous Mao years, which included the devastating man-made famine of the Great Leap Forward (1958–61) and the political chaos of the Cultural Revolution (1966–76). Food was a matter of basic sustenance and survival, not a bourgeois pleasure reflecting refined culinary consumption (Lu 1987; Gong and Seligman 2011). In this immediate postwar period, the centers of Chinese cuisine shifted to Hong Kong and Taiwan, which printed most of the Chinese cookbooks of the time, with only a handful printed in Beijing, Shanghai, or other PRC cities.

It is critical here to note that although Fu was a ROC citizen, her regional background and culinary expertise cannot accurately be described as "Taiwanese" at this moment. Having arrived in Taiwan only in the years around 1949, Fu and her fellow wartime refugees were called "Mainlanders" (外省人 *waishengren*), in contrast to the "native provincials" (本省人 *benshengren*), mostly Hokkien and Hakka ethnicity descendants who were resident on the island from earlier centuries up through the Japanese colonial period (1895–1945). On Taiwan itself, the term "Taiwanese" (台灣人 *Taiwanren*) has historically referred explicitly to this latter group alone (although this narrow definition is rapidly changing today). "Mainlander" cuisine referred to the numerous regional or provincial Chinese cuisines brought by Mainlander migrants to Taiwan after 1949, such as Shanghainese, Sichuanese, Hunanese, Cantonese, or Northern cuisines. Meanwhile, "Taiwanese cuisine" (台灣菜 *Taiwancai* or 台菜 *Taicai*) referred to the tastes and dishes developed on the island of Taiwan itself, a style rooted in Fujianese cuisine, but also influenced by Japanese culture after fifty years of colonial rule. Though the chaos of war had disrupted the lives of millions of Mainlander refugees and native Taiwanese alike, the exodus to Taiwan dramatically altered available culinary choices, concentrating an extraordinary variety of Chinese regional and ethnic cuisines on a single, small island (Tseng 2015).

The historical circumstances of Chinese Civil War that so indelibly shaped Taiwan's culinary landscape also created the perfect social environment and consumer demand for a unifying culinary figure such as Fu Pei-mei. A native of the northern Chinese province of Shandong, Fu built her entire culinary reputation on the notion of having mastered *all* major Chinese regional cuisines. Fu, who did not know how to cook when she first got married in Taiwan, frequently retold the story of how her culinary career got its rocky start (Fu 2000, 88–90). Her husband, a fellow provincial from Shandong, liked to invite his friends over to play mahjong, most of whom were southerners from Jiangsu and Zhejiang provinces, accustomed to a high level of culinary refinement. Fu's lack of skill in offering guests tasty dishes was an embarrassment to her husband, and he frequently berated her for her culinary ineptitude. Resolving to improve, but without recourse to the infinite range of cookbooks and cooking classes familiar to us today, Fu decided to pay a series of chefs at famous regional restaurants to have them instruct her in private cooking lessons. Over the course of two years, Fu studied from chefs from Jiangsu, Zhejiang, Hunan, and Guangdong Provinces. Eventually, as her story went, she developed so much skill with Jiang-Zhe dishes that the mahjong players were asking her to teach their own wives. Fu's description of herself as a simple housewife, mastering both northern and southern Chinese regional cuisines in order to cater to family and friends with broadened regional tastes, exemplifies the changing culinary context of postwar Taiwan.[4]

From the start, Fu Pei-mei envisioned her cookbooks as a way to carry forth lessons about Chinese culture and identity not just to domestic audiences, but to overseas Chinese and foreign readers as well. Her cookbook series was the first to debut in a bilingual, Chinese–English format, with all prefatory materials, recipes, and photo captions presented in both traditional Chinese characters and idiomatic English. Fu explained that the bilingual format was necessary to appease the demands of her diverse students:

> Recently many Chinese and foreign ladies have hoped to buy my lectures or recipes in order to be able to follow the cooking instructions more closely. This need has been especially true of those going abroad or those with friends or relations abroad. Also, many overseas Chinese have hoped to have Chinese food recipes written in English that are both correct and authentic. (Ch)
>
> Fu 1976, 2

While it seems natural for Fu to have attracted many native housewives in Taiwan to her cooking classes, why did she also have so many English-speaking "foreign ladies" as students? Again, Fu's cookbooks reflect their broader Cold War context: as an ally of "Free China," the United States sent military advisers to the ROC from 1951 until the severing of US–ROC diplomatic relations in 1979. Many wives of these American military officers stationed in Taiwan were also avid fans of Fu's cooking classes. Indeed, Fu herself was never fluent in English (although her Japanese was exceptional, having been educated in Japanese-occupied Dalian); she depended on these American students to help with the translation of her cookbooks into idiomatic English.[5] Yet the English translations throughout the three volumes were not of the same quality; some were more faithful than others. These inadvertent linguistic differences point to distinct registers of meaning for Chinese and foreign audiences: what each group needed to know about Chinese food, or about food on Taiwan, was not exactly the same.

Regionalism

Fu's presentation of Chinese cuisine within a clearly defined regional framework was her most compelling contribution to Chinese culinary writing at the time. Fu appears to have been the first modern cookbook author in Taiwan to use Chinese culinary regions as an organizing principle; her predecessors in Taiwan had arranged their cookbooks by cooking method, main ingredient, and even season (Huang 1954, 1957; Wang 1964).[6] In the first volume of her series, Fu used the cardinal directions to divide China into four culinary regions, which encompassed a range of provinces and cities: "The East has Shanghai as its center and contains Jiangsu and Zhejiang cuisines; the South includes Fujian and Guangdong; the West indicates Hunan and Sichuan cuisines; the North primarily indicates Beijing cuisine" (Ch) (Fu 1976, 2). Each regional category contained twenty-five main dish recipes, with an additional list of twenty snacks and desserts at the end.

To be sure, Fu did not invent these long-standing regional categorizations of Chinese culinary traditions. In the early Qing dynasty (1644–1911), the "four major culinary styles" (四大菜系 *sidacaixi*) had already been canonized, which included 鲁菜 *lucai* (roughly the cuisine of Shandong province), 淮揚菜 *huaiyangcai* (roughly the cuisine of Jiangsu province), 粤菜 *yuecai* (roughly the cuisine of Guangdong province), and 川菜 *chuancai* (roughly the cuisine including parts of Sichuan province) (Lü, Ding, and Dai 2009). Later, by the end of the Qing, the culinary canon was expanded to include the "eight major culinary styles" (八大菜系 *badacaixi*), by adding 閩菜 *mincai* (from Fujian province), 湘菜 *xiangcai* (from Hunan province), 浙菜 *zhecai* (from Zhejiang province), and 徽菜 *huicai* (from Anhui province).[7] Fu's cookbook divisions by cardinal direction explicitly mimicked the four traditional, regional culinary designations.

At the same time, Fu consciously kept her American audience in mind when making decisions about how to arrange her cookbooks and which dishes to include, decisions that had to be justified to Chinese readers while remaining hidden from American readers. For example, Fu anticipated that knowledgeable Chinese readers might object to her four-category organization of Chinese regional foods as overly simplistic. Yet such a schema, she explained, was necessary to accommodate foreign readers: "Drawing these boundaries can seem a little too general and sweeping, but for the sake of foreign readers, who will have an easier time grasping the distinctions of China's territories and its many different cuisine types, there is no better way of doing things" (Ch) (Fu 1976, 2–3). She also took into account "the difficulty of buying ingredients or the lack of various ingredients in foreign countries," which led her to "make an effort to select more ordinary dishes" (Ch) (Fu 1976, 3). Thus the majority of dishes feature ordinary cuts of chicken, beef, pork, fish, shrimp, vegetables, and eggs, while only a handful call for what a foreign reader might deem as exotic (though typically Chinese) ingredients, including shark's fin, sea cucumber, chicken gizzards, abalone, or winter melon. Fu even included recipes for dishes that would be most familiar to American Chinese restaurant-goers, even though they might be either too complicated for the amateur cook to replicate successfully at home (Peking Duck) or more Chinese-American than Chinese in origin (Chop Suey).[8] No mention of these accommodations was made to English readers, however, who were instead merely reassured by Fu that the selected dishes were "typical of my country" (E) (Fu 1976, 8).

While Fu's regional designations look and sound a lot like the traditional "four major culinary styles," there are a number of subtle innovations worth mentioning, which underscore Fu's reinscription of tradition into her own framework of Chinese culinary nationalism. Fu included a map of each culinary region at the start of each section, highlighting the provinces whose cuisines were described under that heading. For example, the map for eastern Chinese dishes highlighted Jiangsu, Anhui, and Zhejiang provinces; southern highlighted Fujian and Guangdong provinces; western highlighted Sichuan, Guizhou, and Hunan provinces; and northern highlighted Shanxi, Hebei, Shandong, and Henan Provinces (Figure 3.1). Although these highlighted areas encompassed the regions suggested by the traditional terms *lucai*, *huaiyangcai*, *yuecai*,

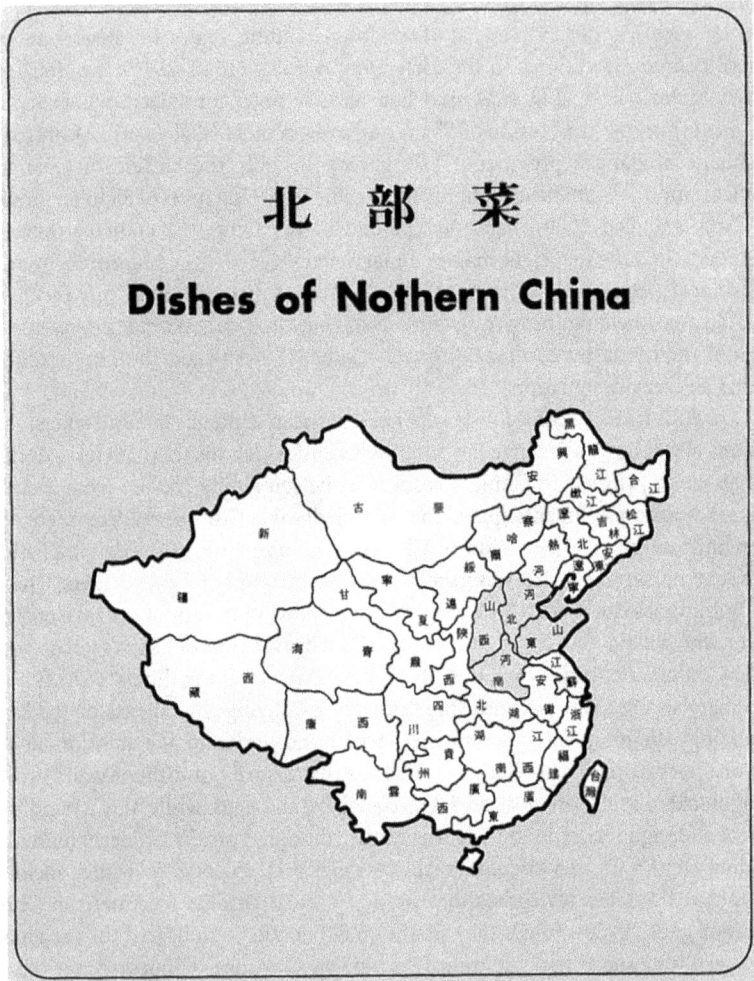

北 部 菜

Dishes of Nothern China

Figure 3.1 Map of the Republic of China (ROC), highlighting the culinary region of "No[r]thern China," which includes Shandong, Hebei, Shanxi, and Henan Provinces. This highlighted region grows out of the allusive category of *Lucai* ("Lu cuisine"), one of the traditional "four major culinary styles" (*sidacaixi*) of China. Lu refers to the historic, but defunct Lu state (1042–249 BCE), revered as the birthplace of Confucius. It is contained by, but not coterminous with modern-day Shandong Province. *Peimei shipu/Pei Mei's Chinese Cook Book* (orig. 1969), Vol. 1: 253. Reproduced by permission from H. H. Cheng.

and *chuancai*, Fu's visual presentation did more than merely match name to place. Instead, Fu's maps fixed in time and space what had formerly been only historico-linguistic, allusive descriptors of regional culinary styles. *Lucai*, for example, took its name from the historic Lu state (1042–249 BCE), revered as the birthplace of Confucius, yet now defunct and not exactly coterminous with the provincial boundaries of Shandong. Fu's explicit delineation of eastern, southern, western, and northern Chinese cuisines in spatial terms allowed the contemporary geopolitical unit of the province and its administrative borders to overdetermine coherent culinary identities.

That all of these regional Chinese culinary styles were to be considered the legitimate cultural inheritance of the ROC on Taiwan as opposed to the PRC on the Mainland was also made manifest by these culinary maps. Although the contours of the national map that Fu deployed look quite similar to what we recognize as modern China, it is not in fact a map of the PRC as we know it today. Rather, the national map included in Fu's cookbook is a map of the pre-1949 *Republic of China*, preserving intact all of its provincial boundaries and territories claimed (such as outer Mongolia), some twenty years later. The overall visual impression of Fu's culinary maps and their implicit reference to a Nationalist version of historical events uniquely illustrate the significance of the cultural arena to the Nationalist Party: although the Nationalists no longer exercised actual *political* authority over any of these Mainland areas, they could and did still claim an inherited *cultural* authority over quintessential Chinese qualities and values, such as cuisine.

For Fu or any of her Mainlander contemporaries in Taiwan to claim a rightful inheritance to the culinary traditions of their home provinces was in line with the political orthodoxy of the day and occasioned no comment from Fu. Yet for a contemporary reader, Fu's map makes manifest a kind of magical thinking, or at least a nostalgic denial of the new territorial realities Mainlanders had to contend with in exile. Tellingly, by the time of the publication of her third cookbook volume in 1979, Fu had expanded her discussion of Chinese culinary regions to also include Fujianese, Hunanese, and Taiwanese cuisines as their own, separate categories. While the addition of Fujian and Hunan was akin to moving from a four-region to eight-region definition of Chinese cuisine, adding Taiwan as its own culinary category was a modern twist from Fu herself, and an obvious response to her new island environment.

Reckoning with this type of internal displacement and its culinary effects has antecedents in China's long history. Michael Freeman (1977) has described a very similar situation occurring during the Song dynasty (960–1279), which has been subdivided into the Northern Song (960–1127), with its capital in Kaifeng, and the Southern Song (1127–1279), with its capital in Hangzhou. The original Song court had been driven out of its northern capital by Jurchen invaders, forcing them to flee south of the Yangtze River in 1127. Writing more than a century after this forced removal, the Southern Song writer Wu Zimu waxed lyrical about the astonishing variety of foods available to residents of the former northern capital, including regional restaurants serving southern food, others serving Sichuanese food, and those serving northern food. However, Wu noted, since moving to the south in the past century, cooking styles had become "mixed up" with "no division of north and south." As Freeman comments,

[R]egional cooking was no longer the unconscious expression of the eating habits of a population defined by locally available ingredients. To cook northern food in Hangchow implied a conscious choice among possible ingredients and possible styles of cooking; it became, in other words, a style of cooking set loose from its local moorings and the product of a consciously maintained tradition.

Freeman 1977, 175

Whether or not Fu and her contemporaries acknowledged it as such, cooking Mainlander cuisine in Taiwan likewise represented a "consciously maintained tradition" "set loose from its local moorings."

There is evidence that Fu was fully aware of the inevitable hybridization of regional cuisines after exile, yet her different audiences were told different messages on the matter of culinary authenticity. For her English-speaking foreign audience, Fu steadily maintained the notion that Taiwan was the last bastion of authentic Chinese regional cooking and the single best place to sample the foods from any Chinese province. In English, Fu (and/or her American collaborator) proudly wrote,

At present, it is only in Taiwan that the pleasure of eating authentic Chinese food from all parts of China can be experienced. China is a vast country, with one of the longest histories of any nation on earth. Thirty-five provinces comprise China, each with it's [sic] own geography, climate, and produce. As a result, ingredients and cooking methods differ from province to province. In Taiwan, there are people from every part of China, and thus there are restaurants representing each province. (E)

Fu 1979, 3

Yet for her Chinese audiences, Fu acknowledged that after the imposed exile of Civil War, Mainlander regional cuisines had become mixed up (just as they had during the Southern Song):

After arriving in Taiwan, because the population of each place gathered all together and contact became frequent, the mutual habits, characteristics, and tastes gradually became closer, tending toward being melted and fused together. Each restaurant, with regard to the taste and style of its dishes, mutually copied or borrowed indiscriminately [from others]. Apart from a few traditional dishes and products, these [dishes] were actually more or less the same, with very little to distinguish them, although their names might be different. (Ch)

Fu 1979, 1

A contradictory logic was thus used to justify the need for a Chinese cookbook with regional distinctions for both Chinese audiences and foreign audiences: American audiences needed to be introduced to the idea of Chinese regional culinary variety, which was most authentically represented on Taiwan, while Chinese audiences in Taiwan needed to learn about the real distinctions of regional Chinese cuisines, since so much of what they ate was inauthentically mixed.

Culinary diplomacy

The significance of Fu's cookbooks and television appearances extends beyond the domestic sphere, in both senses of the word. As her reputation grew through the 1970s and 1980s, Fu frequently traveled overseas to teach Chinese cooking to foreign audiences, with trips to the Philippines, Japan, Singapore, Hong Kong, South Korea, Malaysia, Australia, South Africa, the United States, and the Netherlands. She reached even broader Asian audiences through her cooking programs on both Japanese and Filipino television networks: she was asked to host a instructional program in Japanese for the Fuji Television network from 1978 to 1983, and her TTV cooking program was rebroadcast in the Philippines in both the original Chinese and later dubbed into Tagalog. Her cookbooks, too, frequently traveled overseas in the suitcases of young students from Taiwan going abroad to continue their studies, yet wishing for a taste of home. For all of this international work, Fu was dubbed a "culinary ambassador" by the Taiwan press.

Fu herself gladly took up the mantle of "culinary ambassador," explaining it as the predestined fulfillment of her father's ambitions for her from an early age: "From childhood, my father wished that I would become a talent in something to do with diplomacy. Somehow or other over the years I came to be compared to a 'culinary ambassador.' ... Indeed, I have devoted my entire life, all of my heart and hard work to running around hither and yon [lit., "East and West"] to promote cuisine" (Fu 2000, 19). She shared this gastrodiplomatic message with all manner of foreign audiences. When asked to give the keynote address at the fiftieth anniversary meeting of the Chefs de Cuisine Association of America in Los Angeles in 1976, Fu emphasized in her English speech the role of cuisine in promoting cross-cultural friendship and understanding: "I thank [sic] that cooking is a vital part of a country's culture. All of us in the culinary field have the responsibility to maintain our country's cultures. By sharing our various cuisines. [sic] We can increase mutual understanding and friendship around the world." Again, for her American audience she promoted the notion of Taiwan as the place where authentic Chinese cuisine had been preserved, adding that she "did not forget to conduct a little person-to-person diplomacy" and extended an explicit invitation to the "beautiful island": "You're welcome to visit our country, Taiwan, The Republic of China where you can experience the joy of eating authentic Chinese food." (Fu 2000, 133–4).

Although most of Fu's trips abroad were sponsored by invitations from foreign agencies and private companies, the shadow of the ROC government was never very far away. In 1978, she was awarded a certificate of merit from the ROC Tourism Bureau for "promoting our country's culinary arts" and "seizing the opportunity to expound upon Chinese cultural relics and this treasured island's beautiful scenery to overseas persons, making great contributions in promoting tourism" (Da Fang 1978). In 1985, the Taiwan External Trade Development Council asked her to go with other industry experts to Rotterdam to promote the use of condiments from Taiwan food companies in her cooking demonstrations. During a personal trip to visit her daughter in Florida that same year, she got a phone call from the Taipei Economic and Cultural Representative Office (TECO, the ROC's de facto diplomatic embassy in the United States) in New York City, begging her to come there and talk about Chinese food on television. The TECO representative urged her, "Do something for your country! Enlist your special skills to promote Taiwan!" Fu was happy to engage in "a little person-to-person diplomatic work for the government" by making appearances on television morning programs in various American cities (Fu 2000, 151). Each time she went on the air, she tried to emphasize that "to eat exquisite delicacies, [people] must visit Free China on Taiwan." In so doing, she added, "this had to count as achieving the ultimate goal of the Government Information Office [the ROC's former media and propaganda bureau] in having me going to various places to demonstrate culinary arts, to promote the culture of eating" (Fu 2000, 152).

Though Fu never occupied any formal position in the ROC diplomatic corps, she, her government contacts, and the Taiwan press seemed to believe that her overseas appearances not only promoted the unique cultural and culinary heritage of Taiwan, but also promoted the country's diplomatic agenda to foreign audiences. During her first trip to the Philippines in 1972, for example, one article published in Taiwan extolled Fu's influence abroad, drawing attention to Taiwan in a way that other news items had not:

> English newspapers in the Philippines have never much emphasized news from our country. But during the time of Fu Pei-mei's visit to the Philippines, the four major English-language newspapers, the *Daily Mirror, Manila Daily Bulletin, Daily Express, Manila Evening News*, and *Weekend Magazine*, all had large pictures and lengthy reports on the enthusiasm of Filipino-Chinese women in taking classes and learning [from Fu]. This is successful person-to-person diplomacy through "eating."
>
> Hong 1972

In a more concrete bid to further the ROC's diplomatic agenda, Fu would also sometimes attempt to advocate for the superiority of ingredients available in Taiwan. On Fu's Chinese cooking program for Fuji Television in Japan, for example, Fu referred to the superiority of Taiwan's produce and industrial food products at every opportunity:

> The color of the bean paste available in Japan is not as attractive as that available in Taiwan. Fu Pei-mei can only tell Japanese viewers, "Making this *mapo tofu* in Taiwan, it would be a lot more attractive."
>
> When she has to use rape greens in lieu of green cabbage, she says, "In Taiwan, it's a lot tastier because we use green cabbage, which is both fat and tender."
>
> When making dry-fried green beans, she says, "At this time of year in Taiwan, green beans cost only one-tenth of what they cost here." She is imperceptibly and continuously propagandizing on behalf of our treasured island.
>
> Da Fang 1978

Yet these glowing descriptions in the Taiwan press seem unaware of how foreigners might have interpreted Fu's overseas cooking demonstrations. Just the mention of Taiwan or Taiwanese products did not necessarily mean that foreigners took Fu for anything other than a representative of "Chinese" cooking. In my review of English-language newspapers from the Philippines of the time, for example, I have found two separate instances of coverage of Fu's visit, one in the society pages of the *Manila Daily Bulletin* (Perez 1972), and another in the society pages of the *Philippines Daily Express* (1972). In the former there is one photo of Fu's cooking demonstration with a brief accompanying article about Fu's class, and the latter includes two large photos of Fu plus a caption. Little to no mention is made of Taiwan in either example, while there is a consistent emphasis on Fu's expertise in the realm of "Chinese" cuisine and culture pages. The Taiwan press may have continually celebrated the diplomatic (read: national) side of Fu's gastrodiplomacy, but foreign press coverage of Fu emphasized only the gastronomic (read: cultural) angle of her trips.

Fu herself seems to have undermined this promotion of a Taiwan-specific agenda by presenting herself as a general expert on *Chinese* cuisine to foreigners. A large part of Fu's gastrodiplomatic "work" seems to have consisted of correcting misperceptions among overseas Chinese and foreigners about regional distinctions of Chinese food and its proper preparation. During her first teaching trip to the Philippines in 1972, for example, one article reported that what Filipino-Chinese housewives there understood as Chinese food was "still uniformly a mix of Cantonese dishes and Fujianese dishes. These dishes are sweet, sour and salty, and are actually not all that tasty" (Hong 1972). There, Fu wished to expand palates to encompass a wider variety of Chinese regional tastes. An even clearer example arose during Fu's 1985 trip to Australia, on behalf of the Australian Meat and Livestock Association. The "greatest result of this trip," one article explained, was that Fu " 'taught a lesson' to a group of Australian cooking experts, who had only half-baked understandings of Chinese food" (Zhong 1985). The worst of these self-styled foreign experts was Margaret Fulton (b. 1924), who had a reputation as an "Australian Fu Pei-mei" and even dared to teach Chinese cooking to her fellow Australians early in her career. Fu quickly cut the Australians down to size, judging their questions as "amateur," their understanding of Chinese cuisine as "limited," and their knife skills as "not of very high quality." Fu may have seen no contradiction in both advocating for the ROC and promoting Chinese cuisine in general, but her foreign audiences probably missed any of these subtle distinctions.

Gastrodiplomacy in Taiwan today

In many ways, Fu's position as a media celebrity promoting an appealing and appetizing image of Chinese culture abroad prefigures the explicit emphasis in recent decades on bolstering Taiwan's "soft power," or global influence in cultural arenas outside of the military or economy, first initiated by ROC Vice President Annette Lu in 2000 and echoed again by ROC President Ma Ying-jeou in 2008. Since Thailand first introduced its "Global Thai" program in 2002, with the aim of increasing the number of Thai restaurants around the world and driving foreign tourism, other countries, such as Taiwan, South Korea, Malaysia, and Peru—all middle-state powers with rich food traditions—have followed suit with their own versions of culinary campaigns designed to strengthen recognition of their national "brands" and extend soft power (Haugh et al. 2011). Even the United States has joined these countries in the kitchen, with the

State Department introducing its Diplomatic Culinary Partnership program in 2012. American celebrity chefs have been invited to assist in state dinners, sent abroad to participate in food tours and cooking demonstrations in foreign countries, and served as hosts to foreign chefs on food visits to the United States. All of these gastrodiplomatic programs are built on the same premise—that an excellent way to win friends and influence people is to appeal to their stomachs.

Yet this earlier Cold War example of Fu Pei-mei's cookbooks and gastrodiplomatic mission also underscores the particular difficulty of using food as a tool of diplomacy for Taiwan. For countries such as Thailand or Peru, their culinary traditions and geopolitical futures overlap. Yet for Taiwan, its varied Chinese regional culinary traditions are mapped onto an uncertain geopolitical future. What exactly should Taiwan claim as its gastronomic heritage and its culinary future? Is it still the best place to taste "authentic" Chinese cuisine, or must it recognize the gastronomic, as well as political resurgence and dominance of the PRC? What exactly then is Taiwan cuisine? In the past, the ROC Tourism Bureau attempted to manage its national gastronomic "brand" by describing Mainlander, regional Chinese cuisines as only one strand of culinary influence on the island, alongside Taiwan's own night market street snacks and its plethora of international restaurants. In the 2014 version of its "Tastes of Taiwan" website, for example, many of China's regional culinary styles were represented, including those of Taiwan, Fujian, Guangdong, Jiangzhe (Jiangsu and Zhejiang), Shanghai, Hunan, Sichuan, Beijing, and the Hakkas. But there was also particular emphasis on night market street food, all recognized as Taiwan specialties, such as "pearl milk tea, danzai noodles, shrimp pork soup, oyster omelet, meat rice dumplings (*zongzi*), stinky tofu, Taiwanese meatballs, coffin board, veggie and meat wrap, oyster vermicelli, steamed sandwich (*guabao*), crushed ice dessert, scallion pancakes" (ROC Tourism Bureau, n.d.).[9]

In spite of the ROC's attempts to capitalize on its vibrant culinary diversity, outside of Taiwan there is still the all-important question of how to represent Taiwan's culinary heritage for foreign audiences. The Taipei-based dumpling empire, Din Tai Fung, for example, has overseas locations in Australia, Hong Kong, Indonesia, Japan, Macau, Malaysia, the Philippines, Singapore, South Korea, the United States, Thailand, and Dubai, as well as the PRC. On its US website, the homepage opens with the English phrase, "Tradition that crosses international borders" (E), yet the Chinese phrase underneath explicitly describes "The traditional *Chinese* delicacy that strides over national boundaries" (跨越國界的中華傳統美食 *Kuayue guojie de Zhonghua chuantong meishi*) (Ch; my emphasis) (Din Tai Fung USA, n.d.). That the Chinese version of the phrase uses the term 中華 *Zhonghua* is just as critical as the fact that the English version does not use the word "Chinese." For an English-speaking audience, the term "Chinese" is too easily conflated with the PRC, while the term "Taiwanese" could suggest either a narrower, island-based culinary heritage or a political leaning that the chain seeks to avoid. Meanwhile, for a Chinese-speaking audience, *Zhonghua* is the preferred term on the Republic of China on Taiwan (中華民國 *Zhonghua minguo*), as opposed to the People's Republic of China (中華人民共和國 *Zhonghua renmin gonghe guo*) on the Mainland, which is more commonly identified as *Zhongguo*. Though their dumplings might be equally delicious in any language and in any country, clearly

Din Tai Fung's publicity team has had to consider carefully the impact of its messages in a variety of linguistic and cultural contexts.

Critically, this conundrum of Chinese culinary nationalism exists only for those living in Taiwan, for whom the real political stakes of such a question are that much greater. Just as the PRC claims absolute territorial sovereignty over Taiwan, it also makes claims on Taiwan's local culinary traditions, at least as evidenced by the recent CCTV blockbuster television series, *A Bite of China* (舌尖上的中國 *Shejian shang de Zhongguo*). The first season, which was produced by and aired on the PRC state-run network in 2012, attracted some 100 million Mainland viewers. The title itself is telling: it places the emphasis not on "Chinese food"—an ambiguous term which might be interpreted in a variety of ways—but on the geopolitical entity of "China" (中國 *Zhongguo*), whose territorial integrity is not to be questioned. In the first season of the program, besides exploring a range of regional Chinese culinary specialties, explicit references were made to Taiwan's famous mullet-roe harvest, along with references to Uyghur flatbreads and Tibetan matsutake mushroom gatherers—the latter two being restive ethnic populations that have troubled Chinese leaders in Beijing as much as those agitating for independence in Taiwan. A second season of the hit program quickly followed in 2014; a third season aired in 2018.

The earlier history of Fu Pei-mei, her cookbooks and her overseas cooking demonstrations reminds us that our notions about "Chinese" food are not centuries old and unchanging, but have been continually subject to transformation throughout modern history. Through the decades of her postwar career, Fu and other cookbook authors from Taiwan, Hong Kong, and Singapore really were the arbiters of Chinese taste for both their domestic and international audiences, developing presentations of Chinese cuisine for home cooks and consumers in ways that would not be matched in the PRC until the post-Mao era of economic reform. Fu's culinary star rose during a particular postwar moment, when she could readily substantiate her claims about preserving authentic Chinese culinary traditions, in light of the political chaos on the Mainland, which granted little time for indulging in home cooking as a bourgeois pastime for idle housewives. Meanwhile, the forced migration of Mainlander refugees to Taiwan gave Fu both incentive and the method to fashion herself as a general culinary expert in a wide range of Chinese regional cuisines. For foreigners, Fu presented herself as a genial expert on Chinese food, while at the same time attempting to promote the diplomatic agenda of the ROC. Unfortunately, Fu's three cookbooks, as sturdy as they appear, could not bear the entire burden of this complex and convoluted history: for foreign readers and viewers, Fu was an uncomplicated and authentic representative of "Chinese" food, even as she and her cookbooks attempted to represent both a country and a cultural tradition.

Notes

1   Paul Rockower (2012) makes distinctions among "food diplomacy" (state aid in the
     form of foodstuffs), "culinary diplomacy" (state dinners or other programs
     encompassed by formal state-to-state diplomatic relations), and "gastrodiplomacy"

(nation-branding campaigns to acquaint the global public with one's specific national culinary culture), but it seems that the latter two, in particular, are intimately linked.

2   The recipe for Sweet-and-Sour Fish was taken from *Mrs. Ma's Favorite Chinese Recipes* (1968), written by Nancy Chih Ma (b. 1919), a Chinese woman living in Japan. Her cookbook was published in English by a Japanese press, Kodansha International.

3   In order to mark this distinction clearly, my translations from the Chinese portions of Fu's cookbooks are denoted here by (Ch), and excerpts appearing in the original English will be denoted by (E).

4   The situation in postwar Taiwan parallels the postwar social context described by Appadurai (1988) for India, in his classic description of cookbooks, middle-class housewives, and the creation of a national cuisine.

5   Fu thanks a different American woman in the English prefaces to each of her three cookbooks: Yvonne Zeck (vol. 1), Monica Croghan (vol. 2), and Nancy Murphy (vol. 3). Frank Zeck has confirmed that his mother, Yvonne, accompanied his father, Frank Sr., a colonel in the US Air Force, to Taiwan from 1966 to 1968, where the latter served as an adviser to the ROC Air Force. Yvonne took some of Fu's cooking classes and helped with the English portion of the cookbook, though it is unclear exactly how the women shared the task. Author interview with Frank Zeck, April 2, 2014.

6   The attempt to codify Chinese regional cuisines started earlier on the Mainland, through state institutions. See for example *Zhongguo mingcaipu* (*China's Famous Dishes*) (ed. Dier shangyebu yinshiye guanliju 1958–65), published in eleven volumes by the Food and Drink Industry Management Bureau in Beijing, and *Beijing Fandian mingcaipu* (*Famous Dishes from the Beijing Hotel*) (ed. Beijing Fandian 1959). Notably, the recipes in both were drawn from restaurants, with an intended primary audience of other restaurant professionals, and quantities intended for a ten-person banquet table. Neither work seems to have had the home cook in mind. See Swislocki (2008, 176–218).

7   There is also a version of ten culinary regions (adding Beijing cuisine and Shanghai cuisine as their own entities) and a version of twelve culinary regions (adding Henan province or northeastern cuisine and Shaanxi province or northwestern cuisine). Regardless of the canonical number of cuisines, what is significant is the agreement on the canonical first four—other definitions only ever add regional cuisines, rather than replacing any of the original four.

8   Theresa Lin, Fu's daughter-in-law, explains that the cookbook was conceived of as much as a restaurant ordering guide for foreigners as a cookbook, and purposely bound in hardcover with color photographs in order to appeal as the perfect gift. Author interview with Theresa Lin, November 10, 2016.

9   These references to specific regional Chinese cuisines have entirely disappeared in the current version of the website. This may be due in part to the 2016 election of Tsai Ing-wen and the Democratic Progressive Party to the ROC Presidency. The DPP prefers to distance itself from Mainland ties, in contrast to its Nationalist Party predecessor.

References

Anderson, Lara. 2013. *Cooking Up the Nation: Spanish Culinary Texts and Culinary Nationalization in the Late Nineteenth and Early Twentieth Centuries*. Woodbridge: Boydell & Brewer.

Appadurai, Arjun. 1988. "How to Make a National Cuisine: Cookbooks in Contemporary India." *Comparative Studies in Society and History* 30, no. 1: 3–24.

北京飯店 Beijing Fandian, ed. 1959. 北京飯店名菜譜 *Beijing Fandian mingcaipu* [*Famous Dishes from the Beijing Hotel*]. Beijing: Qinggongye chubanshe.

Chinese Restaurants. 2005. Directed by Cheuk Kwan. Toronto: Tissa Films.

大方 Da Fang. 1978. "烹調大使傅培梅 Pengtiao dashi Fu Peimei" ["Culinary Ambassador Fu Pei-mei"]. 家庭月刊 *Jiating yuekan* [*Families Monthly*] 20: 18–21.

第二商業部飲食業管理局 Dier shangyebu yinshiye guanliju, ed. 1958–65. 中國名菜譜 *Zhongguo mingcaipu* [*China's Famous Dishes*], 11 vols. Beijing: Qinggongye chubanshe.

Din Tai Fung USA. n.d. "Home." http://dintaifungusa.com.

Ferguson, Priscilla Parkhurst. 2004. *Accounting for Taste: The Triumph of French Cuisine.* Chicago: University of Chicago Press.

Ferguson, Priscilla Parkhurst. 2010. "Culinary Nationalism." *Gastronomica* 10, no. 1: 102–9.

Freeman, Michael. 1977. "Sung." In *Food in Chinese Culture: Anthropological and Historical Perspectives*, edited Kwang-chih Chang, 141–76. New Haven, CT: Yale University Press.

傅培梅 Fu Pei-mei. (1969) 1976. *Pei Mei's Chinese Cook Book Volume I* [培梅食譜第一冊 *Peimei shipu, diyice*]. Taipei: T&S Industrial Co., Ltd.

傅培梅 Fu Pei-mei. 1974. *Pei Mei's Chinese Cook Book Volume II* [培梅食譜第二冊 *Peimei shipu, dierce*]. Taipei: T&S Industrial Co., Ltd.

傅培梅 Fu Pei-mei. 1979. *Pei Mei's Chinese Cook Book Volume III* [培梅食譜第三冊 *Peimei shipu, disance*]. Taipei: T&S Industrial Co., Ltd.

傅培梅 Fu Pei-mei. 2000. 五味八珍的歲月 *Wuwei bazhen de suiyue* [*Years of Five Flavors and Eight Delicacies*]. Taipei: Juzi chuban youxian gongsi.

Gong, Sasha, and Scott Seligman. 2011. *The Cultural Revolution Cookbook*. Hong Kong: Earnshaw Books.

Haugh, Shannon, et al., eds. 2014. "Gastrodiplomacy." Special issue, *Public Diplomacy Magazine* 11 (Winter).

鴻蓮特 Hong Liante. 1972. "傅培梅烹飪之旅的收獲 Fu Pei-mei pengren zhi lü de shouhuo" ["The Harvests of Fu Pei-mei's Cooking Travels"]. 中國時報 *Zhongguo shibao*. June 24, 1972.

黃媛珊 Huang Yuanshan. 1954. 媛珊食譜 *Yuanshan shipu* [*Yuanshan Cookbook, Vol. 1*]. Taipei: Sanmin shuju.

黃媛珊 Huang Yuanshan. 1957. 媛珊食譜二集 *Yuanshan shipu erji* [*Yuanshan Cookbook, Vol. 2*]. Taipei: Sanmin shuju.

Lu Wenfu. 1987. *The Gourmet and Other Stories of Modern China*. London: Readers International.

呂曉敏 Lü Xiaomin, 丁驍 Ding Xiao, and 代養勇 Dai Yangyong. 2009. "中國八大菜系的形成歷程和背景 Zhongguo badacaixi de xingcheng licheng he beijing" ["The Process of Formation and Background of China's Eight Major Culinary Systems"]. 中國食物與營養 *Zhongguo shiwu yu yingyang* [*Food and Nutrition in China*] 10: 62–4.

Ma, Nancy Chih. 1968. *Mrs. Ma's Favorite Chinese Recipes*. Tokyo: Kodansha International.

New York Times. 1972. "Two Dishes Served in the Great Hall." February 26, 1972.

Perez, Carmen. 1972. "Day and Night." *Manila Daily Bulletin*. May 28, 1972.

Philippines Daily Express. 1972. Uncredited photo of "Chinese Cook Fu Pei Mei." Society Section. May 28, 1972.

Pilcher, Jeffrey. 1998. *¡Que vivan los tamales! Food and the Making of Mexican Identity*. Albuquerque: University of New Mexico Press.

Pite, Rebekah. 2013. *Creating a Common Table in Twentieth-Century Argentina: Doña Petrona, Women, and Food*. Chapel Hill: The University of North Carolina Press.

ROC Tourism Bureau. n.d. "Tastes of Taiwan." https://eng.taiwan.net.tw/m1.aspx?sno=0002026.

Rockower, Paul. 2012. "Recipes for Gastrodiplomacy." *Place Branding and Public Diplomacy* 8, no. 3: 235–46.

Swislocki, Mark. 2008. *Culinary Nostalgia: Regional Food Culture and the Urban Experience in Shanghai.* Stanford, CA: Stanford University Press.

曾品滄 Tseng Pin-tsang. 2015. "戰時生活體制與民眾飲食生活的發展 (1947–1960s) Zhanhou shenghuo tizhi yu minzhong yinshi shenghuo de fazhan" ["The Development of Postwar Systems and Popular Foodways in the Early Postwar Era of Taiwan"]. In 戰後初期的台灣: 1945–60s *Zhanhou chuqi de Taiwan* [*Taiwan in the Early Postwar Era 1945–60s*], edited by 呂芳上 Lü Fangshang, 585–625. Taipei: Guoshiguan.

王玉環 Wang Yuhuan. 1964. 家庭食譜大全 *Jiating shipu daquan* [*The Complete Home Cookbook*]. Tainan: Donghai chubanshe.

Yenal, Zafer. 2010. "The Myth of Turkish Cuisine: National Appropriation of Local Food Cultures." In *Europa im Nahen Osten, der Nahe Osten in Europa*, edited by Angelika Neuwirth and Günter Stock, 271–83. Berlin: Akademie Verlag.

鐘麗珠 Zhong Lizhu. 1985. "傅培梅到澳洲傳播中國吃的藝術 Fu Peimei dao Aozhou chuanbo Zhongguo chi de yishu" ["Fu Pei-mei Goes to Australia to Transmit the Art of Chinese Food"]. 家庭月刊 *Jiating yuekan* [*Families Monthly*] 100: 107–10.

4

From Military Rations to UNESCO Heritage: A Short History of Korean *Kimchi*

Katarzyna J. Cwiertka
Leiden University

Geographers have argued for decades that "[f]oods do not simply come from places, organically growing out of them, but also make places as symbolic constructs, being deployed in the discursive construction of various imaginative geographies" (Cook and Crang 1996, 140). This statement assumes a new dimension in the era of nation branding, which can be generally defined as deployment of marketing communications techniques to promote a nation's image (Olins 2004; Fan 2006; Kerr and Wiseman 2013; Ahn and Wu 2015). Nation branding has in recent years become a key concept for political decision-makers, cultural diplomats, bureaucrats, and marketing and advertising experts who are concerned with cultural policy (Gienow-Hecht 2016, 236). While the nation has functioned as a brand product since at least the nineteenth century (Gienow-Hecht 2016, 242), the degree to which its image is currently being manipulated through corporate branding strategies is unprecedented. Ample empirical evidence demonstrates that governments around the world have since the turn of the twenty-first century ardently embraced nation branding as a key tactic for enhancing their international reputation (Jaffe and Nebenzahl 2001; Prieto Larraín 2011; Rockower 2011; Kerrigan, Shivanandan, and Hede 2012; Dinnie 2014). What is particularly relevant for this chapter, and the volume as a whole, is that food has assumed an increasingly conspicuous place within those activities.

The recently coined term "gastrodiplomacy" reflects this trend. It is defined as a form of public diplomacy that highlights and promotes the awareness and understanding of a national culinary culture among a foreign public. Simply advocating a food product does not equate with gastrodiplomacy. Rather, very much in the spirit of nation branding, it denotes a more holistic approach to raising international awareness of a country's edible national brand through the promotion of its culinary and cultural heritage (Rockower 2014, 14). The term appeared in print for the first time in a 2002 *Economist* article discussing the global promotion of Thai food, but has since developed into "a field of study within the expanding public diplomacy canon" (Rockower 2014, 13).[1] While economic gain deriving from food-related exports is a welcome by-product of gastrodiplomatic activities, their ultimate goal is to boost the country's international profile reaching far beyond the culinary domain. It has been pointed out by marketing scholars that a positive country image may have far-reaching implications for its overall competitive advantage (Jaffe and Nebenzahl 2001). Food and drink can be effectively employed to manipulate this image, as their long-standing deployment in tourism testifies, due to enormous potential they have as indicators of cultural difference (Woolley and Fishbach 2017). Research confirms that eating the same food may not only have a positive impact on forming first impressions among individuals and influence business negotiations (Spence 2016), but that a positive experience with a country's cuisine can directly modify perceptions of a county as a whole (Murcott 1996; Ruddy 2014, 30–4).

The analysis of forceful gastrodiplomacy campaigns conducted so far reveals that they have involved product marketing (for foods brands and restaurants), along with promotional and educational activities, such as food-tasting events, food festivals, and cooking competitions, not infrequently coordinated by embassies and consulates (Zhang 2015). The campaigns operated a coordinated media strategy, including slogans and logos, YouTube clips, blogs, and sometimes celebrities for additional exposure (Cwiertka 2014). Zhang's study (2015) revealed that governments engaging in gastrodiplomacy customarily build partnerships with the food industry and national and international organizations with potential to enhance awareness and credibility of the nation's culinary brand. Opinion leaders, such as restaurateurs, retailers, and celebrity chefs are deployed worldwide, with priority being given to places renowned as trend-setting culinary capitals, such as Paris, London, and New York.

A common technique applied in nation-branding strategies is the continuous repetition of specific peculiarities of the product/state in an attempt to create a distinctive identity (Gienow-Hecht 2016, 237). Designating specific condiments, dishes, and drinks as symbolic signifiers of a nation has proven a very effective tool in this respect. France and champagne, Italy and pizza, Japan and sushi, Mexico and taco, and England and fish and chips are among the most well-known national symbols (Guy 2003; Helstosky 2008; Sakamoto and Allen 2011; Pilcher 2012; Panayi 2014). In this chapter I will explore *kimchi*, which is the most famous culinary symbol of Korea, according to a 2006 Gallup poll (Pham 2013, 7).

The UNESCO inscription

The *Merriam-Webster* dictionary defines *kimchi* as "a spicy, pungent vegetable dish that consists of one or more pickled and fermented vegetables and especially NAPA CABBAGE and radishes with various seasonings (such as garlic, red chili pepper, ginger, scallions, and anchovy paste)" (*Merriam-Webster* 2018). It has long functioned as a quintessential symbol of Korean identity, officially sanctioned to fulfill this role by the Republic of Korea government. For example, *kimchi* was one of the officially designated foods of the 1988 Seoul Olympics, proclaimed as one of the five most potent Korean cultural symbols by the Ministry of Culture and Sport in 1996, and ten years later included on the Ministry of Culture and Tourism's List of One Hundred Symbols of National Culture (Cho 2006, 213, 220). Yet, the proverbial cherry on the South Korean gastrodiplomatic cake was the inscription of *kimchi* on the UNESCO's Representative List of the Intangible Cultural Heritage of Humanity (ICH) in December 2013. This occurrence generated extensive media attention and added credibility to the subjective claims of the South Korean government that Korean food (and by extension the country it comes from) was worthy of global recognition. The Convention for the Safeguarding of Intangible Cultural Heritage, which forms the legal foundation for the list, was ratified by the UNESCO in 2003 with the aim of enhancing the visibility of the world's intangible cultural heritage and awareness of its significance. Yet, in practice, it has been turned into an arsenal for nation-branding warfare (e.g., Askew 2010; Aykan 2015).

Five years after the ratification of the convention, the first elements began to be added to the list: it now includes such diverse entries as Argentinian tango, Chinese calligraphy, and Indonesian batik.[2] UNESCO defines "intangible cultural heritage" as "practices, representations, expressions, knowledge, skills—as well as the instruments, objects, artefacts and cultural spaces ... that communities, groups and, in some cases, individuals recognize as part of their cultural heritage."[3] Although no direct reference to food and drink is made in the text of the Convention for the Safeguarding of Intangible Cultural Heritage, it is today considered the most prolific instrument of international law used to protect culinary traditions (Maffei 2012, 248).

The first three inscriptions that focused specifically on culinary culture— "Gingerbread craft from Northern Croatia" (UNESCO n.d. c), "Gastronomic meal of the French" (UNESCO n.d. d), and "Traditional Mexican cuisine—ancestral, ongoing community culture, the Michoacán paradigm" (UNESCO n.d. e)—were added in 2010, a year after an expert meeting had been organized (in April 2009) specifically to discuss the role of culinary practices in the implementation of the convention (Maffei 2012, 232). It is worthwhile to point out that one of the issues raised was a high risk of commercial exploitation of the culinary elements inscribed on the ICH list. This has prompted the ICH Committee to emphasize in their communication to the states submitting culinary nominations "to take all the necessary measures in order to avoid any commercial misappropriation of inscribed elements, in particular of generic elements covering several domains, through the use of the Convention's emblem for purposes of commercial instrumentalization and branding" (Maffei 2012, 238).

Nearly a decade after this warning had been issued, we can conclude that such measures, if indeed taken, proved largely ineffective, especially if we consider the central position that food and drink have assumed in nation branding. This can clearly be observed in the example of "Washoku, Traditional Dietary Cultures of the Japanese, Notably for the Celebration of New Year" (UNESCO n.d. f), which was added to the list in December 2013. Not only has the inscription of *washoku* since been extensively utilized commercially, but also, and more importantly, the nomination itself had been considerably tweaked to meet the UNESCO criteria (Cwiertka and Yasuhara 2016; Cwiertka 2018a, 2018b; Cwiertka with Yasuhara, forthcoming).

This is hardly surprising in the context of post-industrial capitalism, where "knowledge, communication, and aesthetics are the most important inputs and outputs of economic activity" (Liagouras 2005, 24). These conditions lead to the shifting of symbolic resources (cognitive, communicative, and aesthetic) to the center of the market, and their subordination to the movement of capital; they are now "having their main objectives totally or partially reoriented by profit imperatives" (Liagouras 2005, 25). In this context "profit" does not necessarily translate into direct monetary gain, but may refer to the overall competitive advantage, which, as we observed above, can be manipulated by the national image.

The approval process for a nomination for inclusion on the Representative List of the Intangible Cultural Heritage of Humanity takes approximately two years. All nominations are to be submitted to the UNESCO Secretariat by March 31 of Year 1 in order to undergo screening by the Evaluating Body and be presented for final examination by the Intangible Cultural Heritage Committee for inscription, which is announced in November/December of Year 2. All successful applications must meet the following five criteria:

R.1:   The element constitutes intangible cultural heritage as defined in Article 2 of the Convention.

R.2:   Inscription of the element will contribute to ensuring visibility and awareness of the significance of the intangible cultural heritage and encourage dialogue, thus reflecting cultural diversity worldwide and testifying to human creativity.

R.3:   Safeguarding measures are elaborated that may protect and promote the element.

R.4:   The element has been nominated following the widest possible participation of the community, group or, if applicable, individuals concerned and with their free, prior and informed consent.

R.5:   The element is included in an inventory of the intangible cultural heritage present in the territory(ies) of the submitting State(s) Party(ies), as defined in Article 11 and Article 12 of the Convention.[4]

"Kimjang, Making and Sharing Kimchi in the Republic of Korea" (UNESCO n.d. h) was added to the Representative List of the Intangible Cultural Heritage of Humanity in December 2013. This means that the nomination had been submitted at the beginning of the previous year and that it successfully met the above-mentioned criteria. *Kimjang* refers to the practice of pickling vegetables into a spicy dish (*kimchi*), which can be preserved for several months and accompanies practically every Korean meal. Like the manufacture of soy sauce, soybean paste, and red chilli pepper paste, for centuries *kimjang* was strictly a homemade affair. Activities surrounding pickling vegetables took place in late autumn, marking the passage of time in every Korean household (Figure 4.1). Nowadays, family members residing in cities often travel to the countryside to join their relatives in *kimjang* chores. Preparation methods and flavors used to vary considerably by region and this is still the case. Each family has its own *kimjang* recipes that have been handed down from generation to generation (Cwiertka and Moriya 2008, 167–9; Kim 2016, 41–2).

This brief description alone seems sufficient to conclude that *kimjang* practices highly qualify for the inclusion on the ICH list. In fact, the nomination was singled out as the model case of the type of intangible heritage that UNESCO aims to protect.[5] At

Figure 4.1 Making *kimchi* at home is a laborious process requiring experience. Ingredients pictured here include napa cabbage, garlic, Asian pears, and daikon radish. Seoul, South Korea (2003). Photograph by Katarzyna J. Cwiertka.

this point, the Republic of Korea government had long-standing experience with UNESCO activities and procedures (Korean National Commission for UNESCO 2015), and enthusiastically embraced the new possibilities of having its intangible heritage recognized. Three South Korean nominations were among the first elements inscribed on the list in 2008 (filed in 2007), followed by additional five the following year (filed in 2008).[6] The nominations filed in 2009 included "Royal cuisine of the Joseon dynasty" (Nomination file no. 00476), the very first attempt at having culinary heritage added to the list.

The timing of the submission coincided with launch of the Global Promotion of Korean Cuisine (*Hansik Segyehwa Ch'ujin*) campaign, a comprehensive government-led initiative, with the following, rather ambitious objectives: (1) quadruple the number of Korean restaurants around the world to 40,000 and recognize qualified restaurants through a government-ordained certification process; (2) elevate the popularity of Korean cuisine so it is included in the world's top five favorite ethnic cuisines; (3) enlist South Korean and foreign celebrities to advertise the campaign; (4) increase investment in the worldwide expansion of the Korean food industry; (5) establish Korean culinary courses at internationally renowned culinary schools, such as Le Cordon Bleu and the Culinary Institute of America; (6) establish a new *kimchi* institute; (7) implement the use of social media platforms for Korean food promotion (Pham 2013, 8). In March 2010, the Korean Food Foundation (KFF, *Hansik Chaedan*), was established in order to coordinate the implementation of those goals. It was made possible by donations of 700 million wŏn (about $620,000) from the Korea Tourism Organization, the Korea Agro-Fisheries Trade Corporation, the Korea Foundation, the National Federation of Fisheries Cooperatives, the National Agricultural Cooperative Federation, the Korean Food Research Institute, and the Korean Racing Authority (Cwiertka 2014, 364).[7]

The nomination for "Royal cuisine of the Joseon dynasty" submitted to the UNESCO secretariat in 2009 refers to a lavish, formal style of dining practiced at the Korean royal court until the end of the nineteenth century, and since 1971 recognized as Important Intangible Cultural Asset No. 38 by the South Korean government within the framework of its own intangible heritage protection system (Cwiertka 2012, 138; Kim 2017, 7–9). Yet, royal court cuisine remained largely obscure for the following three decades until the phenomenal success of the television series *Taejanggŭm* (*Jewel in the Palace*) turned it into a household name. The drama depicted the life story of a sixteenth-century historical character, a woman who combined the career of royal chef with that of the king's private physician. Since intrigues and struggles for power in the highly stratified (all-female) royal kitchen constituted the core of the plot, cooking scenes featured prominently throughout the story. The series began broadcasting in September 2003, twice a week, each Monday and Tuesday, at the prime-time slot of 9:55 p.m. to 10:55 p.m. The viewing rate rose at a spectacular rate, from 19 percent at the time of the second episode to 28 percent two weeks later, and surpassed an astonishing 50 percent by mid-November. Every week millions of South Korean viewers were becoming acquainted with the half-imagined tradition of cooking and eating at the royal court. By March 2004, when the series ended, *Taejanggŭm* was declared the most popular historical drama ever aired on Korean television, and the royal cuisine was transformed into an article of mass consumption (Cwiertka 2012, 139).

The series met with a triumphant reception not only at home, but also in Japan, Taiwan, and other parts of Asia, evidently igniting the popularity of Korean food in the region. It is most likely that this enthusiasm inspired the strategists of the global *hansik* (Korean food) campaign to strengthen its gastrodiplomatic cache by nominating "Royal cuisine of the Joseon dynasty" for inclusion on the UNESCO list of intangible heritage, following the eight applications that had successfully passed the vetting procedure in 2007–8 and 2008–9. The application was rejected on the grounds of not meeting criteria 1, 2, and 4 listed above. The precise wording of the decision was as follows:

R.1: Additional information would be needed to identify more clearly the community concerned with the element and its current social function for them, as well as to describe how the practice is recreated by its bearers and provides them a sense of identity and continuity today;

R.2: The State should demonstrate clearly how inscription of the Royal cuisine of the Joseon dynasty on the Representative List could contribute to ensuring visibility of the intangible cultural heritage and awareness of its significance;

R.4: Although two masters and two Institutes participated in the nomination process and provided their free, prior and informed consent, additional information is needed on the participation of a larger community outside the academic environment (UNESCO 2011, 57–8).

Only a few months after this negative outcome, South Korea submitted a new nomination. It is unclear from the submitted documentation whether this move had already been planned, or whether it was prompted by the rejection of "Royal cuisine of the Joseon dynasty."[8] In any rate, the new nomination checked all the boxes of the UNESCO requirements and passed with flying colors.

Within a few months after "Kimjang, making and sharing kimchi in the Republic of Korea" was added to the Representative List of the Intangible Heritage of Humanity, an almost identical nomination reached the UNESCO secretariat—"Tradition of kimchi-making in the Democratic People's Republic of Korea." It was added to the list in 2015 (UNESCO n.d. i). Since the pickling of *kimchi* is a practice shared by Koreans across the Korean peninsula, it hardly comes as a surprise that the government of the People's Republic of Korea (North Korea) decided to claim rights to it. In fact, this was the second instance of North Korea filing a UNESCO nomination for exactly the same element immediately after its southern neighbor. Two years after "Arirang, lyrical folk song in the Republic of Korea" (UNESCO n.d. j) was added to the list in December 2012, "Arirang folk song in the Democratic People's Republic of Korea" (UNESCO n.d. k) was inscribed. As explained above, the screening process of every dossier takes nearly two years, with a few months lag between the announcement of the previous round and the deadline for the submission of the next year's nominations.

Although definitely less prolific than the gastro-national offensive launched by the South, the North Korean government did not relinquish its claims to the shared intangible heritage of the Korean peninsula. For example, a set of North Korean stamps on the theme "National Food" was issued in 2006, following South Korean stamps featuring Korean dishes unveiled a few years earlier (Cwiertka 2012, 170–2). In July 2014, North Korea launched its own website, www.cooks.org.kp, which includes recipes for over a thousand dishes, hailing from both South and North Korea. Kim (2017, 7–9) interprets this as a projection of a unified vision of Korea, but in my view this instance underscores the gastrodiplomatic competition unleashed by the UNESCO's ICH initiative. Sensitivities surrounding shared heritage by nation-states with territorial disputes had already surfaced in 2009, at the occasion of the inscription of Karagöz (UNESCO n.d. l), a form of shadow theatre practiced in Greece and Turkey, but nominated by Turkey (Aykan 2015). Literature to date has called attention to the misuse of the ICH Convention for such nationalistic purposes (see, e.g., Smith and Akagawa 2009; Askew 2010), and more specifically to the drawbacks of nationalistic descriptions of culinary practices. Tettner and Kalyoncu (2016, 49), for example, warn that this rhetoric leads to many historic, geographic, and political dimensions of food cultures that do not conform to these nationalist perspectives being left out. While highly relevant, this is not the only issue that renders the Intangible Cultural Heritage initiative of UNESCO problematic.

In my view, the glorification of intangible cultural heritage fostered by UNESCO underplays the importance of preserving knowledge about the actual historical trajectories of those practices. In order to meet the requirements specified by the ICH Convention, the focus lies on the contemporary state of affairs, without taking into account the historical development of contemporary practices considered as "heritage." The analysis of their past may reveal inconsistencies in the official narratives presented by nominating states, disclosing connections that often do not fit within their nationalistic agendas. To paraphrase renowned British historian David Lowenthal (1998, 13), in the UNESCO nominations the past is being reshaped to make the heritage palatable for public consumption. In the case of *kimchi*, this is particularly relevant in relation to the industrialization of its manufacture.

Industrializing heritage

While in North Korea the practices related to pickling *kimchi* continue more or less undisturbed, in South Korea they have undergone considerable reconfiguration during the last couple of decades. First of all, per-capita consumption of *kimchi* in South Korea has continued to decline since the 1990s. Over a period of twenty years, between 1991 and 2012, it decreased from roughly 35 kilograms to 22 kilograms per annum. The pace of decline has steadily accelerated. Between 2007 and 2012 alone per-capita consumption declined by 25 percent, from 80 grams to 60 grams per day (Jo 2016, 78).

This decline was caused, in the first place, by a rising standard of living. Dishes prepared with foodstuffs of animal origin such as beef, pork, chicken, and eggs, increasingly replaced *kimchi* as the primary side dish; between 1965 and 1996 their consumption skyrocketed from 5.5 kilograms to 93.7 kilograms. Later, the impact of dietary globalization played a role, as foreign foods, such as American fast-food, pasta, and sushi pushed *kimchi* away from South Korean tables (Cwiertka 2012, 122–8). Yet, despite a drastic decline in the consumption of *kimchi*, the *kimchi* industry has kept thriving. For example, between 1991 and 2000 the production increased six-fold (from 52,000 tons to 309,000 tons). Within only two years, between 1995 and 1997, the number of South Korean *kimchi* manufacturers more than doubled, from 190 to 459 (Jo 2016, 6). By 2010, there were 859 manufacturers, which now also included food-processing giants such as Doosan and Chail Jeadan.

Recently conducted surveys indicate that the home pickling of *kimchi*—once a standard chore performed in every Korean household—is successively declining, as more and more Koreans eat out or rely on store-bought products (Lee, Choi, and Park 2011). The year 2013 (the year of the inscription of *kimjang* on the UNESCO list) marked the first time that the value of factory-made *kimchi* surpassed the share of homemade *kimchi* in South Korea. According to data from 2015, the volume of home-pickled *kimchi* was still slightly larger than the amount produced industrially. However, the gap rapidly diminished. In 2008, the amount of *kimchi* pickled at home was almost double the amount made industrially (832,000 tons against 483,000 tons). Within a period of only seven years, between 2008 and 2015, this difference in volume declined by half – from 349,000 tons to 172,000 tons (Jo 2016, 78).

The very same year *kimjang* obtained ICH status, the consumption of factory-made *kimchi* surpassed the share of homemade *kimchi* on the South Korean market for the first time (Kim 2016, 46). Yet, the industrialization of *kimchi* pickling remains an obscure topic within the burgeoning literature on *kimjang*, despite the critical role it has assumed in the preservation of the custom of *kimchi* consumption. As Chi-Hoon Kim (2016, 51), a graduate student of anthropology at Indiana University, convincingly argued in her study of the construction of *kimjang* as an ICH, commercialization of *kimchi* has played an essential role in retaining this labor-intensive food item on the daily menus of South Koreans, despite the demands of contemporary life, thus preserving *kimchi* heritage. "The failure to acknowledge these transformations presents the practice as a time-honored custom fixed in time and space rather than highlighting how new variations are reviving it as a living heritage" (Kim 2016, 51). Kim's critical analysis echoes the insightful comments offered by food historian Rachel Laudan at the occasion of inscription of "Traditional Mexican cuisine—ancestral, ongoing community culture, the Michoacán" (UNESCO n.d. e) as UNESCO's intangible heritage in 2010: "To try to freeze the cuisines in time is like commanding the tide to stand still" (Laudan 2010).

The remainder of this chapter is an attempt to fill in gaps in the historical understanding of the industrialization of *kimchi*. The 1990s are generally considered a turning point in this respect. Cho (2006, 218) reports that the number of manufacturers more than doubled between 1992 and 2000 (from 160 to 400), and production volume reached 450,000 tons. In 1994 the city of Kwangju held its first World Kimchi Festival, organized on a yearly basis with the aim of setting the city on the map as *kimchi*'s capital (Kim 2016, 50). Ten years later, the Planning and Promotion Unit for the Kimchi Industry was created with government funding in Kwangju Technopark, which was the very first case of government funding for a concrete industrial promotion project of *kimchi* (Cho 2006, 220–1). In the meantime, producers of home electronics teamed up with *kimchi* manufacturers in the development of kimchi refrigerators, and in 2005 the Korean Kimchi Association was set up, with "development of domestic *kimchi* industry" as one of its objectives (Cho 2006, 219).

An important incentive for consolidated action between the industry and government was provided by a dispute between South Korea and Japan often called the "*kimchi* war" (*kimch'i chŏnjaeng*), over the international standardization of *kimchi* by the Codex Alimentarius Commission (CAC), part of the United Nations Food and Agriculture Organization (Han 2010, 158–61). The conflict began in 1996 when Japan proposed designating *kimuchi* (the Japanese pronunciation of *kimchi*) an official Atlanta Olympic food. By then Japanese–Korean trade relations were already under stress because Japan had already been involved in exporting the Japanese "instant" version of *kimchi*, which lacked the distinctive flavor deriving from the fermentation process. In response, South Korea had filed a case with the Codex, arguing that there was a need to establish an international *kimchi* standard, which was officially adopted on July 5, 2001. Point 2.2 of the document delineates fermentation as the defining feature of the product.

Kimchi is the product:
(a) prepared from varieties of Chinese cabbage, Brassica pekinensis Rupr.; such Chinese cabbages shall be free from significant defects, and trimmed to remove inedible parts, salted, washed with fresh water, and drained to remove excess water; they may or may not be cut into suitable sized pieces/parts;
(b) processed with seasoning mixture mainly consisting of red pepper (Capsicum annuum L.) powder, garlic, ginger, edible Allium varieties other than garlic, and radish. These ingredients may be chopped, sliced and broken into pieces; and

(c) fermented before or after being packaged into appropriate containers to ensure the proper ripening and preservation of the product by lactic acid production at low temperatures.

FAO (2001) 2017

These developments had rather unexpected consequences. While the exports of Korean *kimchi* indeed increased following the inclusion of the *kimchi* standard in Codex Alimentarius, generating a slight positive margin for Korea, it also led to the boost of its manufacture in China and growing imports of Chinese *kimchi* to Korea (Lee 2014; Wui 2014).

Ironically, the "*kimchi* war" was brought about by the popularity of the pickle in Japan, the very objective of the global promotion of Korean food campaign. Between 1990 and 2000 the production of the Korean pickle in Japan increased nearly fourfold, while its import from Korea increased from 3,432 tons to 30,000 tons. The growth during the final two years was particularly spectacular—from 15,000 tons to 30,000 tons. In the year 2000 *kimchi* ranked as number one among all the pickled vegetables produced (and consumed) in Japan, far ahead of traditional Japanese products (Cwiertka 2006, 153). A combination of factors stimulated the swift popularization of *kimchi* in Japan. Manufacturers' efforts to revive the stagnating market for pickled vegetables, and the tough competition between them, is considered to have played an important role. The ethnic food boom and health-food fashion that swept Japan during the 1990s were also significant, because they led to shifts in attitude, particularly among women, toward spices and garlic. *Kimchi* was embraced as a delicious food with healthy properties, such as the ability to increase stamina, prevent cancer, and even generate weight loss. The third factor behind the rapidly growing popularity of *kimchi* in Japan was the changing attitude toward Korea, inspired by two international sporting events that took place in Seoul—the Tenth Asian Games in 1986 and the Twenty-Fourth Olympic Games in 1988. The publicity surrounding both events engaged the interest of the Japanese public, leading to the growth of Japanese tourism to South Korea (Cwiertka 2006, 154).

To sum up, the popularity of *kimchi* in Japan offered new business opportunities for Korean manufacturers, who thus far had supplied *kimchi* primarily to institutional consumers such as the armed forces and canteens. The new circumstances provided a strong stimulus for expansion, which was reflected by the skyrocketing number of manufacturers mentioned earlier. As the volume of production increased, so did the quality, resulting in the end-product becoming competitive with the homemade pickle.

The *kimchi* file

Along with the 1990s, which can be considered a turning point in the rise of the South Korean *kimchi* industry, the pivotal role of pioneering efforts toward commercialization of *kimchi* production two decades earlier is equally essential. They were undertaken for a very specific purpose of providing *kimchi* rations to Korean troops in Vietnam. South Koreans comprised roughly two-thirds of the Free World Military Forces, which fought along with American soldiers in the Vietnam War (1955–75). The build-up of the Republic of Korea troops began in 1965 from over 20,000 men to a peak of nearly 50,000 three years later. The deployment continued until 1973, with over 300,000 Korean soldiers serving in Vietnam throughout the war, 5,000 of whom died and 11,000 of whom were injured (Larsen and Collins 1985, 23).

The issue of *kimchi* rations began to surface in the media from the beginning of the deployment of Korean soldiers to Vietnam in the spring of 1965. The April 21 edition of the Korean newsreel *Taehan News*, screened in cinemas and other public places, showed images of a Korean Marine Corps engineer company, known as the "Pigeon Unit," being visited by the wives of the staff of the Korean Embassy in Vietnam.[9] The women were engaged in the preparation of *kimchi*, which, according to a newspaper article that appeared in early March, was the first instance of such activity taking place in Vietnam.[10] By the summer, contradictory accounts of whether or not special rations were being procured for Koreans could be found in the Korean media. For example, the newspaper *Kyŏnghyang Sinmun* reported on July 8 that the Korean parliament had discussed the matter of canned *kimchi* produced in Hawai'i being provided to the Pigeon Unit, but two days later issued a correction that this story was untrue.[11] On July 24, the same newspaper again reported rumors from the Korean parliament. This time, parliamentarian Kim claimed that negotiations were ongoing between the Japanese government and the Americans regarding the provision of Japanese miso to the Korean soldiers in Vietnam.[12] Two weeks earlier, the newspaper *Chosŏn Ilbo* had announced that the American authorities had flatly refused a Korean request to provide Korean soldiers in Vietnam with any special rations.[13]

In the following months, the attention of the media shifted to the hardships of the soldiers who were deprived of *kimchi*[14] and the US prohibition against sending Korean troops packages containing Korean condiments.[15] At the same time, updates on the progress that Korean scientists and manufacturers were making in developing canned *kimchi* were frequently published.[16] In 1967, the public was shown how this spectacular new product was being produced and delivered to the soldiers (Figure 4.2), and a year later the first images of Korean troops in Vietnam consuming canned *kimchi* appeared in a newsreel from January 8, 1968 (Figure 4.3).

Meanwhile, behind-the-scenes negotiations were taking place as to who was to pay the *kimchi* bill. The topic was first raised at the highest level during a private conversation between US President Lyndon Johnson and prime minister of the Republic of Korea Il Kwon Chung on March 14, 1967. The prime minister presented the president with a personal letter from President Chung-hee Park, which mentioned, among other things, the necessity of supplying Korean food to the Korean troops in Vietnam.[17] Referring to the letter, the prime minister re-emphasized the importance of Korean food for the morale of the Korean troops and that President Park had specifically asked him to mention the problem to President Johnson. He added a personal note to the conversation by revealing that he himself "had longed for *kimchi* even more than he had longed for his wife back in Korea" while staying in the United States (Gatz 2000, 356).

In his reply to President Park's letter, written nine days after the meeting, President Johnson stated the following: "I fully understand the desire of your men in the field to enjoy familiar rations. That is the way it has always been with soldiers throughout

Figure 4.2 Newsreel still of production of canned *kimchi* for Korean troops in Vietnam. *Taehan News* (1967), 613 edition. Reproduced by permission from Han'guk Chŏngch'aek Pangsong KTV.

Figure 4.3 Newsreel still of Korean troops in Vietnam consuming canned *kimchi*. *Taehan News* (1968), 656 edition. Reproduced by permission from Han'guk Chŏngch'aek Pangsong KTV.

history. Therefore, I have asked Secretary McNamara to work out with your officials a way to meet your request that the Korean forces be supplied with 'kimchi'" (Gatz 2000, 359).

The National Archives in College Park, Maryland, reveal the interesting correspondence that took place afterward between the US Department of Defense and the Republic of Korea government concerning the extra cost of the *kimchi* ration to be provided for the South Korean soldiers fighting in Vietnam. It was estimated that providing each soldier with a Korean-manufactured combat ration instead of a standard US combat ration once a day would require a budget of $12 million per year. The second option considered was the procurement of Korean-made *kimchi* rations for insertion into the US-manufactured C-Rations, as a supplement to the US standard ration. The budget required for this operation would be much smaller, namely $2.5 million, and a decision was made in favor of the latter option (Barnett 1967).

The issue was rather delicate, as the Department of Defense, which was to pay for the *kimchi* rations, was experiencing financial difficulties at the time, while President Johnson had given his personal endorsement to the Korean request for a *kimchi* ration. It was, therefore, crucial to reach an agreement before the White House could interfere, which might have resulted in an even greater financial burden. The financing of the whole operation remained a problem for years to come (Nooter 1969; Lathram 1970).

The story by no means ends there. The *kimchi* rations to be inserted into the standard American C-Rations were manufactured in Korea by a number of food-processing enterprises. According to the data provided by the newspaper *Maeil Kyŏngje Sinmun*, in the fall of 1967 the following three companies were contracted by the US government for this purpose: Chinkang Wŏnun for 1,000,000 cans, Hwanam Sanch'u for 1,500,000 cans, and Taehwa Sangsa for 7,500,000 cans.[18] The last of the three companies was clearly the biggest player in the *kimchi* canning business, as it delivered three times as many cans as the other two combined. Moreover, this was not the first time that the name Taehwa Sangsa had appeared in the Korean print media. Three years earlier, on October 1, 1964, the newspaper *Kyŏnghyang Sinmun* had reported on the well-being of the Korean sportsmen competing in the Tokyo Olympics. They were allegedly in very good form and mood, largely due to the fact that *kimchi* was readily available in the Olympic Village cafeteria. The article explained that the *kimchi* was provided by a firm called Taehwa Sangsa, which was run by Kim Teiru, a Korean living in Japan.[19]

A search in the printed media for Taehwa Sangsa, or Yamato Shōji (as the characters would have been pronounced in Japanese) did not reveal any new information on the alleged supplier of *kimchi* during the Tokyo Olympics. Registers of the Chamber of Commerce mention neither Yamato Shōji nor Kim Teiru (or alternate pronunciations Taiichi/Teichi). However, registration with the Chamber of Commerce was not compulsory at the time, and smaller enterprises hardly ever took the trouble to do so. Thus, the question of whether the supplier of *kimchi* for Korean athletes during the Tokyo Olympics and for Korean soldiers in Vietnam was the same company—or whether these were two independent enterprises that coincidentally shared the same name—remains unanswered.

Conclusion

Under the impact of culinary globalization, the content of our daily diet has, since at least the 1960s, acquired increasingly diverse cultural roots. Greek yogurt for breakfast, sushi for lunch, and spaghetti for dinner is by no means an unusual option for a citizen of the industrialized world. In the midst of this global culinary amalgamation, we tend to classify different foods by referring to their "nationality," even when they have become fully integrated into our lives (see, e.g., Belasco 1989; Heldke 2003; Pilcher 2008; Panayi 2010; Amenda 2008). We customarily attribute specific dishes and condiments as signifiers of specific cuisines, without questioning the legitimacy of such attributions.

As British sociologists Scott Lash and John Urry (1994) observed more than two decades ago, signs rather than material objects are at the center of contemporary political economies. These include, they argued, the proliferation of informational goods and aesthetic products, as well as the growing aestheticization of material objects (Lash and Urry 1994, 15). This implies not only that design comprises an increasing component of the value of goods, but also that they acquire additional worth through the process of branding, in which marketers and advertisers attach specific images and associations to them. By declaring *kimjang* to be cultural heritage (rather than a chore comparable to the practice of the communal washing of clothes), the South Korean government assumes the position of a marketer and advertiser of the nation. UNESCO's recognition of *kimjang* as intangible world heritage not only enhances the Republic of Korea's overall competitive advantage, but also serves the commercial interests of the *kimchi* industry, which can now market its product to the domestic consumer as their national heritage. Familiarity with foreign food, which has since the 1980s steadily infiltrated daily reality in South Korea, has turned eating Korean food into a matter of conscious decision rather than the taken-for-granted act it was in the past.

In *Retrotopia* (2017), the last book Polish sociologist Zygmunt Bauman published before his death, the author suggests that in the globalized world of post-industrial capitalism, the increasing integration of the world economy and the growing power of international institutions has restricted the abilities of nation-states to shape policy (Wolff 2001). "Once stripped of power to shape the future," Bauman argues, "politics tends to be transferred to the space of collective memory—a space immensely more amenable to manipulation and management" (Bauman 2017, 61). Drawing on the work of Svetlana Boym (2001), Bauman claims that nationalist revivals all over the world are engaged in the creation of the anti-modern myth of the ideal home that has been lost, often confusing the actual home with the imaginary one. Engaging directly with David Lowenthal's acclaimed volume *The Past Is a Foreign Country* (1985), Bauman shrewdly observes that "[b]eing a foreign country stopped being a particular and exclusive quality of the past, and in the result the boundary separating the past from the present has been progressively washed out and border-posts all but vacated" (Bauman 2017, 57). Eliminating the industrialization of manufacture from the *kimchi* narrative is an articulation of this process.

Notes

1 See also Rockower (2002).
2 For the full list, see UNESCO (n.d. a).
3 For the text of the "Convention for the Safeguarding of the Intangible Cultural Heritage," see UNESCO (n.d. b).

4 For the text of the "Procedure of inscription of elements on the Lists and of selection of Good Safeguarding Practices," see UNESCO (n.d. g).

5 The statement made on December 5, 2013 by Bak Sang-mee, the Korean member of Cultural Heritage Committee, was aired on Arirang News (2013) and repeated by other news outlets.

6 For the full inventory of the list, see UNESCO (n.d. a).

7 The campaign closed in 2017, and the Korean Food Foundation was renamed the Korean Food Promotion Institute (*Hansik Chinhŭngwŏn*). For the current activities of the institute, see KFPI (2017).

8 See "Consent of Communities" and "ICH Inventory" documents are available for download from UNESCO's website (UNESCO n.d. h).

9 *Taehan News* 대한뉴스, no. 516, April 21, 1955.

10 *Tonga Ilbo* 동아일보, March 5, 1955.

11 *Kyŏnghyang Sinmun* 경향신문, July 8, 1965 and July 10, 1965.

12 *Kyŏnghyang Sinmun* 경향신문, July 24, 1965.

13 *Chosŏn Ilbo* 조선일보, July 9, 1965.

14 *Kyŏnghyang Sinmun* 경향신문, October 14, 1965; *Chosŏn Ilbo* 조선일보, May 12, 1966.

15 *Tonga Ilbo* 동아일보, December 29, 1965.

16 *Kyŏnghyang Sinmun* 경향신문, September 8, 1965; *Tonga Ilbo* 동아일보, September 13, 1966; *Maeil Kyŏngje* 매일경제, September 28, 1966.

17 A copy of Park's March 8 letter, attached to a March 14 letter from Fleck to Rear Admiral Lemos is in the National Archives and Records Administration, RG 59, Central Files 1967–69, POL 7 KOR S.

18 *Maeil Kyŏngje* 매일경제 November 1, 1967.

19 *Kyŏnghyang Sinmun* 경향신문, October 1, 1964.

References

Ahn, Michael J., and Hsin-Ching Wu. 2015. "The Art of Nation Branding: National Branding Value and the Role of Government and the Arts and Culture Sector." *Public Organization Review* 15, no. 1: 157–73.

Amenda, Lars. 2008. "Food and Otherness: Chinese Restaurants in West European Cities in the 20th Century." *Food and History* 7, no. 2: 157–79.

Arirang News. 2013. "Tradition of Making Kimchi Makes It on UNESCO Cultural Heritage List." YouTube video, 7:23. December 5, 2013. https://www.youtube.com/watch?v=of0IUrFi8Iw.

Askew, Marc. 2010. "The Magic List of Global Status: UNESCO, World Heritage and the Agendas of States." In *Heritage and Globalisation*, edited by Sophia Labadi and Colin Long, 19–44. New York: Routledge.

Aykan, Bahar. 2015. " 'Patenting' Karagöz: UNESCO, Nationalism and Multinational Intangible Heritage." *International Journal of Heritage Studies* 21, no. 10: 949–61.

Barnett, Robert W. 1967. "Korean C-Rations: Telephone Conversation with DOD—Mr. Richard Steadman." National Archives and Records Administration, RG 59 General Records of the Department of State. Lot Files 70D34, 71D81 (NN3-059-99-057 Box 1). College Park, MD.

Bauman, Zygmunt. 2017. *Retrotopia*. Cambridge: Polity Press.

Belasco, Warren J. 1989. *Appetite for Change: How the Counterculture Took on the Food Industry*. New York: Pantheon Books.

Boym, Svetlana. 2001. *The Future of Nostalgia*. New York: Basic Books.

Cho, Hong Sik. 2006. "Food and Nationalism: Kimchi and Korean National Identity." *The Korean Journal of International Studies* 4, no. 1: 207–29.

Cook, Ian, and Philip Crang. 1996. "The World on a Plate: Culinary Culture, Displacement and Geographical Knowledge." *Journal of Material Culture* 1, no. 2: 131–53.

Cwiertka, Katarzyna J. 2006. *Modern Japanese Cuisine: Food, Power, and National Identity*. London: Reaktion Books.

Cwiertka, Katarzyna J. 2012. *Cuisine, Colonialism and Cold War: Food in Twentieth-Century Korea*. London: Reaktion Books.

Cwiertka, Katarzyna J. 2014. "Global *Hansik* Campaign: International Commodification of Korean Cuisine." In *The Korean Popular Culture Reader*, edited by Kyung Hyun Kim and Youngmin Choe, 363–84. Durham, NC: Duke University Press.

Cwiertka, Katarzyna J. 2018a. "*Washoku*, Heritage and National Identity." In *Routledge Handbook of Modern Japanese History*, edited by Sven Saaler and Christopher W. A. Szpilman, 376–88. Abingdon: Routledge.

Cwiertka, Katarzyna J. 2018b. "Serving the Nation: The Myth of Washoku." In *Consuming Life in Post-Bubble Japan: A Transdisciplinary Perspective*, edited by Katarzyna J. Cwiertka and Ewa Machotka, 89–106. Amsterdam: Amsterdam University Press.

Cwiertka, Katarzyna J., and Akiko Moriya. 2008. "Fermented Soyfoods in South Korea: The Industrialization of Tradition." In *The World of Soy*, edited by Christine Du Bois, Chee-Beng Tan, and Sidney Mintz, 161–81. Urbana: University of Illinois Press.

カタジーナ・チフィエルトカ Cwiertka, Katarzyna J., and 安原美帆 Miho Yasuhara. 2016. 秘められた和食史 *Himerareta Washokushi* [*The Hidden History of Washoku*]. Tokyo: Shinsensha.

Cwiertka, Katarzyna J. with Miho Yasuhara. Forthcoming. *Branding Japanese Food: From Meibutsu to Washoku*. Honolulu: University of Hawai'i Press.

Dinnie, Keith, ed. (2008) 2014. *Nation Branding: Concepts, Issues, Practice*. Abingdon: Routledge.

Fan, Ying. 2006. "Branding the Nation: What Is Being Branded?" *Journal of Vacation Marketing* 12, no. 1: 5–14.

FAO. (2001) 2017. "Codex Alimentarius. International Food Standards, Standard for Kimchi." Rome: Food and Agriculture Organization of the United Nations. http://www.fao.org/fao-who-codexalimentarius/sh-proxy/jp/?lnk=1&url=https%253A%252F%252Fworkspace.fao.org%252Fsites%252Fcodex%252FStandards%252FCODEX%2BSTAN%2B223-2001%252FCXS_223e.pdf.

Gatz, Karen L., ed. 2000. *Foreign Relations of the United States, 1964–1968*. Vol. 29, Part 1, *Korea*. Washington, DC: U.S. Department of State, Office of the Historian, Bureau of Public Affairs.

Gienow-Hecht, Jessica C. E. 2016. "Nation Branding." In *Explaining the History of American Foreign Relations*, edited by Frank Costigliola and Michael J. Hogan, 232–44. 3rd ed., Cambridge: Cambridge University Press.

Guy, Kolleen M. 2003. *When Champagne Became French: Wine and the Making of a National Identity*. Baltimore, MD: Johns Hopkins University Press.

Han, Kyung-Koo. 2010. "The 'Kimchi Wars' in Globalizing East Asia: Consuming Class, Gender, Health, and National Identity." In *Consuming Korean Tradition in Early and Late Modernity: Commodification, Tourism, and Performance*, edited by Laurel Kendall, 149–67. Honolulu: University of Hawai'i Press.

Heldke, Lisa. 2003. *Exotic Appetites: Ruminations of a Food Adventurer*. London: Routledge.

Helstosky, Carol. 2008. *Pizza: A Global History*. London: Reaktion Books.

Jaffe, Eugene D., and Israel D. Nebenzahl. 2001. *National Image and Competitive Advantage: The Theory and Practice of Country-of-Origin Effect*. Copenhagen: Copenhagen Business School Press.

조재선 Jo, Jae-sun. 2016. "김치산업의 발달사 Kimch'i san'ŏp ŭi paltalsa" ["The Historical Development of the Kimchi Industry"]. 식품과학과 산업 *Sikp'um kwahak kwa sanŏp* 49, no. 4: 70–81.

Kerr, Pauline, and Geoffrey Wiseman. 2013. *Diplomacy in a Globalizing World: Theories and Practice*. New York: Oxford University Press.

Kerrigan, Finola, Jyotsna Shivanandan, and Anne-Marie Hede. 2012. "Nation Branding: A Critical Appraisal of Incredible India." *Journal of Macromarketing* 32, no. 3: 319–27.

KFPI (Korea Food Promotion Institute). "The Taste of Korea. Hansik." Index. Last modified 2017. http://www.hansik.org.

Kim, Chi-Hoon. 2016. "Kimchi Nation: Constructing Kimjang as an Intangible Korean Heritage." In *Urban Foodways and Communication: Ethnographic Studies in Intangible Cultural Food Heritages Around the World*, edited by Casey Man Kong Lum and Marc de Ferrière le Vayer, 39–53. New York: Rowman & Littlefield.

Kim, Chi-Hoon. 2017. "Let Them Eat Royal Court Cuisine! Heritage Politics of Defining Global Hansik." *Gastronomica* 17, no. 3: 4–14.

Korean National Commission for UNESCO. 2015. *Value and Impact of UNESCO Activities in Korea*. Seoul: Korean National Commission for UNESCO.

Larsen, Stanley Robert, and James Lawton Collins. 1985. *Allied Participation in Vietnam*. Washington, DC: Department of the Army.

Lash, Scott, and John Urry. 1994. *Economies of Signs and Space*. London: SAGE.

Lathram, Wade. 1970. "Letter to Henry Bardach, Country Officer for Korea, Department of State." National Archives and Records Administration, RG 59 General Records of the Department of State. Lot Files 73D360, 74D209 Subject Files of the Office of Korean Affairs, 1966–74 (NN3-059-99-057 Box 5). College Park, MD.

Laudan, Rachel. 2010. "Too Many Designations in the Kitchen." *Los Angeles Times*, November 1, 2010. http://articles.latimes.com/2010/nov/01/opinion/la-oe-laudan-unesco-20101101.

Lee, Yong-sun, Ji-Hyun Choi, and Kyu-eun Park. 2011. "Survey and Research on the Consumption of Kimchi by Households and Foodservice Industry." Korea Rural Economic Institute. http://www.krei.re.kr/eng/researchReportView.do?key=355&pageType=010101&biblioId=384178&pageUnit=10&searchCnd=all&searchKrwd=&pageIndex=45&engView=Y.

Lee, Yusun. 2014. "Kimchi: No Longer Solely Korea's." *Finance & Development* 51, no. 2: 32–3. http://www.imf.org/external/pubs/ft/fandd/2014/06/picture.htm.

Liagouras, George. 2005. "The Political Economy of Post-Industrial Capitalism." *Thesis Eleven* 81, no. 1: 20–35.

Lowenthal, David. 1985. *The Past Is a Foreign Country*. Cambridge: Cambridge University Press.

Lowenthal, David. 1998. "Fabricating Heritage." *History & Memory* 10, no. 1: 5–24.

Maffei, Maria Clara. 2012. "Culinary Traditions as Intangible Cultural Heritage and Expressions of Cultural Diversity." In *Cultural Heritage, Cultural Rights, Cultural Diversity: New Developments in International Law*, edited by Silvia Borelli and Federico Lenzerini, 223–49. Leiden: Nijhoff.

Merriam-Webster. 2018. S.v. "kimchi." https://www.merriam-webster.com/dictionary/kimchi.

Murcott, Anne. 1996. "Food as an Expression of Identity." In *The Future of the Nation State. Essays on Cultural Pluralism and Political Integration*, edited by Sverker Gustavsson and Leif Lewin, 49–77. London: Routledge.

Nooter, Robert. 1969. "Action Memorandum for the Deputy Administrator." National Archives and Records Administration. RG 59 General Records of the Department of State. Lot Files 73D360, Subject Files of the Office of Korean Affairs, 1966–74 (NN3-059-99-057 Box 3). College Park, MD.

Olins, Wally. 2004. "Branding the Nation: The Historical Context." In *Destination Branding: Creating the Unique Destination Proposition*, edited by Nigel Morgan, Annette Pritchard, and Roger Pride, 17–25. 2nd ed., Oxford: Butterworth-Heinemann.

Panayi, Panikos. 2010. *Spicing up Britain: The Multicultural History of British Food.* London: Reaktion Books.

Panayi, Panikos. 2014. *Fish and Chips: A History.* London: Reaktion Books.

Pham, Mary Jo A. 2013. "Food as Communication: A Case Study of South Korea's Gastrodiplomacy." *Journal of International Service* 22, no. 1: 1–22.

Pilcher, Jeffrey M. 2008. "The Globalization of Mexican Cuisine." *History Compass* 6, no. 2: 529–51.

Pilcher, Jeffrey M. 2012. *Planet Taco: A Global History of Mexican Food.* New York: Oxford University Press.

Prieto Larraín, María Cristina. 2011. "Branding the Chilean Nation: Socio-Cultural Change, National Identity and International Image." PhD diss., Leiden University.

Rockower, Paul. 2002. "Food As Ambassador: Thailand's Gastro-Diplomacy." *The Economist*, February 21, 2002. https://www.economist.com/asia/2002/02/21/thailands-gastro-diplomacy.

Rockower, Paul. 2011. "Projecting Taiwan: Taiwan's Public Diplomacy Outreach." *Issues & Studies* 47, no. 1: 107–52.

Rockower, Paul. 2014. "The State of Gastrodiplomacy." *Public Diplomacy Magazine* 11: 13–16.

Ruddy, Braden. 2014. "Hearts, Minds, and Stomachs: Gastrodiplomacy and the Potential of National Cuisine in Changing Public Perceptions of National Image." *Public Diplomacy Magazine* 11: 29–34.

Sakamoto, Rumi, and Matthew Allen. 2011. "There's Something Fishy About that Sushi: How Japan Interprets the Global Sushi Boom." *Japan Forum* 23, no. 1: 99–121.

Smith, Laurajane, and Natsuko Akagawa. 2009. *Intangible Heritage.* New York: Routledge.

Spence, Charles. 2016. "Gastrodiplomacy: Assessing the Role of Food in Decision-Making." *Flavour* 5, no. 4. https://doi.org/10.1186/s13411-016-0050-8.

Tettner, Samuel, and Begum Kalyoncu. 2016. "Gastrodiplomacy 2.0: Culinary Tourism Beyond Nationalism." *Journal of Tourism Research/ARA: Revista de Investigación en Turismo* 6, no. 2: 47–55.

UNESCO, n.d. a. "Browse the Lists of Intangible Cultural Heritage and the Register of Good Safeguarding Practices." Lists. http://www.unesco.org/culture/ich/index.php?lg=en&pg=00559.

UNESCO. n.d. b. "Text of the Convention for the Safeguarding of the Intangible Cultural Heritage." Convention. https://ich.unesco.org/en/convention.

UNESCO. n.d. c. "Gingerbread Craft from Northern Croatia." Lists. https://ich.unesco.org/en/RL/gingerbread-craft-from-northern-croatia-00356.

UNESCO. n.d. d. "Gastronomic Meal of the French." Lists. https://ich.unesco.org/en/RL/gastronomic-meal-of-the-french-00437.

UNESCO. n.d. e. "Traditional Mexican Cuisine—Ancestral Ongoing Community Culture, the Michoacán paradigm." Lists. https://ich.unesco.org/en/RL/traditional-mexican-cuisine-ancestral-ongoing-community-culture-the-michoacan-paradigm-00400.

UNESCO. n.d. f. "Washoku, Traditional Dietary Cultures of the Japanese, Notably for the Celebration of New Year." Lists. https://ich.unesco.org/en/RL/washoku-traditional-dietary-cultures-of-the-japanese-notably-for-the-celebration-of-new-year-00869.

UNESCO. n.d. g. "Procedure of Inscription of Elements on the Lists and of Selection of Good Safeguarding Practices." Lists. https://ich.unesco.org/en/procedure-of-inscription-00809#TOC1.

UNESCO. n.d. h. "Kimjang, Making and Sharing Kimchi in the Republic of Korea." Lists. https://ich.unesco.org/en/RL/kimjang-making-and-sharing-kimchi-in-the-republic-of-korea-00881.

UNESCO. n.d. i. "Tradition of Kimchi-Making in the Democratic People's Republic of Korea." Lists. https://ich.unesco.org/en/RL/tradition-of-kimchi-making-in-the-democratic-people-s-republic-of-korea-01063.

UNESCO. n.d. j. "Arirang, Lyrical Folk Song in the Republic of Korea." Lists. https://ich.unesco.org/en/RL/arirang-lyrical-folk-song-in-the-republic-of-korea-00445.

UNESCO. n.d. k. "Arirang Folk Song in the Democratic People's Republic of Korea." Lists. https://ich.unesco.org/en/RL/arirang-folk-song-in-the-democratic-peoples-republic-of-korea-00914.

UNESCO. n.d. l. "Karagöz." Lists. https://ich.unesco.org/en/RL/karagoz-00180.

UNESCO. 2011. "Report of the Subsidiary Body on its Work in 2011 and Evaluation of Nominations for Inscription in 2011 on the Representative List of the Intangible Cultural Heritage of Humanity: Addendum." Bali: UNESCO, Intergovernmental Committee For Safeguarding of the Intangible Cultural Heritage. https://ich.unesco.org/doc/src/ITH-11-6.COM-CONF.206-13+Corr.+Add.-EN.pdf.

Wolff, Martin. 2001. "Will the Nation-State Survive Globalization?" *Foreign Affairs* 80, no. 1: 178–90.

Woolley, Kaitlin, and Ayelet Fishbach. 2017. "A Recipe for Friendship: Similar Food Consumption Promotes Trust and Cooperation." *Journal of Consumer Psychology* 27, no. 1: 1–10.

Wui, Peter. 2014. "Trade Impacts of Codex Standards on Kimchi." Working paper, Forum for Research in Empirical International Trade. http://www.freit.org/WorkingPapers/Papers/TradePolicyGeneral/FREIT797.pdf (site discontinued).

Zhang, Juyan. 2015. "The Foods of the Worlds: Mapping and Comparing Contemporary Gastrodiplomacy Campaigns." *International Journal of Communication* 9: 568–91.

Part Two

Internal Boundaries

5

Priestess of *Sake*: Woman as Producer in *Natsuko's Sake*

Satoko Kakihara
California State University, Fullerton

Introduction: Regendering the Japanese drink

As it does elsewhere, the act of drinking alcohol in Japan holds historical, political, and social significance. Who is drinking, with whom, and where? Is the drinking for celebration, consolation, or obligation? Who is serving or working behind the counter? In addition to the act, the object of drinking—the identity of the liquor being imbibed—also has significance. What is the drink? Who produced it, where, and how? What are the actors eating with their drinks, and by whom was the food prepared? This chapter focuses on a slice of these questions, examining the representation of the production of Japanese *sake* (also romanized as *saké*) in contemporary Japanese popular culture texts.

Competing against imported alcohol domestically and foreign alcohol internationally, the marketing of Japanese *sake* is framed by a nationalist discourse of upholding an entrenched tradition to be maintained at home domestically and disseminated abroad internationally as representative of Japanese cuisine. Recent discourse surrounding the marketing of *sake* (and alcohol in general) has highlighted women as both consumers and producers. As consumers, the topic of women drinking in bars and restaurants has been discussed more in the media since the early 2010s, and advertisements have increased to make *sake* more approachable for women. As producers, more women in recent years have begun to work in breweries, filling the traditionally male role of the *tōji* (杜氏, the *sake* brewery supervisor) and often being described as young and beautiful on promotional posters for products and breweries.

Yet the figure of the female *sake* maker has appeared in popular culture texts since the late 1980s, including the manga *Natsuko's Sake* (夏子の酒 *Natsuko no sake*, 1988–91). This chapter analyzes Natsuko, the protagonist of the manga by Oze Akira (尾瀬あきら), and her ostensible reconstruction of the traditions of Japanese *sake* production. Natsuko is the daughter of a family that owns a *sake* brewery, and she takes on a leadership role to make *sake* in a traditional method using organically grown rice. The manga's framing of Natsuko as a "priestess"—a female figure who serves a deity, who acts as a liaison between the spiritual world and the material world—denies women their agency, however, and leaves unchallenged gender and class hierarchies in Japan. The chapter ultimately argues that the *sake* industry's leveraging of the female figure, whether by constructing her as a new consumer or by normalizing female sexual and cultural purity, perpetuates the nation-state's management of modern women's subjectivity for both male industrial and national profit. The representation of such a character in popular culture suggests the progressive possibility of women entering and thriving in a male-dominated field, yet it simultaneously reinscribes women's maintenance of culinary traditions as a key component of national construction.

Contemporary discourse surrounding Japanese national cuisine underscores the ways in which "[b]oth tradition and modernity have been ... carriers of patriarchal ideologies"—words originally used to describe the context of colonial India (Sangari and Vaid 1990, 17). This chapter builds on Partha Chatterjee's classic discussion of "the Women's Question," which examines the figure of the modern, new woman as one that arises out of the establishment of new systems of gender and class management within Indian colonial history. In the conflict between modernization and nationalism, the resolution to the question of what role women should play in those projects led to the focus of modernization being placed on the realm of the material, while the focus of nationalism remained in the realm of the spiritual (Chatterjee 1990, 237–8). The national struggle was thus cast as achieving the goal of maintaining both India's "national culture" and "spiritual essence" (Chatterjee 1990, 239). Yet Chatterjee points out how "[t]he 'new' woman defined in this way was subjected to a *new* patriarchy" (1990, 244, emphasis in original), constructed through, and to enforce, a new gender hierarchy. Both modernization and the national project were thus made to be consistent with each other (Chatterjee 1990, 240), operating in tandem to create a national model that recast women as spiritual figures.

Such relationships among different forces—of tradition and modernization, spiritual and material—are also evident in *Natsuko's Sake*. Within the Japanese context, the "New Woman" emerged in the 1920s through middle-class women's consumption of, and desire for, commodities in the urban marketplace (Sato 2003). The figure of modern Japanese femininity was thus constructed in the material realm, in relation to print media such as magazines and advertisements. During the postwar decades of the 1950s and beyond, women's prescribed gender roles, particularly as depicted in popular culture, began to focus on the heteronormative life course that culminated in marriage and motherhood. In the 1980s, popular culture texts often included simplistic characters that "appear as signs that lack the depth and context that are indispensable for a round human character" (Saito 2014, 153). Natsuko is an example of such a female figure, tied to the material realm but also lacking the depth and roundness of a flesh-and-blood human. As a spiritual priestess, Natsuko functions separately from the material and profit-driven efforts of commercial farming and *sake* production; yet as the god's bridge to the material world, she unites those around her to revive and revitalize traditions of *sake* making, which lead to economic profit. That profit, furthermore, is enjoyed by neither the priestess nor the workers who perform the labor, who remain relegated to the realm of culinary tradition and craftsmanship deemed separate from industrialized profit. For the culinary field in Japan, modernizing also means returning to the traditional, as Japanese "tradition" becomes a way to achieve capitalist ends within a global market. Recent efforts in Japanese culinary marketing, therefore, fuse the interests of both state and business, putting women in the position of upholding the spiritual and the national for the sake of material gain.

To begin, the chapter briefly examines the significance of *sake* and alcohol in Japanese history and cuisine. It then positions itself within the larger scholarly discourse, particularly the intersection of Japanese studies and food studies, by discussing previous works in Japanese food studies and other relevant works that point to the construction of an essentialized Japanese-ness through food and culinary practices. After introducing Oze, the writer and artist behind the manga *Natsuko's Sake*, the chapter analyzes how the protagonist Natsuko functions as a preserver of national traditions in the face of modernization and industrialization, particularly in her characterizations as a priestess of *sake*.

Interrogating traditional identity in Japanese food studies

When it was announced by UNESCO in 2013 December, the addition of *washoku* (和食)—the "traditional dietary cultures of the Japanese"—to the list of the Intangible Cultural Heritage of Humanity (UNESCO n.d.) signaled not the end but rather the beginning of a national campaign to invigorate the Japanese culinary world and to promote it internationally. The recognition thus has justified the promotion of *washoku*, a system of national culinary practices in addition to specific dishes and ingredients, in not just Japan but also around the globe.

Yet even while Japan has received this recognition from UNESCO, scholarship about Japanese food has interrogated presentations of, and assumptions about, such purported traditions (Cwiertka 2006; Rath 2016). For example, through historical analyses of primary sources, Eric Rath has investigated the association of Sen no Rikyū (千利休), the sixteenth-century practitioner of the Japanese tea ceremony, with the establishment (or "perfection") of *kaiseki* (懐石 or 会席, tea cuisine). While Rikyū is often described as the figure responsible for outlining the guiding principles of *kaiseki*, Rath points to a more multivalent construction of such traditions, involving other individuals as both direct participants and recorders of what we now think of as Rikyū's contributions to *kaiseki*. Historian George Solt has analyzed the object of *ramen*, the noodle dish often considered the quintessential Japanese fast and street food, both at home and abroad. In his study, Solt analyzes the construction of *ramen* as a Japanese national dish, revealing its ties to the history of labor migration into Japan from other parts of East Asia, as well as to the postwar political and economic relationship between Japan and the United States (Solt 2014). Katarzyna Cwiertka has analyzed the classed construction of culinary traditions in Japan, looking at the political and military motivations behind the hybridization of Japanese and Western foodstuffs and culinary techniques in the first half of the twentieth century (Cwiertka 1996). Her research describes the development of such a culinary practice "under the impact of industrialization, nation-state formation and imperialist expansion" (Cwiertka 2006, 9). These works reveal the carefully controlled processes of constructing traditions for often imperialist purposes.

In addition to specific dishes, both nonalcoholic and alcoholic drinks also comprise an important part of our understandings of national cuisine, and studies have shown how their associations with a Japanese identity have been historically and discursively concocted. For example, Japanese tea and the tea ceremony is a cultural construction that naturalizes its perception as a national practice. Kristine Surak discusses the idea of nation-work, analyzing how tea ceremony functions "as an exceptionally vivid and concentrated illustration of one of the fundamental processes of modernity, the work of making nations" (2012, 15). At the intersection of the larger forces of nationalism and the smaller acts of nation-ness, the tea ceremony serves as a site wherein individuals construct their national identity. Such studies build a body of scholarship that works at dismantling the assumed authenticities and traditions within discourses about food in contemporary Japan—of which *sake* is no exception.

Sake, of course, has as long a history and as much significance as other types of drinks in Japanese cuisine. In Japan, the *kanji* (Chinese character) for *sake* (酒) designates the entire category of alcohol. The character of *sake*, also pronounced "shu," is often attached to other words to indicate an alcohol made out of that particular ingredient—for example, *budōshu* for wine (literally "grape alcohol") and *kajitsushu* for fruit liqueur (such as the popular plum wine of Japan). The category of *sake* thus encompasses a wide variety—from Japanese *shōchū* and German beer to Korean *makgeolli* and Russian vodka. Without any qualification, however, the word *sake* (and the kanji on its own) is often used to refer to what would otherwise be specified as *Nihonshu* (日本酒)—the word that refers to the traditional Japanese rice wine. The referent of *sake* thus has both semantic and historic significance. *Sake*, indeed, has a long history in the Japanese islands, much longer than, for example, the Japanese distilled alcohol of *shōchū*. *Sake* (or at least what evolved into it) and the drinking of it have been recorded in texts such as the classical Chinese text *Lunheng* that dates back to 80 CE, and it is also described as playing an important role in events and spiritual ceremonies recorded in the historico-mythical text of *Nihon Shoki* (日本書紀), which dates back to 720 CE.

While *shōchū* is a popular form of national distilled alcohol produced in Japan, *sake* is a Japanese fermented alcohol made from rice.[1] Making *sake* is difficult work: those who labor in *sake* breweries spend roughly the months from September through April watching over the *sake*, often working in shifts to cover all 24 hours of the day. Many do this at breweries far away from their own hometowns. The industry is also not a thriving one, as many breweries in Japan have closed down over the last several decades (Gingold 2015). The combination of difficult work and shrinking market have left fewer and fewer people in Japan to carry on the tradition, as *sake* production becomes increasingly industrialized and commercialized. As the cycle of *sake* production and consumption in Japan grows smaller in its magnitude, especially given the overall shift in consumption from *sake* and beer to alcoholic cocktails (such as liqueurs and hard alcohol mixed with nonalcoholic drinks like soda, tea, and juice) (National Tax Agency 2016, 3), *sake* producers as well as others working in the broader alcoholic beverage industry must find ways to adapt to changes while also tapping into various (and new) markets.

One way to do so in recent years has been to turn female consumers in Japan on to the practice of drinking alcohol (Alexander 2013, 2).[2] Whereas drinking alcohol was traditionally gendered as masculine (with the proliferation of images of salarymen drinking beer with their colleagues on weeknights, or of Showa-era fathers enjoying warm *sake* that his wife has prepared for him at the living room table), popular media have moved to make drinking both more attractive to, and more accessible for, women. For example, the idea of the *joshikai* (女子会)—a gathering among female friends— has gained popularity since the late 2000s, with media features discussing *joshikai* as they are organized and take place in different forms: at people's houses, at restaurants, as casual meet-ups, or as elaborately-themed parties. These gendered events often provide women (or, at least, those in positions to take part in such *joshikai*) with opportunities to unwind from the daily grind of their work and assert themselves as agents of the act of drinking. At the same time, such events also structure spaces for women to engage in *koibana* (恋話 or 恋バナ)—discussions about their love lives— which reinforces heteronormative expectations that women's primary concerns be the opposite sex and achieving a successful marriage.

Drinking serves as a form of both empowerment and modern feminization in popular contemporary representations. For example, from October 2015 to March 2016, the women's magazine *Nikkei Woman* (日経ウーマン) published a series titled *Moteru biyōgaku* (モテる美容学), which can loosely be translated as "Cosmetology for Being Attractive." The twenty-four stories included in the series explained to readers (presumed to be female, given the magazine's target readership) various beauty and fashion tips to make them more attractive to others, both men and women. The idea of being attractive to other women was not for the reasons of same-sex romance, but simply because a woman whom both men and women find attractive is supposedly "strong" (「モテる女は強い！」, *moteru on'na wa tsuoyoi*). Two stories in the series explained the stylish and "cool ways" that women can enjoy vices previously considered taboo, such as drinking and smoking (「カッコイイ嗜み方」, *kakkoii tashinamikata*), providing details on what to drink, how to drink, and what makeup to wear when going out to drink (Fujimura 2016; Hasegawa 2016). In this way, the media and food service industries are increasingly tapping into the female market to encourage and make fashionable women's consumption of alcohol, whether beer, wine, or *sake*.

Alongside the increased media portrayal and social acceptance of women drinking, the *sake* industry in particular has highlighted the various women who work on the production side in order to reinvigorate itself and refresh its image. Promotional events hosted by brewers and media companies feature female *sake* makers, and brewery websites post profiles of their female employees. By publicizing the inclusion of women in the production of *sake*, the *sake* industry softens its own image and accomplishes two tasks: one, to showcase the new (and feminine) energy being brought into the industry (thus also making it worth entering for other women); and two, to assure women that, because *sake* is something that is meant for women to produce as well, it is also something meant for women to consume. These efforts to welcome new producers and gain new consumers are all attempts to maintain and strengthen the *sake* industry and market in contemporary Japan. At the same time, couched within this discourse of women's freedom to drink is the reinforcement of the idea of women's exploitation for profit-making and the commodifiability of women and their labor.

Preserving the spiritual in *Natsuko's Sake*

This chapter analyzes manga, the Japanese comic book medium, as a site wherein the significance of food in relation to nation and gender is negotiated. Tomoko Aoyama has examined the role of food in modern Japanese literature, looking at how writings about food present an important piece of our understandings about Japanese culture.[3] Within the larger context of food-related popular culture texts,[4] various types of Japanese cultural productions in recent years have featured alcohol-related subjects. From manga and anime to TV shows and documentaries, these texts serve as PR material for specific types of alcoholic drinks, such as *sake* and wine, or for alcohol and drinking culture in general, such as *izakaya* (居酒屋) culture (drinking at establishments where one orders a series of small dishes to accompany drinking over prolonged periods of time). Focusing on the manga medium, works by writer Joh Araki (城アラキ) have been popular and also noted for their ability to educate readers about wine and liqueur. His works—including *Sommelier* (ソムリエ, 1996–9), *Bartender* (バーテンダー, 2004–12), *La Sommelière* (ソムリエール, 2006–12), *Cocktail* (カクテル, 2015–16), and his current serialization *Champagne* (シャンパーニュ, 2018–)—are often adapted into different media, such as television dramas and anime series. A manga that was serialized from 2015 to 2016, *Ippon!! The Sake of Happiness* (いっぽん!! しあわせの日本酒, *Ippon!! Shiawase no Nihon-shu*, written by Masuda Masafumi and illustrated by Matsumoto Kyūjo) features a young woman, age twenty-four, who gradually discovers the various types and flavors of *sake*, and decides to act as an ambassador for *sake* to other consumers as unfamiliar with the drink as she was at the beginning of the story.

In the last two decades in particular, such texts have constructed a discourse that calls attention to drinking as a culture both traditional and modern, in which women as much as men may partake. Yet what is notable is that the producers of most of these texts are themselves male. While numerous works are written by women on the topic of food, fewer works produced by women about drinking alcohol have become commercially successful. One exception is the series *Wakakozake* (ワカコ酒, 2006–) by Shinkyū Chie (新久千映), which began as a webcomic and was adapted into both an anime and a television drama in 2015. This work by Shinkyū, with its young office lady (OL) protagonist, suggests the possibility that male producers need not be the only ones to profit from this genre, while also suggesting fans within an audience of professional women, similar to the titular character of Wakako.

As one of the earlier popular culture texts to focus on Japanese *sake*, *Natsuko's Sake* was originally serialized from 1988 to 1991 in the weekly comic magazine *Morning* (モーニング), published by Kodansha (講談社). Written and illustrated by Oze Akira and consisting of 131 episodes, the story was also adapted into an eleven-episode television drama in 1994. Works by Oze, who was born in 1947 and has been active in the manga industry since 1971, are frequently discussed in Japanese and Anglophone scholarship. These studies analyze Oze's works as representations of authentic Japan and its practices, such as the depiction of rural, agricultural spaces in his works (Ichinomiya 2008). Oze's manga works are also often cited in relation to their use of languages (Japanese and non-Japanese), in both scholarly research and Japanese language study guides (Kiatkobchai 2008; Kuramochi 2011; Lammers 2004; O'Neill 2012), suggesting a tendency for his works to be perceived as exemplifying the use of proper Japanese to be modeled by others. On the other hand, his works also capture how craft is turned into capital, with the potential interpretation of *Natsuko's Sake* as an extended advertisement: in it, the object of its marketing ranges from *sake* and Japanese produce to female youth and beauty (Miyake 2008). These scholarly works suggest that Oze and his works are associated with representations of Japanese-ness as well as the socioeconomic shifts taking place within the country.

Oze certainly does discuss various forms of Japanese traditions in his works, examining how such traditions are affected by industrialization, mass production, and overcommercialization that take place across generations of producers. His work *The Story of My Village* (ぼくの村の話, *Boku no mura no hanashi*, 1991–3), for example, traces the history of what is known as the Sanrizuka Conflict or Narita Conflict (三里塚闘争, 成田闘争). The conflict arose in the 1960s, when the Japanese government took land away from farmers who owned it to build what is now Narita International Airport, in order to accommodate the anticipated increase in domestic and international air traffic coming through the Tokyo area. Another work published after *Natsuko's Sake*, *Kurōdo* (クロード, 2006–9) follows Claude Buttermaker, a biracial fourth-generation Japanese-American who travels from the United States to Japan in order to reestablish his great-grandfather's *sake* brewery. While it, like *Natsuko's Sake*, focuses the spotlight on the Japanese *sake* industry, *Kurōdo* interrogates the position and significance of non-Japanese actors in the maintenance of Japanese tradition. A more recent serialization, Oze's *Prodigal Son* (どうらく息子, *Dōraku musuko*, 2010–17), follows a young man's entrance into, and experience in, the world of *rakugo* (落語), a Japanese storytelling tradition that has been in place since the Edo period (1603–1867). In these ways, Oze's works examine the sociopolitical influences that postwar national development has had on Japanese traditions and practices.

Likewise, *Natsuko's Sake* explores a wide range of issues: the dichotomization of tradition and modernization, gender dynamics in the *sake* industry, relationships within the family institution, interactions between the state and capitalist systems, food safety and organic farming, the decline of rice farming in Japan, and conflict between farming to make a living and farming to make a life—to name just a few. Given these various threads that run through the work, Natsuko—the story's female protagonist—stands out as both a figure and a site wherein these threads intersect. Appearing just before the economic downturn in Japan in the late 1980s, the character of Natsuko represents an integral component in the search (or perhaps reestablishment) of the Japanese tradition of *sake* making. Natsuko, as the character trope of a culturally and sexually pure "priestess" who relays the wishes of the deceased to the living as a way to bridge pre-modernity and modernity (Etō 2014), offers a multilayer object of analysis that problematizes the maintenance of a nationalist tradition that harks back to the spiritual and the dead in a time of industrial advancement and capitalist economies. In the following sections, this chapter examines how her casting as a priestess leaves her character without a dynamic agency, while also highlighting the class differences between the workers who provide the labor, and the capitalists who gain the profit.

Sexual and cultural purity of the priestess

In the first episode of *Natsuko's Sake*, we meet Saeki Natsuko, a woman of twenty-two years who is the daughter of a family that owns a *sake* brewery called Saeki Brewery (佐伯酒造) in Niigata Prefecture, located in the northeastern tip of the Hokuriku region along the Sea of Japan (Map 2). Living away from home, she works in Tokyo as a copywriter for an advertising agency. While in the midst of her first big assignment—writing ad copy for a major Japanese *sake* company—she learns of the death of her older brother, thirty-year-old Yasuo, who had been the managing director (専務, *senmu*) of her family brewery. Devastated by the loss, Natsuko becomes determined to bring into the world what her brother had been working toward before his death: a *sake* made from the legendary rice called Tatsunishiki (龍錦), of which he had found a handful of grains. The story of the twelve-volume manga series follows Natsuko and others at Saeki Brewery in their multiyear quest to harvest, and then turn into *sake*, the Tatsunishiki rice.

The portrayal of Natsuko in this quest to realize her (and her brother's) dream is an ambiguous one. She is criticized by her family at the beginning of the story for having gone away to Tokyo to work in an industry other than *sake* production, one that epitomizes profit-making. Despite the physical and emotional distance that has developed between her and her family, however, she sets for herself a goal that is both admirable and lofty. Yet she is also a young woman who knows very little about farming or the industry side of *sake*. She has youth and beauty (as commented on several times by the other characters, who work in an industry where young women are few), and she also has to be taught by others how to do the things that will enable her to accomplish her goal of making the Tatsunishiki *sake*—what becomes referred to eventually in the manga as "Natsuko's *sake*." As if to signal the higher value placed on her gender and youthful appearance than on her skills as a *sake* producer, the manga artwork also portrays her like a gravure idol—almost a pin-up girl, though very modestly dressed in her representations. The covers of the episodes published in the weekly comic magazine, as well as the front and back covers of the twelve graphic novels later compiled, all feature Natsuko—drinking *sake*, sitting by a rice field, or simply standing, almost as if modeling her outfit or some aspect of Japanese tradition, through clothing and various objects (Figure 5.1). In these depictions, Natsuko is always alone—if anything, she is accompanied by a traditional tool used in the *sake*-making process. While covers of other manga works often feature the protagonist with her romantic counterpart, Natsuko is presented as being separate from such physical, romantic ties. As a priestess, she serves a spiritual role, guarding (and showcasing) Japanese traditions of *sake* making and being present only as a distant object of the viewers' gaze.

Natsuko is characterized—by others and by herself—as a priestess who serves Matsuo-sama (松尾様), the god of Japanese *sake*. Episode 110 of the manga is titled "Priestess" (巫女, *miko*), and in it she declares explicitly to her father that she must be a priestess that serves Matsuo-sama, and thus she will not make incorrect judgments in her efforts to make Natsuko's *sake*, the best *sake* in Japan. These characterizations suggest her need to maintain spiritual purity and to distance herself from romantic attachments, since as a priestess the ability to be in communion with her god is

Figure 5.1 Front covers of the first three (of twelve) volumes of the graphic novel, *Natsuko's Sake*. Reproduced by permission from Oze Akira, *Natsuko no sake* (Tokyo: Kodansha, 1988–9), Vols. 1–3.

expected. Whether she wishes to or not, in other words, Natsuko occupies a position that denies her freedom and agency to experience and act on human desires.

Natsuko herself is torn by this fact that a priestess is one who has given both body and soul to a god—and thus is not permitted to enter into romantic and physical relationships. In the story, Natsuko is desired by three different men, but because of her role (both attributed and chosen) as priestess to Matsuo-sama, she does not actually enter a relationship with any of them in the course of the story. One of the three men is Utsumi Eiji, who runs the Utsumi *Sake* Brewery in Fukui Prefecture, located at the southwestern end of the Hokuriku region. It is in fact Utsumi who first suggests in episode 47 that Natsuko is in love with Matsuo-sama and thus unable to love a human being. Utsumi makes his remark half in jest, half in seriousness. In the scene where he makes this comment, he smiles warmly at Natsuko as he departs on the train, but in his expression there are also hints of sadness, resignation, and a willingness to challenge his own suggestion. Yet his departure nonetheless reinforces both the physical and the spiritual distance between the two characters.

As Natsuko struggles with balancing her dedication to her brother's wish and her own feelings, we see the consequences of her violating the rule of purity associated with her role as priestess tied to a national tradition. Later in the story Natsuko and Utsumi share a kiss (10.109.222),[5] yet what follows is Natsuko's withdrawal as a human being from the people around her; she becomes more and more obsessed with making Natsuko's *sake*, even entering into a trance-like state and walking outside barefoot in the snow (Figure 5.2). In a two-page spread of this scene, the first panel in the upper-right shows Natsuko walking barefoot, a bandage wrapped around her injured left foot that reinforces her physical vulnerability as a human being.[6] Her coworker, Kusakabe, sees her, and he follows her outside in shock. Natsuko continues walking out toward the Tatsunishiki rice fields, her figure clothed in pure white, suggesting an otherworldliness. In the opposing page on the left, the first panel depicts her smiling,

Figure 5.2 Natsuko's coworker discovers her wandering barefoot in the snow at night. Reproduced by permission from Oze Akira, *Natsuko no sake* (Tokyo: Kodansha, 1991), Vol. 12: 96–7.

with her half-closed eyes in a daze. The panel below it shows her back to the reader, as she stares at a sign that indicates the plot of land dedicated to Tatsunishiki. Kusakabe rushes over to her and asks what she is doing in such light clothing on a snowy night, but the eerie smile with which she looks at him gives him pause; her expression seems to strike both worry and fear in him. So powerful is Natsuko's tie to the spiritual realm, that her earlier earthly kiss with Utsumi makes her lose her equilibrium; as either compensation or punishment for her act, she disregards (or is made to disregard) her physical body and can think only of her success in making the Tatsunishiki *sake*.

Despite their shared kiss, when Utsumi proposes to Natsuko in episode 127, she does not accept, telling him that she has decided to carry on the work of Saeki Brewery (12.127.136–9). She says to him, "The only one to succeed my brother is myself" (Figure 5.3)—for, as a priestess, she is responsible for carrying on the will of the deceased, transferring their wishes from the spiritual world to the material world. A two-page spread from the scene begins with a visual separation of Natsuko and Utsumi. Although they stand less than two meters from each other as they converse, the two characters are not depicted in a single panel together, nor even in the same row, at least on the right-hand page. The two are finally captured in the same panel at the top of the left-hand page, in a panel that spans an entire row. The image is a long shot of the two,

Figure 5.3 Natsuko begins to speak after Utsumi has already boarded the train. Reproduced by permission from Oze Akira, *Natsuko no sake* (Tokyo: Kodansha, 1991), Vol. 12: 138–9.

however, showing also the train and snow in the scenery; there is no intimacy between them. In the third panel of that page, Natsuko seems almost desperate to tell Utsumi one more thing, just before his train departs—yet he has already boarded the train, and she remains standing on the platform, unable to join him on his journey home to Fukui, where he has asked her to join him. In the final panel on the bottom row of the page, the two are captured in a close-up, but the train door already has closed, and the two characters are separated both physically and emotionally. They face each other, but Natsuko cannot reach him now. The choice to be Matsuo-sama's priestess and carry on her brother's will causes emotional turmoil for her, as depicted by her simultaneous desire and inability to tell Utsumi how she feels. That inability to foster romantic love for others is not entirely of Natsuko's own choosing, however; it is a consequence of her ascribed role as a priestess.

Toward the end of the story, another man asks Natsuko to marry him—Kusakabe Wataru, a friend of Natsuko's late brother Yasuo, a member of the crew working at Saeki Brewery, and the same one who rescues her from the snow. The marriage proposal is mediated by *sake*: he invites her to participate in a drinking competition and makes a bet: "If I win ... please marry me" (「おれが勝ったら・・・・・・結婚してください」, 12.129.163). Although we see Natsuko lose the competition in the end (perhaps on purpose), we never see the couple actually marry.[7] Without a marriage actually materializing, the character of Natsuko maintains her sexual purity, implying her ability to remain a priestess of *sake*. In fact, during the competition, the others watching the two remark that the two are "not human," given the sheer amount of *sake* they are able to consume (「このふたり 人間じゃねえぞ」, 12.129.171). A marriage proposal to a priestess who is supposed to have given all of herself to the god of *sake* can only be validated if it involves *sake*; furthermore, even if Kusakabe and Natsuko manage to reach an agreement about getting married, they are both labeled as being not human, and we are never shown their marriage, either spiritual or physical, within the story of *Natsuko's Sake*. Their relationship thus remains rooted in their sacred efforts to create the legendary Tatsunishiki *sake*, rather than being tied to the material labor of producing *sake* for profit (or even the reproductive labor expected of Japanese subjects).

Traditions of class and privilege in *sake* production

In *Natsuko's Sake*, as the protagonist carries out the will of her late brother and the god of *sake*—to produce the best *sake* in Japan—the class relationships between Natsuko and those who perform the labor of farming and *sake* brewing become clear. Her project to create Natsuko's *sake* out of Tatsunishiki requires other people's labor, and we see that her spiritual purity and ability to preserve traditions come with class privileges. Chatterjee's discussion of the Women's Question also examines the intersectionality of gender and class, revealing how power dynamics between social and economic classes influenced the construction of other identity categories in colonial India. In this way, we can also analyze the way in which Oze constructs Natsuko's positionality within traditional *sake* production by tying her cultural and sexual purity to ideas of class privilege.

Natsuko, a spiritual priestess, is consistently separated from the material world of business and profit in the story. However, another reading of her character is that she is simply the daughter of an entrepreneurial family who has not had to consider the value of her own labor in the past. She wishes to enlist other farmers' help to grow the Tatsunishiki rice, but she has no response when one of the farmers points out that Saeki Brewery charges 3,000 yen for a bottle of *sake*, while the rice growers are not paid such a large amount for their labor to produce the key ingredient (4.35.53). Natsuko naïvely wonders why the promise of being paid a certain amount for their labor is the only way that people become willing to grow organic rice—particularly for the Tatsunishiki variety of rice, which is more difficult to grow because of its susceptibility to pests and large grain size that makes it fall over toward the ground. In response, one of the farmers offering to help with the rice production screams at her: "Money is more important than life! You can't understand our feelings of having to go that far!" (「命 より金が大事! そこまで思いつめるわしらの気持 あんたにはわからんだろ う!!」, 6.65.214–15). As a daughter of a *sake* brewer, Natsuko has never had to deal with the backbreaking work, the regulations on farming, or the agricultural pricing system that places Japanese farmers in precarious positions. Concerned only with her vision of making her *sake*, Natsuko does not see the hardships that the farmers go through, the hardship that they are willing to undergo in order to help her.

While this is not to say that Natsuko does not care about the farmers, she is consistently unable to consider the toll that her spiritual project takes on those working around her. When Jicchan, the *tōji* who has been working at Saeki Brewery for over thirty years, becomes nearly unable to work because of his old age and declining health, Natsuko is desperate to convince her father that Jicchan is the only one who can realize her and her brother's dream. Even when her father questions her about the pain that they would cause Jicchan if he continued to work and somehow failed to have a successful brewing season, Natsuko is concerned with only one thing: "Then … who will prepare the *sake* with the Tatsunishiki?" (「じゃあ・・・・・・龍錦は 誰が仕込むの・・・・・・？」, 5.51.142–3). Believing that making the Tatsunishiki *sake* is the dying wish left to both her *and* Jicchan by her older brother Yasuo, Natsuko is myopic about realizing the project. She cannot consider the physical and material toll that the work takes on those who actually perform the labor of brewing *sake*.

Natsuko's unwavering focus on creating *sake* from the legendary rice amplifies her ignorance about farming, while also underlining her naïveté about the amount of labor that is required to produce *sake*, from field to bottle. Her lack of consideration, in fact, causes troubles for the others working with her. Early on in the story, when Natsuko is attempting to convince the farmers in her town to stop using pesticides and chemicals in their farming, the representative at the local agricultural co-op office tells her that pesticide-free produce is desired by neither farmers nor consumers. When Natsuko reiterates the issues of safety, the co-op representative tells her that using chemicals makes stronger plants; and that stronger plants enable the use of machines in farming, rather than farming by hand. Gesturing toward an elderly couple visiting the office that continues to work their land, the representative asks Natsuko, "Can you force them to bend over their fields and spend days harvesting their rice?" (「腰を曲げ・・・・・・何日もかけてやるんです。あなたはあの人たちにそれを強いることができますか？」, 4.33.8)—a question which Natsuko cannot answer.

Although Natsuko begins farming rice herself in order to make her (and her brother's) dream come true, she both underestimates the amount of labor required and overestimates her ability to do it. During the second year of harvesting the Tatsunishiki (this time to produce enough rice to make *sake*), Natsuko insists on growing some of her own rice as in the first year, saying that while it is difficult, she wants to do it, for emotional (and not economic) reasons. The other farmers who are growing the rice tell her that it is not her responsibility; one of them, an old friend of Natsuko's, flatly tells her that her reckless ways of tending to the rice cause problems for others. It is not until her father reminds her of her duties as managing director of the brewery—her brother's former position, what is implied as being her rightful and proper position within the production chain of the brewery—that Natsuko relents, giving her share of the rice to another farmer (7.70.89). While her fixation on Natsuko's *sake* exemplifies her devotion to her brother's wish and to Matsuo-sama, Natsuko's lack of experience with the material conditions of labor reinforces the class lines that separate her and the other farmers working with her on the project. A world away from the working class, Natsuko's role in changing the Japanese *sake* industry as a priestess is premised on emphasizing the spiritual without reforming or taking part in the material. Her involvement in the preservation and promotion of a national culinary tradition is therefore also framed by relationships of gender and class. Characterized by both purity and a certain ignorance, Natsuko succeeds through others' labor—yet her separation from the material world prevents her from resolving the issues of agricultural labor that disadvantage the people who make the *sake* production possible in the first place.

Conclusion

The purity and constructed tradition that Natsuko embodies privilege femininity only if it serves the inhuman role of being a non-carnal priestess. Natsuko's characterization as such a spiritual figure strips her of agency and personhood, turning her into a vessel through which her dead brother can realize his dream. Her quest as priestess that serves the Japanese *sake* deity and the spirit of her older brother culminates in the production of "Natsuko's *sake*"—the title also of the manga work itself. Yet the name is ironic in two ways. First, while Natsuko leads the project with unflagging determination, she neither controls the generation of profit at her family's brewery nor has major influence in the larger industry that is still dominated by men. Second, while Natsuko occupies the position of managing director at the brewery, the brewery workers who actually perform the labor of *sake* production remain alienated from the commodity they produce, even more so than does Natsuko. Ultimately, the *sake* is to be marketed under the name of Kōryū—which takes a character each from Natsuko's brother's name and the name of the rice from which the *sake* is made. Suggested by Natsuko herself, the name encapsulates the way in which the priestess, after her spiritual task is done, walks away from the material gains of the quest. The female, in other words, serves the ends of capital through her national and sexual purity, and yet takes little part in the profit.

The story also reinforces patriarchal class differences within capitalism, as it depicts the exploitation of low-wage labor of those who actually produce the *sake*, both farming the key ingredient and processing it. Just as the division of labor leads to material differences, so does the relegation of women and working-class subjects to the realm of the spiritual and the national, separate from the realm of the industrial controlled by men in positions of power. Furthermore, the manga reveals the gendered ways in which popular culture texts that reinterpret and modernize culinary traditions use female (and feminized) objects for the benefit of male subjects. The production of the majority of manga works about Japanese cuisine by men perpetuates representations of female subjectivity through the male gaze. While the Japanese manga industry includes creators of all genders, that such national constructions seem to come mainly from male producers is telling of the fact that the process is still a masculinist project. In representing the role of a woman in the modern *sake* industry, *Natsuko's Sake* highlights the various problematics of the production and consumption of *sake* specifically; yet the reinterpretations of the broader traditions of Japanese culinary practices only reinscribe gender hierarchies and capitalist systems that have been in place since even before Japan's postwar industrialization.

Notes

1 *Shōchū* is most often made from grains (such as barley), sweet potatoes, and sugarcane. Less common ingredients for Japanese *shōchū* include potatoes and chestnuts. *Awamori* (泡盛) is a popular distilled alcohol also made from rice that is produced in Okinawa, Japan.

2 Historian Jeffrey Alexander (2013) traces the history of beer in Japan, from the mid-nineteenth century to the present-day trend of craft beers. He notes how Japanese advertisements for beer in the 1950s were geared toward younger as well as female consumers, often enlisting the star power of celebrities in the marketing.

3 Aoyama (2008) discusses, in fact, how studies about food have taken a backseat in comparison to studies about drinking, given the feminized nature of the former (considering who produces it, and its attachment to the domestic realm) and the masculinized nature of the latter (with drinking often taking place among men in spaces outside the home).

4 While such works have been published in Japan since the late 1950s, significant franchises include *Oishinbo* (1983–), *Cooking Papa* (1985–), and the more recent *Food Wars!* (Shokugeki no Sōma, 2012–).

5 The parenthetical citations for the manga reference the volume, episode, and page number(s).

6 Japanese comic books are typically read from right to left, top to bottom.

7 From 1998 to 2000, ten years after the publication of the original series, Oze serialized a prequel to *Natsuko's Sake*, which was titled *Natsu's Cellar* (奈津の蔵, *Natsu no kura*). The prequel depicts the *sake* brewery in Natsuko's grandmother's time and also indicates that Natsuko is pregnant with the child of her now-husband Kusakabe.

References

Alexander, Jeffrey W. 2013. *Brewed in Japan: The Evolution of the Japanese Beer Industry.* Vancouver: UBC Press.

Aoyama, Tomoko. 2008. *Reading Food in Modern Japanese Literature.* Honolulu: University of Hawai'i Press.

Chatterjee, Partha. 1990. "The Nationalist Resolution of the Women's Question." In *Recasting Women: Essays in Indian Colonial History,* edited by Kumkum Sangari and Sudesh Vaid, 233–53. New Brunswick, NJ: Rutgers University Press.

Cwiertka, Katarzyna. 2006. *Modern Japanese Cuisine: Food, Power and National Identity.* Chicago: University of Chicago Press.

Cwiertka, Katarzyna. 1996. "A Note on the Making of Culinary Tradition—An Example of Modern Japan." *Appetite* 30, no. 2: 117–28.

江藤茂博 Etō Shigehiro 2014. "二十世紀文芸のメディア変換と流通の諸相―物語の構造分析理論と市場性獲得の構図 Nijusseiki bungei no media henkan to ryūtsū no shosō—Monogatari no kōzō bunseki riron to shijōsei kakutoku no kōzu" ["Aspects of Media Conversion and Circulation in Twentieth Century Literature: Structural Analysis Theory of Storytelling and the Composition of Marketability Acquisition"]. PhD diss., Nishogakusha University.

藤村岳 Fujimura Gaku. 2016. "タバコやお酒の嗜み方で問われる、あなたの人間力 Tabako ya osake no tashinamikata de towareru, anata no nin'genryoku" ["Your Value as a Person Tested by the Way You Enjoy Cigarettes and Alcohol"]. *Nikkei Woman Online,* February 24, 2016. http://wol.nikkeibp.co.jp/atcl/column/15/0930/021900022/.

Gaytán, Marie S. 2014. *¡Tequila! Distilling the Spirit of Mexico*. Stanford, CA: Stanford University Press.

Gingold, Naomi. 2015. "Brewing Sake in Japan Is Becoming a Woman's Game—Again." Public Radio International. September 11, 2015. https://www.pri.org/stories/ 2015-09-11/brewing-sake-japan-becoming-womans-game-again.

長谷川真弓 Hasegawa Mayumi. 2016. "タバコもお酒も。。。。。女性のカッコイイ嗜み方とは Tabako mo osake mo ... Josei no kakkoii tashinamikata towa" ["Tobacco and Alcohol Too... Interrogating the Cool Ways for Women to Enjoy Them"]. *Nikkei Woman Online*, March 2, 2016. http://wol.nikkeibp.co.jp/atcl/column/15/0930/022500023/.

一宮真佐子 Ichinomiya Masako. 2008. "ポピュラーカルチャーにおける農業・農村表象とその変化―現代マンガを対象として Popyurā karuchā ni okeru nōgyō • nōson hyōshō to sono henka—Gendai manga wo taishō to shite" ["An Analysis of Representation of 'Agriculture and Rural Space' in Popular Culture and Its Change: Focusing on MANGA"]. 村落社会研究 *Sonraku Shakai Kenkyū* 15, no. 1: 13–24.

キャアコップチャイ・ソムビット Kiatkobchai Sompit. 2008. "「だろう」の四用法について――先行研究の分析から 'Darō' no shiyōhō ni tsuite—Senkō kenkyū no bunseki kara" ["Four Kinds of 'Darou' Usage: From the Analysis of the Early Research"]. 学習院大学人文科学論集 *Gakushūin Daigaku Jinbunkagakuronshū* 17: 73–109.

倉持益子 Kuramochi Masuko. 2011. "「御苦労」系労い言葉の変遷 'Gokurō'kei' negirai kotoba no hensen" ["Transition of 'Gokurō'"]. 明海日本語 *Meikai Nihongo* 16: 13–21.

Lammers, Wayne P. 2004. *Japanese the Manga Way*. Berkeley, CA: Stone Bridge Press.

三宅昭良 Miyake Akiyoshi. 2008. "和醸良酒：「夏子の酒」試論 (I) Wajōryoshu: *Natsuko no sake* shiron (I)" ["Wajōryoshu: An Essay on *Natsuko no sake*"]. 人文学報表象文化論 *Jinbungakuhō Hyōshōbunkaron* 401: 69–89.

National Tax Agency. 2016. "*Sake* Report." National Tax Agency. https://www.nta.go.jp/ taxes/sake/shiori-gaikyo/shiori/2016/pdf/000.pdf [in Japanese].

O'Neill, Ted. 2012. "Uses and Representations of Foreign Language in Storytelling: Oze Akira's *Kuroudo*." *Journal of J. F. Oberlin University Studies in Language and Culture* 1: 73–87.

尾瀬あきら Oze Akira. 1988–91. 夏子の酒 *Natsuko no sake* [*Natsuko's Sake*], 12 vols. Tokyo: Kodansha.

Rath, Eric C. 2013. "Reevaluating Rikyū: *Kaiseki* and the Origins of Japanese Cuisine." *The Journal of Japanese Studies* 39, no. 1: 67–96.

Rath, Eric C. 2016. *Japan's Cuisines: Food, Place and Identity*. London: Reaktion Books.

Saito, Kumiko. 2014. "Magic, *Shōjo*, and Metamorphosis: Magical Girl Anime and the Challenges of Changing Gender Identities in Japanese Society." *The Journal of Asian Studies* 73, no. 1: 143–64.

Sangari, Kumkum, and Sudesh Vaid. 1990. "Recasting Women: An Introduction." In *Recasting Women: Essays in Indian Colonial History*, edited by Kumkum Sangari and Sudesh Vaid, 1–26. New Brunswick, NJ: Rutgers University Press.

Sato, Barbara. 2003. *The New Japanese Woman: Modernity, Media, and Women in Interwar Japan*. Durham, NC: Duke University Press.

Solt, George. 2014. *The Untold History of Ramen: How Political Crisis in Japan Spawned a Global Food Craze*. Berkeley: University of California Press.

Surak, Kristin. 2012. *Making Tea, Making Japan: Cultural Nationalism in Practice*. Stanford, CA: Stanford University Press.

UNESCO. n.d. "Washoku, Traditional Dietary Cultures of the Japanese, Notably for the Celebration of New Year. Japan. Inscribed in 2013 (8.COM) on the Representative List of the Intangible Cultural Heritage of Humanity." Paris: UNESCO. https://ich.unesco. org/en/RL/washoku-traditional-dietary-cultures-of-the-japanese-notably-for-the-celebration-of-new-year-00869.

6

Defining "Modern Malaysian" Cuisine: Fusion or Ingredients?

Gaik Cheng Khoo
University of Nottingham Malaysia

Introduction

If one were to look for the category "modern Malaysian" among numerous Malaysian food blogs and cookbooks, one will be hard-pressed to find it. The label is relatively new, rare, and has not been widely used to describe the kind of contemporary fusion cooking found in fine-dining restaurants, pricey new cafés and eateries that have sprouted up since the late 2000s in hipster suburbs in Kuala Lumpur (Map 4). While several restaurants have either self-identified as such or been reviewed as offering a twist to Malaysian food, only one chef, Darren Teoh (Figure 6.1), has consciously and consistently described the food served at his restaurant, Dewakan, which opened in 2015, as such (Ragavan 2015; Suanie 2015). At a food panel entitled "The Future of Modern Malaysian Cuisine: A Conversation with Darren Teoh and Isadora Chai," organized during the Cooler Lumpur Festival in June 2015, Teoh and Chai, two young Malaysian chefs, discussed what exactly "modern Malaysian food" was or could be (Cooler Lumpur n.d.). Chai, owner of modern French restaurant Bistro à Table, defined "modern Malaysian food" as deploying foreign (French) cooking techniques on local dishes, giving a new twist to modernize Malaysian cuisine. Chai's restaurant Antara, according to its website, serves "luxe modern Malaysian food with French influences," such as Cantonese *mantou* with foie gras and mango chutney, toasted *chapati* with goat's curd and curried mussel cream, and lobster *laksa* (Jamaluddin 2017; Lim n.d.). Several other restaurants deemed to have modern Malaysian cuisine are Manja (modern Malaysian fusion), Ruyi & Lyn ("contemporary Chinese food") and Wondermama, a casual dining restaurant where "traditional meets contemporary" (Lonely Planet n.d.) and where Japanese, Malaysian, and Nyonya influences are evident (CCFoodTravel 2012). Teoh, however, turns to the category almost as a last resort: "I guess [the term "modern Malaysian cuisine"] came from trying to explain to people what we were doing in a nutshell" (Ragavan 2015). Determined to get away from the well-trodden path of "the traditional and the known" in starting up his restaurant—one that reflects his personality and obsessions with origins, history, and terroir—Teoh

Figure 6.1 Malaysian Chef Darren Teoh of Dewakan adds the finishing touches to a dish. Kuala Lumpur, Malaysia (2015). Photograph by Choo Choy May. Courtesy of *Malay Mail*.

chose to center on ingredients instead. This innovative approach shifts the focus away from the discrete cultural origins of Malaysian national cuisine, and instead deconstructs the foundations of the Malaysian palate, ingredient by ingredient.

Malaysian cuisine reflects the multicultural make-up of its population and although it can be subdivided into Malay, Indian, Chinese, Peranakan, and Eurasian cooking, there is a long history of cross-cultural borrowing, adaptation, and hybridity. With regard to the cultural blends unique to the Malaysian peninsula, the Peranakan, creolized Chinese whose cuisine, language, and fashion were heavily influenced by Malay culture through intermarriage and cultural adaptation, are perhaps the most celebrated and recognized (see Duruz, Chapter 12 in this volume). Generally speaking, Malaysians are happy to eat each others' tasty food, barring some religious restrictions, and acknowledge that multicultural diversity is integral to Malaysian identity. In that sense, a close study of Malaysian cuisine and the Malaysian diet very quickly blurs ethnic divisions in the overall society attributed to race politics. At the same time, ethnic divisions still remain the default organizational categories for cookbooks and food blogs describing Malaysian recipes, dishes, and restaurants.

While Malaysians are united by their love and pride in their food diversity, the state exercises racism toward ethnic minorities through affirmative action policies that favor the majority Malay Muslims and facilitates racial divides through supporting a literalist and narrow interpretation of Islam—all in the name of maintaining political power. These policies, propelled by the New Economic Policy (1971–90), include an ethnic quota system to favor *bumiputera* (lit., "sons of the soil"), which refers to all indigenous groups and Malays, for positions in public universities and other public institutions, special discounts on housing, buying shares, etc.[1] This has manifested in the civil service, police, and army being dominated mainly by ethnic Malays, while middle-class ethnic Chinese and Indians often send their children to study in private universities and colleges locally or abroad. A growing consciousness about the need to observe religious strictures coupled with the state's Islamization measures have seen intense mosque building, the establishment of Islamic bodies, an International Islamic University, Islamic banking and financial services, the *halal* food industry, and the strengthening of *Syariah* [Sharia] laws. In other words, it entrenches Malay sociocultural and political hegemony and perpetuates a sense of ethnic entitlement. These measures putatively privilege the ethnic majority, though segments of the Malay Muslim population, such as liberal Muslims and non-Muslims, are disadvantaged by the morally conservative climate.

Such racial politics play out in food through the discourse of *halal* (that which is permissible by Islam) and *haram* (that which is not).[2] The *halal* strictures make it difficult for Muslims and non-Muslims to eat together in non-*halal* spaces and to accommodate the non-Muslim other (Duruz and Khoo 2014). Nevertheless, in the rarified sphere of fine dining and nouveau Malaysian cuisine, the word "halal" seldom surfaces, since alcohol is expected to be served and fine dining assumes an international hue to attract the global cosmopolitan elite. Rather, to appeal to middle- to upper-class, liberal Malay Muslim clients who remain somewhat free from the repressive laws of the Islamic authorities, such restaurants advertise a "pork free" menu.

What this chapter considers is the possibility of conceptualizing a different type of national cuisine, one that is modern and that Malaysians can take pride in—while also transcending standard cultural divisions. This national pride is vested in raising the visibility of Malaysian cuisine on the world stage, though not the kind promoted by the government abroad in its Malaysia Kitchen Programme (Mehta 2015). The latter is less interested in promoting gastronomy and concentrates more on promoting trade and exporting Malaysian food products overseas, such as ready-to-eat sauces, frozen parathas, etc. Moreover, the kind of culinary image of Malaysia that MATRADE (Malaysian External Trade Development Corporation) promotes is pluralistic, associated with classic Malaysian cuisine and embodied by the tourist slogan "Malaysia Truly Asia." For the state, multicultural diversity in the form of food and culture is useful and unthreatening when consumable and commodified, and less so when in the form of demands for rights recognition.

This chapter argues that modern Malaysian cuisine is a chef-headed project to propel classic Malaysian cuisine, often associated with its village and migrant street food origins, onto the global gastronomic stage. It can be read as a form of culinary nationalism but one that is not content with merely displaying Malaysian pluralism. Rather, the strategy, conscious or unconscious, is a cosmopolitanizing endeavor in David Hollinger's sense: to shift from pluralism, which "is more concerned to protect and perpetuate particular, existing cultures" to cosmopolitanism which, by comparison, "is willing to put the future of every culture at risk through the sympathetic scrutiny of other cultures" (Hollinger 1995, 85–6). Teoh's attitude toward culture is characteristically cosmopolitan, with a ready willingness to critically deconstruct what Malaysian food is.

Cosmopolitanism in the case of these chefs and restaurateurs takes the form of embracing global discourses and global culinary trends from the West and other top Asian cuisines while also creating something new: offering ten-course degustation menus, Frenchifying Malaysian food (Antara) or Malaysianizing sushi (Ruyi & Lyn), drawing on California cuisine and its insistence on "local suppliers for a direct 'farm-to-table' experience" (Krich 2015, on Dewakan), or using the latest scientific methods of cooking, such as molecular gastronomy (Dewakan). Cosmopolitanism with its transnational identifications exists in tension with nationalism: in modern Malaysian cuisine, cosmopolitanism modernizes and animates the national. It provides the twist to the national. For Malaysian cuisine to be modern, it has to be cosmopolitan. And to be cosmopolitan is to propagate fusion cooking in one form or another, whether acknowledged or not.

Malaysian cooking: Asia's original fusion food

The classic narrative of how traditional Malaysian cuisine came by its present reputation has to do with its oft-told history. It is a story that combines the felicity of geography (abundant seafood, rice paddies, fresh herbs and tropical fruit, forest produce) with a history of maritime trade, colonialism (Portuguese, Dutch, then British), and labor migration. The ethnic composition of the Malay peninsula changed drastically under British rule, with the highest immigration rates between 1881 and 1939, when Chinese and Indians came to work as indentured laborers and coolies in Malaya and brought their cooking styles and ingredients with them. Perhaps even earlier than the nineteenth century, going back to the Melaka sultanate of the 1400s (Map 4), we find local-born Chinese and Indians who either married Malay women or culturally adapted to native customs, diet, and dress, creating a hybrid culture called Peranakan ("native born"). Together with the descendants of the Eurasian Portuguese, their foods have also become part of the canon of Malaysian cuisine. But arguably, even within what can be called "Indian" or "Chinese" or "Malay" food are some dishes that have emerged out of the meeting of two or more of these cultures that merit Malaysian cuisine's overall moniker as "Asia's original fusion food" (O'Flaherty 2013). The dish *mamak mee goreng* is the result of such a meeting of two cultures: Tamil Muslim hawkers fry Chinese yellow noodles in a spicy tomato sauce with cubed boiled potatoes, crunchy fritters, fried tofu and bean sprouts, and reconstituted dried cuttlefish. This dish does not exist in Tamil Nadu, the province of their ancestors.

Malaysian cookbooks and restaurants (especially overseas) offer a range and mélange of Malay, Chinese, Indian, Peranakan, and sometimes Portuguese Eurasian recipes, as well as carrying neighboring influences from Thai and Indonesian cooking (Saw 2009; Hutton 2005, 5; Rajah 2013; Musa 2016; Lee 2014; Chef Wan [2006] 2011).[3] In practice, Malaysian kitchens of all ethnic groups stock traditionally Chinese products like soya sauce, bean paste, and sweet dark soya sauce (*kicap manis*), dried rice noodles, and tofu. Thus borrowing, adaptation, and incorporation of ingredients and cooking styles occurs among the different groups, making the art of fusion cooking much of the norm and basis of Malaysian food. This is notable, for Malaysians will eat across different cultures (with the Chinese being the most voracious cultural omnivores), though nowadays self-conscious Muslim Malays who observe *halal* regulations will ask first if the food of the Other is *halal*. The liking of certain Chinese dishes can prompt Malays to adapt them to conform to *halal* requirements; for example adopting the famous Penang wok-fried rice noodles (*char koay teow*) and making it their own by excluding pork lard and Chinese sausages, and substituting *kicap manis* to cater to sweeter taste preferences. In short, traditional Malaysian food is both pluralistic and hybrid, with most home-cooked food tending to have a strong basis in one's own culinary traditions.

Notably the diversity and wide variety of food available and consumed make it difficult to generalize what Malaysians eat. Drawing together all these diverse cuisines urges some to attempt to pin down shared national (for lack of a better word) characteristics to describe the Malaysian taste palate. Cookbook author Wendy Hutton, for example, writes about "Malaysian food's irresistible flavors" as embodied in "Malay satay, pungent Indian mutton soup, Nyonya chicken curry with lime leaves, Chinese pepper crab or Eurasian salt fish and pineapple curry" (Hutton 2005, 7). On the one hand, Hutton's description might be considered universal, calling forth strong intense flavors that derive from reliance on aromatic herbs and rhizomes, spices, chilies, coconut milk, and preserved seafood, which can be salty and sweet, hot and sour, or creamy and rich. Indeed, modern Malaysian restaurants like Antara trade on this notion with mottos like "Sample. Savor. Relish. The full flavor of Antara." On the other hand, Hutton's description of the Malaysian culinary palate is once again invariably built on the discrete contributions of different ethnic dishes, whose essentialized palatal profiles seem eternally distinct.

What can be summed up in brief is that Malaysian food reflects the multicultural make-up and history of its population; it is well known for its bold flavors and fusionism. And it is associated with certain ingredients. Moreover Malaysian cookbooks, the epitome of culinary nationalism (Ferguson 2010), reinforce this image of its national cuisine as diverse and plural, with Peranakan cooking signifying its most celebrated form of multicultural hybridity. But a point not given as much emphasis is the middlebrow roots of Malaysian national cuisine, which is closely tied to family recipes, home cooking, and well-known street food. This association with street food is celebrated by ordinary Malaysians and the government, promoted by the Malaysian Tourism Board and the Penang state government (Map 4) who sponsor foreign "food and travel" writers to come to Malaysia. This is the kind of food mostly found in Malaysian restaurants, food festivals, and national food promotions overseas. It is also this same, classic image of Malaysian cuisine that modern, native chefs are trying to change.

Defining "modern Malaysian": A contemporary twist

By general consensus, modern Malaysian cuisine is about novelty and newness.[4] In a survey I conducted with six Malaysian food bloggers, "traditional given a contemporary twist" (Chris Wan of Pure Glutton) seems to be the central theme, with the twist referring to a variety of possibilities: "Malaysian cuisine cooked and presented in a more stylish manner" (Winston Ng), a combination of ingredients and flavors not found in traditional cuisine (KYSpeaks), something that retains its "original flavor but has a unique form" (VKeong) or new scientific cooking methods such as *sous vide*, using a rotisserie oven, or molecular gastronomy (Chris Wan, SyCookies, VKeong, Auntie Lilly).

Presentation matters since, by contrast, traditional dishes are not served in any artistic fashion: "Our *rendang* or *bak kut teh* are just always served in a bowl or pot with hardly any 'decoration,'" notes Pure Glutton reviewer Chris Wan.[5] If delicious home-cooked dishes and traditional street food lack a certain aesthetic finish, modern cuisine on the other hand gives thought to "the beautiful plating and presentation of dishes: the ones that are meticulously arranged to impress and must consist of ingredients that are not foreign to Malaysians"[6] (Figure 6.2).

Figure 6.2 Dewakan's elegant presentation of its smoked chocolate and banana dessert: smooth smoked chocolate Chantilly cream, decorated with dramatic chocolate twigs, drops of nutmeg syrup, sprigs of dill and deep-fried banana (*pisang goreng*) ice cream. Kuala Lumpur, Malaysia (2015). Photograph by Choo Choy May. Courtesy of *Malay Mail*.

Working within a cosmopolitan universe or a field of liquid modernity where constant change is the norm (Bauman 2000), modern Malaysian chefs are constantly experimenting with different styles; their variously themed restaurants become laboratories of a sort to convert traditional Malaysian food from its low- to middlebrow street food image into high cuisine. This perceived need to elevate Malaysian food is dictated by the "global hierarchy of taste" (Ray 2016), where French cuisine and cooking styles still remain the most culturally prestigious. Some of this thinking is behind the modern Malaysian restaurant Antara (meaning "in between"), opened by chef Isadora Chai, who was trained in French cooking in Australia and who runs a French restaurant, Bistro à Table, in Petaling Jaya. Chai explains: "Bistro à Table is 80% French, 20% Malaysian and other stuff; Antara is the flip of that. Why I wanted to do Antara is because I sometimes create very radical things that I could never park in Bistro ... [s]o I decided to just open up another restaurant for all my other cooking experiments that aren't French" (Ng 2016).

Can there be hierarchies of fusion cooking? Many seem to define fusion cooking as a style of cooking that uses traditional, Western techniques on Asian ingredients. This definition would be precisely what Taiwanese scholar Chen Kuan-Hsing critiques in his book *Asia As Method* (2010), for its implication of Western colonial mastery, control, or ownership of theory applied to the Eastern context, as if the East has no theories of its own that are worth applying locally and globally. Such a definition suggests that Western cooking styles are still the universal model to be emulated within "the global hierarchy of taste," and tried out on various minor cuisines (or local ingredients) emerging from developing nations. Minor cuisines need to engage with Western styles of cooking, and chefs need to learn these methods in order to be taken seriously. But of course, this West–East flow of cooking techniques ignores the long-standing influence of even older cuisines from Asia, namely Chinese and Indian, that are ubiquitous on the Malaysian foodscape. It also ignores the changes rendered by culinary influences and taste buds from around the region, as more and more migrant workers from Myanmar and Indonesia are found working in Malaysian kitchens today: "You change the genetic make-up of a community, the food will change."[7]

Such a definition adheres to fusion cooking as "a combination of elements from different culinary traditions," suggesting that modern Malaysian fusion can be fusion with lateral and proximate cultures, and speaks of inter-Asian cultural encounters that may be less hierarchical in conceptualization. For example, the self-titled "modern Chinese hybrid restaurant" Ruyi & Lyn in Bangsar, Kuala Lumpur, serves sushi with Malaysian flavors like nasi lemak, chicken rice, and mango sticky rice.[8] The form and appearance is Japanese but the cooking style, taste, and ingredients, recognizably Malaysian. The restaurant's orientation is eastward or pan-Asian, looking toward Chinese and Japanese cuisine as models. For Valentine's Day 2018, its in-house chef James Ho collaborated with Chef Nik Michael Imran to curate "a distinct yet nostalgic East-meets-West menu" that included salted egg yolk lava cake, inspired by a bun with a runny, golden salted egg yolk custard center (*liu sha bao*) that first emerged in Hong Kong in 2009, and reached the shores of Singapore in 2011 (Lim 2016). Since then it has inspired many new creations in Malaysia and Singapore, ranging from salted duck egg sauce to accompany Malaysian seafood, pastas, burgers, fries, and pizza, to cocktails and desserts like macarons, croissants, donuts, and ice cream. Other pan-Asian dishes with modern inflections available at Ruyi & Lyn include Drunken River Prawn steamed with champagne and egg white beer sauce, pan-seared foie gras with Japanese miso and radish, Thai and Japanese-inspired crunchy soft-shell crab with green mangoes and bonito flakes, and deep-fried soft-shell crab in the form of the Malaysian fruit salad, rojak. Their pan-Asian-ness supports cultural studies scholar Chen's call to Asia-based scholars to derive methods from the Asian region and to learn from each other's experiences and theorizing, rather than relying on the West as the center of universal knowledge generation and the central conduit connecting situated and neighboring locations. Indeed, the restaurant's executive chef, James Ho, is a returning Malaysian with twenty years' experience working in different parts of Asia: Singapore, Indonesia, Hong Kong, Taiwan, Thailand, Korea, and Japan.

A more democratic or egalitarian understanding of modern Malaysian cuisine comes from blogger Auntie Lilly, for whom the term "modern Malaysian cuisine" evokes "a mix of local and international cuisine or recipes, such as Tomyam Pasta, Tandoori Pizza, Roast Pork (Siew Yoke) Biryani."[9] Auntie Lilly's idea of modern fusion is one that does not simply center on an East–West dialogue as found in Antara, but also combines Malaysian with other international cuisines that can come from other parts of Asia, Southeast Asia, and beyond. She also does not associate modern Malaysian cuisine necessarily with a particular price range, stating that "From *pasar malam* [night markets] to cafés and fine-dining restaurants, you are bound to find many kinds of modern Malaysian food accessible to most average foodies." Yet while Malaysian street food and industrial snacks offer their own kind of innovative fusion styles and localization, in dishes and products such as garlic cheese *naan*, *durian* ice cream, salted egg croissants, and *nasi lemak* Kit Kat, these creations do not seem to be encompassed in the general definition of "modern Malaysian cuisine."

Experimentation and change are the engines of this culinary modernity, like in China (see Farrer, Chapter 10 in this volume). Notably, this avant-gardism is driven by cooks and chefs rather than consumers. Thus, every aspect of modern Malaysian cuisine is carefully studied, researched, and tested before emerging in the design of the whole package: the décor, design, and ambience of the restaurant, the service, menu, the presentation (plating), narrative, and thought, and, finally, the food itself. This additional labor and attention to detail is reflected in the high prices. To put it bluntly, that "something extra" about modern Malaysian cuisine might just be its price tag. Most of these restaurants—Antara, Manja, Ruyi & Lyn, and Dewakan—are fine-dining establishments for the highbrow foodie, the kind where dishes are expected to be accompanied by narratives, infused by some kind of intellectual thought (again, see Farrer, Chapter 10 in this volume). Only Wondermama is casual dining. So modern Malaysian cuisine emanates social distinction sought by the class most able to afford to dine there, the class with the cultural capital most able to appreciate the labor, art, and creativity of the chefs that went into manipulating ingredients, mixing flavors, and harmonizing tastes into new pleasing forms and flavors for both the eyes and the palate.

A word about this class: out of all the ethnic groups, Malaysian Chinese make up the largest group who dine out, even though they are only 24.6 percent of the national population (Poulain et al. 2014, 138). This has to do with their urban location, economic status, and earning power relative to the other ethnic groups and perhaps also the idea that most Chinese are dual-income families who do not have time to cook at home. In addition, they make up the largest numbers who migrate due to the racial policies that disadvantage them, yet open up Malaysian restaurants abroad that express pride in their culinary diversity (see Duruz, Chapter 12 in this volume). It is this embrace of the spicy flavors of Malay and Indian dishes on their menus that distinguishes their food from other Chinese cuisines, making their palates first and foremost Malaysian rather than "purely" Chinese. In Malaysia, they are not only the majority diners and customers of the middle- to upper-level restaurants, but also the top food bloggers and self-declared foodies, not to mention cooks and chefs at various levels of the food and beverage sector.[10] I argue that this cultural accommodation and embrace of spices and sambal, of a diverse diet within the nation's existing cuisines, testifies to a culinary cosmopolitan sensibility; one that does not make them less patriotic but one that modern Malaysian chefs seek to tap and expand on.

Modern Malaysian restaurants carve out their niche on home territory rather than overseas because just as they strive to provide something a little different in a highly competitive industry, they are also simultaneously appealing to the knowing customer, the local foodie: those who are already, at base, familiar with the tastes and look of local dishes and ingredients and who wait to be surprised by the chef's playful twists and turns on that which they know. A modern Malaysian restaurant in Chicago would make little sense when most Americans may not even know where Malaysia is, let alone have an inkling of what kinds of foods constitute "Malaysian" cuisine. A 2014 *Huffington Post* feature on Malaysian food in the United States, for example, sounds naïve and rudimentary in its headline: "Malaysian Food Is Hot, Spicy, Delicious . . . and Here!" (Weston 2014). Meanwhile, back at Dewakan, guests may be familiar with local desserts, but will never have experienced them in such novel forms and combinations that enhance visual appearance and taste. Take the Gula Melaka, for example. Conventionally this is an aromatic palm sugar that graces many local desserts. A Malaysian food reviewer of Dewakan enthuses:

> Number two [dessert] is the **Gula Melaka**, which consisted of Gula Melaka marquise, sour meringue and *pulut* (sticky rice) ice cream . . . The *pulut* ice cream is not sweet at all but has a hint of saltiness. This might sound like a silly statement but it also really tastes like sticky rice, so you have one of those mind-boggling moments where it looks like you're eating one thing but your tastebuds and brain are processing something different entirely. Inside the Gula Melaka is caramelised and within it are little nubbins of biscuit to keep the texture play going . . . Every element screams classic Malaysian dessert but reinvented for a modern audience.
>
> Samanthawxlow 2016

Given their presumably "knowing" consumer base, it should come as no surprise that many modern Malaysian fusion restaurants like Wondermama, Manja, and Antara are driven by nostalgia. Nostalgia is "a longing for a different time—the time of our childhood, the slower rhythms of our childhood dreams" (Boym 2001, 8). Its not-so-repressed note resurfaces in the form of colonial ambience—fine-dining restaurants housed in colonial shophouses (Manja), and restored and renovated nearly century-old bungalows (Antara). Antara, established recently in 2016 in the shadow of former prime minister Najib's corrupt regime, hearkens to the more hopeful period of post-Merdeka (Independence) with its centerpiece upstairs of fifty portraits of Tunku Abdul Rahman, the first prime minister who was ousted in a coup in the guise of the 1969 race riots. Songs by female diva Saloma of the same era, and jazz legend of the 1990s, Sheila Majid, provide a charm and character "decidedly steeped in nostalgia" (*Eat Drink KL* 2016). Antara is housed in a restored colonial bungalow, which also houses Chai's other eating outlet, Anson, her nod to "the great old colonial cafés of yore, which she thinks are slowly being wiped out by modernization" (Durai 2017). Manja promises the first-class service connoted in the notion of "old world colonial luxury," in contrast to the general dining scene, dotted by badly trained (and poorly paid) migrant workers, impatient and time-poor diners hooked on their electronic devices, and fast-food joints where self-service is the only reliable form of service: "Step into Manja where old world colonial luxury awaits you. Indulge in our array of local and international dishes with our own modern twists. Revel in the selection of stunning local fruit cocktails. In short, let us Manja [pamper] you!" (Manja 2018). Or nostalgia can stem from the longing for a more innocent past, tied to happy childhood memories. Popsicles and ice cream *potong*[11] appear in new flavors, food is served in vintage enamelware,[12] and retro presentations and settings riff on such a past, with décor that allows one to step back into Malaysia during the 1970s (Wondermama).[13] In that sense, the old is rendered anew and nostalgia "not necessarily opposed to modernity ... [but] coeval with it" (Boym 2001, 8).

Dewakan: Ingredient-based modern Malaysian

I now want to move to a discussion of Dewakan chef Darren Teoh's interpretation of modern Malaysian cuisine. A focus on ingredients instead of the cultural origins of dishes shifts the frame away from "race" and can be treated as a possible deracialization strategy. At the same time, Teoh does not eschew the traditional or the cultural, believing instead that it is so innate in us that it forms the lens through which we approach everything.[14] Yet, in our discussion of his choice to focus on ingredients, many assumptions are deconstructed, not least the concept of the nation and the temporal idea of "modern."

Unlike many of the bloggers who expect it to be fusion, Teoh does not define modern Malaysian as fusion food, although Dewakan's menu has been described as such: "Please call it 'modern Malaysian' rather than 'fusion'—which implies that we want to join something European," he insisted in an interview with John Krich (2015). Teoh maintains a strong postcolonial position, even though the discourse on Dewakan is about modern Malaysian cuisine as fine dining—"the NOMA of Malaysia," exalts a reviewer on Trip Advisor (BV 2015). Championing ingredients and modern cuisine places Teoh alongside other Malaysian chefs of French fine-dining restaurants, James Won of Enfin and Darren Chin of DC, who are inclined toward "La Jeune Cuisine," slow food, and modernist techniques. Yet Teoh's adamant emphasis on local ingredients, which make up 80 percent of what he serves in his restaurant (Krich 2015), evades the discourse of social prestige and class, often associated with expensive, imported ("airflown"), fresh ingredients found in other fine-dining establishments, such as wagyu beef, sea urchin, truffles, caviar, quinoa, etc (Lee 2015).

Indeed, Teoh himself claims that the moniker "fine-dining" comes from the patrons of his restaurant rather than being a self-given label (Ng 2017). This does not mean, however, that the menu is within reach of the average Malaysian diner, although its degustation menu is very reasonably priced compared to its French peers in town, like DC and Enfin: Dewakan's seventeen-course degustation dinner menu is RM370 (US$95) per person while Enfin's four-course degustation dinner menu is RM388 (US$99) per head without wines. The focus on local produce and local flavors brings us back to the notion of terroir, and the specifics of Malaysian food history and geography.

As a proponent of modern Malaysian cuisine, Teoh outrageously claims that "there isn't a modern Malaysian cuisine as yet because we haven't figured out where we came from. We come from a bastardized society, and we just need to draw more lines, just bring a little structure to it."[15] This does not mean that he rejects the culinary pluralism inherent in traditional Malaysian cooking. After all, culture (or racialization) is deeply embedded in Malaysians and it has become our innate way to approach anything. Rather, he feels that focusing on ingredients is more inclusive and can transcend ethnicity/culture and therefore begin a deeper conversation about what makes a culinary nation.[16] He points to wheat flour, certainly an introduced ingredient that comes from far away, that is used by all the ethnic groups: by the Chinese in noodles, by the Indians in *roti*, *chapati*, and *puri*, by the Malays in fritters and a sweet, soupy dessert called *bubur gandum*, and by the Jawi Peranakan (creolized Indians) for a savory *gandum*.[17] He speculates that it was the Chinese and the Indians who would have brought wheat flour with them as migrants, and that it predates British colonization.

Teoh enthuses that rarely used local ingredients like the *rambai*, a tropical fruit similar to the *langsat*, or specially selected "red prawns" and "forbidden black rice" display "a greater pride in what we have and can do here, not in imitation of the West but trying to break from preconceived notions" that have led to "most of our restaurants cooking the same things over and over" (Krich 2015).[18] By this, Teoh means that these local but rare ingredients are seldom used but could yield uniquely original dishes.

At the same time though, one has the feeling that in his pursuit of the representative ingredient or ingredient-based dish, Teoh is a nativist, for whom "the sambal [associated the most with Malay cooking] cannot be the poster boy for Malaysian cooking. I feel the answer has to do with the Orang Asli [the indigenous people of Peninsula Malaysia]."[19] This is because sambal consists of freshly pounded chilies, which is an ingredient introduced to the region by the Portuguese and which has become a key component in Malaysian cooking (Mustafa 2016). Teoh is interested in what the original inhabitants ate as they relied first on the bounty of the forests through foraging and the sea. *Ulam*, a raw salad of local plants, herbs, and vegetables usually served with *sambal belacan* or some spicy condiment and eaten by Malays and indigenous Orang Asli, might be the better answer if eaten plain, without the chili.

These plants and herbs can be classified into two of three categories that Teoh suggests: plants that have been introduced accidentally or intentionally over a time that are now part of our ecosphere, i.e., *ulam raja*,[20] *ciku* (sapodilla from Latin America), starfruit, cucumber, and bitter melon (originally from South Asia), that have become naturalized to Malaysia. Second, there are those plants that are indigenous to the land, which have been part of the ecosphere for far longer. This might include *daun pegaga*, the Asiatic pennywort (*Centella asiatica*); a vegetable fern known as *pucuk paku*; winged bean (native to New Guinea); and *buah petai*, the stink bean (*Parkia speciosa*).

This interest in exploring an almost purist, totally "native" cuisine is unusual as it negates the image of Malaysian culinary diversity that has become such a symbol of Malaysian cuisine. It is this diversity of fusion that most modern Malaysian chefs take as the baseline for further experimentation, but Teoh feels such an approach may not be radical (or modern) enough. Nevertheless, one may have to separate out the speculating purist nativist from the practitioner chef, whose idea of incorporating local and indigenous roots while modernizing Malaysian cuisine is not about returning to a past that is no longer accessible, but more about centralizing local ingredients and produce. Since my interview with Teoh, the new menu "Kayangan" from September/October 2017 features "Temuan chocolate with jaggery ice cream" as dessert (Temuan is an indigenous tribe in Peninsula Malaysia). This chocolate is made from wild cocoa beans sourced from Temuan villagers and is part of a collaboration with Ong Ning Geng, Malaysian artisanal chocolatier of Chocolate Concierge (Goh 2017; Lim 2017, 12).[21]

In the attempt to define and unpack what is modern about modern Malaysian cuisine, a philosophy of modernity is necessary, one that takes into consideration Zygmunt Bauman's concept of modernity as ever changing and in flux: "To 'be modern' means to modernize—compulsively, obsessively; not so much just 'to be,' let alone to keep its identity intact, but forever 'becoming,' avoiding completion, staying underdefined" (2000, viii). Here Darren Teoh seems to echo this sentiment as he shares his philosophy about cuisine, modernity and change:

> Cuisine ALWAYS changes. So, is change modern? Or is it not? And even if change ... were to go backward in process, say maybe from gas to charcoal, is that modern? So we have probably kind of defined what modern is. Now if you're saying that modern is applying a scientific technique or technology to it, that again could be quite simplistic because it's only a medium, right? So at some point what we consider the microwave as modern could no longer be. It would become defunct because it's become a staple in so many homes. So I think that first and probably what we're doing now is just trying to find an identity for what Malaysian cuisine is. And trying to find a loose framework or even just a definition of what Malaysian cooking is. So Malaysian cooking can exist, purely culturally as in the *char koay teow* [Chinese fried rice noodles], the *bah khut teh* [Chinese herbal pork soup], as in whatever we want to consider as Malaysian cuisine. It can exist that way. Or, we can go back to sources and find out where I mean ... or we can go back to ingredients and define cuisine that way as well.

So if you were to look at France for example. Now, because they have cows therefore they have dairy. And dairy makes cheese, and cheese is based out of an ingredient that is naturalized there. Right? What do we have? What is our equivalent to an ingredient-based product? You have things like *budu* [fish sauce], *belacan* [shrimp paste], which come from our seas, they are shipped and they are processed here. The fish and they are processed there and that just kind of makes that connect. So it's not impossible to define what the cuisine is and once we have been able to have that then we'll probably be able to define what a *modern* cuisine is.[22]

From this passage it's clear that Teoh is struggling to define what classic national cuisine is before even venturing to answer what its modern version would look like. He would like the definitive national cuisine or ingredient to be something that is sourced and produced locally: for example, fish sauce and shrimp paste. But arguably, these ingredients are only found in Malay cooking and by extension, Peranakan cooking (Peranakans being Chinese and Indians who have adapted, localized, and integrated Malay cooking styles and local ingredients into their own cooking and whose food can be described as creolized). In other words, to claim Malaysian national identity, ethnic minorities have still to adopt, adapt, and identify with indigenous ingredients and indigenous cuisine, more likely Malay than Orang Asli, as there is more likelihood of interacting with the former (consisting of 60 percent of the population) than the latter.[23] One way of reading Teoh's injunction that "the answer lies with the Orang Asli" may be the connotation of marginalized indigenous folk knowledge that makes edible little-known forest produce. Teoh's question to me about what people used to flavor their food before the introduction of garlic can perhaps be answered by a Temuan activist, Jenita: "We don't use garlic here but semomok leaves," she explains, though the jungle leaf is hard to find nowadays (Augustin 2016). Teoh's idea of tracing the roots of ingredients is new, even if the ingredients themselves are not. It may equally be the case that the local ingredient's potential has not been fully realized in cooking, nutrition, and health.

But returning to Teoh's version of modern Malaysian cuisine, one senses genuine intellectual curiosity behind the questions, even if the questions about the source of what our ancestors ate may not yield clear-sighted implications. After all, how far back need one go in order to find ingredients or plants that are indigenous, or to find foodways that end up being not as "pure" or local as we assume?[24] To give him credit, Teoh downplays molecular gastronomic techniques as merely a medium to signify modernity because in twenty to thirty years' time, it will be a newer technique that will be modern. His interest still prioritizes ingredients and the tastes and flavors they yield. This is not to undermine the prowess and creativity that goes into his technique. Dewakan delivers flavors that cater to the local taste profile through focusing on familiar ingredients offered up in unique forms and textures, widening the expanse of that ingredient's possibilities. Several bloggers deem its technique of molecular gastronomy as the epitome of modern Malaysian cuisine. Take its opening *amuse*: beef tendon crackers (that mimic the Indonesian *emping belinjo*) served with blended watercress, and *sawi* crackers (made from blended greens, *sawi*, which have been dehydrated before being fried) served with *budu* (fish sauce from the east coast of Peninsular Malaysia) mayonnaise.

Teoh's background in molecular gastronomy shows up in his technical manipulation of local ingredients like sticky rice to make *pulut* ice cream, offered at Dewakan. He explained that the starch in overcooked sticky rice has a similar texture and mouth feel as *crème anglaise* that is used to make ice cream base. " 'We removed ourselves from the traditional box and we started thinking that, as a Malaysian, if we did not have any of these influences, how would we make ice cream?' Darren says. 'And rice came to mind' " (Ragavan 2015).

Teoh demonstrates an uncanny predilection for finding the universal common denominator across cultural traditions by thinking about the science of the ingredient. One has to be objective, he says. This same objectivity is conducted through the "critical scrutiny" of all culinary traditions (both East and West) and existing approaches, to achieve taste profiles that are worthy of a true cosmopolitan nationalist. In a way, these dishes described above, the amuse-bouche and the dessert, come in Western-now-universalist forms—crackers, mayonnaise, and ice cream—but their local ingredients provide a twist, both to the universalist form as well as the way such local ingredients are divorced from their original or common, local concoctions. Thus local Malaysians like blogger Samanthawxlow, mentioned earlier, can recognize the flavors despite the estranged appearance. Elsewhere in Malaysia, sticky rice desserts still often resemble sticky rice in appearance, and beef tendon usually looks like a heavy meat entrée rather than a light cracker.

Modernity, as Fa-ti Fan explains, "is based in part on Eurocentric narratives of scientific progress" but at the same time, is "a site of imaginings where futures, presents, and pasts are inscribed and contested" (2016, 366). Like every new or young nation, modern Malaysian chefs yearn for international recognition by participating in the global discourses and practices of culinary modernity and science in which (unfortunately) French technique still dominates. I would characterize Teoh's molecular gastronomic techniques as not really about the old fusion "in the sense of a seamless melding of the older with newer cuisines," but rather about picking up ingredients, tools, techniques that can be incorporated without violating his culinary philosophy, which is also influenced by embracing globalization and rejecting cultural imperialism (Laudan 2013, 21). Insofar as molecular gastronomic techniques may still hold some novelty in Malaysia, they are the current "modern," but as Teoh reminds us, only a medium to enhance our sensory taste of featured ingredients. To put it another way, he wants to "interpret Malaysian produce through contemporary lens" (Jessica 2016). Perhaps part of Teoh's philosophy is not all that different from French molecular gastronomists' notion of "culture [as] an object of chemistry" and the reversal of valuing authenticity over technoscience in the belief that science can discover more deliciousness and contribute to our culinary pleasure (Roosth 2013, 5–6).

Conclusion

To sum up, modern Malaysian cuisine, led by Malaysian chefs, can be characterized as a cosmopolitan nationalist project: cosmopolitan in embracing diversity within

Malaysia and welcoming and engaging in global discourses and trends. Make no mistake about it, the discourse of modern Malaysian cooking, with its twists and a sense of bringing novelty, is definitely occurring at the level of haute cuisine and attracting talk of Michelin stars (see Farrer, Chapter 10 in this volume). This is in opposition to what is middle- to lowbrow "traditional" Malaysian ethnic cuisine associated with street food, the village, and home cooking. The only difference between Teoh and the rest is that he wants to return problematically to a purist precontact era by tracing the roots and routes of ingredients, while others take the path of least resistance by accepting the view of Malaysian cuisine's Chinese and Indian migrant heritage as the starting point of further fusion. His curiosity about botanical indigeneity helps push the discourse further, beyond the realm of existing culinary possibilities. Questions such as what the traditional inhabitants used before garlic was introduced lead to the revelation about a local jungle leaf only known to indigenous people, *semomok* leaves, "the secret ingredient" of their cooking (Augustin 2016). Although tracing the roots of ingredients may not yield answers about any gastronomic potential, the ingredients are important only in so far as providing a reference point to start interrogating possibilities. It should be said that such musings do not stem from ethnic self-negation: Teoh is himself half-Chinese and half-Indian. His concocted mango curry is a tribute to his grandmother's late Malayalee friend's cooking: a rich, spicy, creamy mango pureed soup with a glass of frozen mango laid on the top.

As for the average Malaysian eater, while adventurous and willing to try anything once, she is less likely to "frequent" fine-dining modern Malaysian restaurants. She might try out *nasi lemak* ice cream just for novelty's sake but will soon revert to the separation of spheres—ice cream should remain a dessert and *nasi lemak*, a savory staple—that have assured the popularity of each dish for so long. With hawker food encapsulating all that is flavorful and cheap, why go in search of more esoteric and expensive nouveau cuisine that is more than likely to be expensive, pretentious, and come in too small portions, especially when economic times are difficult (with the shrinking ringgit, the goods and services tax, and rising costs)?[25] Food blogger VKeong gave examples of some of the fusion, updates, and revisions on current dishes that he knew, saying they were slight modifications and there was nothing "modern" about them: stir frying *bak khut teh* with chili and dark soya sauce instead of the soupy version, using wagyu beef to make beef *rendang* or adding lobster to *Sarawak laksa*. The food and beverage industry will also continue to cater to the demand for that something slightly new, revised, updated, localized, and globalized—but all are mostly minor tinkering within a system of well-worn traditional dishes and predictable flavor profiles. The luxury class who remain ever above the economic fray will still be able to afford the experience of fine dining. But whether dishes that challenge their conventional approach to taste profiles, appearances of ingredients, etc., may provoke them to demand more of other restaurants in future has yet to be seen.

Notes

1   The NEP was a series of five-year plans to address the unequal ethnic share of the economy, dominated then by the Chinese. In essence it continued after 1990 under different names.

2   *Halal* includes the proper ritual slaughter of cows, goats, sheep, and chicken; no pork or alcohol in any part of the dish; and the observation of hygiene standards (ensuring meat does not come into contact with impurities) in the full food cycle from farm to table. Having Muslim workers in the kitchen helps to ensure that the process is kept *halal*. These are in strict accordance with JAKIM, the Islamic body that awards *halal* certification. A restaurant must have *halal* certification from JAKIM to claim this status.

3   Cookbooks on indigenous peoples' cuisine are rarer; the only one I found was a reference in the early section of *Perak: A Journey for Food Lovers* (Aznan and Ariffin 2015).

4   The definitions that follow are taken from surveys with six Malaysian food bloggers, the author's interview with Darren Teoh, chef of Dewakan, and an analysis of restaurant webpages and current discourse on dining out in Kuala Lumpur.

5   Email to author, February 25, 2017.

6   Email to author, January 24, 2017.

7   Author interview with Darren Teoh, January 21, 2017.

8   Thanks go to food blogger V Keong for recommending Ruyi & Lyn. Phone conversation, February 8, 2017.

9   Email to author, March 6, 2017.

10 I am of course speaking generally. Malays and Indians are also involved in all tiers of the food and beverage sector. But in terms of the percentages within each ethnic group, there are fewer seen eating at these middle- to upper-class establishments.

11 Ice cream *potong* (lit., "cut") refers to the way ice cream used to be sold on the street by mobile ice cream vendors who would cut them into small rectangular blocks and serve them sandwiched between wafers.

12 Wondermama serves its ice cream in an enamel mug. See also Masak Masak, a Malaysian restaurant in Collingwood, Melbourne, Australia (Winston 2013). Even the name of the restaurant hearkens to a childhood game of pretend cooking (from the root verb in Malay, *masak*, meaning to cook).

13 Iron House Kopitiam does not purport to be "modern Malaysian," as it sells traditional Malaysian hawker food, but it trades on a newness (the owners are twenty-something graduates) that relies on memories of "the good old days": zinc roof, enamel plates, "old school decorations like an old television set, PVC cord chairs and even long forgotten snacks like haw flakes" (Lee 2016).

14 Author interview with Darren Teoh, January 21, 2017.

15 Author interview with Darren Teoh, January 21, 2017.

16 This is despite his qualms about the petty food wars between Malaysia and Singapore, fighting over claims about which nation invented chicken rice.

17 The Malay word *gandum* is an Urdu word meaning "wheat." The fact that it is in Urdu might explain wheat's routes/roots to Malaysia.

18 *Rambai*, a fruit that grows in the wild, has not been commercialized, and is thus not well known locally. Moreover, due to rapid urbanization and deforestation, it is becoming rarer. It is usually eaten raw, in a tossed salad (*ulam*), or by cooking the skin of the fruit, lending a sour taste to coconut curry (*masak lemak*).

19 Author interview with Darren Teoh, January 21, 2017.

20 *Ulam raja* (lit., "the king of salads") (*Cosmos caudatus*) is originally from Latin America, but was brought by the Spaniards to the Philippines and then to the rest of Southeast Asia (Bodeker 2009).

21 Cocoa was first grown in Melaka in 1778, but entered Southeast Asia via the Philippines in the late 1660s from Latin America (Streak 2003, 64).

22 Author interview with Darren Teoh, January 21, 2017.

23 The overall indigenous population is 13.8 percent but the majority of this includes groups from East Malaysia. The indigenous population of Peninsular Malaysia constitutes a mere 0.7 percent of the national population (IWGIA n.d.).

24 For example, Johor *laksa* uses spaghetti instead of rice noodles "because Sultan Abu Bakar—known as the 'Founder of Modern Johor' and said to be the first Malay ruler to visit Europe in 1866—instructed his royal chefs to use spaghetti instead of the traditional rice noodles in his laksa Johor" (Soon 2016).

25 Blogger VKeong concurs: "No, it's for really well-to-do people, they are not cheap, modern Malaysian restaurants." He also says that for most Malaysians, Malaysian food is still hawker food (VKeong, phone conversation with the author, February 8, 2017). The GST was removed by the new government after the May 9, 2018 general elections.

References

Augustin, Kerry-Ann. 2016. "The Good Earth." *New Straits Times*, July 31, 2016. https://www.nst.com.my/news/2016/07/161935/good-earth.

Aznan, Azmelia, and Omar Ariff Kamarul Ariffin. 2015. *Perak: A Journey for Food Lovers*. Kuala Lumpur: RNS Publications.

Bauman, Zygmunt. 2000. *Liquid Modernity*. Cambridge, MA: Polity Press.

Bodeker, Gerard. 2009. *Health and Beauty from the Rainforest: Malaysian Traditions of Ramuan*. Kuala Lumpur: Didier Millet.

Boym, Svetlana. 2001. *The Future of Nostalgia*. New York: Basic Books.

BV. 2015. "The NOMA of Malaysia" (review). *TripAdvisor.com*. December 15, 2015. https://www.tripadvisor.com.my/ShowUserReviews-g298316-d7785726-r334865796-Dewakan_Restaurant-Shah_Alam_Petaling_District_Selangor.html.

CCFoodTravel. 2012. "Wondermama @ Bangsar Village, Bangsar." *CCFoodTravel.com* (blog). July 23, 2012. https://ccfoodtravel.com/2012/07/wondermama-bangsar-village-bangsar/.

Chef Wan. [2006] 2011. *The Best of Chef Wan: A Taste of Malaysia*. Singapore: Marshall Cavendish International (Asia) Pte Ltd.

Chen Kuan-Hsing. 2010. *Asia As Method: Toward Deimperialization*. Durham, NC: Duke University Press.

Cooler Lumpur. n.d. "The Future of Modern Malaysian Cuisine: A Conversation with Darren Teoh and Isadora Chai." Big Food Fringe Festival. http://www.coolerlumpur.com/dangerousideas/programme.

Durai, Abirami. 2017. "A Modern Reworking of Colonial Hainanese Food." Star2.com. February 7, 2017. http://www.star2.com/food/eating-out/2017/02/07/a-modern-reworking-of-colonial-hainanese-food-anson-colonial-cafe/#Swilg5jcp8pXVYaq.99.

Duruz, Jean, and Gaik Cheng Khoo. 2014. *Eating Together: Food, Space, and Identity in Malaysia and Singapore*. Lanham, MD: Rowman and Littlefield.

Eat Drink KL. 2016. "Antara Restaurant @ Raja Chulan." *Eat Drink KL* (blog). June 19, 2016. http://eatdrinkkl.blogspot.my/2016/06/antara-restaurant-raja-chulan.html.

Fan, Fa-ti. 2016. "Modernity, Religion and Technoscience: One Small Cheer for Asia As Method." *Cultural Sociology* 10, no. 3: 352–68.

Ferguson, Priscilla Parkhurst. 2010. "Culinary Nationalism." *Gastronomica* 10, no. 1: 102–9.

Goh, Daniel. 2017. "Home Grown—The Peak Follows the Cocoa Bean as It Goes From Farm to Table. Featuring Chef Darren Teoh of Dewakan and Ong Ning Geng of Chocolate Concierge." *The Peak*. December 14, 2017. http://thepeak.com.my/palate/home-grown-peak-follows-cocoa-bean-goes-farm-table/.

Hollinger, David. 1995. *Postethnic America: Beyond Multiculturalism*. New York: Basic Books.

Hutton, Wendy. 2005. *The Food of Malaysia: 62 Easy-to-Follow and Delicious Recipes from the Crossroads of Asia*. Singapore: Periplus.

IWGIA (International Work Group of Indigenous Affairs). n.d. "Malaysia." Home. http://www.iwgia.org/regions/asia/malaysia.

Jamaluddin, Lira. 2017. "MC Mentor Mentee: Isadora Chai." *Marie Claire*, March 20, 2017. http://marieclaire.com.my/lifestyle/mentor-mentee/mc-mentor-mentee-isadora-chai/.

Jessica. 2016. "The Culinary Genius of Dewakan's Darren Teoh." *Going Places Magazine*, February 19, 2016. http://www.goingplacesmagazine.com/the-culinary-genius-of-dewakans-darren-teoh.

Krich, John. 2015. " 'Nouvelle Malaysian' Chefs Break Gastro-Boundaries." *Nikkei Asian Review*, October 6, 2015. https://asia.nikkei.com/NAR/Articles/Nouvelle-Malaysian-chefs-break-gastro-boundaries.

Laudan, Rachel. 2013. *Cuisine and Empire: Cooking in World History*. Berkeley: University of California Press.

Lee, Khang Yi. 2015. "Dewakan Shakes Up the Dining Scene With Modern Malaysian Cuisine." Malaymail.com, July 19, 2015. https://www.malaymail.com/news/eat-drink/2015/07/19/dewakan-shakes-up-the-dining-scene-with-modern-malaysian-cuisine/935779.

Lee, Khang Yi. 2016. "Iron House Kopitiam: Pulling in the Crowd with Delicious Local Food." *The Malay Mail Online*, March 6, 2016. http://www.themalaymailonline.com/eat-drink/article/iron-house-kopitiam-pulling-in-the-crowd-with-delicious-local-food.

Lee, Sook Ching. 2014. *Malaysian Home Cooking: A Treasury of Authentic Malaysian Recipes*. Singapore: Marshall Cavendish International (Asia) Private Limited.

Lim, Grace. 2017. "Cocoa High: Chocolate Concierge Makes Its Chocolate Bars Entirely in Malaysia." *Focus Malaysia Business Weekly*, July 29–August 4, 2017. http://www.chocconcierge.com/press/2017-07-29_Focus_Indulgence.pdf.

Lim, John. n.d. "Where Chefs Eat: Isadora Chai." Sea.askmen.com. http://sea.askmen.com/where-chefs-eat/1733/article/where-chefs-eat-isadora-chai.

Lim, Stephanie. 2016. "#HotRightNow: Salted Egg Yolks: 5 Things You Should Know about Singapore's Trendiest Ingredient." Michelin Guide Singapore. April 26, 2016. https://guide.michelin.sg/en/salted-egg-yolks.

Lonely Planet. n.d. "Wondermama: Malaysian in Lake Gardens, Brickfields & Bangsar." Last accessed March 10, 2018. https://www.lonelyplanet.com/malaysia/kuala-lumpur/restaurants/wondermama/a/poi-eat/1316742/356949.

Manja. 2018. "About Us." http://manja.com.my/index.php#abouut-us.

Mehta, Manik. 2015. "New York MATRADE's Malaysian Food Promotion Gets 'Great Response.' " *BERNAMA*, December 7, 2015. http://www.ssig.gov.my/blog/2015/12/07/new-york-matrades-malaysian-food-promotion-gets-great-response/.

Musa, Norman. 2016. *Amazing Malaysian: Recipes for Vibrant Malaysian Home-Cooking*. London: Square Peg.

Mustafa, Marina. 2016. *Everything Sambal*. Kuala Lumpur: MPH Books.

Ng, Karmun. 2016. "Leading Ladies of F&B: Isadora Chai of Bistro à Table and Antara Restaurant." *Malaysia Tatler*. November 18, 2016. http://my.dining.asiatatler.com/features/leading-ladies-of-f-and-b-isadora-chai-bistro-a-table-antara-restaurant.

Ng, Nicholas. 2017. "Dewakan." Food For Thought. September 25, 2017. http://foodforthought.com.my/dewakan-review/.

O'Flaherty, Mark C. 2013. "Asia's Original Fusion Food." *Independent*, July 6, 2013. http://www.independent.co.uk/travel/asia/asias-original-fusion-food-8690141.html.

Poulain, Jean-Pierre, Laurence Tibère, Cyrille Laporte, and Elise Mognard. 2014. *Malaysian Food Barometer: An Initiative of the Chair of Food Studies, Food, Cultures and Health*. Malaysia. Subang Jaya: Taylor's Press.

Ragavan, Surekha. 2015. "Dewakan and Modern Malaysian Cuisine." *Time Out KL*, May 24, 2015. https://www.timeout.com/kuala-lumpur/food-and-drink/dewakan-and-modern-malaysian-cuisine.

Rajah, Carol Selva. 2013. *Malaysian Cooking: A Master Cook Reveals Her Best Recipes*. Singapore: Tuttle Publishing.

Ray, Krishnendu. 2016. *The Ethnic Restaurateur*. New York: Bloomsbury.

Roosth, Sophia. 2013. "Of Foams and Formalisms: Scientific Expertise and Craft Practice in Molecular Gastronomy." *American Anthropologist* 115, no. 1: 4–16.

Samanthawxlow. 2016. "Dewakan, Malaysia." *Will Be* (blog). September 9, 2016. http://www.samanthawxlow.com/2016/09/dewakan/.

Saw, Betty. 2009. *The Complete Malaysian Cookbook*. Singapore: Marshall Cavendish.

Soon, Ivy. 2016. "Laksa Johor." *The Star Online*, September 16, 2016. http://www.thestar.com.my/news/nation/2016/09/16/laksa-johor/#h1AwmRBKlHj8FAkz.99.

Streak, Judith. 2003. "An Analysis of the Cocoa Frontier in the Indian Ocean Rim Region." In *The Indian Ocean Rim: Southern Africa and Regional Cooperation*, edited by Gwyn Campbell, 64–76. London: RoutledgeCurzon.

Suanie. 2015. "Dewakan—Modern Malaysian Cuisine." *As Suanie Sees It* (blog). November 14, 2015. http://www.suanie.net/2015/11/dewakan-modern-malaysian-cuisine/.

Weston, Jay. 2014. "Malaysian Food Is Hot, Spicy, Delicious . . . and Here!" *Huff Post* (blog). August 20, 2014. https://www.huffingtonpost.com/jay-weston/malaysian-food-is-hot-spi_b_5691991.html.

Winston. 2013. "Eating Malaysian in Melbourne: Masak Masak & PappaRich." *The Hungry Excavator* (blog). July 7, 2013. http://www.thehungryexcavator.com/2013/07/eating-malaysian-in-melbourne-masak.html.

7

Eating to Live: Sustaining the Body and Feeding the Spirit in the Films of Tsai Ming-liang

Michelle E. Bloom

University of California, Riverside

The films of Malaysian-born Taiwanese auteur Tsai Ming-liang have received much scholarly attention but have not been studied through the optic of food. This is not surprising, since Tsai's slow-paced art-house films are not "food films," meaning that food preparation is not depicted, and food is rarely shown in close-up. Food does not play a central role in the life of any of the characters, nor is it crucial to their plots.[1] For Tsai, who evokes acts that rarely appear in feature films, such as urination and masturbation, eating is another bodily function rather than a source of pleasure. Though not an obvious object of study in Tsai's oeuvre, food plays important roles and focusing on it will offer an innovative reading of two of his films, his first Sino-French work, *What Time Is It There?* (你那邊幾點 *Ni neibian jidian*, 2001; hereafter, *What Time?*) and the Venice International Film Festival Grand Jury Prize winner, *Stray Dogs* (郊遊 *Jiaoyou*, 2013).

Tsai's films omit the culinary and aesthetic qualities of food, thereby challenging the concept of a glorified culinary nationalism. Along with the films of other art-house directors, such as the late Iranian auteur Abbas Kiarostami, Tsai's work has already been considered "international" rather than "Taiwanese" or even "Asian" (De Luca 2016, 24; Neri 2006, 66). A self-described drifter (Bloom 2015, 75), Tsai downplays the specificity of his adoptive country, Taiwan, and connects with European and especially French cinema (Neri 2006, 66; see also Bloom 2015). Like his hybrid national identity and his drifting, Tsai's films blur boundaries, such as those between nations; between haves and have-nots; and between life and death.

Although Tsai's intention to minimize indices of place, and thus nationality (Bloom 2015, 77–80), applies to food, the erasure is no more complete in terms of food than with respect to cultural and tourist icons. Traces of nationality remain in all cases, even if the national is plural, with Taiwanese elements melding with Asian ones (Nakano 2009; Moskin 2008). The Taiwanese-style boxed lunch and chopsticks seen in *Stray Dogs*, for example, together constitute Asian plating and utensils. Taiwanese boxed lunches (便當 *bian dang*) are inspired by the Japanese bento box paradigm for take-out food, and chopsticks are originally Chinese but used in slightly varying forms in multiple Asian countries (China, Japan, Korea) (Wang 2015). Utensils and plating thus embody intra-Asian crossover. However, since Taiwan is itself a linguistically and ethnically hybrid nation, its culinary and para-culinary (plating, utensils) hybridity simultaneously embody specific Taiwanese elements of eating practices and more general Asian elements.

In light of Tsai's conceptions of filmmaking and film viewing, one can view the notion of consuming the culinary "Other" or the unfamiliar in a different light. Tsai aims to make consumers of images uncomfortable, through unfamiliar slowness, and, doing so, unsettles us as much as coffee upsets the stomach of one of his Taiwanese characters visiting Paris. Whether the difference lies in fast versus slow or another dimension of unfamiliarity, Tsai evokes the positive dimension of being unsettled, of uncertainty and liminality, like that of Buddhist conceptions of the passage from one's human body into another form after death. Crossing borders, be they between types of film, national cuisines, social classes, or life and death, entails discomfort with the unfamiliar. Such border crossing encourages resisting the ease of what is known and embracing the more challenging, the slower, the less familiar, or getting outside of one's cinematic or culinary comfort zone. Tsai represents food as functional, commensal, and representative of psychic hunger, particularly through the depiction of family and commensality (or lack thereof), and Buddhist rites of passage between life and death.

Asian food films

Many of the best known Asian food films resonate with their non-Asian counterparts in that the culinary provokes transformation from repression to fulfillment. They also frequently represent iconic dishes of national or cultural importance. Meanwhile, Tsai's films depict nondescript foodstuffs with no portrayal of food preparation. Juzo Itami's early food film, the Japanese "noodle Western" *Tampopo* (1985), exemplifies the central role of an iconic dish, *ramen*. *Tampopo* also entails the narrative arc of transformation in portraying the eponymous character's training, the improvement of her *ramen*, and the renovation of her *ramen* shop. Another successful Asian food film, Taiwanese-American director Ang Lee's *Eat Drink Man Woman* (1994), depicts a former chef and patriarch who regains his sense of taste and, along with it, his lust for life, alongside his three daughters' self-fulfillment. Other examples of the genre, depicting triumphs in cooking competitions, include Taiwanese director Lin Cheng-sheng's biopic *27 °C: Loaf Rock* (2013); Raymond Yip's Hong Kong film *Cooking Up a Storm* (2017); Korean director Jeon Yun-su's *Le Grand Chef* (2007); and Hong Kong helmer Steven Chow's *The Gods of Cookery* (1996).

In contrast to these commercial films, Tsai Ming-liang's art-house oeuvre distances food from pleasure or other positive feelings. In this way, his films and some of his food scenes resonate more with images in Asian films depicting food in relation to trauma and violence. Such Asian films include Korean auteur Park Chul-soo's *301/302* (1995), which portrays the two female protagonists' obsessions with food. Like *301/302*, Hong Kong director Fruit Chan's *Dumplings* (2006) depicts a form of cannibalism. Compared to *301/302* and *Dumplings*, Tsai's films depict food most often in understated fashion, consistent with his undramatic portrayals of even the most taboo and potentially shocking physical acts, such as incest (*The River*, 1997). Nevertheless, he evokes food powerfully, with the intensity lying in the act of consuming, not in the images of the foodstuffs themselves. In *What Time?* and *Stray Dogs*, food serves as the object onto which psychic hunger or the longing for connection are projected. Tsai depicts food as a basic human need, but even for the marginalized, it is not only a means of sustenance, but also plays important psychic roles. Food blurs the distinctions between the physical and the spiritual, with the latter transcending the world of the living, for whom food serves as a means of connection to the dead.

Tsai's oeuvre: Intratextuality and Slow Cinema

Tsai's filmography constitutes an intratextual network of films that relate to each other (Lim 2007, 226), with the reappearance of characters from one to the next blurring the boundaries between the individual works. All ten of his feature films star Lee Kang-sheng, beginning with his early career "Taipei Trilogy" (*Rebels of the Neon God*, 1991; *Vive L'Amour*, 1994; and *The River*, 1997) and culminating in *Stray Dogs*.[2] The Taipei Trilogy, comprising Tsai's first three full-length films, inaugurates his tendency to recast the same actors, often as the same characters, with Lee Kang-sheng as Hsiao-kang, along with Lu Yi-ching as his mother in all three films.[3] The family constituted by Lee Kang-sheng as the son, Miao Tien as the father, and Lu Yi-ching as the mother seems to reappear beyond the trilogy, for instance shortly thereafter in *What Time?* Lee Kang-sheng once again plays Hsiao-kang, this time as a watch vendor who lives alone with his mother, and who sells his dual time zone watch to Shiang-chyi, a young woman headed for Paris.

A dozen years and five films later, Tsai stated that he would not have made *Stray Dogs* (2013), his tenth and most recent full-length film, if he had not worked with Lee Kang-sheng for twenty years (Jaivin 2015). Tsai was motivated by the desire to show his signature actor's aging face (Homegreen Films 2013). In the later film, Lee Kang-sheng no longer plays a young adult son. Instead, he has become a middle-aged father, homeless for most of the film, and with two children. However, to mix things up on a couple levels and to add to the ambiguity regarding the actors and characters, three different actresses play the maternal counterpart of Lee Kang-sheng as the father: Lu Yi-ching, the eldest of the trio, who was cast as Hsiao-kang's mother in *What Time?*; Chen Shiang-chyi, who was the much younger watch buyer destined for Paris in the same film; and Yang Kuei-mei who played a real estate agent in *Vive l'Amour*. The pragmatic reason that Tsai cast all three actresses was that he wanted to work with all of them again in what he thought might be his last film, since he was very ill at the time (Homegreen Films 2013). This unusual variation on the more common practice of actors and actresses reappearing time and again in films, which Tsai himself also and more often engages in, also evokes the Buddhist notion of reincarnation.

Born in 1957 in the small, peaceful town of Kuching, Malaysia, Tsai benefited from early exposure not only to film (the town had a dozen movie theatres), but also to the "very slow pace of life," which he brought to his filmmaking (Rivière 1994, 79, 81). In

Taiwan, and especially in Taipei, where he moved in the 1970s to pursue his education in theatre, because film was not an option, the pace of life was accelerated (Rivière 1994, 104). When he returned to Kuching, Malaysia as a "young person in the Chinese diaspora," he still found that "it's much slower, things hardly move there" (Rivière 1994, 83). The same pace applies to his cinematic oeuvre. In the excellent study, *Tsai Ming-liang and a Cinema of Slowness* (2014), Song Hwee Lim studies the most striking feature of the auteur's work. Tiago De Luca also lists Tsai as one of the practitioners of Slow Cinema, a movement named by the French critic Michel Ciment in 2003 and characterized by "measured pace, minimalist mise-en-scène, opaque and laconic narratives, and an adherence to the long take" (De Luca 2016, 24).

What Time? and *Stray Dogs* adhere to all of these characteristics. Both films consist of well under 100 shots each, as opposed to the approximately 500 to 1,900 shots in over 117,000 feature films from 151 countries from 1998 to 2017.[4] Although the range is great, even the genre at the lowest end, documentary, comprises five-fold more shots than Tsai's films. The length of shots in *Stray Dogs* ranges from under a minute to a fourteen-minute extreme long take. However, even at the lower end of the spectrum, a shot lasting between thirty seconds and a minute is still long by the Hollywood standard Average Shot Length (ASL) of four to six seconds.[5] Amplifying the sense of slowness in Tsai's films is the tendency toward a fixed camera and minimal dialogue. The minimal dialogue of *What Time?* is typical for Tsai, with his 2003 film *Goodbye Dragon Inn* counting only ten lines (Wang and Fujiwara 2006). *Stray Dogs* includes speech in about 25 percent of the shots. This figure, based on my own analysis, includes scenes with merely a word or two within a long take.[6] The words that are spoken stand out more because they are so few and infrequent.

Even though Tsai tends to downplay the importance of place in his films, he does characterize the lack of verbal communication as a phenomenon prevalent in his adoptive country: "The family members [in *The River*] don't have much to say to each other, because they're that type of family, one which is quite common in Taiwan" (Rivière 1994, 110). The same family appears in *What Time?* as in *The River*. Rather than unilaterally critiquing the families, or the Taiwanese cultural construction thereof, Tsai calls into question the power of dialogue to facilitate communication, instead suggesting the power of silence, or non-verbal communication and sound (Rivière 1994, 110). Because dialogue is minimal, those rare scenes when characters interact verbally are almost jarring, heightening the viewers' attention and bringing us into more familiar territory which has become unfamiliar in Tsai's soundscape.

Tsai's signature Slow Cinema provides the ideal means of depicting slow eating. The parallel processes of slow eating and Slow Cinema both offer critiques of postmodern urban life's fast pace, and attempt to put brakes on it, making consumers of food and images engage more mindfully. The Slow Food Movement was founded by Carlo Petrini and other activists in Bra, Italy in the 1980s in order to promote "good food, gastronomic pleasure, and a slow pace of life." (www.slowfood.com) The movement's Manifesto proposes slow food as an alternative to fast food, and a counter to the "fast life" that has "changed our lifestyle and now threatens our environment and our land (and city) scapes" (Slow Food 1989). Like Slow Cinema, Slow Food is reserved for those privileged enough to have the resources, time, and education to consume slowly. The underprivileged, the poor, and the uneducated may not have the means to take advantage, much less to appreciate slowness. They eat for sustenance, even if their engagement with food spills over into psychic terrain.

Homelessness

Tsai questions the very notions of food as choice and food as pleasure. For his homeless characters, who struggle to survive, food is merely a necessity. They eat to live, rather than live to eat. Food choice is presumably based on availability and price, not luxuries like health and sustainability. The Hsiao-kang character of *Stray Dogs* is not unemployed, but underemployed, as he ekes out a living as a "human billboard," holding signs for real estate. Such low-paid work, yielding 700–800 new Taiwan dollars, or about US$25 per day, puts the family near poverty level. Hsiao-kang does not earn enough to pay for housing, but can at least feed himself and his daughter, Yi-chieh, and his son, Yi-cheng, minimally, thus accounting for *Stray Dog*'s food scenes. This low-paying job helps explain the family's homelessness and food insecurity, while his advertising luxury real estate offers an ironic comment on his homelessness (Lisiak 2016, 837).

Tsai denies that *Stray Dogs* is about marginality or homelessness and reviewers such as Andrew Schenker (2013) concur that it is not a "social-problem film," consistent with Tsai's work in general. We may extrapolate from this claim that the director is not interested in the socioeconomic issue of food insecurity of the homeless or otherwise. Indeed, he says, "My films are not really about society. I'm not really interested in social questions" despite the notion that, "People think of this film as a film about people who live on the margins, who live in the lower strata of society" (Jaivin 2015). However, *Stray Dogs* goes beyond Tsai's intentions, raising important "social questions" despite the director's self-proclaimed disinterest in them.

Even Tsai contradicts his own stance, revealing his concern about social issues, for instance, in response to a question by interviewer Charles Tesson, the artistic director of the Critics' Week at the Cannes Film Festival. Tesson notes that *Stray Dogs* paints an even more miserable portrait than Tsai's earlier films, and that the more recent work is about "the vicissitudes of sustaining life (finding food and shelter)" (Homegreen Films 2013). Rather than refute that claim, Tsai himself expresses serious concern about socioeconomic issues:

> The world seems to change all the time, and yet it seems never to have changed. All the problems remain, and become worse: poverty, starvation, war, power, desire, avarice, hatred . . . When shooting this film, I often thought of one expression from Laozi, 'Heaven and Earth do not act out of benevolence; they treat all things as straw dogs.' [*Dao De Jing*, Ch. 5] Those poor people and their children seem to have been abandoned by the world, but they still have to live.
>
> Homegreen Films 2013, n.p.

In another response from 2013, Tsai told Agence France Presse that, "This is not a film about hope or despair. It's about a man who gives up, who lets himself go completely ... Everywhere we look, unemployment is increasing, homelessness is rising. Life is becoming more difficult for many, and it is those difficulties I wanted to explore" (DeHart 2013). Although he makes no reference to food, food insecurity of course goes part and parcel with homelessness. In the context of what one critic calls an "audaciously enigmatic vision of urban poverty" (Young 2013), *Stray Dogs* calls attention to the food insecurity of the homeless.

Commensality

In the absence of a table or even a home, the father and two children in *Stray Dogs* sit on a covered bench outdoors at night above a busy traffic intersection to consume their dinner. In this makeshift site for sharing a family meal, they nevertheless come together, eating, and even talking to each other.[7] Rather than sitting around a table or across from each other, they sit in a row, with the children on either side of their father, making him the center and allowing for dialogue between him and each of his children (Figure 7.1). Using disposable wooden chopsticks, they eat Taiwanese box lunches of the sort one might buy at a 7–11 in Asia and inspired by the Japanese bento box. The meals comprise what looks like fried chicken (or another fried protein), both noodles and rice, and some green and red foodstuffs, perhaps vegetables. Each character also has a paper cup presumably containing soup or hot water. The meals are unhealthy by

Figure 7.1 Film still of Hsiao-kang (Lee Kang-sheng) (center), his daughter, Yi-chieh (Lee Yi-chieh) (left), and his son, Yi-cheng (Lee Yi-cheng) (right), eating their boxed meal dinners outside on a covered bench. *Stray Dogs* (2013), dir. Tsai Ming-liang. Photograph by William Laxton. Reproduced by permission from Homegreen Films.

some standards, due to the fried entrée and the inclusion of two carbohydrates, which offer volume for low cost. However, the boxed meals are also copious and varied.[8]

Conversation enriches the basic but filling meal, going beyond silence to rudimentary exchange, which takes on added significance given the default of lack of dialogue in *Stray Dogs* as in Tsai's oeuvre more generally. Hsiao-kang asks his daughter what she did that day, expressing interest in her in a manner unprecedented in terms of human interactions between adults in Tsai's films, which also do not typically depict children. The conversation also touches on food, as the girl tells her father that she bought "stuff" (東西 *dongxi*), but then answers his follow-up question by specifying "cabbage" (高麗菜 *gaoli cai*), which plays a major role in a scene to be examined below. The lunch box foods appear as details in a larger shot. Hsiao-kang rebukes his daughter, Yi-chieh, for eating only the dried tofu. The father is clearly offering typical parental encouragement for a child to clear her plate, to eat everything rather than picking out selected items, for her well-being and to avoid food waste. In a rare moment in the film, not only because it contains dialogue, but also because it addresses the nutritional value of food rather than merely treating it as sustenance, Hsiao-kang tells Yi-chieh to "Eat to grow big and strong." He also gives her something visually and verbally unidentified from his plate, calling it "nice." His daughter's hesitant eating, not unusual for a child, indicates that she is not so food-deprived that she will gobble up anything.

The daughter's slow-paced eating serves as a compelling parallel for Tsai's long takes and the resulting pace of *Stray Dogs* and his films in general. At 2.5 minutes, the family meal sequence is not one of Tsai's longer scenes even if it consists of a single shot. In addition, due to the exceptional dialogue and the relatively high level of activity (eating), this rhythm reflects the father and son's wish to fight against the slowness characterizing Tsai's filmmaking. Hsiao-kang says to his daughter, "Eat properly, or we'll have to wait for you," suggesting that proper eating is faster paced and that they need to move on rather than linger. Such an attitude makes sense given that they are eating outdoors in poor weather and without a table. The attitude also reflects that even though homeless and sleeping in an abandoned space, they still adhere to a schedule which includes hygiene: the next family activity is washing up, including brushing their teeth, together, in a public restroom. Yi-cheng's comment to his sister Yi-chieh that she should "hurry up and finish" might apply equally to the virtual spectator addressing the director or his cinematographers (Liao Pen-jung, Lu Ching-hsin and Shong Woon-chong) as well, contrary to Tsai's favoring of slowness. Hsiao-kang and Yi-cheng's concern that Yi-chieh won't finish eating if she continues at such a slow pace parallels the impatient viewers' wondering if *Stray Dogs*, like Tsai's other films, will ever end. Tsai joked about the soporific qualities of his films prior to a screening of *Stray Dogs* at Australian National University (Jaivin 2015), even as he aims to challenge the passive viewer.

Solo eating

Another slow food scene, in which Hsiao-kang, on break from sign holding, consumes chicken, including a chicken leg (Figure 7.2), entails the sole image of clearly identifiable

Figure 7.2 Film still of Hsiao-kang devouring chicken on a meal break from his job as a human billboard. *Stray Dogs* (2013), dir. Tsai Ming-liang. Photograph by William Laxton. Reproduced by permission from Homegreen Films.

food in *Stray Dogs*. The framing precludes seeing where or how Hsiao-kang is seated; whether squatting or standing, for instance. The image also fails to portray the poultry photogenically, unlike close-up shots, which tend to do so in food films. The chicken is as drably colored as the gray sky. The scene highlights Hsiao-kang's hunger, his unrestrained consumption of the meal. The single shot sequence begins *in media res*, when Hsiao-kang is already in the midst of devouring the piece of fowl, which he holds in the same hand as a pair of disposable chopsticks. After putting down the chicken bone, Hsiao-kang uses the chopsticks to shovel the rice and cabbage accompanying the poultry into his mouth. We hear not only Hsiao-kang breathing and chewing but also the sound of chicken bones being torn apart. We also occasionally see Hsiao-kang's teeth and scraps of food in his mouth and on his chin as he chews and sucks the bones. At one point, he licks a crumb of chicken off his lip.

This close-up, even intimate, view of the act of eating, of the exterior and even a bit into the interior of Hsiao-kang's oral cavity, resonates with the portrayal by Franco-Tunisian director Abdellatif Kechiche of his characters eating couscous in *Secret of the Grain* (2008), complete with shots capturing food in their mouths as they chew. Kechiche himself comments on these shots as intentional efforts to create intimate connections between his characters and viewers, and of showing the minute details of their existence (Kechiche 2007). Such unglamorous and detailed depictions of body parts in action, engaged in a mundane daily activity, resonate with Tsai's portrayals. The more than three minute close-up in *Stray Dogs* of Hsiao-kang eating chicken contains no camera movement, no action other than chewing and the movement of the tall windswept grass and no dialogue. These absences amplify the slowness of the sequence shot (Lisiak 2016, 842), while the close-up focuses on the person consuming and the process of consumption, not on the food being eaten, since the meal is unremarkable, in terms of ingredients and presentation alike. The antithesis of "food porn," the images make us empathize with Hsiao-kang but fail to whet our appetite for his meal. Tsai's films offer the cinematic equivalent of meals to contemplate and remember, rather than fast food, which offers immediate gratification with little investment.

Hypermarket

Unlikely as it seems, the corporate hypermarket provides food, shelter, and even nurturing for homeless children, ironically from a "broken home," within the alienating urban space of contemporary Taipei. The hypermarket, which serves as a repeated setting in the film, often intercuts with the blustery, rainy Taipei streets where Hsiao-kang holds signs. Carrefour, a French chain of hypermarkets (defined by the company as a large store of 2,400–23,000 square meters), first entered the Taiwan market in 1989. This hypermarket offers "a wide range of food and non-food items, low prices and targeted promotions" (Carrefour, n.d.). This is the only site where we see the characters in *Stray Dogs* acquire food. Given that the hypermarket is a capitalist enterprise, it is ironic that the store is also a source of human contact and caring. In terms of both literal and emotional sustenance, Carrefour, the food store equivalent of a blockbuster movie and thus the antithesis of Tsai's Slow Cinema, provides a positive role in Hsiao-kang's children's lives. Nicely distinguishing between the color palette of the exterior or urban space, on the one hand, and the interior of the store, on the other hand, Schenker (2013) comments upon the "stark contrast" between the "greys of Taipei," and the store's "eye-bleeding neon which suggests something of a wonderland for the youngsters." The glaring difference between exterior and interior contrasts Tsai's more general blurring of boundaries.

The first Carrefour scene, more alienating than the subsequent ones, portrays people sitting at tables in what is presumably an in-store food court, without any connection and in one case, without any food. This sequence shot, offering a diagonal view of rows of tables in the food court, requires the viewer to watch the young girl restlessly fidgeting while seated, with her feet in motion. The camera stays still, capturing her for much of the more than a minute-long shot as she looks longingly at the ample bowl of noodle soup that the man across the table from her is consuming (Figure 7.3). The juxtaposition of the unidentified man and Hsiao-kang's daughter distinguishes between "have" and "have-not." We watch the anonymous man consume his food, oblivious to Yi-chieh. This calls into question the power of the table as anything more than a literal structure, a symbol of commensality lacking the power to bring people together around food and conversation, in the absence of existing connections or efforts to reach out. In this case, the man shows no sign of concern for the little girl; not a word or look is exchanged between them.

Within the space of the store, free samples which the brother (Yi-cheng) and sister (Yi-chieh) consume offer tastes of food, bits of sustenance, with minimal visual

Figure 7.3 Film still of Yi-chieh, at a table with an unidentified man consuming soup in the food court at the Carrefour hypermarket. *Stray Dogs* (2013), dir. Tsai Ming-liang. Photograph by William Laxton. Reproduced by permission from Homegreen Films.

attention to the particular foodstuffs in question. The minute-long scene is far denser than most in the film, between the crowd of people and plethora of merchandise in conjunction or disjunction with various types of sound with ambiguous sources and meanings. It is often unclear who is saying what and what they are saying.[9] The first sample that the siblings consume is unidentified. Echoing the vendor's warning and answering his younger sister's question, the brother tells her that the contents of the cup are hot and advises her to blow on it, but it is only a food sample used here to satisfy the appetite. The camera focuses on the dense crowd of shoppers and the products for sale rather than on foodstuffs, although a vendor dishes out what are identifiable visually as noodles, offered with a choice of thirteen different sauces. The choice among so many options reflects the proliferation of products in the global capitalist economy, as seen in mainland Chinese artist Liu Bolin's 2010 "Supermarket" photographs in his "Hiding in the City" series (MEP 2017). Just as Yi-chieh is dwarfed by the size of the products and displays, and the sampled products come in numerous varieties, Liu Bolin's own image "disappears" into the shelves holding multiple products in myriad varieties.

The Carrefour hypermarket develops the relationship between the homeless family and food, portraying the girl as a consumer instead of a marginal observer. The size of the hypermarket accentuates the age-appropriate diminutive stature of Hsiao-kang's daughter, an underaged consumer. The girl's size and youth are underscored within the store, densely packed with food products and consumers alike, her head barely reaching above her shopping cart. Similarly, Yi-chieh can barely reach her chosen cabbage, as the mountain of them on the counter rises above her head. This gives the store manager, played by Lu Yi-ching, cast as Hsiao-kang's mother in Tsai's previous films, a chance to perform a maternal role. Extending this role, the store manager later helps the girl wash her smelly hair in the restroom, cautions her to be careful and aids her in putting the cabbage in the bag and then the cart. A basic dialogue ensues: the girl utters, *xie xie* (謝謝 "Thank you"), eliciting the store manager's *bukeqi* (不客氣 "You're welcome"). The dialogue, which consists of polite formalities, takes on great significance since silence is the default in Tsai's films. Here, it evokes human connection even in the sterile, capitalist space of the supermarket.

Through the character of the Carrefour store manager, *Stray Dogs* highlights the food waste in the face of food insecurity. This problem is addressed explicitly in documentaries such as French director Agnès Varda's *The Gleaners and I* (1995), in which potatoes and other produce which do not conform to normative standards of size and shape, metaphors for non-normative humans, are deemed unfit to sit on grocery store shelves, while people go hungry. Tsai's art-house film brings to light this contradiction powerfully, as the manager checks expiration dates on merchandise, then removes it from shelves, even though such dates are marketing tools rather than true indicators that the contents are no longer viable (Bloom 2010, 162–7). A shot showing the manager washing her hands in the warehouse area, not once but twice after smelling them, includes images of packages of ostensibly expired meat in the background. As Neil Young (2013) puts it, the store manager takes "out-of-date but perfectly edible supermarket produce to a pack of placid stray dogs." Consistent with Buddhist philosophy, which blurs the boundaries between animals and humans in terms of reincarnation, Tsai suggests that humans, and specifically Hsiao-kang and his children, are "stray dogs." In an alienating postmodern world, human beings and non-human animals need food for survival and caring for nourishment.

Ravaging cabbage

Slowness characterizes most but not all shots in *Stray Dogs* as well as *What Time?* Similarly, a languid pace characterizes the eating in the films, but not consistently so and certainly not always, or in any case, with different rhythmic nuances. Hsiao-kang's consumption of the chicken meal, which may be read as reflecting physical hunger, is voracious but not fast at least in terms of screen time, lasting the duration of a nearly four-minute sequence shot. But the intensity of Hsiao-kang's later ravaging of the cabbage that his daughter buys should not be mistaken for its speed. The shot lasts more than thirteen minutes, almost as long as the film's longest take. Beyond the differing levels of intensity, an important distinction between the cabbage sequence and the chicken scene lies in the latter reflecting physical hunger, and the former evoking figurative hunger, even despair about his life. Of course, physical and psychic hunger overlap.

The children's personification of the cabbage sets the stage for the father's eroticization of it. Indeed, anthropomorphizing or "gynomorphizing" the cabbage is quite apt, as the unit of the produce is already called a "head" in both English and

Chinese (頭 *tou*). Yi-chieh draws a face on it. She and Yi-cheng then play with naming options, including the family surname (Lee), as well as "Miss Cabbage" or "Miss Big Boobs." The children are playful, breaking into a laughing fit upon mention of the second epithet, anticipating their father's uncontrollable crying. Yi-chieh calling her prepubescent brother's evocation of large breasts "weird" foreshadows her father's violent and sexual treatment of the cabbage.

In the hands of the middle-aged actor (Lee Kang-sheng), the scene takes a violent turn, reflecting the character's desperation and psychic hunger. When Hsiao-kang rejoins his children in the space where the family is squatting, he finds the cabbage in bed next to him. Tsai gave his signature actor the cabbage and free rein to do with it what he wanted (Homegreen Films 2013). The father character smothers the personified cabbage with a pillow, then uses his fingers to penetrate the eyes drawn on with lipstick, in a form of rape. He rips off leaves and chews them, progressing from one at a time to a bunch in hand to biting directly into the head, ravaging it. Hsiao-kang pulls the cabbage apart with both hands and then stuffs bunches of leaves into his mouth until they fall from the orifice and hands. As Jonathan Rosenbaum (2017) says of the cabbage, the father "attack[s], shred[s], and devour[s] it in a paroxysmal frenzy." Hsiao-kang finally sobs, the tears falling from his eyes in this heart-wrenching scene paralleling the downpour throughout this scene and much of the film. As a father unable to house his children and stuck doing dehumanizing work in a dreary environment, Hsiao-kang wails in a despair he is unable to articulate, but can enact, embodying it before a simulation and symbol of a human. The profound sobs speak volumes more than the basic dialogue he engages in with his children at the family dinner scene. Although he maintains a mere facade of an intact self in the face of his children, the act of expressing paternal care and concern is valuable and authentic.

Hsiao-kang's breakdown recalls the meltdown of Alfred Molina as the Count Reynaud in Lasse Hallström's food film *Chocolat* (2000). Prompted by his Lenten and conjugal abstemiousness, Reynaud breaks the window to enter the French village *chocolaterie*, ravages the Easter display, then laughs hysterically until that turns into sobbing. The scenes of ravaging in *Chocolat* and *Stray Dogs* both depict breakdowns resulting from deep longing. In each, hysterical laughter becomes uncontrollable crying. The chocolate and the cabbage are foodstuffs onto which the Count Reynaud and Hsiao-kang project their deprivation, which is so deep that the psychological becomes physical. Reynaud's wife has left him, so he has experienced sexual deprivation as well as the renunciation of certain foods during Lent. Hsiao-kang's deprivation stems more from the despair of an undignified job and homelessness. Both characters' desperate needs for human connection manifest as uncontrollable violence, albeit toward inanimate objects that are surrogates for humans and specifically females. The count begins by decapitating and fully fragmenting a chocolate statue of a female nude and Hsiao-kang ravages the anthropomorphized cabbage which his children have personified as female. The Chinese phrase 性饑渴 *xingjike*, meaning "hunger for sex," like the English language connotation of appetite in terms of food and sex, explains the violent, erotic nature of both characters' breakdowns even if the hunger is not for food.[10]

Offering food

Blurring the boundaries between life and death in the context of Buddhism, food in *What Time?* is served but not always eaten—at least not by the living. As opposed to feeding the living, one of the more important roles of food in the film is to nourish the spirits of the dead. Therefore, images of foodstuffs are consumed visually by the film's spectators, but the food itself remains intact. Whether offered to the dead or the living, or those in liminal or ambiguous states, food offerings are symbolic. Corrado Neri (2006, 67) suggests that *What Time?* "situates itself in a perverse magical realism—a dreamlike, indefinite space where living and dead can communicate and interact." In Taiwan, as Neri explains, "there is a strong interest in spirits and mediums, a deep faith in the interaction between living and dead ... The popular culture of everyday life is absorbed by both its narrative (infinite ghost stories, spectres everywhere) and visual aspects (temples and offerings in every household, shop and bus)" (Neri 2006, 70).

Hsiao-kang's father, played by Miao Tien, has a ghostly presence even in the film's opening scene, in which he appears to be alive. Blurring the boundaries between father and son, Hsiao-kang's absence from this scene sets the stage for his father's disappearance in the sense of death. Miao Tien's death in turn foreshadows his reapparition in Paris at the end of the film. At the outset of *What Time?* the central foodstuff is dumplings, a quintessentially Chinese and specifically Northern Chinese dish popularized throughout Asia and beyond. The food preparation is not entirely visible nor is it fully offscreen or implied; instead, it is conjured up partially, both visually and sonically. The wide shot of Miao Tien offers a full view of his back and leg, cut off by the frame of the half-open kitchen door, which covers his head as well. Tsai reveals little through the yellow-tinted translucent panel in the door: the partly obstructed and filtered view sets the stage for Miao Tien's role as an apparition. The half-open kitchen door allows us to hear the staccato sounds of food preparation, anticipating another ghostly moment, when Shiang-chyi, in her Paris hotel room, hears footsteps. Miao Tien turns off the light before he emerges fully from the kitchen about ten seconds later, the darkness contributing to the already ambiguous, eerie scene.

After walking from the kitchen with the plate of dumplings, he sets it down on the table next to the rice cooker, puts down a pair of chopsticks and a pack of cigarettes, lights up (Figure 7.4), and then leaves the table twice, within a shot of nearly four minutes with a fixed camera. Miao Tien gets up to call out to Hsiao-kang to come to the table—but elicits no response or exchange: this total absence of dialogue stands at the extreme of the spectrum from dialogue to silence even in Tsai's films. Hsiao-kang appears only after an abrupt cut, holding an urn of what are presumably his father's ashes as he sits in the back of a car. Miao Tien makes what amounts to an unintended offering to his son, who turns out to be absent, setting a precedent for the father's subsequent substitution in the posthumous role of the absentee at the table: Miao Tien's widow later makes a ritual offering of food for her late husband through a similar place setting intended for a person who is missing in body but present in spirit.

Ritual offerings and hawker food converge in one of the film's rare representations of food preparation, when the widow stops at a stand selling duck on a Taipei street. Framed by the stall with the hawker's body and head interrupting the long row of full,

Figure 7.4 Film still of Miao Tien (Miao Tien), with a plate of dumplings he has prepared for his absent son, Hsiao-kang. *What Time Is It There?* (2001), dir. Tsai Ming-liang. Photograph by Lin Meng-Shan. Reproduced by permission from Homegreen Films.

cooked ducks hanging from above, the vendor uses his knife skills in a manner recalling the manual manipulations of Chef Chu cutting a live fish at the opening of Ang Lee's *Eat Drink Man Woman* (1994). In *What Time?* we watch Lu Yi-ching from behind, to the left of the hawker, as she in turn watches the preparation of the duck for take-away. The quick percussive clanks of the hawker's knife hitting the chopping block are as significant as the image. A cut immediately to the widow bowing at the home altar, where she places incense and then the duck, indicates that it is an offering for her late husband. The duck, like the dumplings, is a quintessentially Chinese dish, with both specialties hailing from Northern China. Neither is exclusively Chinese, as other Asian and non-Asian national culinary traditions offer their own styles of both dishes (Polish *pirogi*, French *canard à l'orange*, among endless other varieties). However, the concept of food as ritual offering narrows the scope to Buddhist and other religious traditions with such food-related rites. Ritual offerings do not necessarily go uneaten. Unlike the dumplings prior to Miao Tien's death, the duck is consumed, as the widow retrieves it to place it among the other dinner offerings on the table where she eats with her son.

Tsai's version of commensality not only omits dialogue, substituting unspoken language, but also includes those absent in human bodily form because they are deceased. Hsiao-kang and Lu Yi-ching have a conflict about their absent father and husband, respectively: the son calls his mother "crazy" for taping up the windows because the light will bother her deceased husband, but he himself urinates into a bag at night for fear of encountering his father's ghost if he goes to the bathroom. Lu Yi-ching sips plum wine at a romantic table set for two, with a candle and glass of wine

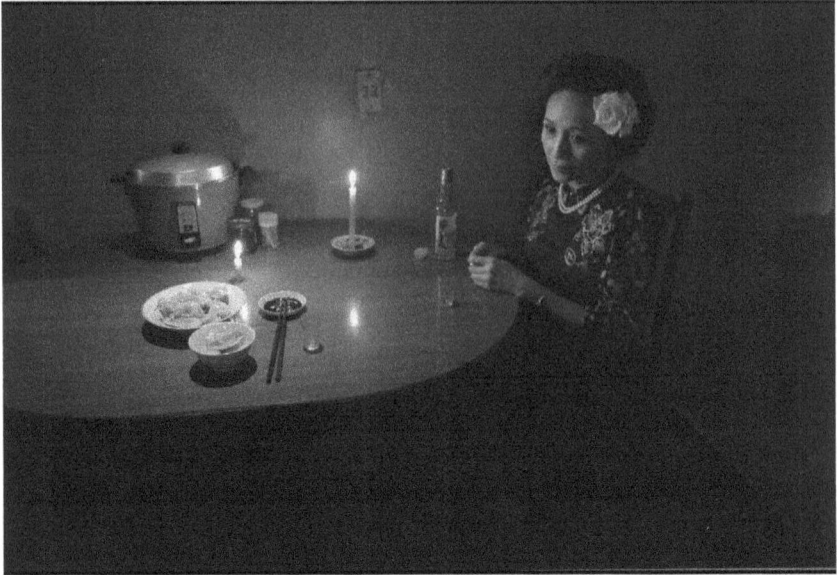

Figure 7.5 Film still of Hsiao-kang's mother (Lu Yi-ching), dressed up for dinner and seated next to a place setting for her deceased husband, Miao Tien. *What Time Is It There?* (2001), dir. Tsai Ming-liang. Photograph by Lin Meng-Shan. Reproduced by permission from Homegreen Films.

presumably for Miao Tien's ghostly presence (Figure 7.5). The scene immediately following, in which the widow masturbates with a cane headrest in the presence of her husband's photographic portrait (Martin 2003), affirms her attentions to his lingering ghostly presence. Indeed, Hsiao-kang's mother wakes up her son at midnight because she notices a time change on the clock and interprets it as the return of her husband and his request for food, rather than recognizing it as her son's effort to synchronize the clock to Paris time. Lu Yi-ching puts out chopsticks for three, including Miao Tien, whose place setting lies between hers and her son's. When his mother gives him an Asian-style ceramic soup spoon holding expensive, unidentified Chinese medicinal pills, he slides it toward his father's place setting, in a sarcastic remark on his mother's belief in his father's presence and as a means to avoid taking the pills. By contrast with Hsiao-kang, who is skeptical, his mother believes she is fulfilling her responsibilities toward her husband, according to the Buddhist "belief in the power of ritual action, performed by others on the deceased's behalf" to ensure a superior rebirth (Cuevas and Stone 2007, 8; Ladwig and Williams 2012, 1).

Alienation from French food

Meanwhile, in Paris, the character played by Shiang-chyi, to whom Hsiao-kang has sold his watch, encounters French food, but not as a source of pleasure. Instead, it embodies her misery and alienation. At a lively bistro with shared tables and red-and-white gingham tablecloths marking the establishment as casual, Shiang-chyi turns to others to seek help ordering from a French language menu she studies but cannot decipher (Figure 7.6). Responding to her query for help, a Frenchman seated with a group at the table behind hers recommends the *tartare*, repeating the word several times, but Shiang-chyi does not understand. The man explains, in English, the *lingua franca*, that *tartare* is "French meat which is very fine." He does not specify that it is raw. Unlike Japanese food, contemporary Chinese cuisine includes little raw meat or fish.[11] Thus, *tartare* represents an unfamiliar word and concept for Shiang-chyi. Lost among French people speaking their language, which is foreign to her, she asks the young man if there is an English menu, but the camera cuts away from the scene before Shiang-chyi receives one, much less orders or eats. Tsai never returns to the scene, so her meal is not even started much less finished. By depicting numerous people in most of the bistro shots, Tsai suggests the commensality surrounding Shiang-chyi but not including her. He also amplifies it through sounds of lively conversation rather than through images. In terms of consumables, a basket of bread and glasses of wine appear, as adornment. The plates portray food vaguely, with the medium wide shots meaning that the contents on the plates, presumably meat and potatoes, are not large enough to appear as clearly identifiable. Tsai depicts French food as a distinct national culinary tradition no more than Taiwanese food.

Consistent with Shiang-chyi's culinary alienation and failure to engage in commensality in Paris, following the restaurant experience, she next appears in relation

Figure 7.6 Film still of Shiang-chyi (Chen Shiang-chyi) trying in vain to read a French menu at a Parisian bistro, before the Frenchman seated behind her offers his help. *What Time Is It There?* (2001), dir. Tsai Ming-liang. Photograph by Lin Meng-Shan. Reproduced by permission from Homegreen Films.

to food at a convenience store and, alone in her hotel room, she consumes the comestibles that she has purchased. Although such a small, neighborhood grocery store might offer a warmer exchange and environment than a supermarket, the notion that the grocer is wearing a winter jacket inside the establishment reflects the literal, wintry cold, which opposes Taiwan's tropical climate and serves as a metaphor for the emotional coldness the young woman experiences in Paris. The grocer even offers her a kind word of warning about her plastic bag and a courteous "Au revoir," but challenged by her lack of knowledge of French and her state of mind, Shiang-chyi remains silent. Her failure to engage in even basic pleasantries reflects her inability to connect, her distance, as opposed to warm, non-verbal communication, such as a smile would suggest.

What Time?'s final food scene portrays Shiang-chyi eating her packaged food items and fruit in very un-French fashion; namely, sitting on her hotel room bed rather than at a table in a home or a restaurant. Her solo eating of convenience-store food reflects how out of place she is in the City of Lights, where one typically or, at least, stereotypically eats well. Shiang-chyi's failure to engage in commensality reflects the isolation of being solo, away from her home country. The image of her sitting alone on her hotel bed, eating packaged cookies, along with a banana, reveals that she is not appreciating the "traditional" culinary benefits of being in France by buying food from *pâtisseries* (pastry shops) or *marchés* (outdoor markets), where food tends to be fresh rather than processed. The qualification of "traditional" implies accurately that France has moved in the direction of processed and fast foods in recent years, with the chain store Picard devoted to packaged frozen foods. Certainly, a large number of people living in France, as opposed to visitors, eat processed and fast foods. However, in the diegetic world of *What Time?*, Shiang-chyi's inability to take pleasure from the stereotypical French culinary delights, be they foods or restaurants, reads as alienation, not as a mere reflection of social reality.

Images of food are no more appetizing than shots of Paris are beautified. Like the city, food is functional. Shiang-chyi buys and drinks Vittel brand French bottled water, which she might just as easily have purchased at the Carrefour hypermarket in Taipei. Solitary consumption of food and drink contrasts the commensality characteristic of eating in general but especially in both France and Taiwan where, at least historically and on special occasions, meals tend to entail familial or social gatherings and lingering over multi-course meals. Despite socioeconomic disadvantage, the middle-aged father Hsiao-kang in *Stray Dogs* engages in more commensality during the take-out meal outdoors in the rain with his children than Shiang-chyi does in the crowded Parisian bistro in *What Time?* Although familial connections fail to alleviate the pain of homelessness, neither does socioeconomic comfort (the means to travel from Taiwan to Paris and to eat "out" rather than simply outside) ensure breaking down barriers between self and other to avoid alienation and solitude.

Conclusions

What Time? and *Stray Dogs* provide windows onto Taiwanese culture and society from vantage points that stray from the norm of eating as pleasure. Despite Tsai's lack of intention to call attention to the plight of the homeless, *Stray Dogs* demonstrates that the lack of means accounts in part for divorcing eating from pleasure. Consuming food is a bodily act, like excreting or urinating, masturbating or having intercourse. *What Time?* confirms this view: even though the characters have a place to live (an apartment), it does not necessarily qualify as a home in terms of emotional warmth. *Stray Dogs* expands the discussion of food security to show urban Taiwanese homelessness, focusing on those who live in precarity but are sometimes sheltered, other times not, who occupy liminal spaces between homelessness and having roofs over their heads, and who are thus ignored, forgotten, nearly invisible. *What Time?* broadens the parameters to the invisible: to humans who are no longer alive, ghosts, who have no bodily life but may appear on screen through Buddhist ritual offerings that keep the dead vital.

Tsai evokes Asian food, plating, and utensils in the context of Buddhist rituals rather than Taiwanese culinary nationalism. The urban Taiwanese culinary context, in the form take-out food or the poverty of its margins, emerges subtly despite the backgrounding of place and minimal cultural specificity. The failure to highlight French cuisine in the Paris scenes of *What Time?* confirms the minimal role of national cuisine. As seen in the cabbage scene in *Stray Dogs*, violence is intense but not directed to other humans, except symbolically, since the cabbage is anthropomorphized. The consumption of food in the literal, physical sense notably entails neither the typical culinary pleasure seen in the majority of food films nor the trauma portrayed in films depicting food disorders, starvation, and the like. Tsai's films focus on psychic hunger more than physical appetite. Food serves as either purely functional or symbolic of despair or of the liminal state between life and death. Tsai's cinematic representations of food in the context of socioeconomics, religion, and a hybrid nation are understated, nuanced contributions to the study of culinary nationalism, which call into question both the "culinary" and the "national."

Notes

1 These are four of Steve Zimmerman and Ken Weiss's (2005, 112) five criteria defining food films.
2 Ironically in light of its name, "The Taipei Trilogy" downplays the specificity of the city in question (Hong 2011), as do all of his films.
3 Regarding Tsai's tendency to work with the same actors and actresses from film to film, see Rivière (1994, 108).
4 Stephen Follows (2017) uses the Cinemetrics database to analyze the range of shots in movies by genre, beginning with documentaries and culminating in action films.
5 See Bordwell (n.d.) on ASL.
6 Tsai does focus on sound other than dialogue and includes musical numbers in *The Hole* and in *Face*, as Lisiak (2016, 846) points out.
7 For further discussion of talking (and writing) about food, see Ferguson (2014).
8 Thanks to Han-Hua Chao for her assistance with analysis of the foodstuffs in this scene.
9 My gratitude goes to Chenshu Zhou for her insights into this scene.
10 Thanks to Han-hua Chao for sharing her linguistic expertise.

11 In *Food of China*, Anderson (1990, 138) notes that boiling, steaming, and stir-frying
    are the most common methods of cooking in contemporary China, whereas eating
    foodstuffs raw is "quite rare," without limiting the comment to meat.

References

Anderson, Eugene N. 1990. *The Food of China*. New Haven, CT: Yale University Press.

Bloom, Jonathan. 2010. *American Wasteland: How America Throws Away Nearly Half of Its Food (and What We Can Do About It)*. Boston, MA: Da Capo Press.

Bloom, Michelle E. 2015. *Contemporary Sino-French Cinemas: Absent Fathers, Banned Books, and Red Balloons*. Honolulu: University of Hawai'i Press.

Bordwell, David. n.d. "Precise Tools in Film Studies (Brief Survey, 1974–2005)." Cinemetrics. http://www.cinemetrics.lv/bordwell.php.

Carrefour. n.d. "Hypermarkets." http://www.carrefour.com/content/hypermarkets.

Ciment, Michel. 2003. "The State of Cinema (M. Ciment)." Unspoken Cinema (blog), San Francisco Film Society. October 10, 2006. http://unspokencinema.blogspot.fr/2006/10/state-of-cinema-m-ciment.html.

Cuevas, Bryan J., and Jacqueline I. Stone, eds. 2007. *The Buddhist Dead: Practices, Discourses, Representations*. Honolulu: University of Hawai'i Press.

De Luca, Tiago. 2016. "Slow Time, Visible Cinema: Duration, Experience, and Spectatorship." *Cinema Journal* 56, no. 1: 23–42.

DeHart, Jonathan. 2013. "*Stray Dogs*: Tsai Ming Liang's Last Film Urges Us to Slow Down." *The Diplomat*, September 17, 2013. http://thediplomat.com/2013/09/stray-dogs-tsai-ming-liangs-last-film-urges-us-to-slow-down/.

Ferguson, Priscilla. 2014. *Word of Mouth: What We Talk About When We Talk About Food*. Berkeley: University of California Press.

Follows, Stephen. 2017. "How Many Shots Are in the Average Movie?" *Film Data and Education* (blog). July 3, 2017. https://stephenfollows.com/many-shots-average-movie/.

Homegreen Films. 2013. *Stray Dogs* (Pressbook). Homegreen Films: Taipei; JBA Production: Paris. http://newwavefilms.co.uk/assets/1066/Stray_Dogs_Pressbook__1_.pdf.

Hong, Guo-Juin. 2011. "Anywhere but Here: The Postcolonial City in Tsai Ming-Liang's Taipei Trilogy." In *Taiwan Cinema: A Contested Nation on Screen*, edited by Guo-Juin Hong, 159–81. New York: Palgrave Macmillan.

Jaivin, Linda. 2015. "In Conversation with Director Tsai Ming-lang [*sic*]: Stray Dogs." Published January 19, 2015. View from the South Conference, Australian National University TV. Video, 43:54. https://www.youtube.com/watch?v=IlSrm5zJ2Ag&t=10s.

Kechiche, Abdellatif. 2007. *Secret of the Grain (La Graine et le mulet)*. Interview with Kechiche/DVD Extra. UK: Criterion.

Ladwig, Patrice, and Paul Williams. 2012. "Introduction: Buddhist Funeral Cultures." In *Buddhist Funeral Cultures of Southeast Asia and China*, edited by Paul Williams and Patrice Ladwig, 1–20. Cambridge: Cambridge University Press.

Lim, Song Hwee. 2007. "Positioning Auteur Theory in Chinese Cinemas Studies: Intratextuality, Intertextuality and Paratextuality in the Films of Tsai Ming-liang." *Journal of Chinese Cinemas* 1, no. 3: 223–45.

Lim, Song Hwee. 2014. *Tsai Ming-liang and a Cinema of Slowness*. Honolulu: University of Hawai'i Press.

Lisiak, Agata A. 2016. "Making Sense of Absence: Tsai Ming-liang's Cinematic Portrayals of Cities." *City* 19, no. 6: 837–56.

Martin, Fran. 2003. "The European Undead: Tsai Ming-liang's Temporal Dysphoria." *Senses of Cinema* 27. http://sensesofcinema.com/2003/feature-articles/tsai_european_undead/.

MEP (Maison Européenne de la Photographie). 2017. "Liu Bolin: Ghost Stories." Exhibit. Maison Européenne de la Photographie. Paris, France. June–October.

Moskin, Julia. 2008. "The Steamy Way to Dinner." *The New York Times*, September 30, 2008. http://www.nytimes.com/2008/10/01/dining/01rice.html.

Nakano, Yoshiko. 2009. *Where There Are Asians, There Are Rice Cookers: How "National" Went Global via Hong Kong*. Hong Kong: Hong Kong University Press.

Neri, Corrado. 2006. "Past Masters, New Waves: Tsai Ming-liang/François Truffaut." 跨文本跨文化 *Transtext(e)s Transcultures: Journal of Global Cultural Studies* 1: 64–79.

Rivière, Danièle. 1994. "Scouting," translated by Andrew Rothwell. In *Tsai Ming-liang*, edited by Jean-Pierre Rehm, Olivier Joyard, and Daniele Rivière, 79–121. Paris: Dis-Voir.

Rosenbaum, Jonathan. 2017. "Performing Spectators: The Audience as Stray Dogs." Jonathan Rosenbaum. Last modified September 6, 2018. http://www.jonathanrosenbaum.net/2018/09/performing-spectators-the-audience-as-stray-dogs/.

Schenker, Andrew. 2013. "Stray Dogs." Review of *Stray Dogs*, by Tsai Ming-liang. *Slant Magazine*, September 25, 2013. http://www.slantmagazine.com/film/review/stray-dogs.

Slow Food. 1989. "Slow Food Manifesto." https://slowfood.com/filemanager/Convivium%20Leader%20Area/Manifesto_ENG.pdf

Tsai Ming-liang, dir. 2002. *What Time Is It There? (Ni neibian jidian)*. New York: Fox Lorber.

Tsai Ming-liang, dir. 2013. *Stray Dogs (Jiao you)*. New York: Cinema Guild.

Varda, Agnès, dir. 1995. *The Gleaners and I (Les glaneurs et la glaneuse)*. New York: Zeitgeist.

Wang, Q. Edward. 2015. *Chopsticks: A Cultural and Culinary History*. Cambridge: Cambridge University Press.

Wang, Shujen, and Chris Fujiwara. 2006. " 'My Films Reflect My Living Situation': An Interview with Tsai Ming-liang on Film Spaces, Audiences, and Distribution." *Positions: East Asia Cultures Critique* 14, no. 1: 219–41.

Young, Neil. 2013. "Of Cabbages and Kings: Tsai Ming-liang's 'Stray Dogs.'" Neil Young's Film Lounge. Last modified November 19, 2013. http://www.jigsawlounge.co.uk/film/reviews/straydogs/.

Zimmerman, Steve, and Ken Weiss. 2005. *Food in the Movies*. Jefferson, NC: McFarland.

8

The Politicization of Beef and Meat in Contemporary India: Protecting Animals and Alienating Minorities

Michaël Bruckert

French Agricultural Research Centre for International Development (CIRAD)

In September 2015 in Dadri, Uttar Pradesh (Map 3), a Muslim man named Mohammed Ikhlaq was beaten to death with sticks and bricks in his house by an angry Hindu mob over a rumor, spread by the local Hindu temple, that he had slaughtered a cow calf and consumed its flesh at home with his family. The police arrested eight of the presumed attackers, but some locals protested against these arrests, opposing the authorities and destroying shops. Threatened, the family of the victim had to move away from the village. When alleged links between some of the assailants and the Bharatiya Janata Party (BJP), the Hindu nationalist party ruling the country, were uncovered, Prime Minister Narendra Modi implicitly rejected such criticisms, deeming the lynching only as "saddening." A local villager later filed a petition in court, urging the police to register a First Information Report against Ikhlaq's family on charges of cow slaughter and animal cruelty. The rumor that sparked the murder eventually proved unfounded: the suspected meat seized in the fridge was only mutton (*The Hindu* 2015a, 2015b; *The Indian Express* 2016). Yet this fact adds only a bitter twist to an already disturbing outcome: above all else, this incident shows that in contemporary India people can be harassed or even killed for their food preferences. Several other attacks of the same kind have occurred over the ensuing three years, triggering a wave of outraged criticism for their political overtones, but also for the lack of unequivocal reaction by the Hindu Right.

It is well known that cattle has a special status in India. But it is perhaps less well known that beef has been consumed since ancient times and is still consumed now by some sectors of society. As a matter of fact, slaughtering cattle and eating bovine meat have never been homogeneously prohibited throughout the subcontinent. Yet the Hindu Right, stimulated by its recent political successes, has made the battle against beef and, to some extent, against meat in general, one of the priorities of its communal agenda. In this chapter, I will argue that the protection of the "holy cow" and the larger stigmatization of meat eaters in India are both the expression of deep-rooted structures of feelings and the result of a political mobilization of voters around the defense of a so-called "Hindu identity" (*hindutva*).

The case of contemporary India highlights the way food produces identities in an always polyvocal and never definitive way (Ray 2013). In the Hindu context, food is theoretically perceived as a bundle of fluid substances that circulate through and between the bodies (Daniel 1984). As a biological and moral matter, these substances connect and define the human, the divine, and the material realms, while participating in the stabilization, differentiation, and hierarchization of the socio-cosmic order. These highly transactional and relational properties give food the power to "encode messages" (Appadurai 1981, 508) and to convey multiform meanings and feelings, making it fit for emotional empowerment and for ideological appropriation (Berger 2011).

How has meat become a political tool in the hands of Hindu nationalists? In this chapter, I will unpack the cultural and political construction of meat and vegetarianism in India. Drawing on public discourse and action, on legislation, and on individual representations and practices that I studied in Chennai, the capital of the southern State of Tamil Nadu (Map 3), between 2012 and 2015, I will show how Hindu nationalism shapes the significations attributed to meat, and especially to bovine meat. At the same time, subaltern groups are resisting this process in multiple ways. I will argue that, in contemporary India, meat and cows are powerful objects, leveraged for electoral strategies and political control: they are used to draw a line between those considered as "good citizens" and those seen, at best, as "misguided fellows" or, at worst, as "traitors to the nation."

The politics of food in India raises questions about how communal divides are entrenched by producing and disciplining "eating subjects" whose stomachs and bodies are barred from ingesting allegedly immoral, impure, and "anti-national" foods. The global mobility of goods, capital, and people tends to foster uncontrolled food transactions, blurring the lines between people and social groups. By essentializing and subjugating foodways, the nation-state ensures the stabilization and polarization of imagined communities, making them prone to political mobilization.

Meat consumption in India

According to the figures provided by the National Sample Survey Office in 2011 (Ministry of Statistics of the Government of India), Indians eat an annual average of 3 to 4 kilograms of meat per person: 2 kilograms of chicken, 1 kilogram of mutton and less than 0.5 kilogram of beef. Fish consumption is also low with an annual average of 3 kilograms per person (NSSO 2012). (By way of comparison, the annual average of meat consumption in the United States exceeds 120 kilograms.) Though meat consumption is low in India compared to international standards, it still cannot be entirely dismissed. Only 30 percent of the population is strictly vegetarian (Yadav and Kumar 2006). Cereals and other carbohydrates account for almost half of caloric intake, yet animal flesh, mostly served as side dishes, supplies valuable protein in a context of prevalent malnutrition and anemia.

Individual meat consumption is the highest in the northeastern and southern states (respectively around 10 kilograms and around 5 kilograms) and extremely low in the northwestern states of the country (less than 1 kilogram). Far from portraying India as a country of culinary homogeneity and evenly distributed vegetarianism, these statistics draw a complex picture of contrasts in meat consumption. Remarkably, this uneven geography does not pertain to developmental indices, such as per-capita revenue, urbanization rate, or literacy rate. On the contrary, it appears to be correlated with cultural factors alone, such as the dominant religious and ethnolinguistic groups, the castes locally present, etc. Generally speaking, meat consumption is the highest where the percentages of Muslims, Christians, tribal populations, or members of the "low castes" are also the highest. Indeed, the status of meat is defined by lingering conceptions about religion and purity (Dumont 1970). Many Indians, especially Hindu Brahmins, followers of Vishnu (called Vaishyas) and Jains, embrace a pure vegetarian diet. For these groups claiming a superior ritual and moral status, meat is still seen as an impure food.

Even for those who do not strictly eschew "non-vegetarian" food, meat can be shunned as much as three times per week. Many Hindus still refrain from eating meat on days considered as auspicious by the Hindu calendar, when visiting a major temple, or preparing for a pilgrimage. "I don't want to be impure in front of god," a man in his forties told me to explain why he maintains a vegetarian diet before praying to his family deity. A temporary state of ritual defilement, for instance after the death of a relative or during menstruation, also implies meat abstinence: meat impurity should not be added to an already existing bodily impurity. Certain patterns of temporary meat abstinence are also commonly followed by Christians.

If a vegetarian diet is often considered as superior to a "non-vegetarian" diet, different meats are also ranked on a hierarchical scale. In South India, chicken and mutton (the flesh of goat or sheep) are the most commonly accepted meats. Although pork is seen as an impure food, beef definitely ranks the lowest. During the interviews, some families could not even pronounce the word "beef." Sometimes, a disgusted grimace was the only answer to my question "Do you eat beef?" In the context of caste, people are often defined by what they eat and do not eat. Ingesting bovine flesh is a taboo that few middle-caste and high-caste Hindus transgress, at least inside the house. Even Christian families who converted from Hinduism two or three generations ago, as well as Muslims claiming a superior social status, usually eschew beef. In broad terms, eating beef is still often associated with "untouchability." Indeed, Dalits (members of the castes formerly known as "untouchables") have long been responsible for removing and flaying cow carcasses. Even B. R. Ambedkar, a tireless champion of Dalits' rights, sought to end this practice of carrion eating to enhance Dalit respectability (Nair 2016, 14). Some Dalit families I visited in rural Tamil Nadu first tried to conceal their beef consumption in order to appear more respectable. However, many among the lower castes also praise beef for its economic affordability, its appetizing taste, and its medicinal virtues.

What do we exactly mean by "beef" in India? In fact, the flesh of cattle (the species *Bos taurus*) and that of buffalo (*Bubalus bubalis*) are often amalgamated, both in terms of organoleptic and "ritual" qualities: few Indians reject the former and accept the latter. However, the live animals do not share the same status. Although their role in the agropastoral life is rather similar (supplying milk, plowing the fields, providing manure and fuel, expanding the herd, etc.), cows' and buffaloes' respective religious attributes differ strongly. Indeed, buffaloes are rarely, not to say never worshiped in India. On the contrary, they are often seen as malevolent creatures: mythology associates them with Yama, the god of death, or with the demon Mahishasura, culled by the goddess Durga (Hoffpauir 1982). These opposing symbolic properties result in different bovine legal statuses, as will be mentioned later in this chapter.

A short history of vegetarianism and cow veneration

Due to the long prevailing ethos of high-caste Hindus, meat, particularly beef, is a contentious food in India—yet this has not always been the case. The impurity associated with animal flesh is a cultural and political construct, developed over many centuries. It has now been well documented that early Indians were meat eaters. In the Vedic period (around the first millennium BCE), the Brahmins (members of the priesthood) were in charge of sacrificing animals. These ritual sacrifices were at the center of the politico-religious order. The doctrine of *ahimsa* (non-violence), based on the "dread of destroying life" (Alsdorf 2010, viii) was then used as a "protective technique against the effects of the necessary violence in ritual" (Ghassem-Fachandi 2012, 11). Around 600 BCE, new ideologies started competing with this early form of Hinduism (called Brahmanism). Buddhism, Jainism, and the doctrine of renunciation reshaped the understanding of *ahimsa* and turned it into an ethical tool to oppose the blood baths performed by the Brahmins. At first, *ahimsa* had nothing to do with vegetarianism: the Buddha himself was a meat eater. However, fearing to be surpassed by these powerful spiritual rivals, Brahmins started integrating *ahimsa* in their conceptual repertoire, gradually giving up animal sacrifice. Over several centuries, legal texts such as the Laws of Manu set out contradictory prescriptions regarding meat eating (Robbins 1999, 403). It was not until medieval times that Brahmins and other groups claiming a high status (such as the Vaishyas) embraced a strict vegetarian diet as a marker of their supposed moral and ritual superiority.

In the Vedic period, cattle were the most prestigious animals, conferring power and wealth on their owners. Beside this economic and political dimension, a "mystical relationship between the cow and the universe" (Korom 2000, 187) is described in the Rigveda, canonical sacred texts dating approximately to the first millennium BCE. But this prestige also made cattle the favorite animals for sacrifice. It was only after the adoption of *ahimsa* by the Brahmins after the fifth century BCE that massive bovine sacrifices gradually stopped. The formal proscription to eat their flesh emerged quite late, in the fourth century CE.

Throughout the centuries, the enforcement of vegetarianism and of cow protection has been subject to different political and religious configurations. Abstinence from meat and beef consumption has benefited primarily from the spread of Brahmanism to South India long before the beginning of the Common Era, the conversion of the emperor Asoka to Buddhism in the third century BCE, as well as the emergence of the *bhakti* (devotion) movement (twelfth century) and the rise of its associated cult of Krishna (sixteenth century). However, although the appropriateness of beef consumption has been debated for centuries (Sébastia 2017, 106), it is mainly the emergence of Hindu reformist and nationalist movements in the nineteenth century, as well as Gandhi's rhetoric in the early twentieth century, that have reinforced the devotion toward the *gau mata* (mother cow) and the stigmatization of meat consumption in general.

The politicization of cow veneration and protection in India

Gandhi depicted cow protection as "the gift of Hinduism to the world" (quoted in Alsdorf 2010, 58). However, he tried not to make it a religious issue. Instead, he based his discourse in agronomic and economic arguments. Gandhi was not in favor of a full-fledged ban on cattle slaughter; rather, he hoped that Muslims themselves would freely decide to refrain from cow slaughter (Noronha 1994, 1447). In their time, reform and nationalist movements that emerged in the late nineteenth century did not adopt this supposed religious neutrality. The Arya Samaj, a reformist movement founded by Dayananda Saraswati in 1875, championed a return to an alleged Vedic "golden age." Its main objectives included the end of religious sacrifice, the protection of cattle, and, to some extent, the promotion of vegetarianism. Its sway and ascendency over Indian society strongly contributed to making the cow into an icon of Hindu identity. The first Indian cow protection society was created in 1882 under the authority of Bal Gangadhar Tilak, a radical Hindu nationalist. In the 1920s, the creation of the RSS (Rashtriya Swayamsevak Sangh—Organization of National Volunteers) marked the birth of modern Hindu nationalism. This paramilitary organization, inspired by Hitler's youth movements, sought, and still seeks, to promote the ideology of *hindutva*, implying that it is other groups that need to yield to mainstream religious culture.

Although the RSS and other Hindu nationalist organizations (often drawn together under the term Sangh Parivar, or the "family of organizations") did eventually open up to middle and low-caste members, their ideology still mostly draws upon high-caste Hinduism. These different movements tried to rally Hindus around their common opposition to both British colonialists and Muslims. Such a strategy paved the way to more frequent and violent communal confrontations in the late nineteenth century, most of them revolving around the issue of cow protection (Van der Veer 1994).

Legislation regarding cattle slaughter

At the time of Independence in 1947, Gandhi's views were taken into account when drafting the Constitution of the Republic of India: Article 48, entitled "Organisation of Agriculture and Animal Husbandry," stipulates as a directive principle that individual states shall "endeavour to organise agriculture and animal husbandry on modern and scientific lines and shall, in particular, take steps for preserving and improving the breeds, and prohibiting the slaughter of cows and calves and other milch and draught cattle" (Indian Kanoon n.d.). No explicit reference to religion is made in this article, which anchors the protection of cattle in utilitarian arguments and makes it a state responsibility.

Despite the rarity of cattle slaughter in the post-Independence period, Hindu nationalist movements did not relent: in 1952, their manifesto to strictly ban this practice gathered hundreds of thousands of signatures. In 1966, they organized massive demonstrations and protests in Delhi that ended in riots (Robbins 1999, 414). More recently, the proliferation of efforts to protect cows on a broad, communal basis made headlines with the political successes achieved by the Hindu Right. When it came to power in the territory of Delhi in 1994, the BJP passed the *Delhi Agricultural Cattle Protection Act*, making cattle slaughter a non-bailable offence with imprisonment up to five years and a fine of 10,000 rupees (Noronha 1994, 1447).[1] In 2006 in Chhattisgarh, the slaughter of any type of bovine, including buffaloes, was banned by the ruling BJP. In Madhya Pradesh too, beef consumption was made illegal in 2010—a step termed "draconian" by human rights activists (*The Times of India* 2012a; Mahaprashasta 2012). The story could have been similar in neighboring Karnataka. When he became the state's new chief minister in 2012, Jagadish Shettar, a politician affiliated with the BJP, passed a *Prevention of Cow Slaughter and Preservation (Amendment) Bill*, stipulating that only buffaloes and bullocks aged fifteen years or above could be slaughtered after obtaining a permission from a competent authority. The culling of any other cattle was considered as an offence with imprisonment up to seven years and a fine of 50,000 rupees (Kumar 2012). Opposition leaders termed this bill "anti-people." Activists campaigning for the rights of low-caste and Muslim workers argued that such a ban would affect the already poor laborers involved in the cattle, meat, and leather business. After it came back to power in the state in 2013, the Congress Party withdrew the bill, triggering hostile reactions among BJP members.

In 2014, during the campaign for general elections, the ban on cattle slaughter was once again made into one of the Hindu Right's priorities: the BJP candidate Narendra Modi blamed the ruling Congress Party for having orchestrated a "pink revolution," namely a boom in meat production epitomized by India's new position as the world's largest beef exporter (Singh and Jaipuria 2015). Although officially the exported bovine meat is only buffalo meat (termed carabeef), right-wing politicians tend to confuse the voters by lumping it together with cattle meat. After Modi was elected as prime minister of India in May 2014, these "cowlitics" became even more stringent. RSS offshoots asked again for a strict ban on cattle slaughter throughout the country and pushed to grant the cow the status of "national animal." At the state level, politicians have gained confidence: in 2015, a BJP-led government enforced an Act to ban the slaughter of bulls and oxen in Maharashtra, once again threatening livestock merchants', butchers', and tannery workers' livelihoods (Lukose 2015).

As animal husbandry is a state responsibility, the legislation regarding slaughter is divided along political and religious lines. The rules are stricter in the northwestern segment of the country, a region nicknamed the "Hindu belt," where Hinduism is both more conservative and more political. Elsewhere, such as in the northeast where large religious minorities and tribal groups eat beef, states tend to be less coercive. Other multi-confessional states, such as Kerala and West Bengal, which share a communist past and an attachment to secularism, are also more liberal in terms of cattle slaughter, imposing few restrictions.

Such regional clemency appears as an obstacle to the nationwide politics of *hindutva*. In May 2017, the central government issued a notification imposing restrictions on cattle sales on a national scale: anyone purchasing a bovine in a livestock market would have to prove that s/he was an agriculturist who had no intention to sell the animal within a period of six months (Rajalakshmi 2017a). The goal was a de facto ban on the sale of cattle and buffalo for slaughter throughout the country, preventing the production of beef. After a few months, following public upheaval and numerous petitions filed by activists and butchers, the Supreme Court suspended this notification.

The cow as a symbol of differentiation

In their defense of the "sacred cow," nationalist politicians easily find allies among right-wing groups. For several decades, paramilitary militias, whose members call themselves "cow vigilantes" (*gau rakshaks*), attack those suspected of indulging in beef production, transportation, or consumption. The infamous lynching of Mohammed Ikhlaq mentioned in the introduction is just one among many. Such attacks have actually intensified since the BJP took the power in 2014. In April 2017, two milk producers from Haryana were beaten by Hindu activists after they had bought cows at a cattle fair in Rajasthan. One of them succumbed to his injuries. In June of the same year, a teenager allegedly carrying beef was stabbed to death on a train in Haryana, while three Muslims suspected of stealing cows were beaten to death in a village in West Bengal (*Daily Sabah* 2017). In July, the truck in which Tamil Nadu Husbandry Department officials were legally transporting milk cows was burnt in Rajasthan by vigilantes suspecting them of smuggling cattle for slaughter (*The Hindu* 2017). Seventy-five attacks of this kind have been recorded between January 2010 and August 2017 by the Indian website IndiaSpend. Of the twenty-eight people who have died from such attacks, twenty-four were Muslim. More than half of these incidents happened in states ruled by the BJP (Abraham and Rao 2017).

The protection of the cow is therefore politically constructed in government offices, in Hindu nationalist organizations, and in the streets. Alongside repressive legislation and violent action, the Sangh Parivar nurtures the image of cow as a divine and generous benefactor: building on century-old medical treatises praising bovine products for their purity, it promotes the use of cow urine and excrement in the manufacturing of "traditional" medicine and agricultural inputs (Sébastia 2010).

Right-wing movements also strive to give a nationalist account of the cow's place in Indian history. While numerous historians have shown that Brahmins were sacrificing bovines and eating their flesh during the Vedic period, Hindu nationalist activists deny these practices, claiming loud and clear that slaughtering cows and consuming beef are exogenous habits, brought to India by foreign invaders (Ilaiah 1996, 1444). In *Holy Cow: Beef in Indian Dietary Traditions* (2001), D. N. Jha, a former professor of history at the Delhi University, provided evidence shedding light on the history of beef consumption in ancient India.[2] The VHP (Vishva Hindu Parishad, or World Hindu Council) argued that this book was insulting the Hindu faith and succeeded in temporarily banning it. The author was accused of blaspheme and threatened with death by *hindutva* hardliners (Ahmad 2014, 23).

In the years since Modi became prime minister, cow politics carried out by the Sangh Parivar have created a sense of fear among farmers. Instead of being sold to traders, herds of unproductive cattle are being released into public space, generating social, economic, and ecological threats.[3] The increasing number of stray cattle in North India results in overgrazing, encroachment on wildlife sanctuaries, and crop destruction. Lack of fodder and of public investment prevents cow protection institutions (*gaushalas*) from taking in the abandoned animals. The growing impossibility of turning these animals into meat also lessens the revenues of those involved in this sector, notably small-scale herders, cattle traders, and butchers, but also leather producers and merchants. Restrictions on cattle slaughter jeopardize a livestock sector that accounts for almost 5 percent of the total national gross domestic product (Panwar 2017). Besides harming the livelihoods of marginalized sectors of Indian society, these restrictions also affect their foodways. Beef, once the cheapest meat, mostly eaten by Muslims, Christians, Dalits, and other low-caste Hindu groups, has become practically unavailable in states ruled by Hindu nationalists. Though Ernesto Noronha (1994, 1447) noted twenty-five years ago that "the issue of cow slaughter has never occupied the centre stage in Hindutva politics," it can surely be argued today that the cow and its meat have become central symbols and political tools to antagonize communities along religious lines.

Admittedly, the sacredness of the cow is not only a political construct. For several centuries, Hindus have built up a specific economic and symbolic relationship with this bovine. For many Indians, the cow is seen as a mother or as a deity. Because of these manifold dimensions, this animal "not only reflects Hindu reality but also embodies and defines it" (Korom 2000, 193).[4] Being a key symbol of Hinduism, the cow is therefore easily leveraged for ideological strategies, primarily to alienate Muslims and to win Hindu votes. Hindu nationalists use this symbol to polarize the communities, drawing a line between the "good Indians" that would worship the cow and refrain from eating its flesh, and the "bad Indians" that would recklessly kill it and devour it. Equating "Indian-ness" with high-caste "Hindu-ness," they depict Islam as a factor of civilizational decadence and the Muslims as enemies, whose beef consumption marks their relative barbarity and allegiance to foreign powers.

A more general battle against meat

Beyond the issue of beef alone, many nationalist politicians and activists are now fighting a more general battle against meat. As with the defense of cows, the promotion of vegetarianism is not merely a political construct. At the same time, even though many Brahmin castes and other groups claiming a high status have historically adopted vegetarianism, food habits have nonetheless never been unified throughout India. On the contrary, medical scriptures have long advocated specific diets adapted to the season, to one's place of living, bodily constitution, occupation, etc. (Zimmermann 1987). Moreover, pure vegetarianism today is practiced only by a minority of the population. The hierarchy of castes does not strictly overlap with the hierarchy of diets. In Northern India for instance, some Brahmin castes and lineages occasionally indulge in meat eating (Khare 1966). Yet, food practices are more than ever at the center of an ideological and political struggle that strives for their homogenization.

Significantly, Sangh Parivar members seek to link a meat-based diet to violence, immorality, and obscurantism. While some nationalists longing for independence associated Indian's perceived physical weakness with vegetarianism—thereby echoing the debates taking place in Japan in the early twentieth century about the alleged association between meat eating and bodily strength (see Mitsuda, Chapter 1 in this volume)—the Arya Samaj promoted vegetarianism as a return to a putatively pristine Hindu civilization (Chatterjee and Souvik 2014, 29).[5] More than a century later, in 2003, when he was still the chief minister of Gujarat, Narendra Modi argued in a public speech that "vegetarianism is unavoidable for the purity of thoughts and action," comparing non-vegetarian stomachs with a funeral pyre (cited by Ghassem-Fachandi 2012, 154). In the 2000s, BJP leaders protested against serving eggs in schools, claiming that it was a *tamasik* (i.e., impure, dark) food (Nagaraj 2007), while village headmen from Uttar Pradesh and Haryana blamed non-vegetarian food for inducing inter-caste marriages and rapes (Mahaprashasta 2014).

Such arguments are not found only in the rhetoric of village politicians: in 2014, Maneka Gandhi, the Minister for Women and Child Development and an animal-rights activist, stated that India was until recently a vegetarian country, condemning her "misguided" fellow citizens for starting to eat meat, a foodstuff she refers to as "a drug" (Gandhi 2014). More recently, she argued that humans are "natural vegetarians," meat being an "alien substance" that, sooner or later, destroys the eater's body. Likewise, in a book published in 2008, Arun Kumar Jain, the former president of the BJP, put forward ecological and moral arguments in favor of vegetarianism (Sébastia 2010). In this way, those promoting a religious conception of the Indian nation are also fighting a cultural battle to impart specific significations to meat and meat eating.

The discourse against meat sometimes takes on a more virulent and political tone, directly targeting the meat industry. BJP politicians governing in Delhi in the 1990s argued that meat exports to the Gulf were "a robbery of India's 'cattle wealth'" (quoted in Robbins 1999, 415). Even more controversial were Maneka Gandhi's assertions that "money through trade of slaughtered animals goes into terrorism, therefore goes into killing us" (*International Business Times* 2014). Knowing that the meat sector is mostly in the hands of Indian Muslims, such allegations, uttered by a BJP minister, shamelessly associate meat, Islam, and anti-Hindu violence. Animals and meat are encompassed in a geopolitical discourse and become pivotal in defining irreconcilable entities, clearly distinguishing "us, vegetarian animal lovers" from "them, animal and man killers."

Restricting sites of meat production, marking vegetarian territories

In their defense of a meat-free diet, Hindu nationalist leaders have moved quickly from words to action, restricting sites of meat production and marking vegetarian territories. In 1994, after it took office in the municipality of Delhi, the BJP actively participated in the closure of the municipal slaughterhouse. Although the main arguments given to account for this closure were related to sanitation and hygiene, this secular discourse has been analyzed as "window dressing for deep-rooted religious biases" (Ahmad 2014, 28). Over the past few years, Sangh Parivar activists have relentlessly demonstrated against planned or operating abattoirs across the country. In 2014, for instance, VHP members screened propaganda films in the city of Ghanauri (Punjab), protesting against a projected mechanized slaughterhouse (Sharma 2014). In many respects, slaughterhouses, as spatial epitomes of meat production, concentrate Hindu nationalist opposition and anger.

More recently, following BJP electoral successes in the north of the country, the meat industry has been facing drastic controls and restrictions. After he was elected as chief minister of Uttar Pradesh in March 2017, the extremist monk Yogi Adityanath decided to clamp down on non-licensed slaughterhouses and butcher shops. The rules to open a meat shop were made tougher, if not impossible to comply with: walls had to be tiled, water tanks and freezers installed, tinted glass put up to prevent the public's gaze, animal slaughter was prohibited on the premises, etc. Many retailers had to close their shops as their application for a license was denied. During Navaratri, a nine-day Hindu festival, local political leaders forced meat shops to shut down, professing respect for religious sensibilities (Rajalakshmi 2017b). At the same period, in the nearby state of Haryana, the chief minister declared that butcher shops and slaughterhouses were not allowed near religious establishments and schools, resulting in the closure of 666 small-scale businesses and unemployment for thousands of laborers (Rajalakshmi 2017c).

For many decades, nationalist leaders, high-caste Hindus, and members of the Jain community have been trying to restrict the space dedicated to meat-related activities, thereby delimiting, de facto or de jure, vegetarian territories. In Haryana, the slaughter of animals and the sale of meat are banned in Kurukshetra and Pehowa, two towns considered as "holy" by many Hindus (*The Indian Express* 2012). Likewise, meat products are allowed neither in Rishikesh and Haridwar in Uttarakhand, nor in Badrinath and Kedarnath in Uttaranchal (Beauty Without Cruelty—India 2018). In Delhi, butchers cannot open a shop in the vicinity of temples (Ahmad 2014, 26), and no meat can be served during festivities held in buildings bearing the name of leading religious figures.

Such rules do not remain uncontested. In 2014 in Palitana in Gujarat, answering the demand of Jain monks, officials declared the city a "vegetarian-only zone," putting an end to the activity of 260 butchers and triggering waves of opposition by the large Muslim minority (Niazi 2014). Unsurprisingly, the coercive closures of meat shops by authorities operating under the sway of Hindu nationalist groups often end up in violent confrontations with meat sellers eager to maintain their livelihoods (see, e.g., *The Hindu* 2011).

These spatial restrictions on meat production and sales contribute to what I call a "territorialization of vegetarianism." Such a territorialization is not always politically enforced: it can also result from cultural hegemony. The areas surrounding major Hindu temples, usually referred to as *agraharam*, are de facto vegetarian territories: Brahmin priests enforce informal, unwritten bans on meat sale and meat consumption in the adjacent streets. In Chennai, around the Kapaleeshwarar temple, in the neighborhood of Mylapore, even non-Brahmin people acknowledge that "this is a pure vegetarian area." Announcements in newspapers often specify that apartments for rent are for "veg only."

The butchers established in the fringes of such areas argue that they would face huge troubles if they were to move their shops closer to the temple. In the cosmopolitan city of Mumbai, the Jain and high-caste residents of Malabar Hills have managed to turn their neighborhood into a vegetarian enclave (Bengali 2014). Thus, the enforcement of vegetarianism in public space, be it political or cultural, reflects and contributes to the drawing of boundaries between the communities, spatializing a diet-related hierarchy. Meat and vegetarianism are used to exercise power, to rule, and to control.

Nor are semipublic spaces safe from the hegemonic views of conservative and nationalist Hindus. In 2014, the Ministry of Human Resource Development of India sent a letter to all the prestigious Indian Institutes of Technology (IITs), asking their directors to consider operating a separate canteen for vegetarian students. Such a request stemmed from an RSS member's demand, blaming these institutions for spoiling the students' minds and behaviors with Western and non-vegetarian—in other words, impure—food. While the head of the IIT Madras (Chennai) answered that the campus already had a vegetarian mess, many observers criticized the BJP for its desire to enforce a politics of religiously motivated vegetarianism on allegedly secular places.

The Vedic notion of *ahimsa* and Gandhi's heritage are often put forward by *hindutva* advocates to justify their actions against the meat sector. But, as Parvis Ghassem-Fachandi has clearly shown, by targeting the activities, foodways, and sometimes the very existence of subaltern communities, "the doctrine of non-violence becomes implicated in the production of violence" (2010, 172).

Vegetarianism, environmentalism, and religion

In their struggle against meat and meat eating, political leaders and nationalist activists do not only put forward respect for religious tradition as the primary motivating factor. Sanitary, environmental, and moral arguments are often made to conceal the ideological basis of their endeavors.

In many cases, *hindutva* ideologues receive the support of animalist and environmentalist activists eager to promote vegetarianism or veganism. For several decades now, nationalist groups and members of PETA (People for the Ethical Treatment of Animals) have gathered in front of the Deonar abattoir in Mumbai to condemn the sacrifice of cattle during the Muslim Bakr Eid—also known as Eid al-Adha or "sacrifice feast" (Saglio-Yatzimirsky 2009, 805–6). When the state of Maharashtra banned the slaughter of bulls and bullocks in 2015, depriving thousands of traders and butchers of their livelihood, the vice-president of PETA argued that such a step toward a total ban on animal killing should be supported by "forward-thinking liberals" (Joshipura 2015). In Chennai also, at the Pulianthope slaughterhouse, animal-rights activists and environmentalists sometimes rally with Hindu nationalists to denounce the ill-treatment of animals and the poor slaughtering conditions.

Interestingly, several Indian animal-rights activists and environmentalists come from a high-caste background. Some of them maintain a close link with politico-religious groups. The most famous of them is probably Maneka Gandhi, already mentioned, a member of the BJP and founder of People for Animals (India). Her organization's website perfectly illustrates the conflation of a religious ethos and animalism: it calls for the protection of cows for ecological reasons while referring to Hindu cosmology (People for Animals 2013). Maybe even more famous abroad, the ecofeminist activist Vandana Shiva, head of the Research Foundation for Science, Technology, and Natural Resource Policy, is similarly promoting a ban on livestock slaughter. In a book chapter entitled "Ecological Balance in an Era of Globalization," she argues that the massive slaughter of buffaloes and sheep leads to a lack of manure, therefore requiring the costly importation of chemical fertilizers (Shiva 1999, 60). Although at first her argumentation seems to be based only on scientific nutrient calculations, she thereafter asserts that abstaining from killing animals "is preserving the Indian Cultural Heritage, of which we claim proud [*sic*]," terming the ecology "the true and common Dharma for all civilizations" (Shiva 1999, 61).[6] Another of these environmental and animal-rights activists is Nanditha Krishna, president of the C. P. Ramaswami Aiyar Foundation in Chennai, which has set up an environmental education center. Though the goals of this institution appear to be secular, Mrs. Krishna is nonetheless a proclaimed Hindu and an author whose books oppose animal sacrifice and *halal* killing, blaming Muslim rulers and British colonialists for having harmed the wisdom of ancient India and "the great legacy of ahimsa" (Krishna 2010, xii).

Even if these two latter activists are not officially affiliated with the Sangh Parivar, they contribute to the circulation of a pro-vegetarian environmentalist discourse that is imbued with Hindu religious values. In what Mukul Sharma calls the "intermeshing of green and saffron," environmental issues such as the ecological impacts of meat eating and the protection of animals are rephrased in the terms of Hindu politics (Sharma 2011). Critical theorists deplore these bonds made between the defense of nature and the defense of religion, which have prevented the emergence of a secular and progressive approach to animal well-being in India (Srinivasan and Rao 2015).

As argued by Zarin Ahmad, in India, meat is "a site of margin-making" (2014, 28–9), a food around which identities are formulated, divided, and contested. In this cultural battle to impart specific significations to meat, Hindu nationalists seem to have taken the upper hand, often alluding to secular repertoires such as environmentalism, prevention of cruelty to animals, morality, or hygiene to command their religious agenda. But the politicization of vegetarianism does not remain unchallenged. It is notably resisted by low-caste and left-wing activists, but also, in a less political way, by the middle class that sees consumption as an opportunity to endow meat eating with new meanings.

Resisting the politicization of meat

Meat can be politicized "from the top," but also "from the bottom." The most spectacular cases of such a counter-politicization of meat in contemporary India are perhaps the "beef festivals" organized since the early 2010s by student unions in different universities. One of them has been well documented by Brigitte Sébastia (2017): in April 2012 at Osmania University in Hyderabad, students mostly from Dalit backgrounds tried to distribute beef *biriyani*, a rice dish cooked with spices and meat, in order to persuade the university mess to serve bovine meat. The food distribution ended up in great turmoil and violence: paramilitary groups tried to destroy the equipment, a bus and a car were burnt, and the police used teargas to disband the crowd (Sébastia 2017, 110). Before the festival, the organizers had been threatened by the Akhil Bharatiya Vidyarthi Parishad (All-Indian Student Council), an association affiliated with the Hindu Right that blamed them for degrading Indian culture. They had also received a notification from the police ordering them to distribute the food outside the campus in order not to offend non-beef eaters (Sébastia 2017, 109).

Beyond the inclusion of beef on their mess menus, students organizing such festivals pursue three main political objectives: defending university campuses as secular places, promoting their food culture, and presenting beef as a respectable and nutritious food. For them, serving beef on university campuses is a way to contest a social hierarchy based on food habits. In doing so, they denounce high-caste Hinduism and Hindu nationalism for their hegemonic and undemocratic views and politics regarding food (Gundimeda 2009). "Our aim is to fight against this food fascism," said Suraj Beri, a student who planned to organize a beef and pork festival at Jawaharlal Nehru University in Delhi in 2012—an unsuccessful move as the Delhi High Court asked the police and the university administration to ensure that the festival would not take place (*The Times of India* 2012b). While historically, many low-caste Hindus and tribal groups have abandoned beef consumption as a strategy of upward social mobility (Eichinger Ferro-Luzzi 1975, 413), Dalit groups are now trying to disrupt and subvert the principles of the hierarchy itself: in their words, upward mobility should be achieved not through the erasure of differences, but through the recognition, or even the praise, of these very differences (Chigateri 2008, 12).

Student organizations' defense of food secularism often receives the support of scholars and activists. In numerous newspapers and websites, the carnivorous past of India and the pivotal role of vegetarianism and beef abstinence in the caste hierarchy have been exposed and discussed (Sattar 2014). A prominent intellectual such as Kancha Ilaiah, a low-caste activist and a professor of political science at Maulana Azad National Urdu University in Hyderabad, regularly expresses his views against food nationalism. As early as 1996, he claimed that "a political party or a government cannot suspend food rights of people simply because the leadership of a ruling party does not like the taste of a particular food, or because it considers some animals sacred" (Ilaiah 1996, 1445). From such a perspective, meat and beef consumption are seen as inalienable rights in a purportedly secular and multicultural society. Ilaiah (2004) also provocatively promotes a "buffalo nationalism": in his view, this animal epitomizes the qualities of the Dalits and their struggle to legitimate their identity.

The defense of meat eating often takes on a lower political intensity. Members of the lower castes, as well as Muslims and Christians, even when they do not openly campaign against high-caste Hindu hegemony, assert their pride in eating meats deemed "impure" such as beef and pork. A Christian Dalit who retired from the Indian Air Force told me, "I am a pure non-vegetarian, eating meat 365 days per year, two times per day!" adding that eating beef was his individual way to resist conservatism and to struggle against what he termed a "segregationist system" that induces social hierarchy and malnutrition.

Most of the time, carnivorism is not overtly political. James Staples has aptly shown that many Christian communities in Andhra Pradesh eat meat, and particularly beef, as a marker of religious identity (Staples 2008, 42), but also on the ground that it is beneficial for growth and health (Staples 2017, 243). In many contexts, animal flesh is not seen as an impure food. On the contrary, its consumption can also denote a higher status. Festivals held by low-caste Hindus, Muslims, and Christians have long since required the ceremonial presence of meat, and global capitalism and the rise of a consumer culture are now creating new opportunities and places where meat is valued in and of itself (Bruckert 2015). Non-vegetarian restaurants have mushroomed in urban Tamil Nadu, serving a wide range of food, from "Arabian" to "Chinese" to "Chettinadu" (a region of Tamil Nadu famous for its spicy meat dishes). These venues are patronized by young male professionals and middle-class families who can enjoy a chicken kebab or a mutton biriyani there. Interviews carried out in Chennai reveal that, in these contexts, meat is praised for its taste, for the change it brings from the usual vegetarian food, for its connection with modernity, and also for the higher purchasing power it denotes. Many people told me that they would eat more meat if they had the means.

In India, vegetarianism has long since been conflated with social, moral, and religious superiority, while meat eating has been associated with the Kshatriyas— namely the *varna* (meta-caste) of soldiers and rulers—and, later on, with the British colonial power. Today, this "Kshatriya rationale," whereby eating meat denotes material power, boldness, and also often masculinity, has been renewed and recoded in the urban space (Bruckert 2018). Yet, the practice of conspicuous carnivorism does not extend to beef consumption. Apart from high-end cosmopolitan restaurants situated on star hotel rooftops and Muslim roadside eateries set away from the public gaze, few places offer bovine meat. Deeply embodied regimes of palatability and a more political association of beef eating with low-class citizens still prevent any transformation in the significations endowed to the flesh of cattle in contemporary urban India.

Conclusion

Food practices are fields of power and domination. While there was no sense of an Indian national cuisine before the postcolonial period (Appadurai 1988), culinary traditions are now being interpreted and reshaped by a nationalist discourse that seeks to promote the image of India as a Hindu, vegetarian, and cow-worshipping country, threatened by bloodthirsty, meat-eating primitives and invaders. In the nationalist discourse, meat and beef simultaneously embody immorality, "unnaturalness," backwardness, otherness, and barbarism. Cow protection and meat abhorrence, as Eliza Kent has described regarding the broader *hindutva* movement, are thus made up of two dimensions: a homogenizing dimension that seeks to "encompass a broad range of communities," and an antagonizing dimension that heightens the contrasts between Hindus and "foreign others" (Kent 2013, 171).

The political will to decide who is accepted and what food is served at the national table proliferates at a time when caste boundaries are blurred by global capitalism and urban life, notably in the context of eating out. Therefore, the culinary nationalism cooked in the Sangh Parivar's cauldron is a very modern recipe. Far from being an outdated whim, and despite its regular references to a pristine past, the political promotion of vegetarianism has been largely crafted by a contemporary, educated, Hindu middle class living in cosmopolitan cities. Its appropriation of very topical issues, such as animal well-being, environmental protection, public health, or respect for religious sensibilities, sheds light on the interplay between localism and globalism that lies at the heart of identity politics in the contemporary era.[7] As mentioned in this chapter, advocates of *hindutva* look back with nostalgia to the Vedic times, when the pure essence of what is now India was deemed to be preserved from invaders' impurities. Yet paradoxically, Hinduism, with its variegated, profuse, and often contradictory scriptures and practices spanning thousands of years, is actually more an obstacle than an asset for such a culinary nationalism: the standardization of diets can be achieved only in a modern nation-state where power is centralized. In this framework, subjects are disciplined and controlled through a regulated access to food and through the ascription, by the highest levels of the government, of specific significations to sensitive foodstuffs such as meat.

These narratives and politics of homogeneity obviously deny the manifold and complex culinary histories of India. A "negative" definition of culinary identity is promoted: according to the Sangh Parivar, Indians should not be defined by what they *do eat* but by what they *do not eat*. The case of India makes us think differently about culinary nationalism: instead of promoting national dishes, such a culinary nationalism is a process of exclusion, of purification. Behind the abstinence from alien foodstuffs (meat and notably beef), the exclusion of alien people (Muslims, Christians, low-caste Hindus, etc.) underpins the national interpretation of India's culinary history and identity.

In the introduction, I argued that, due to its "semiotic virtuosity" (Appadurai 1981) and relational properties, food is fit for political appropriation in the Indian context. Perhaps more than any other type of food, meat has a capacity to take on various significations. It is a volatile and contextual symbol, ripe for appropriation to serve diverse and often contradictory strategies (Staples 2018, 74). Originating in animal bodies, meat is a vector of intercorporeality between differentiated beings. Necessitating an (often violent) act of killing to obtain it, its legitimacy is definitely never taken for granted. These inherent biological and moral dimensions enable meat to support acts of identification and differentiation, entailing a specific way to feel, to know, and to shape worlds (Evans and Miele 2012, 303). Supporting organic and mental transactions, it carries both matter and meaning. People maintain a metabolic, ethical, and aesthetic relationship with meat. The way they interact with it contributes to drawing material and immaterial geographies, to mapping, fixing, and blurring spatial, ontological, and political boundaries between living entities and within social groups. Such communicative properties make meat a substance prone to provoke contestation. In contemporary India, the negotiations and conflicts over the significations imparted to meat and to meat eating have opened the way to new episodes of communal tension and violence. Arguably, the more meat is accepted and commodified, the more it is also contested and politicized.

Notes

1 Approximately US$150 in 2017.
2 See also K. T. Achaya (1994) for a detailed account of meat eating in ancient India.
3 This "cow menace" is well documented in a cover story for the Indian magazine *Frontline* (Ramakrishnan 2017).
4 It seems needless to add that, contrary to what Marvin Harris argued, the reason for the sacredness of the cow is not to be found primarily in ecological factors (Harris 1966).
5 Notably, the Hindu monk Vivekananda (1863–1902) promoted meat consumption to increase stamina and energy.
6 In Indian religions, the Dharma refers to the socio-cosmic law.
7 Interestingly, Gandhi's defense of vegetarianism also did not directly stem from his own caste ethos but from his acquaintance with the Vegetarian Society in London.

References

Abraham, Delna, and Ojaswi Rao. 2017. "84% Dead in Cow-Related Violence Since 2010 Are Muslim; 97% Attacks After 2014." IndiaSpend. Last modified December 8, 2017. http://www.indiaspend.com/cover-story/86-dead-in-cow-related-violence-since-2010-are-muslim-97-attacks-after-2014-2014.

Achaya, K. T. 1994. *Indian Food: A Historical Companion*. Delhi: Oxford University Press.

Ahmad, Zarin. 2014. "Delhi's Meatscapes: Cultural Politics of Meat in a Globalizing City." *IIM Kozhikode Society & Management Review* 3, no. 1: 21–31.

Alsdorf, Ludwig. 2010. *The History of Vegetarianism and Cow-Veneration in India*. Translated by Bal Patil. New York: Routledge.

Appadurai, Arjun. 1981. "Gastro-Politics in Hindu South Asia." *American Ethnologist* 8, no. 3: 494–511.

Appadurai, Arjun. 1988. "How to Make a National Cuisine: Cookbooks in Contemporary India." *Comparative Studies in Society and History* 30, 1: 3–24.

Beauty Without Cruelty—India. 2018. "Vegetarian and Animal Religious Observances." Awareness. Learn About. Last modified April 10, 2018. http://bwcindia.org/Web/Awareness/LearnAbout/VegetarianandAnimalReligiousObservances.html.

Bengali, Shashank. 2014. "Mumbai's Strictly Vegetarian Enclave Gives Flesh-Eaters the Evil Eye." *Los Angeles Times*, November 24, 2014. http://www.latimes.com/world/asia/la-fg-india-vegetarianism-20141124-story.html.

Berger, Peter. 2011. "Food." In *Brill's Encyclopedia of Hinduism Volume III: Society, Religious Specialists, Religious Traditions, Philosophy*, edited by Knut A. Jacobsen, Helene Basu, Angelika Malinar, and Vasudha Narayanan, 68–75. Leiden: Brill.

Bruckert, Michaël. 2015. "Changing Food Habits in Contemporary India: Discourses and Practices from the Middle Classes in Chennai (Tamil Nadu)." In *Routledge Handbook of Contemporary India*, edited by Knut A. Jacobsen, 457–73. Abingdon: Routledge.

Bruckert, Michaël. 2018. *La Chair, Les Hommes et Les Dieux: La Viande En Inde* [*Flesh, Men, and Gods: Meat in India*], Paris: CNRS Editions.

Chatterjee, Amitava, and Souvik Naha. 2014. "The Muscular Monk: Vivekananda, Sports and Physical Culture in Colonial Bengal." *Economic and Political Weekly* 49, no. 11: 25–9.

Chigateri, Shraddha. 2008. " 'Glory to the Cow': Cultural Difference and Social Justice in the Food Hierarchy in India." *South Asia: Journal of South Asian Studies* 31, no. 1: 10–35.

Daily Sabah. 2017. "Two Muslims Transporting Cattle Beaten to Death in India." August 27, 2017. https://www.dailysabah.com/asia/2017/08/27/two-muslims-transporting-cattle-beaten-to-death-in-india.

Daniel, E. Valentine. 1984. *Fluid Signs: Being a Person the Tamil Way*. Berkeley: University of California Press.

Dumont, Louis. 1970. *Homo Hierarchicus: The Caste System and Its Implications*. Chicago: University of Chicago Press.

Eichinger Ferro-Luzzi, Gabriella. 1975. "Food Avoidances of Indian Tribes." *Anthropos* 70, no. 3/4: 385–427.

Evans, Adrian B., and Mara Miele. 2012. "Between Food and Flesh: How Animals Are Made to Matter (and Not Matter) Within Food Consumption Practices." *Environment and Planning D: Society and Space* 30, no. 2: 298–314.

Gandhi, Maneka Sanjay. 2014. "Mock Meat in Market." *Daily Excelsior*, March 2, 2014. http://www.dailyexcelsior.com/mock-meat-in-market/.

Ghassem-Fachandi, Parvis. 2010. "Ahimsa, Identification and Sacrifice in the Gujarat Pogrom." *Social Anthropology* 18, no. 2: 155–75.

Ghassem-Fachandi, Parvis. 2012. *Pogrom in Gujarat: Hindu Nationalism and Anti-Muslim Violence in India*. Princeton, NJ: Princeton University Press.

Gundimeda, Sambaiah. 2009. "Democratisation of the Public Sphere: The Beef Stall Case in Hyderabad's *Sukoon* Festival." *South Asia Research* 29, no. 2: 127–49.

Harris, Marvin. 1966. "The Cultural Ecology of India's Sacred Cattle." *Current Anthropology* 7, no. 1: 51–66.

Hindu, The. 2011. "Officials Attacked for Stopping Sale of Meat." January 21, 2011. https://www.thehindu.com/news/national/tamil-nadu/Officials-attacked-for-stopping-sale-of-meat/article15526200.ece.

Hindu, The. 2015a. "UP Launches Probe into Killing over Beef." September 30, 2015. Last modified September 6, 2016. https://www.thehindu.com/news/national/other-states/muslim-man-killed-for-eating-beef-in-uttar-pradesh/article7706825.ece.

Hindu, The. 2015b. "Lynching Is Saddening, but Centre Is Not to Blame." October 14, 2015. Last modified March 25, 2015. https://www.thehindu.com/news/national/why-blame-the-centre-modi-on-dadri-lynching/article7760342.ece.

Hindu, The. 2017. "Rajasthan Vigilantes Attack TN Team Transporting Cattle." June 12, 2017. https://www.thehindu.com/news/national/tamil-nadu-government-officials-attacked-by-cow-vigilantes-in-rajasthan/article18965787.ece.

Hoffpauir, Robert. 1982. "The Water Buffalo: India's Other Bovine." *Anthropos* 77, no. 1/2: 215–38.

Ilaiah, Kancha. 1996. "Beef, BJP and Food Rights of People." *Economic and Political Weekly* 31: 1443–5.

Ilaiah, Kancha. 2004. *Buffalo Nationalism: A Critique of Spiritual Fascism*. Kolkata: Popular Prakashan.

Indian Express, The. 2012. "Haryana Bans Meat in Holy Towns of Kurukshetra, Pehowa." August 25, 2012. https://indianexpress.com/article/news-archive/punjab-and-haryana/haryana-bans-meat-in-holy-towns-of-kurukshetra-pehowa/.

Indian Express, The. 2016. "Dadri Lynching: Hearing on Petition Against Akhlaq's Family Adjourned Till June 23." June 13, 2016. https://indianexpress.com/article/india/india-news-india/dadri-lynching-hearing-on-petition-against-akhlaqs-family-adjourned-till-june-23-2850458/.

Indian Kanoon. n.d. "Article 48 in The Constitution of India 1949." Constitution. https://indiankanoon.org/doc/1452355/.

International Business Times. 2014. "Money from Cow Slaughter Feeding Terrorism, Alleges Minister." September 15, 2014. https://www.ibtimes.co.uk/india-money-cow-slaughter-feeding-terrorism-alleges-minister-1465447.

Jha, D. N. 2001. *Holy Cow: Beef in Indian Dietary Traditions.* New Dehli: Matrix Books.

Joshipura, Poorva. 2015. "Why Forward-Thinking Liberals Should Support the Beef Ban." *The Blog* (blog), *HuffPost India.* Last modified July 7, 2016. http://www.huffingtonpost.in/poorva-joshipura/forwardthinking-liberals-_b_6798590.html?utm_hp_ref=india.

Kent, Eliza F. 2013. *Sacred Groves and Local Gods: Religion and Environmentalism in South India.* Oxford: Oxford University Press.

Khare, Ravindra S. 1966. "A Case of Anomalous Values in Indian Civilization: Meat-Eating Among the Kanya-Kubja Brahmans of Katyayan Gotra." *The Journal of Asian Studies* 25, no. 2: 229–40.

Korom, Frank J. 2000. "Holy Cow! The Apotheosis of Zebu, or Why the Cow Is Sacred in Hinduism." *Asian Folklore Studies* 59, no. 2: 181–203.

Krishna, Nanditha. 2010. *Sacred Animals of India.* Delhi: Penguin.

Kumar, N. D. Shiva. 2012. "Anti Cow Slaughter Bill Is Tougher." *The Times of India,* December 16, 2012. https://timesofindia.indiatimes.com/city/bengaluru/Anti-cow-slaughter-bill-is-tougher/articleshow/17640071.cms.

Lukose, Anjali. 2015. "At Asia's Largest Abattoir, Butchers Fear Livelihood Loss As Beef Ban Sets In." *The Indian Express,* March 23, 2015. https://indianexpress.com/article/india/india-others/at-asias-largest-abattoir-butchers-fear-livelihood-loss-as-beef-ban-sets-in/.

Mahaprashasta, Ajoy Ashirwad. 2012. "Sacred Cow." *Frontline* 29, no. 3, February 11–24, 2012. https://www.frontline.in/static/html/fl2903/stories/20120224290301400.htm.

Mahaprashasta, Ajoy Ashirwad. 2014. "Messing with Food Habits." *Frontline,* December 26, 2014. https://www.frontline.in/cover-story/messing-with-food-habits/article6672291.ece.

Nagaraj, G. N. 2007. "Sangh Parivar Again Incites Communal Violence." *People's Democracy* 31, no. 5. http://archives.peoplesdemocracy.in/2007/0204/02042007_karnataka.htm.

Nair, Gayatri. 2016. "The Bitter Aftertaste of Beef Ban: 'Choice', Caste and Consumption." *Economic and Political Weekly* 51, no. 10: 14–16.

Niazi, Shuriah. 2014. "Controversy over Indian Pilgrim Town Declared 'Veg-Only.'" *Anadolu Agency,* August 26, 2014. http://www.aa.com.tr/en/world/379213--controversy-over-indian-pilgrim-town-declared-quotveg-only-quot.

Noronha, Ernesto. 1994. "BJP: Cow as a Political Symbol." *Economic and Political Weekly* 29, no. 24: 1447–8.

NSSO (National Sample Survey Office). 2012. "Household Consumption of Various Goods and Services in India." New Delhi: Government of India, National Sample Survey Office. http://mospi.nic.in/sites/default/files/publication_reports/nss_report_541.pdf.

Panwar, Sudhir. 2017. "Running Roughshod over Livelihoods." *Frontline,* November 10, 2017. https://www.frontline.in/cover-story/running-roughshod-over-livelihoods/article9920919.ece.

People for Animals. 2013. "Home" Last modified. 2013. http://www.peopleforanimalsindia.org/index.php.

Rajalakshmi, T. K. 2017a. "Big Backlash." *Frontline,* July 7, 2017. https://www.frontline.in/cover-story/big-backlash/article9731099.ece.

Rajalakshmi, T. K. 2017b. "License to Harass." *Frontline,* October 27, 2017. https://www.frontline.in/the-nation/licence-to-harass/article9897745.ece.

Rajalakshmi, T. K. 2017c. "Held to Ransom." *Frontline*, November 10, 2017. https://www.frontline.in/cover-story/held-to-ransom/article9920916.ece.

Ramakrishnan, Venkitesh. 2017. "The Cow Menace." *Frontline*, November 10, 2017. https://www.frontline.in/cover-story/the-cow-menace/article9920842.ece.

Ray, Krishnendu. 2013. "Food and Identity." In *The Handbook of Food Research*, edited by Anne Murcott, Warren Belasco, and Peter Jackson, 363–76. London: Bloomsbury.

Robbins, Paul. 1999. "Meat Matters: Cultural Politics Along the Commodity Chain in India." *Cultural Geographies* 6, no. 4: 399–423.

Saglio-Yatzimirsky, Marie-Caroline. 2009. "L'abattoir de Deonar (Mumbai, Inde): centre industriel ou autel sacrificiel? Représentations de l'animal de boucherie dans le monde indien" ["The slaughterhouse of Deonar (Mumbai, India): representations of butchered animals in the Indian world"]. In *Penser, dire et représenter l'animal dans le monde indien*, edited by Nalini Balbir and Georges-Jean Pinault, 791–810. Paris: Champion, Bibliothèque de l'Ecole des Hautes Etudes.

Sattar, Arshia. 2014. "Non-Vegetarianism a Choice: Let's Respect It." *Bangalore Mirror*, November 26, 2014. http://bangaloremirror.indiatimes.com/opinion/views//articleshow/45279955.cms.

Sébastia, Brigitte. 2010. "Be a Vegetarian! Discours en Inde sur les bienfaits du végétarisme pour un corps pur et sain" ["Discussion in India on the benefits of vegetarianism for a pure and healthy body"]. Observatoire Cniel des Habitudes Alimentaires. Last modified August 2, 2010. http://www.lemangeur-ocha.com/texte/be-a-vegetarian-discours-en-inde-sur-les-bienfaits-du-vegetarisme-pour-un-corps-pur-et-sain/.

Sébastia, Brigitte. 2017. " 'Beef Is Our Secret of Life': Controversial Consumption of Beef in Andhra Pradesh, India." In *Eating Traditional Food : Politics, Identity and Practices*, edited by Brigitte Sébastia, 104–28. New York: Routledge.

Sharma, Amaninder. 2014. "Sangh Protests Against Mechanised Slaughterhouse in Punjab." *The Times of India*, December 25, 2014. https://timesofindia.indiatimes.com/city/chandigarh/Sangh-protests-against-mechanised-slaughterhouse-in-Punjab/articleshow/45635708.cms.

Sharma, Mukul. 2011. *Green and Saffron: Hindu Nationalism and Indian Environmental Politics*. Ranikhet: Orient BlackSwan.

Shiva, Vandana. 1999. "Ecological Balance in an Era of Globalization." In *Global Ethics and Environment*, edited by Nicholas Low, 47–69. New York: Routledge.

Singh, D. K., and Timsy Jaipuria. 2015. "Pink Revolution? Meat Exports up in NDA Regime." *Hindustan Times*, January 6, 2015. https://www.hindustantimes.com/business/pink-revolution-meat-exports-up-in-nda-regime/story-6GuGjvgHgPcnFyscGTqJ0O.html.

Srinivasan, Krithika, and Smitha Rao. 2015. " 'Will Eat Anything That Moves': Meat Cultures in Globalising India." *Economic and Political Weekly* 50, no. 39: 13–15.

Staples, James. 2008. " 'Go On, Just Try Some!': Meat and Meaning-Making Among South Indian Christians." *South Asia: Journal of South Asian Studies* 31, no. 1: 36–55.

Staples, James. 2017. "Beef and Beyond: Exploring the Meat Consumption Practices of Christians in India." *Ethnos* 82, no. 2: 232–51.

Staples, James. 2018. "Appropriating the Cow: Beef and Identity Politics in Contemporary India." In *Farms to Fingers: The Culture and Politics of Food in Contemporary India*, edited by Kiranmayi Bhushi, 58–79. Cambridge: Cambridge University Press.

Times of India, The. 2012a. "MP Goes Tough on Cow Slaughter." January 4, 2012. https://timesofindia.indiatimes.com/india/MP-goes-tough-on-cow-slaughter/articleshow/11358042.cms.

Times of India, The. 2012b. "Meat of the Campaign at JNU." October 15, 2012. https://timesofindia.indiatimes.com/home/education/news/Meat-of-the-campaign-at-JNU/articleshow/16817601.cms.

Van der Veer, Peter. 1994. *Religious Nationalism: Hindus and Muslims in India.* Berkeley: University of California Press.

Yadav, Yogendra, and Sanjay Kumar. 2006. "The Food Habits of a Nation." *The Hindu,* August 14, 2006. Last modified March 22, 2012. https://www.thehindu.com/todays-paper/the-food-habits-of-a-nation/article3089973.ece.

Zimmermann, Francis. 1987. *The Jungle and the Aroma of Meats: An Ecological Theme in Hindu Medicine.* Berkeley: University of California Press.

Part Three

Global Contexts

9

Writing an "International" Cuisine in Japan: Murai Gensai's 1903 Culinary Novel *Kuidōraku*

Eric C. Rath

University of Kansas

The words for Japanese cuisine (*washoku* 和食, *Nihon ryōri* 日本料理, and *honpō ryōri* 本邦料理) date from the late nineteenth century and are meant to identify a native dietary culture against Western and Asian foods that became more available as Japan developed into a nation with imperialistic ambitions and overseas colonies (Rath 2016, 248). Today, the Japanese government—specifically the Agency for Cultural Affairs and the Ministry of Agriculture, Forestry, and Fisheries—has made a noticeable intervention in the shaping of the meaning of one these terms: in 2013 UNESCO accepted the government's application to add *washoku*, defined as the "traditional dietary cultures of the Japanese," to the Representative List of the Intangible Cultural Heritage of Humanity. In contrast to this definition of *washoku*, which purports to be derived from the social and cultural customs as well as the foodways of the rural past, this chapter is about a model of cuisine from Japan more than a century older that rejects tradition, promotes urban over rural dining habits, and prioritizes international culinary science over the preservation of native customs of cooking and eating. At the same time, this earlier culinary vision articulates aesthetics and values familiar in discussions about the essence of Japanese cuisine today.

The person a century ago who imagined and promoted a cuisine in Japan shorn of tradition and transcending national boundaries was the author Murai Gensai (1863–1927). Murai wrote forty novels and hundreds of articles, as well as plays, advice manuals, and books about food, but many people in Japan today do not recognize his name (Kuroiwa 2007, 10).[1] Those acquainted with his work know Murai for his 1903 culinary novel *Kuidōraku* (later retitled *Shokudōraku*), one of the best-selling books of the early twentieth century, which launched numerous spinoffs including a kabuki play, theme restaurants, clothing, and Japan's first monthly gourmet magazine.[2]

Murai might be better known today had he not written so disparagingly of traditional Japanese dietary cultures in contrast to ascribing more advanced practices to the West. There is ample evidence in *Kuidōraku* to support the idea that his novel is meant to critique and reform Japanese cooking and eating habits, bringing them in line with "enlightened" Western practices.[3] But rather than simply try to modernize or

Westernize Japanese cuisine, this chapter contends that Murai's ultimate goal was to create an "international" style of cooking in Japan based on scientific principles.[4] In other words, while Murai's writings exemplified and helped to fuel the popularity for Western foods among the urban middle class after the turn of the twentieth century, his vision was not simply to promote Western cooking, but to build a new cuisine that combined Japanese sensibilities and methods with a scientific approach derived from Western science.

Murai's contributions are important because he not only articulated a vision for a cuisine at a time when cooking and the nation were first understood as being in conjunction, but he also recognized the shortcomings of any cuisine defined solely on the basis of native ingredients, cooking techniques, and indigenous culture. From Murai's perspective, national cuisines were lacking when compared to an international cuisine developed from the most nutritious foods and the best ways to prepare them taken from around the world. Instead of looking backward to static traditions, Murai's international cuisine, like the scientific methods he endorsed, represented a forward-looking approach. He tested foods and then informed a wider public about them, first as recipes in his culinary novel, and then in his non-fiction writings about his experiments with different diets. National cuisines (like the aforementioned *washoku*) are often invoked against modernization and globalization, but Murai had no fear in looking beyond his country's borders and welcoming new approaches to food while also publicizing the best aspects of Japanese cooking to an audience outside of his country.

The chapter begins by briefly recounting Murai's career, asking how a newspaper reporter became a food novelist. It then introduces the characters and plots of *Kuidōraku* and his English novel *Hana: A Daughter of Japan* to explore Murai's process of thought about creating an international style of cuisine. The chapter concludes by examining some of Murai's later writings to understand why he turned to experimentations on his own diet as a means to discover universally relevant ideas about eating and food applicable toward developing an international cuisine.

How Murai Gensai became a food writer

Murai Gensai was born in a samurai household five years before the Meiji Restoration of 1868. His father, a Confucian scholar teaching in the school for Yoshida domain in Toyohashi (modern Aichi prefecture), opposed the Restoration and subsequently lost his position. Eventually the family resettled in Tokyo in 1871. Murai attended primary school and then the Tokyo School of Foreign Languages, where he began learning Russian. He left school at eighteen in 1881, and then traveled to California in 1884, where he lived for a year (Suzuki et al. 2016, 24–5; Kuroiwa 2004, 411–12).[5] No doubt Murai picked up some English during that time.

On his return to Japan he found employment in 1887 at the *Hōchi Shimbun* newspaper. In 1890, *Hōchi Shimbun* became the first major newspaper to try to expand its readership by including serialized tales and novels, and Murai contributed several stories for publication that year (Kuroiwa 2007, 22–3).[6] His domestic novel *The Kitten*

(*Koneko*) appeared in *Hōchi Shimbun* in 1891, and its positive reception allowed Murai to focus on writing fiction for the paper. Murai's *Island of the Sun Rise* (*Hinodejima*) ran for six years in the *Hōchi Shimbun*, from 1896 to 1901, making it one of the longest novels written in the Meiji period (1868–1912), filling thirteen volumes when published in book form (Kuroiwa 2004, 5–6).[7] After completing this opus, Murai planned to write a hundred novelettes exploring different hobbies such as reading, archery, research, Japanese chess (*shogi*), theater, biking, travel, photos, and dogs; he sketched out plans for twenty-nine of these works (Kuroiwa 2004, 10–11, 2007, 17). *Pleasures of Women* (*Onna dōraku*) and *Pleasures of Sake* (*Sake dōraku*) appeared in 1902. Both novels explored how the "way of pleasure" (*dōraku*) was a road to ruin as when alcoholism or adultery damaged health and family relationships.[8] His first translator, Kawai Unkichi, detected the moralizing tone of the son of a Confucian scholar in Murai's writing. In 1904 Kawai wrote, Murai's "vast experience in the world has persuaded him to write didactic novels to teach the public how to make their homes happy, and to rebuke social evils, and to save people from them" (Unkichi 1904, xxxvi).

The title of his culinary novel, *Kuidōraku* (食道楽), which ran in *Hōchi Shimbun* in 1903, suggests that the story will be a diatribe against over "eating" (*kui*, 食い) (Kuroiwa 2004, 12–13).[9] The dialogue in the novel is frequently reminiscent of a Confucian text: someone poses a simple question to an authority figure and receives a lengthy instructional reply. But the novel also betrays Murai's sense of humor. *Kuidōraku* opens on New Year's Day with a stomachache told from the perspective of the stomach complaining to his neighbor the intestine (Murai 1978a, 1). The upset stomach and irritable bowel are an internal dialogue in the dreams of the novel's protagonist, Ōhara Mitsuru (大原満), a recent university graduate who is hung over. Ōhara Mitsuru's name suggests someone with a bloated or worn out stomach.[10] Indeed, Ōhara's compulsive overeating caused him to fail his university graduation exams three times.

Listening to his complaints, his friend's wife offers Ōhara a sweet, curative soup made from peanuts (Murai 1978a, 7–8).[11] She then leads him into the kitchen, causing Ōhara to rethink his understanding of this space as a remarkable site of food preparation in the home. "Hearing the word kitchen evokes something dark, smoky, and untidy, but Ōhara discovers that the kitchen in this household, which the wife proudly leads her guest into, shows her propensity for hygiene and beauty. The scrubbed surfaces, the well-tended stove, and the wood floor all sparkle with light, and all the while the maid servants bustle around in view" (Murai 1978a, 9).

The modern kitchen produced the novel dish made from peanuts—a food that became more prominent in the Meiji period, and one that the wife reports eating daily as a tastier substitute for sesame seeds in salads (*goma'ae*) and as having more protein than walnuts (Murai 1978a, 10).[12] So begins a major theme of the novel that new foods, better eating habits, and modern cooking are the solution to long-standing health problems.

The storyline of *Kuidōraku* follows Ōhara Mitsuru as he reforms his diet and outlook on food, especially after falling for the heroine Otowa, who is an expert chef. As Ōhara deepens his appreciation of good cooking, his depth of affection for Otowa grows. Otowa embodies the practical side of cooking, while her brother,

Nakagawa, is the theorist. Nakagawa, who works as an editor for a literary magazine, serves as the voice of authority in the novel, holding forth on the state of Japan and its food culture. In contrast, Otowa wields her influence in the home. With the hopes of emulating Nakagawa and wedding Otowa someday—and to escape an arranged marriage with his cousin named Odai—Ōhara decides to travel to the West to study about food.

Murai planned to write *Kuidōraku* for only half a year, but the novel quickly became too popular to cut short and he continued it for a full year. At the time of publication of *Kuidōraku*, circulation of *Hōchi Shimbun* was 83,000 issues per day, but that climbed to 100,000 by 1904. Sales of the first volume of the book version of *Kuidōraku*, also published in 1903, reached 100,000 copies, making it one of the best-selling novels in the period. When Murai became editor at his newspaper in 1904, he built on the popularity of *Kuidōraku* and its themes to include columns about cooking and the household, making *Hōchi Shimbun* more appealing to female readers but provoking some critics to call it the "*Kuidōraku* newspaper" (Kuroiwa 2004, 13, 21, 25, 247).

Kuidōraku contains 630 recipes for Japanese, Western, and a few Chinese dishes, but before writing it, Murai had no experience as a chef or gourmet. The major culinary influence on his work was his wife Takako whom he married in 1900 (Figure 9.1).[13] In the sequel to *Kuidōraku*, Murai credited Takako as his inspiration for his interest in food and as the model for the heroine, Otowa (Murai 1906–7, i–ii). Takako later became a noted food writer, contributing recipes to women's magazines and the newspapers *Yomiuri Shimbun* and *Asahi Shimbun* in the 1910s–1940s.[14] Many of the dishes in the first volume of *Kuidōraku* probably derive their inspiration from her, but Murai also employed two professional chefs to test recipes, one of whom, Katō Masutarō, had worked for seven years as a cook at the American legation.[15] Murai also sought advice from chefs working at Chinese restaurants (Iida 2010, 35; Kuroiwa 2007, 72, 2004, 157–8).

If Takako was the inspiration for the character Otowa, Murai's voice in the novel is Nakagawa, who discourses about cuisine, displays his knowledge about the caloric content of certain foods, and designs menus, but does not prepare food himself, mirroring Murai's own lack of experience of cooking.[16] *Kuidōraku* reproduces the heteronormative gender roles for the Meiji period in which the man as husband represents the public face of the household in society while the woman is the "good wife and wise mother" who manages the home. "Good wife, wise mother" was the slogan used to signify the Meiji government's program for women, which sought to mobilize women as wives (*shufu*) in support of the household and by extension the state while at the same time denying them the right to vote or even to discuss politics in public. Culinary texts including *Kuidōraku*, as well as cooking education in middle-school home economics courses for girls, which began in 1899, reinforced the gendered division of labor in food preparation, charging women with the role of providing nutritious, varied, and appealing meals for their families and allowing men (apart from professional chefs) to enjoy food as a gourmet or intellectual pursuit without having to learn to cook.[17] Murai's novel gained acclaim because its characters embodied and appealed to both readerships: women who were supposed to gain mastery of home cooking and men who fancied themselves as gourmets.[18]

（本誌第七頁參照）

人夫同氏齋弦井村

Figure 9.1 Murai Gensai (*left*) and Murai Takako (*right*). Frontispiece photograph from *Kuidōraku* magazine (1905), Vol. 2.

A novel about eating well, not a gourmet novel

Kuidōraku was a novel that doubled as a cookbook with recipes that readers could prepare themselves, but *Kuidōraku* also presented delicacies outside the reach of typical Japanese.[19] In one scene, Otowa describes a Western-style banquet containing thirty separate dishes, costing ¥25–30 per person, the equivalent of the monthly living expenses for a middle-class family of four (Murai 1978b, 169–72; Kuroiwa 2007, 93). Otowa reveals that there are even more costly dishes: Chinese bird's nest soup, which costs ¥50–60 per serving; a Western dish made with house martin chicks; and a recipe at a French hotel that includes the tips of baby asparagus grown in a greenhouse (Murai 1978b, 173–4). At a time when only some 1 percent of the population drank milk and per capita pork and poultry consumption was negligible, *Kuidōraku*'s recipes for ice cream, butter cake, and pork with macaroni, which might be considered humble today, would have been beyond the ken of most of the novel's readers (Smil and Kobayashi 2012, 2; Murai 1978c, 216, 257, 1978a, 30).[20] *Kuidōraku* helped play an important role in educating readers about these novel Western dishes as well as new vegetables such as "red eggplant" (tomatoes), and modern cooking utensils. An appendix in the final volume of *Kuidōraku* contains illustrations of a potato masher, pudding mold, coffee grinder, and other Western kitchen tools.

Murai's novel helped propel the assimilation of Western cuisine, transforming it from an elite practice to one where Western cooking methods like frying became part of the daily culinary repertoire in urban kitchens. The ready assimilation of Western cooking into the diet of urban households is exemplified by the ease that dishes like potato croquettes (*korokke*) could be added as a side dish to a Japanese meal. Croquettes, which could be inexpensively purchased from stores or made at home, could be eaten with chopsticks like Japanese food, thus requiring no knowledge or use of Western cutlery. Croquettes also gained the reputation of being filling and healthy, and their taste, especially when slathered in Worcestershire sauce, made them a favorite of Japanese consumers (Okada 2012, 212).

However, not all of the recipes in *Kuidōraku* could be easily incorporated into daily meals, and Murai recognized that new and exotic dishes like blancmange and bavarois were part of the novel's appeal for both wealthy and middle-class readers who wanted to learn about gourmet dining (Yoshida 2012, 183). Thus, when he turned his novel into a kabuki play in 1905, he had the Kabukiza theater install a gas stove on stage, allowing the actors to make Western sweets such as *choux de crème* (*shūkurīmu*) for distribution to the audience (Murase 2000, 192).[21] Murai further stoked interest in fine dining in his role in Japan's first gourmet monthly, *Kuidōraku*, which was named after his novel and also bore the English masthead *Culinary Magazine*. The magazine heavily excerpted Murai's writings, interviewed him at his home, showcased an "Otowa-style" apron designed by Murai's wife, and featured reviews of *Kuidōraku* themed restaurants (Rath 2017).[22] Katō Masutarō, the chef who had crafted many of the recipes used in *Kuidōraku*, was one of the entrepreneurs who opened a Western-style restaurant based on Murai's novel. Katō's establishment in Mita in Tokyo competed with the Otowa-tei in Hongyoku, an eatery named after *Kuidōraku*'s female protagonist. Otowa-tei proved so successful it opened three branches by 1905 (Kuroiwa 2004, 157–8). "Murai-style" dishes could also be found in restaurants outside of the capital (Ishida 2000, 45–6). Murai's popular nickname "*Kuidōraku* Gensai" speaks to the way he had become synonymous with his novel and with gourmet food. His home in Hiratsuka was called a "palace to gastronomy" (*bishoku no dendō*). There he entertained leaders in the culinary world including the owner of the historic Tokyo restaurant Yaozen, the founder of the confectionery company Morinaga, and the head of Ajinomoto, marketers of MSG (Kuroiwa 2004, 5).

As much as Murai tried to cultivate the interest of would-be gourmands and restaurateurs who might seek inspiration from his novel, Murai nevertheless condemned restaurant food several times in *Kuidōraku* through the voice of the pedantic Nakagawa. In one scene Nakagawa declares that the food in Western-style restaurants tastes bad. In another he testifies that dining out could never compare to eating at home where the wife makes daily efforts to please her husband (Murai 1978b, 69; 1978c, 271).

Rather than an exposition on gourmet food, "the main lesson of Murai's novel," as Jordan Sand has noted, "was the moral and physiological, as well as the pleasure, of *katei ryōri* (home cooking)" (Sand 2003, 73). Nakagawa declares, "in whatever country the very best cuisine is none other than home cooking, because there is nothing tastier than preparing food as one likes in one's own home" (Murai 1978c, 27). Nakagawa advocates for the ideals of home cooking while his sister Otowa is the person actually able to prepare meals according to these specifications.

Home cooking was a task that Odai utterly fails when she tries to make sushi. Odai is the country cousin that Ōhara seeks to avoid marrying in the novel.[23] Odai and her parents have taken up residence in Ōhara's home in a bid to try to force him to marry her, and Ōhara expresses his exasperation at Odai's eating habits that rely on purchasing food instead of preparing it herself:

> "Odai, ever since you came from that place in the countryside you haven't cooked at all, and all you do is order and eat take out from sushi restaurants and food sellers noon and night. That's not economical. If you want to eat sushi, make it yourself. It's a real problem if you don't know anything at all about home cooking."
>   Odai replies defensively, "But I don't know how. How am I gonna make sushi?"
>   Ōhara responds: "You could at least make sushi rolls at home. You can do that by just adding vinegar to rice, mixing it, placing some pieces of dried gourd in the middle, and rolling it up in nori. Even if it's not perfect, you can make a lot you can eat."
>
> Murai 1978b, 157–8

But even with the help of her servant, Odai makes a mess. She adds too much vinegar and makes the rice soggy. She burns the nori when she tries to toast it. She cannot roll the sushi; and when she tries to cut the rolls, rice squirts out the ends. "Ugh, tastes terrible. I can't eat it," she declares, spitting it out. Luckily, Ōhara's friend arrives with some homemade scattered (*gomoku*) sushi, which Odai quickly opens and sniffs in appreciation. "What's this? Oh, looks good," she says (Murai 1978b, 159–60). Odai's mistake provides an opportunity for Ōhara's friend Koyama to explain the correct way to make sushi (Murai 1978b, 160–3). Odai's failure to cook even a simple dish reveals that successfully managing a household is beyond her capacity and she serves as the foil for the ever capable Otowa in the novel.

The earliest English translation of the title of *Kuidōraku* was *The Pleasure of House-keeping*, a choice that reveals the centrality of home cooking and the household to Murai's novel.[24] Managing the household is not only important for the proper health of the family: the novel famously declares that the state of the household speaks to the level of modernity of a nation in its progress toward "enlightenment," borrowing part of the catchphrase "civilization and enlightenment" (*bunmei kaika*), which the Meiji government invoked to advocate for Western-style cultural and social reforms. Koyama, one of Nakagawa's friends, opines: "People talk about an enlightened country, but an enlightenment that is not based on the household is a superficial enlightenment. A true enlightenment is one in which people's households advance to enlightenment first, then society moves toward enlightenment" (Murai 1978d, 151).

Proper home cooking was integral to the creation of an enlightened household as seen in the architecture of an ideal home. "An enlightened lifestyle requires an enlightened kitchen," declares a caption at the beginning of the first volume of *Kuidōraku,* which has a color illustration of the kitchen in the residence of Ōkuma Shigenobu (1838–1922) (Figure 9.2). Ōkuma served as prime minister in 1898 (and again from 1914 to 1918) and his kitchen is described in the caption as equipped with glass windows, a cement floor, and an expensive gas range, providing a spectacular example of hygiene and efficiency. Able to prepare food for more than fifty people at a time, the kitchen is larger than a three-bedroom apartment (3LDK) in Japan today (Kuroiwa 2007, 37).

Beyond such grand examples, Nakagawa expounds in *Kuidōraku* that the kitchen should become the center of every home. It is where the family's meals are cooked three times a day, where delicacies are prepared for guests, and where the health of the family is determined. Thus, a kitchen deserves more attention than any other place in a

Figure 9.2 The kitchen in the residence of Ōkuma Shigenobu. Frontispiece illustration from Murai Gensai, *Kuidōraku* (1903), Vol. 1.

house. Nakagawa convinces his wealthy friend Hiroumi Shishaku to invest in remodeling the older cooking space in his home into a spacious, well-lit kitchen, saying "it's impossible to create the foods of the Meiji period in a kitchen of the 1830s" (Murai 1978b, 239–41, 243).

Having a modern kitchen is only the first step toward an enlightened household because the family, including the men, have to know how to best make use of it. Otowa observes to her brother Nakagawa that unless husbands take an interest in food, home cooking will not improve regardless of a wife's efforts. Nakagawa agrees, "Japanese men who disregard food are the main reason why home cooking is not able to advance" (Murai 1978b, 336). He proposes that men should study household management until they reach the age of forty. Nakagawa does not call for men to learn to cook, but to know instead what good cooking is. Women, Nakagawa observes, are sufficiently schooled in domestic matters that they can stop their formal studies when they marry; presumably that is when women will take over the responsibility of cooking for the husband, who, thanks to his knowledge of home cooking, will know what to expect (Murai 1978d, 164–7). Nakagawa's diatribe about cooking provides the intellectual pretext for Ōhara to travel to England to research home economics, while Otowa will later join him and pursue her own studies.

The international cuisine of *Kuidōraku*

That home cooking is the pinnacle of any type of meal and that the novel's hero and heroine need to travel abroad to study it are telling points about Murai Gensai's ideas about cuisine. This section will examine *Kuidōraku*'s message that good cooking needs to be something larger than a repertoire of native ingredients, flavors, and culinary techniques ascribed to a particular country. In other words, an evidence-based approach, which treats cooking like a science must replace obeisance to culinary tradition, and the resulting cuisine will have an international character, not a national one.

Murai wrote at a time before Japanese cuisine was represented as "traditional," and he clearly opposed the idea of preserving old ways of doing things for their own sake. In one scene Nakagawa proclaims, "with impartial analysis one can see that Westerners are more advanced than Japanese in their research on matters of food such as physiology and hygiene." Clearly there is much to be learned from the West, and Nakagawa advocates that Japanese create their own style of Western food (*seiyō ryōri*) by taking the best from the cuisines of countries from around the world (Murai 1978c, 273–4). In another episode, Nakagawa pontificates that the ideal home cooking will be a pastiche that blends Western, Chinese, and Japanese cooking, showing no preference for native dishes over those of other countries (Murai 1978b, 218).[25] A few years after the publication of *Kuidōraku*, Murai referred to his novel to urge readers of the magazine *Ladies' World* (*Fujin sekai*) to serve both Western and Japanese foods for breakfast. Murai explained that in his home, the servants consumed a Japanese meal of rice and miso soup, but he and his wife (who by implication were more sophisticated) ate oatmeal, muffins, rolls, French toast, and rolled oats (Murai 1907, 71–2).

In his later career, Murai experimented with a diet of grains and gathered foods reminiscent of long practiced strategies of subsistence in rural areas of Japan, but he was dismissive of rustic eating habits in *Kuidōraku*. Ōhara's initial health problems are due to his rural background and his fiancée Odai, who failed to make sushi rolls, embodies a stark rural diet. Ōhara describes Odai as a "country daughter from the middle of the northern mountains, lacking education and ill mannered." She is physically larger than Ōhara "with a red face, messy hair, a dumpling shaped nose, and eyeballs like acorns" (Murai 1978a, 15). Grain dumplings and acorns were associated with less desirable aspects of the rural diet that Odai personified. The beautiful heroine Otowa, in contrast, is "very advanced in her cooking" having lived in Nagasaki, Kobe, and Osaka, a background that explains her familiarity with Chinese food from Nagasaki's Chinese settlement, Western food from the treaty port of Kobe, and Japanese food from Osaka, known for centuries as the city where people "go broke for good food" (*Ōsaka no kuidaore*) (Murai 1978a, 17).

Otowa's home cooking is advanced not just in terms of her culinary skills, but also because with her brother's guidance she approaches home cooking as a science, derived from universal principles that transcend both tradition and political boundaries. Nakagawa, imparts this modern approach to cooking to his fiancée, Tamae, stating:

> An enlightened home needs enlightened appliances. If someone spends as much as ¥300–500 on a famous hanging scroll for their alcove, they can at least purchase one microscope for their kitchen. Count Ōkuma's residence now has a microscope room adjacent to the kitchen … Enlightened appliances are a necessity to give rise to and live an enlightened life. It is impossible to use things from the 1830s to create the enlightened foods of today.
>
> Murai 1978b, 126–7

Nakagawa explains that the purpose of a microscope is to detect adulterated food. In an age before refrigeration and consumer protection laws, having a microscope might indeed prove handy, but at the cost of building a single family home, the instrument was outside the reach of nearly all of the novel's readers (Nihon Tosho Sentā 2014, 46). As a less expensive means to test the quality of milk, Nakagawa recommends the Fesel lactoscope, priced at just ¥1.17 (Murai 1978b, 128).[26] In the aforementioned monologue, the real-life Count Ōkuma serves again as an exemplar to *Kuidōraku*'s readers as someone who lives a modern life by virtue of having enlightened kitchen appliances.[27]

The West can provide a source for modern technology, but there are a few things that Japan can contribute to the international science of cooking. Nakagawa proclaims that he wants to tell the world about *konbu*, a natural source of MSG, and a flavor enhancer that he states that Westerners do not know about. *Kuidōraku* contains a recipe for a soup with a broth combining *konbu* and beef, well suited for Western cooking (Murai 1978c, 37). After the publication of *Kuidōraku*, Murai Gensai became one of the earliest advocates for artificial MSG, created by the company Ajinomoto and marketed under the same name. The first advertisements for Ajinomoto in 1909 carried Murai's endorsement (Ishida 2000, 41; Kuroiwa 2004, 244).

Hana, Murai's message to the West

Another expression of Murai's interest in creating an international cuisine can be found in his novel *Hana: A Daughter of Japan*, published only in English translation in 1904.[28] Appearing in print the year after he wrote *Kuidōraku* and during the Russo-Japanese War (1904–5), *Hana* is a didactic novel intended for Western readers. Murai never published a Japanese language version and the original Japanese manuscript does not survive. *Hana* opens with a preface that provides a justification for Japan's war efforts. "The little Island-Empire has unsheathed her sword, sanctified and blessed, against gigantic Russia. Japan knows what she is fighting for; it is on behalf of humanity, civilization and the world's peace. It will never astound us if the war continues many years. England struggled with Napoleon for twenty-two years: she is our example" (Murai 1904b, liv).

The larger conflict is the backdrop to a contest between two characters, an American and a Russian, who struggle over the affections of a Japanese women named Hana. The story opens at the Fujiya Hotel near Hakone where Connor, an American from Chicago, has traveled under doctor's orders to soak in the hot springs in hopes of curing his dyspeptic stomach. Hana befriends Connor after he rescues her dog. He then meets Hana's father, Dr. Hayashi, who introduces himself:

> I treat the diet; I follow one of the old Chinese schools of medicine, called *shokui*. I do not know what you call it in English—perhaps a diet-physician, or a diet-specialist may convey the meaning. So I might call myself a diet-physician. My special study is the food men eat ... The medical doctors treat the patients after they are ill, but my system treats men so that they will not suffer from sickness.
>
> Murai 1904b, 12–13

Dr. Hayashi exhibits the same eclectic approach to the study of food as found in *Kuidōraku*, extending his interests beyond Japanese cuisine. He explains: "Besides our own Japanese food, there is Chinese and European cookery; and European, again, is subdivided into French, English, German, and Russian styles, etc. I study all these and take the best from all of them, and I make food in what I may call a new international style" (Murai 1904b, 13). With Dr. Hayashi's guidance, Connor's health improves, and he becomes infatuated with Hana, who is an "excellent cook" (Murai 1904b, 19). Their love triumphs over the treacherous Russian spy, Danski, who first attempts to blackmail Hana and then tries to kill her.

Besides defending Japan's role in the Russo–Japanese War, *Hana* is a message to English readers about possible points of culinary collaboration between Japan and the West in developing an international cuisine. At the same time that Connor defeats Danski and wins Hana's love, her father Dr. Hayashi gains fame for his study of food to the point that a "new cooking of the 'Hayashian style' was gradually gaining a place in Japan as the best sanitary diet." Connor attests to the virtues of Dr. Hayashi's diet and seeks to serve as the doctor's ambassador to the West. He echoes Nakagawa's plans in *Kuidōraku* to introduce soup made with konbu, which Connor states "will surely be welcomed by Western [*sic*] people" (Murai 1904b, 234–5). He urges Dr. Hayashi to write a book about his methods and allow Hana to travel with him back to America so that she could become a cooking teacher. The last line of *Hana* indicates the success of this venture: "Dr. Hayashi's new method of cooking has been gradually taking hold in America, and people say it has succeeded through the aid of Mr. Connor and his beloved wife Hana" (Murai 1904b, 239).

Hana clearly has many parallels with *Kuidōraku*. In both novels, a man with stomach problems benefits from the sage advice of a male authority and becomes infatuated with that man's female relative. Hana and Otowa embody the principles their respective male culinary experts in their novels espouse. Despite being able to actually cook— something that Dr. Hayashi and Nakagawa do not even attempt—both Hana and Otowa exist in the shadows of these men much like Murai Takako who published her cookbooks under the title "Gensai's Wife" (Murai and Ishizuka 1910, 1912). Unlike *Kuidōraku*, *Hana* only contains one recipe, and in *Hana* Connor wins and marries his love.[29] In *Kuidōraku*, Ōhara's future with Otowa remains uncertain even in the sequel. *Hana* also presents the fruition of the development of an international style of cuisine, a process that had only been in the making in *Kuidōraku*. Dr. Hayashi's new international cuisine is created in Japan as an adaptation of different national cuisines and scientific methods, and then exported to the West by Japanese and American collaborators: one grasps the theoretical basis for healthy food and the other is actually able to prepare it. Hana and Connor's interracial marriage can be read as symbolizing a fusion of Western and Japanese food that has given rise to an international cuisine.

Murai took up the topic of interracial marriage in his book *Advice to Ladies and Men* (*Fujin oyobi danshi no sankō*), published in 1910, a work compiled from columns he wrote for *Ladies' World* magazine. Murai observed that interracial marriages between Japanese and Westerners typified the Meiji era. Some people, Murai explained, saw this hybridization of race as a way to improve Japan's genetic stock, but Murai disputed that notion, explaining that victory over Russia proved that Japan was as advanced as any Western country. Instead of nationalistic terms, such marriages should be viewed on a case-by-case basis. He noted that an interracial marriage could only succeed if the couple shared the same taste in food (Murai 1910, 334–6, 354). By that logic, the development of an international cuisine would help bring people of different nationalities together.

Healthy eating after *Kuidōraku*

Home cooking, household management, and above all the attempt to view cuisine as a science with universal applications rather than through the lens of national identity remained a focus of Murai's writings after the publication of *Kuidōraku*. In 1906, *Hōchi Shimbun* ran the sequel to *Kuidōraku*, which was later published in book form in 1906 and 1907 under the title *The Sequel to Shokudōraku* (*Shokudōraku zokuhen*). *Shokudōraku* uses the same Chinese characters as *Kuidōraku*, but Murai presents a different reading of the first *kanji* as *shoku*, meaning "food" as opposed to *kui*, representing "eating," suggesting an attempt to emphasize cooking instead of consuming. By 1906 Murai had severed ties with the gourmet magazine *Kuidōraku* named for his novel, and that might have also provoked his decision to change the book's title for the sequel. *Shokudōraku zokuhen* failed to win the same popularity as *Kuidōraku* and it did not resolve the romance introduced in the original. Otowa remains in Japan while Ōhara is off studying in Europe so they are unable to consummate their affections. Odai, however, transforms from a country bumpkin to a proper middle-class lady.

In the same year that *Hōchi Shimbun* ran the sequel to *Kuidōraku*, Murai left the newspaper to join the editorial board of a newly founded magazine, *Ladies' World* (*Fujin sekai*), where he worked the next two decades. Apart from two short novels serialized in *Ladies' World*, Murai gave up writing fiction, focusing instead on advice columns for housewives. Circulation of *Ladies' World* climbed to an average of 200,000 issues per month after he joined that publication (Kuroiwa 2007, 273).

Kuidōraku made Murai famous for home cooking, but in his career writing for *Ladies' World*, he became obsessed with making drastic adjustments to his own diet in the pursuit of the healthiest way of eating. At a time when the cause of beriberi was still under debate, in 1910 Murai read about an experiment in which beriberi in chickens had been cured by adding rice bran to their feed. He tested this with his own flock and discovered the same result. From 1911 to 1912, he launched a "bran campaign" in *Ladies' World* magazine, which he advertised in other publications, promising that his "Murai soup" containing rice bran was a cure for beriberi. Physicians looking for a bacteriological cause for the ailment scoffed at Murai, but readers of *Ladies' World* wrote letters testifying that "Murai soup" had cured them (Ishida 2000, 44–4; Kuroiwa 2007, 83–4).[30]

Emboldened with the idea of experimenting with different foods as medicines, from 1915 Murai began making radical changes to his diet. He practiced fasting, building up to a thirty-five-day period when he only ate two bowls of gruel and a pickled apricot once a week. He reported the results in *Ladies' World* and wrote a 647-page book, *The Gensai Method for Health by Fasting* (*Gensaishiki danjiki ryōhō*) (Murai 1917). Murai went on to explore the curative properties of other foodstuffs. He tried a number of food restriction diets, eating only fruits, nuts, shoots, buckwheat, and tofu in turn. He then switched to a paleo diet composed only of foods that he had hunted, caught, or gathered by himself while living for half a year as a recluse on Mount Mitake in Tokyo prefecture (Kuroiwa 2007, 276–80). In an interview twenty-eight years after Murai Gensai's death, Murai Takako commented on her husband's culinary journey. She explained, "because he changed from *Kuidōraku* to fasting to a diet of nuts, everyone was surprised, but it was all part of his consistent aspiration to ask what to do to make life better" (Murai 1955, 79). Murai's literary characters traveled abroad to deepen their knowledge of food science. Murai himself seems to have exhausted all available textual and informant resources on food in Japan, so he experimented on his own body in the effort to make discoveries he could share with others, following a scientific method to improve cooking and develop an international cuisine.

Conclusion

Murai Gensai used the neologisms Japanese, Chinese, and Western cuisine in his writings, but his vision for cooking transcended national boundaries. He determined that cuisine should not be limited to a catalog of a country's dietary traditions, but rather should demarcate a scientific method that people around the world could use to improve their health and well-being and thereby enlighten society. He envisioned Japanese homemakers who employed principles of cooking developed in other countries taking a leading role in the pursuit of culinary knowledge, creating their own home cooking with merits that would rise above national boundaries. Outside of his fiction, Murai experimented on the effects of food (and fasting) on his own body in an effort to make new gastronomic and medical discoveries.

Today, "traditional" Japanese meals are typified as healthy due to their small serving sizes and for preferencing vegetables over beef, but those were qualities Murai attributed to Western cooking in his novel, which not only shows how dominant perceptions of Japanese food have changed since his time, but also how Japanese cuisine has become closer to the ideals that Murai promoted.[31] In *Kuidōraku*, the authoritative Nakagawa describes a home-cooked meal in the West made up of varieties of dishes "served as if for a doll." He then criticizes Japanese imitators of Western food who grilled beefsteak large enough to feed three people. Authentic Western cuisine actually uses more vegetables than meat, he explains (Murai 1978a, 91–3) (Figure 9.3).

Learning about proper portion size and to preference vegetables over meat falls under the rubric of "food education" (*shokuiku*), a term found in Murai's novel that has become popular again thanks to government campaigns since 2005.[32] For his program

Figure 9.3 Otowa shows a diagram of different cuts of beef. Illustration from Murai Gensai, *Kuidōraku* (1903), Vol. 4.

of food education, Murai wanted his readers to embrace authentic Western dietary practices and abandon indigenous ones, but the recent food education campaigns in Japan, as Stephanie Assmann has described, seek to steer people away from Western foods to adopt a supposedly healthier native diet (Assmann 2015). In the chapter in *Kuidōraku* titled "A Discourse on *Shokuiku*," Ōhara complains how Japanese schools fail to include practical learning. Otowa concurs, stating, "more important than intellectual knowledge and physical education, is food education, so it would be unwise to omit studying it" (Murai 1978c, 242–3). Food education as depicted in *Kuidōraku* was a progressive, scientific approach to creating a healthy lifestyle that borrowed from foreign models and technology, not the attempt to provoke a return to an idealized version of a nation's "traditional" diet as evidenced by the Japanese government's recent *shokuiku* and *washoku* campaigns.[33]

Kuidōraku debuted at an opportune time for critiquing native foodways and for envisioning an international cuisine. In the first decade of the twentieth century, the Japanese government was making strides in establishing political parity with Western powers such as by signing the Anglo–Japanese Alliance in 1902, whereby Britain and Japan pledged to protect each other's territorial interests against Russian expansion. In *Hana* Murai expressed confidence in his country's victory over Russia in the Russo-Japanese War and that a cuisine based on scientific principles could cross cultures. Writing in an era before an essentialized national cuisine had yet to appear in Japan, Murai had the freedom to imagine transnational culinary possibilities placing him in sharp contrast with the culinary expert Kitaōji Rosanjin (1883–1959), who wrote decades later about the superiority of Japanese cuisine.[34]

In 1920, Murai printed a revised version of *Kuidōraku*, which included an extended preface of 211 pages developed, he explained, from his eighteen years of further research about food. He added supplemental essays on the alimentary qualities of adlay, tofu, and rice bran. He included his recipe for "Murai [rice bran] soup." And he set forth four rules for cuisine: (1) preserve natural flavors; (2) follow natural ways of combining [foods]; (3) endeavor to harmonize eating and digestion; and (4) impart cuisine with beautiful taste, smell, color, and shape, and use fine serving ware (Murai 1920).

Although he advocated for developing an international cuisine rather than elevating the foods of his own country, Murai's ideas echo most strongly today in familiar expressions about the aesthetics of "traditional" Japanese cuisine that emphasize enhancing the natural flavors of food and appealing to all of the senses through delicate cooking and careful plating.[35] A hundred years after the publication of *Kuidōraku*, food author Ruth Reichl wrote in the preface to a famous Japanese cookbook: "to truly appreciate Japanese cuisine means learning to appreciate quality and paying attention to every bite" (Reichl 2011, 9). Were Murai alive today he might ask why Reichl ascribed those qualities to a national cuisine when they should be international. The fact that today the category of "cuisine" is so closely defined according to national boundaries provides all the more reason to return to the ideas of Murai Gensai, who imagined creating an international cuisine that would be elegant, healthy, and would bring people of different nationalities together to collaborate as cooks and as eaters.

Notes

1   Unlike other major authors, Murai Gensai lacks a collected works (*zenshū*) (Kuroiwa 2004, 27). Two books by Kuroiwa Hisako are the major studies of Murai's life and works. *Shokuiku no susume* (2007) is a close reading of *Kuidōraku* and *"Kuidōraku" no hito Murai Gensai* (2004) is a biography. I relied on both greatly in this chapter.

2   I discuss *Kuidōraku* magazine and its relationship with Murai Gensai in Rath (2017). The novel also spawned literary parodies with Kōda Rohan's (1867–1947) 1904 story *The Delicacy Competition* (*Chinsenkai*) the most prominent example (see Aoyama 2008, 55–7).

3   Sand (2003, 74) discusses how Murai's novel promoted "home cooking" (*katei ryōri*). Kushner observes how Murai promoted Western ways of eating over Japanese, citing Murai as declaring that Western food was "more nutritious, hygienic, practical, modern and democratic than traditional Japanese fare" (Kushner 2012, 109; see also Aoyama 2008, 103).

4   As described later, the term "international style" of cooking appears in English in Murai's novel *Hana: A Daughter of Japan*, and was used separately from Western cooking in the same text. We do not know the original term Murai used in Japanese for "international style," but the word meant something different than Western food.

5   The Tokyo School of Foreign Languages (Gaikokugo Gakkō) is now the Tokyo University of Foreign Studies.

6   In 1894, *Hōchi Shimbun* shortened its name from the *Yūbin Hōchi Shimbun*.

7   The length of *Hinodejima* means that most readers find it too daunting to read today and it is no longer in print.

8   Not all of Murai's *dōraku* novels warned readers off pleasures. In *Pleasures of Fishing* (*Tsuri dōraku*), Murai expounded on the joy of angling (Murai 1901).

9   The novel was later published in four volumes organized by the four seasons. The first three volumes appeared in 1903 with spring in June, summer in October, and fall in December. The winter volume was published in March 1904.

10 Kuroiwa interprets the name Ōhara Mitsuru to mean a large stomach that is full; Aoyama concurs with this reading (Kuroiwa 2007, 46; Aoyama 2003, 253).

11 The peanut soup is identified in the text as *nankinmame shiruko*.

12 Peanuts arrived in the eighteenth century, but peanut farming only became prominent in the Meiji period (Adachi 1981, 308–9).

13 Kuroiwa Hisako observes that there were no references to food in Murai's writings before his marriage to Takako in 1900 (Kuroiwa 2007, 49).

14 For instance, Murai Takako wrote the column "Gensai's Wife Discusses Cooking" in *Fujin sekai* magazine for six years. The recipes were later republished as a four-volume book *Gensai's Wife's Cooking Talks: Easy and Practical* (Murai and Ishizuka 1910, 1912). The title presents Takako's authority as deriving from being Gensai's spouse when in fact she knew more about cooking than he did.

15 The chef is mentioned in passing under the name Katō Masujirō in *Kuidōraku*.

16 The one exception to Murai's lack of interest in kitchen work was that he loved grilled eel and wanted to be able to prepare it himself. He sought guidance from a professional chef, and sometimes prepared grilled eel three times a day to try to perfect his recipe (Kuroiwa 2007, 167).

17 In 1881, the government mandated that elementary and middle schools for girls include home economics in their curriculum. The extent and emphasis of cooking instruction varied by locality, but the overall goal of girl's education was, according to

the Ministry of Education in 1899, to socialize young women to become "good wives and wise mothers" (Ehara 2012, 103–8).

18 This gendered division of readership also influenced *Kuidōraku* magazine, inspired by Murai's novel. The magazine included restaurant reviews that catered to male readers and home cooking articles for housewives (Rath 2017).

19 Regarding the use of *Kuidōraku* as a cookbook, see Kuroiwa (2007, 200). English translations of the title as *Gourmandism* and *The Gourmand*, suggest the novel is about gourmet food (Aoyama 2003, 252; Kushner 2012, 109).

20 In his 1904 parody of *Kuidōraku*, Kōda Rohan caricatured how Murai introduced new and strange foods. Kōda's work, *The Delicacy Competition*, describes an eating contest of baby mice, monkey lips, and steamed toads (Aoyama 2003, 255–6).

21 Spectators could also purchase a boxed lunch specific to the play from the theater's restaurant (Murai 1955, 77).

22 The magazine ran from 1905 to 1907. A magazine with the same title was published from 1928 to 1941.

23 The *kanji* for the name Odai (お代) can also be read as *oshiro*, making Odai "the 'price' or the 'cost' of the financial support Ōhara received" to attend university from Odai's father (Aoyama 2003, 253). The homonym *odai* (お台) meant the wife of a high-ranking aristocrat or warrior and is short for *odaidokoro*, which also meant kitchen. In the Edo period, the wife of the shogun was called *odaidokoro* or *odaisama* (Yamaguchi and Kenkyūjo 1980, 17). Thus, Odai also personifies a feudal method of food preparation, marriage, and society that Gensai critiqued in his novel.

24 The translated title appeared in the preface of a 1904 translation of Murai's novel *Hana*, introduced below.

25 Murai referred to Chinese cuisine by the derogatory term *Shina ryōri*, "Chink cooking" as opposed to Nanjing cuisine (*Nankin ryōri*), another term for Chinese food in the Meiji period (Han 2014, 85).

26 The Fesel lactoscope is used to measure the butter fat content of milk, and hence its purity. I am grateful to Takashi Domoto and Demet Guzey for an explanation of this device.

27 Murai frequently mentions Ōkuma Shigenobu in *Kuidōraku*. The first volume of *Kuidōraku* opens with a color frontispiece depicting the modern kitchen in Ōkuma's home (Figure 9.2) and the fourth volume shows him seated at a Western-style banquet table entertaining foreign dignitaries. Ōkuma had close personal ties with Murai through Murai's wife, Takako, who was the daughter of Ōkuma's cousin. When Murai began serializing his novel, Ōkuma sent his personal chef to live with Murai to provide advice about cooking (Kuroiwa 2007, 206–7).

28 *Hana* was one of three works Murai wrote to be translated into English (Murai 1904b). The other two were for adolescent readers (Murai 1904a, 1905).

29 The recipe in *Hana* is for crumbly pork (*soboro*), usually served as a topping for rice (Murai 1904b, 198–9).

30 For an account of the history of beriberi in modern Japan and a discussion of the debate over the causes of the condition, see Bay (2012).

31 M. F. K. Fisher exclaimed: "The Japanese *ryōri* says, 'Let little seem like much, as long as it is fresh and beautiful'" (Fisher 2011, 21).

32 The term *shokuiku* was not widely used until the Japanese government's 2005 Fundamental Law on Food Education (*Shokuiku kihon hō*) (Kuroiwa 2007, 15–16).

33 "Perpetuation of traditional food culture," is one of the aims of the Ministry of Agriculture, Forestry, and Fisheries *shokuiku* programs (Ministry of Agriculture, Forestry, and Fisheries n.d., 5).

34 The first Japanese national cuisine was "national people's cuisine" (*kokuminshoku*) a
    government project to economize resources and mobilize the population during the
    Second World War (Rath 2016, 127–45).
35 Kitaōji Rosanjin observed, "the mountains and seas of Japan are blessed with beautiful
    vegetables and seafood. It is the responsibility and the pleasure of people who cook to
    either give life to or kill these sacred flavors" (Kitaōji and Hirano 1980, 280).

References

安達巌 Adachi Iwao. 1981. 日本食物文化の起原 *Nihon shokumotsu bunka no kigen* [*The
    Arrival and Culture of Japanese Foodstuffs*]. Tokyo: Jiyū Kokuminsha.

Aoyama, Tomoko. 2003. "Romancing Food: The Gastronomic Quest in Early Twentieth-
    Century Japanese Literature." *Japanese Studies* 23, no. 3: 251–64.

Aoyama, Tomoko. 2008. *Reading Food in Modern Japanese Literature*. Honolulu: University
    of Hawai'i Press.

Assmann, Stephanie. 2015. "The Remaking of a National Cuisine: The Food Education
    Campaign in Japan." In *The Globalization of Asian Cuisines: Transnational Networks
    and Culinary Contact Zones*, edited by James Farrer, 165–85. New York: Palgrave
    Macmillan.

Bay, Alexander R. 2012. *Beriberi in Modern Japan: The Making of a National Disease*.
    Rochester, NY: University of Rochester Press.

江原絢子 Ehara Ayako. 2012. 家庭料理の近代 *Katei ryōri no kindai* [*Home Cooking in
    the Modern Age*]. Tokyo: Yoshikawa Kōbunkan.

Fisher, M. F. K. 2011. Introduction to *Japanese Cooking: A Simple Art* by Shizuo Tsuji,
    11–21. New York: Kodansha.

Han, Eric C. 2014. *Rise of a Japanese Chinatown: Yokohama 1894–1972*. Cambridge, MA:
    Harvard University Asia Center Press.

飯田喜代子 Iida Kiyoko. 2010. "「食道楽」における西洋料理の導入について
    Kuidōraku ni okeru seiyō ryōri no dōnyū ni tsuite" ["The Introduction of Western
    Cooking in *Kuidōraku*"]. 生活文化研究 *Seikatsu bunka kenkyū* 19: 33–50.

石田あゆう Ishida Ayū. 2000. "「食道楽」作家・村井弦斎にみる消費者教育 *Kuidōraku
    sakka, Murai Gensai ni miru shōhisha kyōiku*" ["Consumer Education As Seen in the
    Work of Murai Gensai Author of *Kuidōraku*"]. *Kyōto shakai kagaku nenpyō* [*Kyoto
    Social Science Annual*] 8: 31–50.

北大路魯山人 Kitaōji Rosanjin, and 平野雅章 Hirano Masaaki. 1980. 魯山人味道
    Rosanjin midō [*Rosanjin's Way of Taste*]. Tokyo: Chūō Kōronsha.

黒岩比佐子 Kuroiwa Hisako. 2004. 「食道楽」の人村井弦斎 *"Kuidōraku" no hito
    Murai Gensai* [*Murai Gensai, the Man of "Kuidōraku"*]. Tokyo: Iwanami Shoten.

黒岩比佐子 Kuroiwa Hisako. 2007. 食育のススメ *Shokuiku no susume* [*Promoting Food
    Education*]. Tokyo: Bungei Shunjū.

Kushner, Barak. 2012. *Slurp! A Social and Culinary History of Ramen—Japan's Favorite
    Noodle Soup*. Boston, MA: Brill Global Oriental.

Ministry of Agriculture, Forestry and Fisheries. n.d. "What is Shokuiku (Food
    Education)?" http://www.maff.go.jp/e/pdf/shokuiku.pdf.

Murai, Gensai. 1904a. *Kibun Daizin; Or, From Shark-Boy to Merchant Prince*. New York:
    Century Co.

Murai, Gensai. 1904b. *Hana: A Daughter of Japan*. Translated by Unkichi Kawai. Tokyo:
    Hochi Shinbun.

Murai, Gensai. 1905. *Ordeal by Music; The Tale of Akoya.* Translated by Unkichi Kawai, Tokyo: Hochi Shinbun.

村井弦斎 Murai Gensai. 1906-7. 食道楽 統編 *Shokudōraku zokuhen* [*The Sequel to Shokudōraku*]. Tokyo: Hōchisha.

村井弦斎 Murai Gensai. 1907. 婦人の日常生活法 *Fujin no nichijō seikatsuhō* [*Rules for Daily Life for Ladies*]. Tokyo: Jitsugyō no Nihonsha.

村井弦斎 Murai Gensai. 1910. 婦人及男子の参考 *Fujin oyobi danshi no sankō* [*Advice to Ladies and Men*]. Tokyo: Jitsugyō no Nihonsha.

村井弦斎 Murai Gensai. 1917. 弦斎式断食療法 *Gensaishiki danjiki ryōhō* [*The Gensai Method for Health by Fasting*]. Tokyo: Jitsugyō no Nihonsha.

村井弦斎 Murai Gensai. 1920. 十八年間の研究を増補したる食道樂 *Jūhachinenkan no kenkyū o zōhoshitaru shokudōraku* [*The Expanded Shokudōraku Based on Eighteen Years of Research*]. Tokyo: Shinbashidō.

村井弦斎 Murai Gensai. 1978a. 食道楽 *Kuidōraku* [*The Pleasures of Housekeeping*], edited by 村井米子 Murai Yoneko, Vol. 1. Tokyo: Shin Jinbutsu Ōraisha.

村井弦斎 Murai Gensai. 1978b. 食道楽 *Kuidōraku* [*The Pleasures of Housekeeping*], edited by 村井米子 Murai Yoneko, Vol. 2. Tokyo: Shin Jinbutsu Ōraisha.

村井弦斎 Murai Gensai. 1978c. 食道楽 *Kuidōraku* [*The Pleasures of Housekeeping*], edited by 村井米子 Murai Yoneko, Vol. 3. Tokyo: Shin Jinbutsu Ōraisha.

村井弦斎 Murai Gensai. 1978d. 食道楽 *Kuidōraku* [*The Pleasures of Housekeeping*], edited by 村井米子 Murai Yoneko, Vol. 4. Tokyo: Shin Jinbutsu Ōraisha.

村井多嘉[子] Murai Taka[ko]. 1955. "思い出の絵巻：その二 Omoide no emaki: Sono ni" ["Picture Scroll of Memories: Part Two"]. 婦人の友 *Fujin no tomo* [*Ladies' Companion*] 12 (December): 73-9.

村井多嘉子 Murai Takako, and 石塚月亭 Ishizuka Gettei. 1910. 弦斎夫人の料理談：手軽実用 *Gensai fujin no ryōridan: Tegaru jitsuyō* [*Gensai's Wife's Cooking Talks: Easy and Practical*]. Vols. 1-3. Tokyo: Jitsugyō no Nihonsha.

村井多嘉子 Murai Takako, and 石塚月亭 Ishizuka Gettei. 1912. 弦斎夫人の料理談：手軽実用 *Gensai fujin no ryōridan* [*Gensai's Wife's Cooking Talks: Easy and Practical*]. Vol. 4. Tokyo, Jitsugyō no Nihonsha.

村瀬士郎 Murase Shirō. 2002. "「食」を「道楽」にする方法（マニュアル）：明治三十年代消費生活の手引き 'Shoku' o 'dōraku' suru hōhō (manyuaru): Meiji sanjū nendai shōhi seikatsu no tebiki" ["Manual for Turning Food into a Pleasure: A Consumer's Guide from the Meiji 30s"]. In ディスクールの帝国：明治三〇年代の文化研究 *Disukūru no teikoku: Meiji sanjū nendai no bunka kenkyū* [*Discourse of Imperialism: Cultural Studies of the Meiji 30s*], edited by 金子明雄 Akio Kaneko, 高橋修 Takahashi Osamu, and 吉田司雄 Yoshida Morio, 165-98. Tokyo: Shin'yōsha.

日本図書センター Nihon Tosho Sentā. 2014. 明治・大正庶民生活史 *Meiji, Taishō shomin seikatsushi* [*A History of People's Daily Life in the Meiji and Taishō Periods*]. Tokyo: Nihon Tosho Sentā.

岡田哲 Okada Tetsu. 2012. 明治洋食事始め：とんかつの誕生 *Meiji yōshoku kotohajime: Tonkatsu no tanjō* [*The Beginning of Western Food in the Meiji Period: The Origin of the Pork Cutlet*]. Tokyo: Kōdansha Gakujutsu Bunko.

Rath, Eric C. 2016. *Japan's Cuisines: Food, Place and Identity.* London: Reaktion Books.

Rath, Eric C. 2017. "For Gluttons Not Housewives, Japan's First Gourmet Magazine, *Kuidōraku.*" In *Feeding Japan: The Cultural and Political Issues of Dependency and Risk*, edited by Andreas Niehaus and Tine Walravens, 83-111. London: Palgrave Macmillan.

Reichl, Ruth. 2011. "Foreword." In *Japanese Cooking: A Simple Art*, edited by Shizuo Tsuji, 7-9. New York: Kodansha.

Sand, Jordan. 2003. *House and Home in Modern Japan: Architecture, Domestic Space, and Bourgeois Culture, 1880–1930.* Cambridge, MA: Harvard University Asia Center Press.

Smil, Vaclav, and Kazuhiko Kobayashi. 2012. *Japan's Dietary Transition and Its Impacts.* Cambridge, MA: The MIT Press.

鈴木良昌 Suzuki Yoshimasa, 岩瀬彰利 Iwase Akitoshi, 藤田大貴 Fujita Daiki, and 中野裕子 Nakano Yūko. 2016. 食道楽豊橋版：グルメ小説の再現レシピ *Shokudōraku Toyohashiban: Gurume shōsetsu no saigen reshipi* [*The Toyohashi Shokudōraku Book: Reproductions of Recipes from a Gourmet Novel*]. Aichi, Toyohashi: Toyohashi-shi Toshokan.

Unkichi Kawai. 1904. "Gensai Murai: His Life and Works." Foreword to *Hana: A Daughter of Japan*, by Gensai Murai, v–xlvii. Tokyo: Hochi Shinbun.

山口昌伴 Yamaguchi Masatomo, and G. K. 研究所 G. K. Kenkyūjo. 1980. 図説台所道具の歴史 *Zuzetsu daidokoro dōgu no rekishi* [*An Illustrated History of Kitchen Utensils*]. Tokyo: Shibata Shoten.

吉田 菊次郎 Yoshida Kikujirō. 2012. 西洋菓子：日本のあゆみ *Seiyōgashi: Nihon no ayumi*, [*Western Sweets: Developments in Japan*]. Tokyo: Chōbunsa.

10

Red (Michelin) Stars Over China: Seeking Recognition in a Transnational Culinary Field

James Farrer
Sophia University

Everyone hates Michelin...

The first Michelin city guide to a Mainland Chinese city was published in Shanghai (Map 2) in September 2016. In a pointed contrast to the inaugural Michelin guide for Tokyo, which awarded 227 stars in 2011 (Farrer 2010), only thirty-five stars were awarded to Shanghai restaurants. Tang Court, the Shanghai branch of a Hong Kong-based Cantonese restaurant located in a luxury hotel, was the only restaurant to be awarded three stars. Seven Shanghai eateries received two stars, and eighteen received one. Most surprisingly perhaps, only twenty-five restaurants were listed in the Bib Gourmand, defined in China as a selection of dining establishments that offer good food for under 200 yuan per person (Xu 2016). The publication of a culinary guidebook may seem trivial, but I will argue that it represents a characteristic, perhaps even key, event in the integration of Chinese gastronomy into a globalizing culinary field, shaping not only the expression of cuisine but also its politics.

The night after the guide was published I attended a catered "chef's dinner" at a small Shanghai eatery with several Shanghai-based Western chefs, Chinese chefs, and food writers. They grumbled that Michelin had failed to produce a convincing guide to Shanghai's fine-dining scene. There were too many hotel restaurants and too many chain (or branch) restaurants (including the Tang Court). Given that many of my dinner companions worked in Shanghai's Western fine-dining restaurants, they focused on the several locally run fine-dining Western restaurants that did not make the list, including Bistro 321 Le Bec, a widely acclaimed restaurant run by French chef Nicolas Le Bec, who had operated a two-starred Michelin restaurant in Lyon. Others were surprised that locally based French chef Paul Pairet's experimental restaurant Ultraviolet only received two stars, while a clone restaurant by global celebrity chef Joel Robuchon was awarded two stars despite having just opened in the city. Most chefs attributed this pattern to inexperienced out-of-town judges, who seem to have spent too much time in hotels and shopping malls.[1] Some groused about corrupt judges, though without any evidence.

Broader Chinese reactions to the Michelin guide were also sharply negative but focused on slights to the city's local culinary traditions. Most significantly, Shanghai-based Chinese media outlets criticized the bias of the guide toward Cantonese fare and the failure to include many Shanghainese (本帮菜 *benbangcai*) restaurants. Many noted that only one of the Michelin judges was a native Shanghainese. Others questioned the awarding of stars to old state-owned restaurants generally considered to be serving tired versions of Shanghai cuisine with notoriously inconsistent quality (*Jie Fang Daily* 2016).

Revealing a strong current of Chinese culinary nationalism, critics of Michelin emphasized the inability of foreign judges to understand the culinary techniques and skills involved in producing fine Chinese cuisine. As Chen Shuo, the director of the enormously popular CCTV food documentary series, *A Bite of China* (舌尖上的中國 *Shejian Shang de Zhongguo*) wrote in the *Shanghai Morning Post*: "It is quite likely that Michelin was not able to truly understand the essence of Chinese cuisine ... *A Bite of China* is much more sensitive to the emotional experience of our compatriots, and is based on identifying with the culture. In terms of its emotional sensitivity, the Michelin cannot compare" (Jin 2016).

Indeed, the iconic documentary serial *A Bite of China* could be seen as the best representative of an orthodox Chinese culinary nationalism that focuses on regional dishes, represented in the program as traditional, simple fare that is close to the land and lives of ordinary people. Neither fine-dining restaurant cuisine, nor foreign and fusion cuisine have a place in its pantheon of "authentic" Chinese culinary culture. What matters rather is identification with the culture and "emotional sensitivity" (lit., "temperature of emotion" 感情上的温度 *ganqing shang de wendu*) of a place, presumably something foreigners can rarely feel.

Others, however, regarded Michelin as a wake-up call to reform Shanghainese traditional cuisine. Shen Jialu, a prominent Shanghai food critic, wrote: "Don't be angry, my good brethren! We really need to reflect. Could it be that traditional Shanghainese cuisine, with its oily and soy-laden style that hasn't changed for decades, is in contradiction with the ideas of contemporary culinary culture? While it [Shanghai-style cuisine] has ruled the restaurant market for years, how many innovative dishes actually have been created?" Shen continues with a critique of some traditional Shanghai dishes, such as the cloying "Eight Treasure Chicken" which "fills you up as soon as you start eating." He argues that Shanghai chefs should thank Michelin for the giving them the impetus to modify their cooking styles to better match international culinary trends toward lighter fare (Shen 2016).

In these reactions, we see two faces of culinary nationalism in China—and perhaps Chinese nationalism more generally. The first takes foreign commentary on China as an example of how foreign views, and perhaps foreigners more generally, cannot be trusted when it comes to Chinese matters. Only Chinese really can judge Chinese food. Another uses foreign commentary to prod the Chinese to action. Chinese must rise to the meet the international culinary challenge by learning from its better points and participating in the competition. Underpinning both reactions is a set of assumptions about national unity, ethnic identity, and national culture. In Chinese culinary politics, Chinese cuisine is regarded as an exemplary element of Chinese civilization that only

Chinese people can truly appreciate. At the same time, there is the sense that Chinese culinary culture should also be recognized abroad, and that Chinese should be excelling in the global arena of culinary stars. The close association of nation, national belonging, and traditional culinary culture are emphasized in both these versions of culinary nationalist rhetoric.

Finally, we can see in these reactions that culinary regionalism is embedded within this culinary nationalism, since Shanghainese were most incensed by the domination of Cantonese cuisine in Michelin choices. Yet culinary nationalism and regionalism are not the end of the story here. With Michelin, we also are seeing the partial incorporation of Shanghai into a global culinary field, a pattern we can also see all over the world (Farrer 2015a). This globalization of culinary logics and culinary authority represented in the idea of a global culinary field does not mean the end of culinary nationalism and regionalism, but shapes the expression of both.

. . . but everyone wants a star

The resistance to Michelin in Shanghai may have been shaped by the local circumstances, including the paucity of awarded stars, China's prickly culinary nationalism, the snubbing of the local cuisine in favor of a regional rival, and the relative isolation of the country's cooks from global culinary trends over the past decades. However, in other respects the reactions were predictable and even typical. Shanghai's response to Michelin follows a pattern we can see in the guide book's expansion beyond France and beyond Europe. In Michelin's first non-European venture, the city guide to New York in 2005, local critics' complaints focused on similar factors as in Shanghai: the absence of local tasters on Michelin's panel, the inability to understand local culinary trends and the unsuitability of the standards to the New York scene (Ferguson 2008). Yet after a few years, New Yorkers and the local media largely accepted Michelin as one of the legitimate gatekeepers of culinary excellence (Bouty, Gomez, and Drucker-Godard 2013, 13).

A similar pattern was found in the introduction of Michelin to Asia, starting with Tokyo in 2008, where critics initially focused on many of the same problems—the lack of local tasters, the incompatibility with Japanese cuisine, and the imposition of French tastes, etc. However, similar to the case in New York, most Tokyo restaurateurs also came to accept the usefulness of the guide, particularly its economic value: the city's high-end restaurant scene has come to rely increasingly on international tourists, particularly Chinese tourists (Bouty, Gomez, and Drucker-Godard 2013, 14–17). This is not to say that the guide is fully accepted in these cities, but it has come to serve as a legitimating authority in fine dining, with stars conferring prestige and measurable economic benefits (Gergaud, Guzman, and Verardi 2007).

We can see similar processes in the entry of Michelin in Hong Kong in 2009 and Singapore in 2016. Resistance focused on the same elements—foreign tasters, foreign tastes, and foreign standards—but, for individual restaurants, the recognition by this established international authority generally proved too valuable for most recipients of these rewards to ignore. There may be complaints of unfortunate side effects, such as rising rents on Michelin restaurants in Hong Kong (Wong 2012)—and there are always complaints of particular restaurants that are excluded or included, but the influence of such global legitimating culinary authorities is now widely acknowledged, if not always positively appreciated in the local press (Henderson 2017; Lau 2008).

In the case of Shanghai, the publication of the second (2018) Michelin guide received grudging praise for its recognition of two local Western cuisine favorites— Jean Georges (which received a star) and Ultraviolet (now awarded three)—and for improving its coverage of local Shanghainese cuisine. There were now five Michelin-starred Shanghainese cuisine restaurants, and one Hangzhou-style and one Ningbo-style restaurant (*Xinwen Chenbao* 2017). Nonetheless, many local critics still were unhappy with the "over-representation" of Cantonese- or Hong Kong–style restaurants (Sun 2017). Other critics pointed out that Japanese restaurants continued to be snubbed in the Shanghai guide (while not in Hong Kong) (*That's Shanghai* 2017). On the other hand, the guide had managed to stay in the news, and, if the difficulties of getting a reservation are a clue, stars have clear economic value in Shanghai, as in other cities.

As a former official of Michelin China (himself a People's Republic of China (PRC) national) said to me, "Always there is a negative reaction. When we first went to Tokyo, they hated us, but now they love us. It was the same in Hong Kong." He predicted that the guide would also be accepted in Shanghai. Some ratings could be questioned, he conceded. However, he defended the low ratings given to Shanghainese cuisine restaurants overall, arguing that unlike its more refined Cantonese rival, Shanghainese cuisine lacked complexity and would rarely rate more than one star. Although presented as the personal views of a former Michelin official, such comments reveal implicit hierarchies of taste that may underlie Michelin judgments.[2]

As these discussions show, culinary nationalism is almost always part of the reaction against culinary globalization, but this reaction should not be understood as simple opposition. Rather it may also be part of the process of incorporation, as chefs challenge themselves to meet global standards, often resulting in a partial adjustment of their practices. As Simmel's writing on conflict suggests, conflict is always part of social integration rather than simply a sign of continued opposition and refusal (Simmel 1904).

From a comparative sociological perspective, this is also an example of the increasing importance of global legitimating authorities in many fields, from credit agencies to university rankings (Bouty, Gomez, and Drucker-Godard 2013). The concept of "fields" has been deployed in sociology widely as a way of describing the social organization of strategic action among various actors engaged in a common endeavor (Fligstein and McAdam 2012). In gastronomy, we can think of the culinary field as a space of interactions among all the actors who produce and sustain the "rules of the game" of modern restaurant cuisine—chefs, critics, regulators, consumers, guidebook writers, etc. (see Farrer 2015a). Legitimating authorities, who provide certifications of quality, legality, or authenticity, are key actors in any field. In the culinary field, expert opinion plays a crucial role both in legitimating prices and providing information on choices (Chossat and Gergaud 2003; Gergaud, Guzman, and Verardi 2007; Bouty, Gomez, and Drucker-Godard 2013).

The globalization of social fields—in areas from finance to education to travel—has made such legitimating authorities increasingly important. As is the case with Michelin, legitimating authorities may be contested while growing in importance. We can see this in the case of the relatively recent acceptance of global university rankings. At first these were met with near universal derision, but increasingly they are impossible to ignore, particularly among institutions eager for broader recognition (Ishikawa 2009).

With China's economic rise, Chinese consumers have become important players in culinary globalization. With more than 100 million foreign trips a year, Chinese have become the world's largest group of global travelers. Wealthy Chinese tourists engage in Michelin "star collecting" in culinary destinations in Europe and Japan. Upon returning to China, many globe-trotting gourmets seek out chefs with an overseas Michelin pedigree. Within China, events focused on Michelin-starred chefs proved popular even before the Michelin guide appeared in Shanghai. For example, tickets for a gala dinner cooked by Michelin three-star chefs priced at 4,888 yuan (US$787) per person at Park Hyatt Shanghai in November 2014 sold out six months before the meal. The rise of this global culinary field is linked to the rise of a transnational capitalist class—both tourists and rich Chinese—as the chief audience for such standards.

Indeed, it may have been easier to make a career in Shanghai with the imprimatur of Michelin before the guidebook actually arrived locally in 2016, than it is now. That is, if one already had worked at a starred restaurant in Europe, it was relatively easy to market these stars in Shanghai, since no local guide existed to validate (or invalidate) them. One typical example is the French chef Nicolas Le Bec. In the summer of 2012, Le Bec, the former owner of the eponymous two-star Michelin restaurant in Lyon, shuttered his Lyon restaurant and moved to Shanghai with his Shanghainese wife. In April 2014 Le Bec opened in a sumptuous villa on Xinhua Road. Unlike other "flying Michelin chefs," like Vongerichten or Robuchon, who simply put their name on the door while spending most of their time organizing culinary ventures elsewhere, Le Bec had his feet planted firmly on Chinese soil. As the manager, Guillaume, from Lyon, explained, "We are changing the game of French cuisine in Shanghai. We have a two-star Michelin chef in the kitchen cooking lunch and dinner." Without any advertising, Le Bec's pricey bistro attracted a stream of customers, 80 percent of whom were Chinese. So far, Le Bec has been frustrated in his attempts to win Michelin stars in Shanghai, but his early success clearly owes to the reflected glory of his French Michelin résumé.

The rise of a global modernist culinary field

Although perhaps the most famous, Michelin is only one of many legitimating authorities in an emerging global culinary field. A much more recent, but highly influential player is a web-based list-producing organization called "The World's 50 Best Restaurants." The World's 50 Best list first appeared in *Restaurant* magazine in 2002, as a provocative feature. It is now independently managed by William Reed Business Media. Consumers and restaurant insiders worldwide now follow the results on the World's 50 Best Restaurants website (www.theworlds50best.com). There are global and regional awards ceremonies, which many awardees attend, often becoming judges themselves.

Unlike Michelin, World's 50 Best does not employ professional judges. Rather, one thousand anonymous "academy" members—chefs, food writers, and other "gourmets"— vote for the list. A much more limited group of publicly known "academy chairs" choose the academy members, and because they are known, these individuals become the targets of intense gastro-diplomacy efforts. National and regional tourist bureaus, and even well-heeled restaurateurs, assiduously court academy chairs, flying them over to visit not only restaurants but suppliers of key local ingredients.

The World's 50 Best list is but the latest model of culinary authority. As Ferguson (2008) writes, the earliest culinary authority was the lone critic, who acts as a "judge" of what is good or bad, tasty or terrible. Such critics include classic food writers but also modern food journalists. The Michelin guide reviewers, Ferguson writes, are a "tribunal," making decisions collectively (and anonymously). Starting with the Zagat guides, but now extending to online platforms such as China's dianping.com, consumer-produced guides are a "plebiscite" in which quality is determined by popular democracy. All of these forms of food critique remain important, but only the last is easily scaled up to a global level, since a single critic can scarcely cover the whole planet, and Michelin-style "tribunals" are essentially local organizations. Consumer-produced reviews, however, are widely regarded as unreliable guides to fine dining and easily manipulated by unscrupulous restaurant owners to achieve artificially high rankings through paid reviews.

The World's 50 Best list, in contrast, is an attempt to incorporate actors in the culinary field—chefs, critics, and elite consumers—into the process of judging restaurants. Based on Ferguson's categories of "judges," "tribunals," and "plebiscites," I would add the concept of a culinary "plenum" to describe this new model. Although World's 50 Best does not involve all the key players directly, the thousand-member academy serves as a plenum of representatives of all sectors in a globalized culinary field, who, at least ideally, pass judgment based on insider knowledge, not outside authority. The standards of academy members are entirely subjective, but are presumably well-informed because of their immersion within the field itself.

Shanghai-based food journalist Crystyl Mo is academy chair for China and Korea. I have accompanied her to many restaurants in Shanghai and Tokyo, and she is a chief informant for this chapter. As she pointed out to me in an interview, the World's 50 Best Restaurants started off as a very small operation, but it had an immediate global impact that shocked the early organizers. The list can create a culinary reputation, not just for a restaurant, but for a country or a whole region. As Mo said: "No one went to Copenhagen before Noma became the best restaurant in the world. Now there are multiple restaurant destinations there. This created a huge growth in tourism for them. So, governments are willing to spend money bringing in these culinary opinion leaders."[3]

Restaurants get rewards, but the focus is increasingly on chefs. "Chefs must now be much more than good cooks," said Melinda Joe, a Tokyo-based food writer and online opinion leader. "They must be able to communicate, speak multiple languages, travel the world and explain their concepts."[4]

The rise of global legitimating authorities in the culinary field—from food journalists to guidebooks—has been accompanied by a rise in the status of culinary producers and a redefinition of their profession. This has meant the elevation of cook to chef, and chef to artist, along with the celebration of culinary innovation over traditions, and of culinary process over culinary products (Trubek 2000; Rao, Monin, and Durand 2005; Ottenbacher and Harrington 2007; Leschziner 2015; Otero 2017). Together, this revolution in restaurant cooking has been described as a "modernist revolution" that has redefined the relation between the chef and client, with the former gaining a prestige and authority never before enjoyed (Myhrvold 2011; Svejenova, Mazza, and Planellas 2007).

In the West, this modernization of the culinary field and its separation from other spheres of domestic work had already begun in nineteenth-century France, with the professional distinction of the "chef" as opposed to the "cook." This new role of chef was associated with the new institution of the restaurant, with its other innovations such as waiters, printed menus, and private dining tables (Spang 2001). Throughout the nineteenth and early twentieth centuries, the professionalization of the chef was a slow, fitful process because of the associations of culinary work with unskilled labor and unpaid domestic female labor (Trubek 2000). In the mid-twentieth century, the rise of food journalism and the advent of "nouvelle cuisine" among an increasingly professionalized network of chefs in postwar France led to a greater elevation of the chef role. Nouvelle cuisine not only challenged traditional recipes but also put the chef in the kitchen in charge of plating, creating a new stage for culinary artistry. With the rise of "nouvelle cuisine," chefs created dishes that referred to literature and the chef's imagination, employing novel ingredients from distant regions and techniques outside the standard repertoire (Weiss 2001; Rao, Monin, and Durand 2005).

The rise of what has been termed "molecular gastronomy" in Spain represented an even more radical stage in the redefinition of cuisine as art and chef as artist. It also signified a break in the identification of high cuisine with French cooking, and a globalization of the culinary field beyond the imaginary boundaries of national cuisines altogether. The chef Ferran Adrià is central to this story. Adrià redefined the dialogue between chef and diner, making the chef the arbiter of tastes and an innovator responsible to his art rather than to the naïve preferences of diners. Adria's intellectual and conceptual approach to cuisine at his restaurant elBulli was based on the principle that it "was not enough for the food to be delicious; it also had to elicit thoughts and feelings" (Myhrvold 2011). Cuisine was now governed by the logic of the avant-garde, in which innovation is a cardinal value and the consumer (though still the person paying the bill) is dethroned as the arbiter of taste.

If the rise of "nouvelle cuisine" was closely associated with the legitimating authority of French journalists (Rao, Monin, and Durand 2005), the artistic revolution at elBulli has been driven by the rise of a global internet-based food journalism, reviewers, and list makers such as the World's 50 Best. Esoteric concepts, restaurants formed around social ideals, cutting-edge design and novel, even shocking, dining experiences are rewarded much more readily in the World's 50 Best list than they are by Michelin. Tradition seems to play little role. Nor does the adherence to an idea of national culinary authenticity. The list represents a type of culinary authority largely divorced from the concerns of ordinary consumers, though, as Crystyl Mo argues, ideas from leading chefs filter out into the larger, mass-market culinary field. As Mo points out, chefs must be communicators and conceptual innovators; it is not enough to simply cook tasty food. As one young Shanghai chef explained in somewhat less flattering terms, "Michelin is about consistency, getting the same taste right, night after night. With World's 50 Best, it's more about the creative idea, the food doesn't have to even taste good!"[5]

In short, this rapid emergence of a global culinary field, based on modernist ideals, has been elevating the status of chefs and transforming culinary work worldwide. These influences are dramatic in the booming cities on the expanding periphery of global capitalism. In Istanbul, for example, we see "a fundamental change in the role of the chef: from a nameless and faceless kitchen worker to—frequently and in various combinations—cook, restaurateur, businessperson, author and researcher, media personality, celebrity and brand name, innovator or traditionalist, activist and campaigner." Many of the new star chefs have more middle-class upbringings, unlike traditional cooks (Yenal and Kubiena 2016, 64). Also in Russia, we see that professional associations among chefs, the rise of culinary journalism, and culinary fairs have raised the profile of chefs (Shectman 2009). This process is not without its contradictions and stresses. In Turkey, for example, many customers still value expensive ingredients and exclusivity over culinary innovation, making the work of creative young chefs difficult (Yenal and Kubiena 2016, 71–2). East Asia has also experienced the rise of modernist cuisine associated with culinary globalization. Sana Ho argues that the Michelin guide has shaped the tastes offered in Korean restaurants as they reach for Michelin stars through modernist fusion dishes (Ho 2017).

In China, outside of Hong Kong, the influence of this globalized modernist culinary field is recent and limited. Chinese restaurant cuisine has been based on principles more analogous to classical—or even medieval—European cuisines rather than its modernist forms. Chinese cooking, while highly elaborate, is artisanal rather than artsy, with attention to reproducing classical dishes rather than modernist provocations. Pricing has been based more on rare ingredients rather than the chef's pedigree. Writings about Chinese cuisine typically celebrate its classical roots as far back as the Han Dynasty rather than modern innovations. Foreign influences have been rarely emphasized (Huang 1990; Li 2008). Moreover, as in medieval European foodways, considerations of humoral medicine still run through discussions of Chinese dietary choices (Anderson 1988).

Even the social organization of Chinese dining mitigates against the modernist culinary aesthetic. Eating out in China has been a collective experience of banqueting focused on cultivating or celebrating social relations rather than the individualistic and conceptual focus of modernist dining (Yang 1994). Classical Chinese writings on food have celebrated the gourmet rather than the chef. Even now, the high-status individual ordering dishes is arguably the most important author of a Chinese meal, in stark opposition to the (often inscrutable) set menus composed by star chefs in modernist fine dining. Chinese cooks are still seen as lowly paid and unskilled workers, even those working in fine dining (Fung 2007, 144; Farrer 2015b). Though there are now notable exceptions, as discussed later, most cooks are often anonymous workers specializing in a few dishes, while owners are the public face of a restaurant.

In short, the Chinese culinary field seems to operate on principles largely at odds with the globalized modernist culinary field described earlier. However, culinary globalization has become a disruptive influence on Chinese gastronomy. Some of these disruptors come directly from abroad, while others are responses by traditional Chinese culinary workers to the global culinary field represented by legitimating authorities such as Michelin.

The globalization of Shanghai's culinary field: Western chefs chasing stars in Shanghai

Given the Western origins of this transnational field of modernist fine dining, most early beneficiaries of culinary "Michelinization" in Shanghai were foreign chefs with Michelin pedigrees. In 2004, a luxury retail development called Three on the Bund opened in Shanghai, featuring venues by globally established restaurateurs, most notably Jean-Georges Vongerichten, whose Michelin three-star restaurant and several other highly regarded ventures in New York City, London, and Paris had earned him international recognition. Vongerichten's flagship Shanghai restaurant relied on his global Michelin star power, finally winning its own star in 2018. For chefs and consumers, these restaurants served as a local window onto global fine dining.

By 2015, the star of the Bund dining scene was the locally based French chef Paul Pairet. A peripatetic master of avant-garde cuisine and protégé of Alain Ducasse, Pairet came to the city in 2005 to work at Jade 36 in the Peninsula Hotel, where he introduced a technical style of "molecular gastronomy" to Shanghai. I first encountered Pairet at this restaurant in 2007. After tasting what was for me an exotic modernist dinner, I asked him if he had to make adjustments to the tastes of diners who were not used to such adventurous reconstructions of familiar tastes. He shrugged and replied that he really wasn't too concerned about the response of diners who could not understand what he was doing. "You cannot cook for an audience," he said. "If a lot of people tell me that they do not like something on the menu maybe I will think about taking it off. But I will replace it with something I want. Maybe it will not be something they like either." His answer intrigued me. Nearly all chefs I interviewed to this point strictly adhered to the "customer is king" motif in describing guest-relations. Here I was faced with a new figure in Shanghai, not the classic gastronome, but a self-styled culinary artist.[6]

Not even Pairet's colleagues in fine dining in Shanghai were confident the concept would work. As Eric Johnson, the head chef at Shanghai's Jean Georges, said to me in 2005,

> They're doing creative modern food in such a way that I personally find to be interesting. I have my doubts, but it'll be interesting to see whether it works here because if you have a deconstructed version of a lemon tart, you have to know what a lemon tart is in the first place in order for it to be interesting. And I'll be fascinated by that. I can't wait to eat there. But is it viable here? I don't know. I mean, it's not even viable in the States.[7]

Possibly molecular gastronomy was too much for Shanghai in 2005, so in 2009 Pairet opened a relatively conventional French bistro, Mr. and Mrs. Bund at Bund 18, which became the most highly acclaimed Western restaurant in the city. However, in 2012, with financial backing from the Taiwanese VOL group, Pairet launched an ambitious and highly modernist project, Ultraviolet, where a single table of ten diners are bused from the Bund to a nearby hidden location to savor a degustation menu of intricate delicacies accompanied by carefully choreographed sounds, images, and scents, all intended to provide a multisensory pairing to the flavors of the meal. The menu revived some avant-garde items from the Jade 36 menu, such as "Foie gras can't quit," which was an edible "cigarette" of foie gras wrapped in a shining fruit-flavored "paper" and presented in a silver ashtray. Diners dipped the "cigarette" in "cabbage ash" while a projection of cigarette smoke swirled around them on screen. Initially, course menus started at 3,000 yuan (roughly US$480) per person, which some restaurant industry insiders still described as a "bargain," given that twenty-five chefs and waiters entertained ten guests every night. By 2018 the price had soared to 6,000 yuan, or close to US$1,000 (Mo 2012). From its inception, Pairet clearly was shooting for the (Michelin) stars. In 2017, it was No. 8 on the list of Asia's 50 Best restaurants and No. 41 on the global list (William Reed Business Media 2017a). A French restaurant thus represented the pinnacle of culinary artistry in Shanghai to a transnational gastronomic audience. Although Pairet accepted his two stars with visible disappointment at the ceremony in 2017, he was vindicated with three stars in the 2018 guidebook, justifying his efforts and the extraordinary high prices charged at Ultraviolet, even for restaurants in this category.

Chinese restaurateurs take up the Michelin challenge

Chinese restaurateurs have not been immune to the lure of the Michelin stars. One chef who exemplifies the desire to change the reputation and presentation of Chinese cuisine is a young Shanghainese named Qian Yibin. Qian is both a widely traveled culinary cosmopolitan, but also a culinary nationalist whose dream is to raise the standards of Chinese cuisine to compete globally. Qian runs four mid-priced restaurants in Shanghai, but his dream is to produce a Michelin-quality Chinese restaurant in Shanghai. The charge for a course menu, of over twenty individually plated courses, will be 5,000 yuan, or over US$800. The models for this restaurant are the restaurants outside China, and also in Shanghai, that have been written about as the greatest restaurants in the world. Qian has visited many of them from Alinea in Chicago to Noma in Copenhagen. His local inspiration in Shanghai is Paul Pairet's Ultraviolet. Instead of simply showing videos on four walls (and even on the plate and table) as Ultraviolet does, Qian plans a holographic display in the middle of the table. He has even developed plates that float magnetically above the table, suspended in a force field (though placing them was devilishly tricky, as I learned from trying). The dishes he plans are photogenic, also tasty, reconstructions based on traditional Shanghai flavors, but also a variety of influences from around the world.

Qian's concept of a restaurant is designed for the age of WeChat in which taking photos of every dish is the norm. With his background as an accomplished food photographer, Qian's goal is to create a visually spectacular Chinese cuisine that can rival the creations at restaurants such as elBulli and Noma. He not only plans his own restaurant, but trains other chefs in a specialized kitchen atelier that I visited. He also wants to break Shanghai chefs out of the doldrums of repetitive menus and traditional sugary, soy-laden sauces. The goal is to bring Shanghai cooking into the modernist culinary field (cf. Khoo on the similar impulses of Malaysian chef Darren Teoh, Chapter 6 in this volume). His is clearly a "Chinese culinary dream," whose goal is to gain positions on the lists of the World's 50 Best restaurants and in Michelin guidebooks. By 2017, Qian's Michelin-level concept had yet to take off, but Qian remains active in educating aspiring cooks about the value of presentation and innovation in remaking Shanghai cuisine (Figure 10.1).[8]

Some Shanghai culinary entrepreneurs have met with more immediate Michelin success. Perhaps the most prominent example is restaurateur Song Yuanbo, a Taiwanese restaurant owner who has lived in Shanghai for twenty years. Song is not a chef, and has unique motives in running restaurants. A devout Buddhist, Song pledged to become a vegetarian when his mother became ill. Since then he has made it a personal mission to promulgate vegetarian food by persuading meat eaters that it is superior in taste.[9] After interviewing Song, I was invited to dine at his flagship Wujie restaurant on the Bund together with Sidney Schutte, a Michelin two-star chef from the Netherlands. Schutte had been a guest of the Waldorf Astoria for Shanghai restaurant week, doing a series of private and public culinary exhibitions.

Figure 10.1 Pink pickled radishes and shallots served on a black grooved slate plate at chef Qian Yibin's culinary atelier. Shanghai, PRC (2014). Photograph by James Farrer.

The exquisite dinner began with a set of delicate appetizers presented in a French-styled individual plating. One was candied hawthorn, another an almond pastry puff. Menu items could loosely be described as Chinese or Western in inspiration. They both featured rare or unusual ingredients from around China. Given that this was a vegetarian restaurant there was a large variety of soy and mushroom products, many very labor intensive. The faux beefsteak was made with lion's mane mushrooms that had been squeezed and roasted, then soaked in egg white for four hours. The roasting desiccates them so that they will absorb the egg white, then they are formed into squares in baking forms and grilled (Figure 10.2).

Over dinner, Song's questions for Schutte focused intently on Michelin standards, and how to meet them. Schutte replied frankly that the flavors in the Western-style dishes were not savory enough. "The Asian dishes are powerful," he said. "But the Western dishes are not powerful enough. The risotto, is not a risotto. It is nice, but after you eat it there is no flavor left on the palate ... The presentation is there, but not the powerful flavors."[10]

Schutte also emphasized that for Michelin, presentation is key. Indeed, he said, presentation may occupy as much effort as taste, and personally, he wasn't sure it was worth it. A look at Wujie's Facebook page shows that such advice has not been ignored. Dishes now look complex, three-dimensional, and spectacular.

Figure 10.2 Black truffle lion's mane mushroom with yellow bell pepper carrot basil sauce, served at the high-end vegetarian restaurant, Wujie. Shanghai, PRC (2015). Photograph by James Farrer.

Over dinner, Schutte invited Song's chefs to Amsterdam and expressed his own hope to visit as a cook at Wujie. Song seemed surprised at this suggestion and it became apparent that there was a gap in expectations about the practice of chefs visiting restaurant kitchens, known globally by the French term *stage*, a type of short professional internship. Whereas this is a common practice in European kitchens, it is not widespread in Chinese gastronomy. To build expertise, Chinese restaurants typically must hire chefs who have experience in other restaurants. In any case, Song's chefs, particularly the young female pastry chef, responded enthusiastically to this invitation, and a few months later they actually went, interning in Schutte's kitchen and visiting other Michelin-starred venues in Amsterdam. Later, Schutte returned to Shanghai as a guest chef in Wujie's kitchen. For the young head chef Ivan Xu, originally from Anhui, these were formative experiences in building up a Michelin-style menu (Figure 10.3).[11]

Song's ideas about gastronomy, while idiosyncratic, match well with the conceptual focus of the global culinary field, providing intellectual fodder for food writers. Beyond Buddhism, Song prioritizes the health and safety of customers, workers, and suppliers. For example, chefs at Wujie use some atypical oils in their cooking. Some dishes are sautéed in olive oil whereas high temperature cooking is done with tea seed oil (Camellia oil) which is quite expensive but has a very high smoking

Figure 10.3 Almond mousse with orange chrysanthemum, candied cherry stuffed with walnuts, and avocado beetroot jelly roll, served at the high-end vegetarian restaurant, Wujie. Shanghai, PRC (2015). Photograph by James Farrer.

point. They do this to protect the chefs from being burnt, Song said. Song also has toothpicks made out of starch, so that they soften in liquids. This means that when the dishwashers wash dishes they do not prick their hands on the toothpicks. Song and the chefs showed pride in explaining their trips to Yunnan Province to find mushrooms. They said that they also believe strongly in "fair trade" and sustainable trade. The idea is that if you treat the suppliers well, they will introduce others to you. Moreover, it means paying not only a fair price but paying enough to help people sustain their business.

All of these discourses relate to Song's Buddhist ideals and at the same time play to a sophisticated gourmet audience that wants to hear a philosophy articulated with its meals. Song was aiming at the Michelin stars, not by abandoning, but highlighting his Buddhist ideas for creating both a tasty and virtuous meal. In the 2018 guide, he achieved his goal and was awarded a Michelin star for his flagship Wujie restaurant on the Bund, while two other branches of this restaurant retained the Bib Gourmet rankings they had garnered in the inaugural Michelin guide. According to Wujie's manager, chef Ivan Xu was the force behind the Michelin efforts. Still Xu remained mostly in the kitchen instead of performing the "star chef" role of greeting guests, a practice quite common in Shanghai's Western restaurants.[12]

Transnational culinary modernism in China

Increasingly, it is not the coastal cities, but Chengdu, that may be emerging as the center of Chinese culinary modernism. This movement seems to have been founded by a single chef, Yu Bo, whose restaurant Yu's Family Kitchen has absorbed much of the spirit of global modernist cooking into its elaborate tasting menus, influenced by Japanese models, as well as the molecular cuisine of elBulli. He incorporates the avant-garde spirit of culinary innovation rather than emphasizing tradition. Presentation, including humor or surprise, is key. Yu Bo's signature dish is a calligraphy brush whose tip is made of flaky pastry with minced pork, to be eaten dipped in a red, inky sauce. This playful modernist approach quickly garnered Yu Family Kitchen attention from global food critics, though initially it was met by skepticism in his home city, in which culinary traditionalism still prevails (Lim 2009).

Another of Chengdu's rising stars is Lan Guijin, who began his career working with his famed contemporary Yu Bo (Dunlop 2014). Lan's restaurant Yu Zhi Lan, featured by food writer Fuchsia Dunlop in the *Financial Times*, embodies many of the principles of global modernist cooking and a desire to see Chinese cuisine recognized on a global stage. As a young chef, he worked in Japan for two years and was inspired by the small and personal scale of Japanese fine-dining restaurants. In 2004, along with Yu Bo and another Chengdu chef, Xiao Jianming, Lan Guijun joined Dunlop in California for a conference at the Culinary Institute of America, where he made an impressive show of Sichuan noodle-making. After the conference, the three chefs dined with Dunlop at the French Laundry, an experience that had a profound impact on Lan. "Writing for a Chinese food magazine some years later," Dunlop writes, "he said he had decided that a revival of Chinese cuisine would require that kind of small-scale culinary perfection, along with a renewed concern for fine ingredients and unfussy, naturalistic presentation" (Dunlop 2014).

Like its fine-dining models abroad, Yu Zhi Lan is a small and expensive restaurant frequented by celebrities and featuring square tables rather than the traditional round banqueting tables. Lan has also adopted individual plating at the table, which is not only part of a conscious effort to raise the level of Chinese cuisine by appealing to international standards, but a way to make sure that the flavors are enjoyed by each diner visually and on the palate. Lan also freely incorporates Mediterranean and Japanese flavors into his cooking, arguing against an obsession with culinary authenticity (cf. Khoo's discussion of pan-Asian culinary borrowing in modernist restaurants in Malaysia in Chapter 6 of this volume). He has his own pottery made in Jingdezhen, where he also intensively studied pottery making himself. This penchant for self-designed tableware is also notable in Shanghai restaurants inspired by Japanese fine dining.

Perhaps because Sichuan is on the fringes of China's own culinary field, there is a greater incentive to engage with global modernist concepts, or perhaps the boom in Sichuan food overseas creates greater unique opportunities for chefs from Chengdu. In any case, we see a new trend toward globalist modernist dining that is also regarded by its practitioners as an expression of regional and Chinese culinary excellence, in short, culinary nationalism expressed in the norms of the global culinary field.

Culinary nationalism and professional mobility in the transnational culinary field

As Chinese cuisine expert Fuchsia Dunlop writes in the *Financial Times*, "Chinese cuisine is the ghost at the feast of global gastronomy. Despite a rich gastronomic tradition dating back more than two millennia and a remarkable history of culinary innovation, Chinese food is almost invisible at the highest international levels" (Dunlop 2014).

Dunlop cites several problems. One she describes as a "culture clash" between Chinese consumption practices and those of foreign reviewers. Restaurant reviewers usually review alone (or in pairs) whereas Chinese cuisine usually is served banquet style for groups. Other problems are China's profound food safety scares, a shortage of good staff, and the recent anti-corruption campaign that has limited fine-dining consumption. At the same time, as Dunlop's own writings show, one reaction of chefs to the marginalization of Chinese cuisine globally has been to join in the fray, participating in the global culinary field in an attempt to gain not only a personal reputation, but also often in the name of rescuing China's culinary reputation. In other words, one significant new expression of China's culinary nationalism is the involvement of younger chefs in the global culinary field.

The emergence of a transitional culinary field of fine dining thus structures not only professional strategies of culinary "star making" but also the expression of Chinese culinary nationalism. This now is reformulated by these chefs in the global vernacular of fine-dining culture, including ideas such as fair trade, local supplies, and pairings with local alcoholic beverages. This new style of culinary nationalism echoes less the voices of traditional culinary gatekeepers—Chinese food writers with little international experience—than a cohort of younger social media–based writers eager to see Chinese restaurants achieve globally recognized standards.

I do not want to exaggerate these trends. The extent of global culinary authority into Asia is limited. Local pundits are eager to push back against what they perceive as Western culinary imperialism and ignorance of local standards. From Singapore to Tokyo, chefs, critics, and consumers have reacted negatively or ambivalently to the Michelin guides. However, as argued previously, even the resistance to Michelin may involve a deeper acknowledgment of the significance of international authorities. As one Hong Kong food writer and restaurant owner told me, "Giving stars to noodle booths is a sign of disrespect to Asian restaurants."[13] As this comment indicates, this chef criticizes Michelin, but he remains invested in a global culinary field that celebrates fine dining as an expression of service quality and culinary sophistication. Chefs may repudiate Michelin as an authority, but they are too embedded in this culinary culture to reject the assumptions that govern the restaurant ratings business as a whole. The essential idea is that high cuisine is creative expression, not just business, and restaurants must be subject to expert judgment. The food critic may be criticized, but food criticism is essential.

At the more abstract level, the global culinary field is an example of a social field. Social fields are not only games of position but give both meaning and purpose to a large set of actors within the field, from the major players who create the rules of the game, to marginal players who struggle to find a position in the field. All these players, however, find their meanings and purposes in their interactions within the field. They are thus invested in the field itself, not just their positions within it (Fligstein and McAdam 2012). As fields emerge or change, new positions and opportunities emerge within them. One new status group that has clearly emerged in this transnational culinary field is the Asian celebrity chef, such as Singapore's Andre Chiang, originally from Taiwan, with accolades from both Asia's 50 Best and Michelin (though he is quite critical of the latter). Another is the globe-trotting food writer, such as Crystyl Mo, a bilingual Chinese-American with family ties to Shanghai, or Fuchsia Dunlop, a white British woman who speaks Chinese. Of course, China has its own domestic culinary field that remains partially insulated from global influences. Most Chinese chefs and Chinese food writers ignore overseas audiences and refuse to play the global game. As in other fields, there is plenty of profit and status to be gained from having thousands of domestic followers on WeChat or WeiBo. Meanwhile, the global culinary field remains biased toward Western culinary standards, and perhaps even toward white faces (Wei 2017). Andre Chiang remains the only ethnic Chinese on the World's 50 Best List, yet his flagship restaurant is not traditionally Chinese, but "high concept Mediterranean inspired fine dining" based on his cosmopolitan "Octaphilosophy" of the eight elements of cuisine (William Reed Business Media 2017b).

Still, the transnational culinary field that has emerged around fine dining has given opportunities for Chinese chefs such as Yu Bo to become global stars independently of the domestic context. Andre Chiang is an idol for young aspiring Chinese chefs. The informal networks within the transnational culinary field also provide opportunities for geographical and social mobility for workers in one of the largest industries in nearly every nation. The culture of fine dining elevates the ordinary cook from unskilled laborer to artisan, and the head chef from artisan to artist. It promises high rewards and high profile for a few elite star chefs. It also makes chefs spokespeople for national cuisines, despite the global fusions of their actual offerings.

A culture of star chefs in China may be emerging and this would be a revolutionary change. Culinary work in China is traditionally a working-class and low-status job. However, the transition to the system of star chefs will not occur easily. Complicating factors include the tradition of investor-dominated restaurants. The public face of the restaurant in China is generally an owner, not a chef. Any celebration of the chef as artist is perceived as a threat to the ownership of a brand (for example, the chef opening his or her own shop). Rather than chefs going on to open new restaurants, we see a pattern of chain restaurants created by the same owners, indicated also in awards to chain restaurants in the Shanghai Michelin guide. Even Song's Wujie could be seen as an example of this trend.

As many informants told me, the low status of culinary work in Chinese contexts is likely the greatest obstacle to the full participation of Chinese chefs in the globalized culture of fine dining. Few have the education, training, and life experience to appeal to diners in transnational contexts. Within Shanghai, most cooks come from the provinces and are socially marginal migrant workers. A similar situation prevails in Hong Kong kitchens. For these migrant cooks, the possibilities for upward social mobility are limited by a low level of formal education, inadequate language skills, and a near total unfamiliarity with the social worlds and lifestyles of the elite diners they serve (Farrer 2015b).

In short, a new transnational culinary field has emerged, globally and in China, but it is unclear yet who will benefit in the Chinese context. As the ethnography above shows, some fine-dining restaurant owners in China yearn for global recognition. Some chefs such as Yu Bo have already achieved it. Most Chinese cooks (and even many accomplished chefs), however, are not well placed as participants in this transnational field. Locally entrenched actors, including owners of large restaurant chains, may continue to dominate the national culinary field in a way that limits both culinary globalism and the social mobility of chefs.

Notes

1 Author fieldnotes, September 23, 2016.
2 Author fieldnotes, March 5, 2018.
3 Author interview, September 16, 2016.
4 Author interview, February 10, 2017.
5 Author fieldnotes, March 7, 2018.
6 Author fieldnotes, September 15, 2007.
7 Author interview, November 2, 2005.
8 Author fieldnotes, August 24, 2014.
9 Author interview, September 14, 2015.
10 Author fieldnotes, September 14, 2015.
11 Author fieldnotes, March 4, 2018.

12 Author fieldnotes, March 4, 2018.
13 Author interview, September 30, 2016.

References

Anderson, E. N. 1988. *The Food of China*. New Haven, CT: Yale University Press.

Bouty, Isabelle, Marie-Léandre Gomez, and Carole Drucker-Godard. 2013. "Maintaining an Institution: The Institutional Work of Michelin in Haute Cuisine Around the World." Working paper 1302, Centre De Recherche de l'ESSEC.

Chossat, Véronique, and Olivier Gergaud. 2003. "Expert Opinion and Gastronomy: The Recipe for Success." *Journal of Cultural Economics* 27, no. 2: 127–41.

Dunlop, Fuchsia. 2014. "Chengdu Chef Lan Guijun: The New Emperor of Chinese Gastronomy." *Financial Times*, August 22, 2014. https://www.ft.com/content/20f3d64e-27f5-11e4-ae44-00144feabdc0.

Farrer, James. 2010. "Eating the West and Beating the Rest: Culinary Occidentalism and Urban Soft Power in Asia's Global Food Cities." In *Globalization, Food and Social Identities in the Asia Pacific Region*, edited by James Farrer. Papers presented at the symposium, "Globalization, Food, and Social Identities in the Pacific Region," February 21–2, 2009, Sophia University, Tokyo. Tokyo: Sophia University Institute of Comparative Culture. http://icc.fla.sophia.ac.jp/global%20food%20papers/html/farrer.html.

Farrer, James. 2015a. "Introduction: Traveling Cuisines in and out of Asia: Toward a Framework for Studying Culinary Globalization." In *Globalization and Asian Cuisines: Transnational Networks and Culinary Contact Zones*, edited by James Farrer, 1–20. New York: Palgrave Macmillan.

Farrer, James. 2015b. "Shanghai's Western Restaurants as Culinary Contact Zones in a Transnational Culinary Field." In *Globalization and Asian Cuisines: Transnational Networks and Culinary Contact Zones*, edited by James Farrer, 103–24. New York: Palgrave Macmillan.

Ferguson, Priscilla Parkhurst. 2008. "Michelin in America." *Gastronomica* 8, no. 1: 49–55.

Fligstein, Neil, and Doug McAdam. 2012. *A Theory of Fields*. Oxford: Oxford University Press.

Fung, Luke Y. C. 2007. "Authenticity and Professionalism in Restaurant Kitchens." In *Food and Foodways in Asia: Resource, Tradition and Cooking*, edited by Sidney C. H. Cheung and Tan Chee-Beng, 143–55. Abingdon: Routledge.

Gergaud, Olivier, Linett Montano Guzman, and Vincenzo Verardi. 2007. "Stardust over Paris Gastronomic Restaurants." *Journal of Wine Economics* 2, no. 1: 24–39.

Henderson, Joan C. 2017. "Street Food, Hawkers and the Michelin Guide in Singapore." *British Food Journal* 119, no. 4: 790–802.

Ho, Sana. 2017. "Michelinization of Korean Food in Seoul." Paper presented at the Conférence internationale: Les échelles de l'alimentation entre Asie et Europe: Connexions, syncrétismes, fusions. École des hautes études en sciences sociales, Paris.

Huang, H. T. 1990. "Han Gastronomy—Chinese Cuisine *In Statu Nascendi*." *Interdisciplinary Science Reviews* 15, no. 2: 139–52.

Ishikawa, Mayumi. 2009. "University Rankings, Global Models, and Emerging Hegemony: Critical Analysis from Japan." *Journal of Studies in International Education* 13, no. 2: 159–73.

解放日报 *Jie Fang Daily*. 2016. "米其林这次评出真正的中国美食了吗？ Miqilin zheci pingchu zhenzheng de Zhongguo meishi le ma?" ["Did Michelin Review Authentic Chinese Cuisine This Time?"] September 23, 2016. https://web.archive.org/

web/20160930074527/http://newspaper.jfdaily.com/jfrb/html/2016-09/23/content_
218589.htm.

金淼 Jin Miao. 2016. "'舌尖上的中国' 导演陈硕：这份榜单看不出米其林深度调研
的痕迹 'Shejianshang de Zhongguo' daoyan Chen Shuo: zhefen bangdan kanbuchu
Miqilin shendu diaoyan de henji" ["'A Bite of China' Director Chen Shuo: This List
Does Not Reveal Traces of Michelin's In-Depth Research"]. *Shanghai Morning Post*,
September 22, 2016.

Lau, Joyce Hor-Chung. 2008. "Michelin Rates Hong Kong, but with Which Yardstick?" *New
York Times*, November 2, 2008.

Leschziner, Vanina. 2015. *At the Chef's Table: Culinary Creativity in Elite Restaurants*.
Stanford, CA: Stanford University Press.

季鸿昆 Li Hongkun. 2008. 食在中国：中国人饮食生活大视野 *Shi zai Zhongguo:
Zhongguoren yinshi shenghuo dashiye* [*Eating in China: A Broad Perspective on Chinese
Food and Drink*]. Jinan: Shandong chubanshe.

Lim, Louisa. 2009. "Chengdu: Marathon Meal of Experimental Cuisine." NPR. Last modified
January 28, 2009. https://www.npr.org/templates/story/story.php?storyId=99917119.

Mo, Crystyl. 2012. "Paul Pairet's Multi-Sensory Concept Restaurant." *Time Out Shanghai*,
June 29, 2012. http://www.timeoutshanghai.com/venue/Restaurants-European-
French/6008/Ultraviolet.html.

Myhrvold, Nathan. 2011. "The Art in Gastronomy: A Modernist Perspective."
Gastronomica: The Journal of Critical Food Studies 11, no. 1: 13–23.

Otero, J. 2017. "High-Status Food Is Changing: New Gastronomic Perspectives."
International Journal of Gastronomy and Food Science 11: 35–40.

Ottenbacher, Michael, and Robert J. Harrington. 2007. "The Innovation Development
Process of Michelin-Starred Chefs." *International Journal of Contemporary Hospitality
Management* 19, no. 6: 444–60.

Rao, Hayagreeva, Philippe Monin, and Rodolphe Durand. 2005. "Border Crossing:
Bricolage and the Erosion of Categorical Boundaries in French Gastronomy." *American
Sociological Review* 70, no. 6: 968–91.

Shectman, Stas. 2009. "A Celebration of Masterstvo: Professional Cooking, Culinary Art,
and Cultural Production in Russia." In *Food & Everyday Life in the Postsocialist World*,
edited by Melissa L. Caldwell, 154–87. Bloomington: Indiana University Press.

沈嘉禄 Shen Jialu. 2016. "沈嘉禄：可以不上米其林的星，但不能失去大厨应有的腔调！
Shen Jialu: keyi bushang Miqilin de xing, dan buneng shiqu dachu yingyou de
qiangdiao!" ["Shen Jialu: You Can Fail to Get Michelin stars, but You Shouldn't Lose
the Proper Form of a Great Chef!"]. *Wenhui Bao*. Last modified September 21, 2016.
http://dbsqp.com/article/32409.

Simmel, Georg. 1904. "The Sociology of Conflict." *American Journal of Sociology* 9, no. 4:
490–525.

Spang, Rebecca L. 2001. *The Invention of the Restaurant: Paris and Modern Gastronomic
Culture*. Cambridge, MA: Harvard University Press.

孙祺 Sun Qi. 2017. "又有一堆餐厅入围米其林上海指南：你钱包准备好了嘛？
Youyou yi dui canting ruwei Miqilin Shanghai zhinan: ni qianbao zhunbei haole ma?"
["Another Group of Restaurants Has Been Selected for Michelin's Shanghai Guide:
Have You Prepared Your Wallet for It?"]. 第一财经 *Yicai*. Last modified September 20,
2017. https://www.yicai.com/news/5347864.html.

Svejenova, Silviya, Carmelo Mazza, and Marcel Planellas. 2007. "Cooking up Change in
Haute Cuisine: Ferran Adrià as an Institutional Entrepreneur." *Journal of
Organizational Behavior* 28, no. 5: 539–61.

That's Shanghai. 2017. "What 5 Shanghai Chefs Really Think of the 2018 Michelin Guide." September 20, 2017. http://www.thatsmags.com/shanghai/post/20676/what-5-chefs-really-think-of-the-2018-michelin-guide-shanghai.

Trubek, Amy B. 2000. *Haute Cuisine: How the French Invented the Culinary Profession*. Philadelphia: University of Pennsylvania Press.

Wei, Clarissa. 2017. "The Struggles of Writing About Chinese Food as a Chinese Person." *Vice*, April 18, 2017. https://munchies.vice.com/en_us/article/yp7bx5/the-struggles-of-writing-about-chinese-food-as-a-chinese-person.

Weiss, Allen S. 2001. "Tractacus Logico-Gastronomicus." In *French Food: On the Table, on the Page, and French Culture*, edited by Lawrence R. Schehr and Allen S. Weiss, 229–41. New York: Routledge.

William Reed Business Media. 2017a. "Ultraviolet by Paul Pairet." The World's 50 Best 2017. Last modified 2018. https://www.theworlds50best.com/The-List-2017/41-50/Ultraviolet-by-Paul-Pairet.html.

William Reed Business Media. 2017b. "Restaurant André." The World's 50 Best 2017. Last modified 2018. https://www.theworlds50best.com/The-List-2017/11-20/Restaurant-Andre.html.

Wong, Maggie Hiufu. 2012. "Michelin Star Wars: Recognition Not the Tastiest Dish." CNN. Last modified December 6, 2012. http://travel.cnn.com/hong-kong-michelin-guide-rent-increase-895366/.

新闻晨报 *Xinwen Chenbao*. 2017. "【吃货快看】沪上有兩家餐厅摘得三星！《米其林指南上海2018》发布! 'Chihuo kuaikan' Hushang you liangjia canting zhaide sanxing! Miqilin zhinan Shanghai 2018 fabu!" ["Foodie Alert! Shanghai Has Two Restaurants Earning Three Stars! *Michelin's Shanghai Guide 2018* Just Released!"]. 新闻晨报 *Xinwen Chenbao*. Last modified September 20, 2017. https://mp.weixin.qq.com/s?__biz=Nzg1MzAxMTgx&mid=2654449096&idx=1&sn=6b5d604653ae4a73696dcf6c5f6a1155&chksm=1d32441a2a45cd0c4a2e497d17020a55e62b38ab39af8867af069b8454de19016f24085f3c97&scene=0.

Xu Junqian. 2016. "Stirring Up Controversy." *China Daily*, November 19, 2016. https://web.archive.org/web/20161230014201/http://www.chinadaily.com.cn/weekend/2016-11/19/content_27428390.htm.

Yang, Mayfair Mei-hui. 1994. *Gifts, Favors, and Banquets: The Art of Social Relationships in China*. Ithaca, NY: Cornell University Press.

Yenal, Zafer, and Michael Kubiena. 2016. "Culinary Work at the Crossroads in Istanbul." *Gastronomica: The Journal of Critical Food Studies* 16, no. 1: 63–78.

11

Drinking Scorpions at Trader Vic's: Polynesian Parties, Caribbean Rum, Chinese Cooks, and American Tourists

Daniel E. Bender

University of Toronto

It was a typical tourist's day in 1959 with a bit of local color (a visit to a nearby school), a shopping outing, and a lingering lunch. Nina Khrushchev was visiting with her husband, the Soviet premier Nikita Khrushchev, and the newspapers reported on her every consumer choice. So, it was first page news when she decided on lunch at Trader Vic's, the popular—and expensive, reporters smirked—restaurant that offered a taste of tropical leisure to this visitor from the worker's paradise (*Chicago Daily Tribune* 1959).

Khrushchev was curious about the Polynesian food that had become so popular in the United States and in former colonial capitals (like London). The food excited diners not because it actually was a faithful introduction to the multiple cuisines and ingredients of the Pacific but because the drinks, lascivious atmosphere, Asian service labor, and a few ingredients (especially tropical fruits) evoked a Polynesian paradise. Referencing Hawai'i, Tahiti, and other tropical Pacific islands, Polynesian food married ingredients like pineapples or papayas to a handful of "Continental" dishes and, above all, to many standards of Chinese-American restaurants.

If Chinese-American food was a downscale staple of the American food landscape, Polynesian restaurants—especially the expensive Trader Vic's—were decidedly not. Polynesian food, as it was enjoyed by Khrushchev and millions of American business travelers and tourists, mixed fantasies of a Pacific tropical paradise, Caribbean rums, and Chinese and Chinese-American food and labor. The Cold War Polynesian idyll digested the real world of diasporic Chinese food tastes into a make-believe Pacific archipelago, divorced from history, nation, and empire, and ready for tourists (Kirsten 2000; Rennie 2013; Sherman 2011; Matsuda 2012; Lepofsky 1999; Connell 2003). Tropical tourism turned diasporic Chinese dishes into a fanciful Polynesian paradise, not only obscuring the reality of the US empire in the Pacific but also denying connections between diasporic foodways and their Asian nationalist expressions.

The food was tasty enough and the drinks were sweet and powerful, but in replacing tradition with tourism, Trader Vic's (and its many competitors) produced a cuisine without country. It substituted make-believe beach resorts for independent Asian and

Pacific countries and colonies. The Polynesian fantasy was a crucial way that Americans with ever increasing opportunities for global travel sought to relate to a Pacific now at the center of an expanding American military empire. Rather than accept realities of war, revolution, and nationhood, they escaped into Polynesian fantasy. Soldiers may have discovered the South Seas while on service during the war, but Trader Vic's, with its windowless rooms filled with Polynesian bric-a-brac, invited former soldiers, their children, and their families on holidays that recalled wartime R&R. They went as tourists, not colonists, but they still expected Islanders to serve as jolly hosts (Padoongpatt 2013; Lovegren 2005).

Drawing from Brian Roberts and Michelle Stephens' articulation of an archipelagic American Studies, this chapter understands Polynesian foods and their popularity among tourists as a direct response to decolonization, Asian nationalism, and American military expansion (Roberts and Stephens 2013). The end of one form of imperium and the rapid installation of another rendered the postwar Pacific of particular importance and raised questions simultaneously about its relationship to both Asia and America. The United States claimed governance over a series of islands chains and set up a range of military bases and missile testing sites. Like the Pacific itself, the postwar empire, politically anti-colonial, resembled an archipelago (Perez 2015).

Roberts and Stephens invite scholars to consider the "island" as a geopolitical and geocultural construct. An island can represent a model for a pure nation-state in which borders—where water meets land—are naturally visible. Yet the history of the Polynesian idyll that ultimately shaped Trader Vic's pushed toward a different notion of the Pacific islands as individually insignificant formations jutting out of a vast ocean and linked as part of a far-reaching archipelago. The Pacific islands climbed more than ever before into postwar American consciousness in three ways: how they related to the American "mainland," how Asia related to them, and how they related strategically to each other in a chain of army bases and tourist resorts. Missing in this list, of course, is the distinctiveness of their indigenous and labor migrant cultures, relationships between diasporic Chinese and revolutionary China, or nationalist and independence movements in both Asia and the Pacific. The Second World War strategy of island hopping encouraged the American military to consider the islands as identical bases. In a similar peacetime gesture, explorer Thor Heyerdahl's Kon-Tiki adventure—that name would lend itself to one of Trader Vic's copycat chains—described the potential journey of Pacific Islanders to the Americas, a journey that, like the American naval strategy before it, literally mapped an archipelago of common cultures.

The menu and tastes at Trader Vic's, its service labor, the décor, and even the encouraged drunkenness reveal how Polynesian restaurants helped map the postwar US empire by submerging Pacific cultures and sovereignties in a sea of rum and soy sauce. By joining Chinese-American recipes to the notion of a shared Pacific love of a good party, Polynesian food updated an older imperial strategy that envisioned the Pacific islands less as important spaces in and of themselves, but rather as gateways to Asia (China specifically). Polynesian foods also connected Asia into the Pacific and denied diasporic connections to postwar Asian culinary nationalisms by resurrecting older models of racialized service labor to enable tropical tourist pleasures. Drunk and full, Trader Vic's customers were articulating their visions of what relationships should be between (white) Americans, Asians, and Pacific Islanders in the postwar US empire. Relying on older visions of Polynesia as a tropical paradise and on colonial models of service, these were ties not of nations but of hosts and tourists (Imada 2008; O'Conner 2008; Laudan 1996).

Bootlegging rum

Walk through the palm frond gateway, out of late imperial London, and into the tourist's Polynesia. Victor Bergeron, Trader Vic's owner, was meticulous in his interior design and worked to create a make-believe Pacific island paradise that would serve (mostly) exoticized versions of Chinese-American foods. The London Trader Vic's, ensconced in the city's Hilton and occupying some of the most expensive real estate in the world, was far removed from Bergeron's first restaurant. In the two decades after the Second World War, Bergeron built a global chain of expensive theme restaurants that began with a rickety hunting-themed dive bar he called Hinky Dink's in working-class Oakland, California. By the 1950s, Bergeron managed an empire of restaurants, serving potent, sweet rum drinks and just-as-sweet, soy-laced foods, in an atmosphere of Polynesian bric-a-brac. His restaurants became key attractions in Hilton hotels in destinations like Havana, New York, London, Chicago, and San Juan. In smaller cities and smaller hotels, Trader Vic's Outrigger restaurants served the familiar blend of rum, sugar, and soy.

A working-class saloon keeper, the son of French immigrants, Bergeron built a chain that more than any other popularized "Polynesian" foods, a cuisine of Asian tastes divorced from any real geography. As a child, Bergeron suffered from a recurring case of tuberculosis that eventually required amputating a leg. The leg injury kept him home during the world war, but made him seem like a latter-day pirate to customers and restaurant reviewers and, for the sake of publicity, he blamed the loss of his leg on sharks. As an adult, Bergeron, discontented with a humdrum life and low salary running a gas station, turned to drinks and humble cooking to make a living.[1]

Hinky Dink's was a rough-hewn bar that served a cheap free lunch. War, tourism, and his appreciation of local Chinese-American restaurants helped Bergeron progress from small-time bar owner to global impresario. On holiday in the Caribbean, he savored the daiquiri at the Le Floride Hotel, then Havana's leading hotel. Back in Oakland, he visited local tropical theme bars and restaurants, most notably Don the Beachcomber's. For new food ideas, he turned to one of his cooks, Paul Wong, who acted as Bergeron's guide to Chinese-American restaurants ubiquitous throughout the Bay Area.[2] Bergeron soon tore down Hinky Dink's original hunting theme décor and replaced it with tropical souvenirs.

Trader Vic's sweet soy-based foods were staple Chinese-American favorites dressed up with the kinds of rum drinks Bergeron learned on holiday. The name "Trader Vic" wasn't the moniker of a genuine world traveler, just a self-given nickname that fictionally placed him in a long genealogy of Pacific traders selling rum to the "natives." When Victor Bergeron became Trader Vic he cast himself as a latter-day Robert Louis Stevenson connecting Polynesian myths to Caribbean pirates.

There was just one more ingredient to stir into the Polynesian cocktail: war and soldiers. During the Second World War, thousands of American men traveled to bases in the Caribbean and even more island hopped across the Pacific to Japan. Bergeron sold them booze. Working with an officer on a nearby base, he sold cartons of gin, bourbon, whiskey, and especially rum as part of a wartime Pacific bootlegging ring. The idea of a postwar Polynesia and booze-themed chain was already taking shape, as Bergeron thrilled to hear that officers' clubs across the Pacific were laughingly called "Trader Vic's" (Mayland 1957).

As the war ended, Bergeron began to dream of spreading Trader Vic's beyond Oakland. In the midst of the Cold War, the jet age, and in the nationalist headwinds in Asia and the Caribbean, Trader Vic's was a formula that worked. There were plenty of copycat competitors. Don the Beachcomber, which actually predated Trader Vic's, was also expanding. Joseph Stephen Crane, a former actor turned restaurateur, founded a chain he called Kon-Tiki. Bergeron knew that to realize dreams of expansion, he would need an ally with a great deal more capital than a saloonkeeper with just one successful restaurant.[3]

A foreign policy of hotels

Trader Vic's grew with Hilton International hotels. Postwar, Conrad Hilton was searching for restaurants to match the flavor of his new international hotels. His international brand, founded in 1948, represented a conscious departure from older, elite, colonial hotels. Hilton International hotels catered to tourists with money, but not necessarily pedigree. Hilton opened his first international hotels in Cold War hotspots like Cairo and Istanbul. By 1964, in addition to thirty-four domestic hotels, the Hilton chain operated twenty-six international hotels. By then, about a quarter of the chain's 49,298 rooms were in international hotels. Hilton regarded the spread of the leisure travel as the best way to combat communism, especially in former European colonies. Tourism, he argued, was Americanism and Americanism was anti-communism—and Hilton put that sentiment into a prayer he called "America on Its Knees." The published prayer was popular enough that he sent out thousands of copies. Hilton announced a new "foreign policy for hotels." "When we were children, gentlemen," he told the Rotary Club, the world seemed like a mansion owned by "white men." The "servants' quarters were occupied by the yellow men, black men, even a handful of red men." Hilton didn't much care for "a colonial empire," but he hated "communist gangsters" even more. Sometimes, he insisted, the "little peoples of the earth" were not ready for self-government and their new countries thus became breeding grounds for communism. Guns had their role, but hotels brought currency, travelers, and profitable encounters.[4]

Pause for a moment on the Hilton's choice of metaphor to explain collapsing European empires and their systems of racial hierarchy. Even Hilton must have realized the tense similarity between a hotel and a "rich man's house." In Hilton's vision, the hotel was not "colonialism" or a refuge for "big rich Americans," but a "business fellowship." Only local labor and "native supplies" would build the hotel and Hilton would supply managerial "know how." One-third would be American—Hilton's—profit. It was a vision of capitalism as "fellowship" and race relations as hospitality offered by "natives" to Americans.[5] Hilton envisioned Americans on their knees in prayer, but also at the bar drinking and partying. The expanding American economic and military empire would stay at Hilton hotels and, in return for money they spent, tourists would expect hospitality. Trader Vic's added a party room to the imperial mansion, but the legacy of the servants' quarters remained. That was precisely why Trader Vic's fit in Hilton hotels. Trader Vic's advanced a postwar vision of touristic leisure that linked Asia, the Pacific, and the Caribbean. The rum was Caribbean, Pacific Islanders provided the party, and Asians were the servers (Lowe 2015, 21).[6]

Bergeron didn't outwardly share Hilton's anti-communist zeal, but he did seek to expand and he didn't have the capital to do it himself. Hilton put his first Trader Vic's in his flagship Beverly Hills hotel to complement its fancy French dining. Later he expanded to the Palmer House in Chicago. By 1957, Hilton made an offer for the Trader Vic's brand itself. The final partnership proved a good deal for the hotelier. He guaranteed Bergeron a salary of only $65,000 and paid a paltry $2,000,000 for the brand. In return, Bergeron would decorate any new restaurants, train and hire the staff, and provide the Chinese ovens.[7]

Personal relations between Hilton and Bergeron were strained, but the fact that they endured suggests how much Hilton understood how tropical drinks and Chinese-American food could reframe hotels as island resorts for tourists with money, rather than colonial clubs for elites (Bergeron 1946, 91). At a time when French haute cuisine still defined global fine dining, middlebrow Polynesian themed restaurants were earning far more impressive profits and it was easy to understand why. The food was plentiful—but not cheap—and liquor flowed in crowded rooms. Hilton estimated that overall the Trader Vic's in Hilton hotels earned about $5 million a year. For that money, Hilton was willing to be "subjected to Vic's tirades."[8] Sheraton soon answered with its own Ports O' Call brand and with Kon-Tiki. Hilton even suspected that Crane and the architects had stealthily copied the Trader Vic's design for restaurants in Dallas and Montreal.[9] Polynesian food became hotel food for the jet age.

Trader Vic knows how to pamper

"Curl up in the shadowy depths of our Tonga Queen's chair and watch the gardenia floating in your cocktail." More than a meal, Polynesian food was an invitation to tourists to enjoy paradise—and the service it offered. Soft music "murmurs like the song of the Islands." The fashionable, white woman relaxed into the exotic chair, sipping her rum drink—at least in the advertisement. "Trader Vic knows how to pamper," read the ad (*London Life* 1966, 17).

The Park Lane Trader Vic's offered cues referencing the older colonial idea of Polynesia as a primitive paradise of sensuous women, native hospitality, abundant fruits and foods, and luxurious tropical climate. This ideal was first articulated in the seventeenth century and expanded upon by artists, botanists, writers, colonial officials, and myriad other travelers who passed through the many colonized islands of the Pacific. When visitors walked into a Trader Vic's, they were met by familiar images of tropical paradise, especially the exotic fruits. After a dinner of Cho Cho (broiled skewered and marinated flank steak) and the signature crabmeat Rangoon (crab and cream cheese in a fried wonton) came fresh tropical fruit embedded in chipped ice. It was the kind of abundance "that the Polynesian restaurants do so well," noted one reviewer. To complete the fantasy of tropical cornucopia and luxurious service, the waiter arrived with pineapple daiquiris (Loring 1968, 1).

The Pacific also had its imperial history as an intensely contested space where before the world wars, the German, American, French, British, and Japanese empires had jostled for vital coaling stations and lucrative plantation and guano islands. Samoa, Tahiti, and Hawai'i were valuable island colonies with productive plantation economies and essential naval bases (Teaiwa 1999). Combat operations in the Second World War turned the Pacific into a vast battleground, but only reinforced—and broadly popularized—notions of the Pacific as a tropical idyll. After the Japanese attack on Pearl Harbor, American soldiers and sailors depended on Hawai'i as a place for rest and relaxation—complete with plenty of drinking. After the war, as the American military spread its influence everywhere from Guam to Okinawa, integrating colonial possessions into a network of military bases, popular cultural descriptions recast former South Pacific battlefields as tourist havens. For example, *South Pacific*, the 1949 Rodgers and Hammerstein musical (and then 1958 movie) based on a set of stories by popular author James Michener, described a wartime love story between an American army nurse and a local French plantation owner who had fathered two mixed-race children. In the musical's final scene the American woman and the French colonial plantation owner confirm their love—and new mixed-race family—at a table set amid luxurious palm fronds. Between them sat a tureen and bowls. Orientalized by the addition of Chinese-style soup spoons, it could have been a meal at Trader Vic's.

Literary scholar Christina Klein argues that the musical's message of mixed-race adoption and romance recognized that the spread of American power throughout the Pacific and in Asia demanded the repudiation of the imperial racial logic. Like Hilton's "Foreign Policy of Hotels," *South Pacific* imagined replacing the strict racial hierarchies of empire with joyful (and sometimes sexually charged) cross-cultural encounters. Responding to the vast reconfiguration of the Pacific and its incorporation into an American military empire, Teresia Teaiwa demonstrates that tourism and the military work together to obscure histories of colonial conquest. "*Militourism*," she defines, "is a phenomenon by which military or paramilitary force ensures the smooth running of a tourist industry, and the same tourist industry masks the military force behind it" (Teaiwa 1999, 251, original emphasis; Klein 2003).

The antecedent of the Polynesian meal wasn't, in fact, the fine dining of an earlier era of grand hotels. Rather, it was militourism: the combination of leisure travel and military R&R. Trader Vic's also turned militourism into gastrotourism using exoticized Chinese-American foodways to remove Pacific Islanders from modern history. Customers at Trader Vic's even acted as if a Polynesian meal was a tourist trip that demanded material souvenirs. They tried to touch the outrigger canoes on the ceiling and steal the tiki figurines. Waiters were even specially trained about how to assuage the embarrassment of would-be thieves.

Trader Vic's was culinary R&R—"to help us relax and have fun" (Bergeron 1946, 17). Writing just at the end of the Second World War, the budding restaurant impresario insisted that Polynesia and its foods were just what "war-torn civilization" needed. Here, the overtly "inauthentic" recipes reveal how Bergeron had little interest in presenting traditional customs and rituals. Rather, as Bergeron explained: "I have tried to capture the spirit of their feast and fun-making for you here on the mainland" (Bergeron 1946, 135–6). "[T]he Polynesians," he wrote, "just know how to have fun in simple unaffected ways" (Bergeron 1946, 17). So (in his telling), a typical Tahitian party began with dumping wine, rum, and every imaginable tropical fruit into an old wine barrel. To "stir the mess," the host grabbed a paddle from a canoe. Somehow "music appeared from the clouds," and the party magically began. Hardly traditional, it was a three-day party lubricated by Caribbean rum. "The Tahitian has incredible staying powers when it comes to having a good time" (Bergeron 1946, 75). In this representation of the Polynesian way of life, hospitality was naturally given and happily taken by American tourists. US expansion, on the menu at Trader Vic's, was simply mutuality.

Caribbean rum at the *luau*

Vic claimed that he drank his first "Scorpion" at a *luau* in Manoa, Hawai'i. The air was perfumed with exotic flowers while a gentle rain fell to the tempo of soft Hawai'ian music. The table was laid in "true luau fashion," with leaves, blossoms, and orchids. A Chinese punch bowl was, incongruously, the centerpiece and filled with "Honolulu's famous scorpion, a Caribbean rum drink which does not shilly-shally or mess around in getting you under way." Bergeron gave license to see the *luau* not as anything remotely indigenous or traditional, but as drunken excess hosted for the tourist in paradise (Bergeron 1946, 76–7). The addition of Caribbean rum to the Pacific (and as an accompaniment for Asian flavors) not only matched the contours of the US empire but also helped redefine the Pacific, less as a patchwork of newly independent island nations, American military outposts, or distinct communities, than as an everlasting party hosted by a generous people.

Trader Vic's was an invitation to inebriation. Reading the drinks menu at Trader Vic's is an exercise in identifying where history mattered for the Polynesian restaurant and where its denial was just as crucial. Bergeron's own illicit rum selling recollected colonial histories of Pacific rum sellers, selling the cheapest booze in barrels to communities throughout the tropical and arctic Pacific. Bergeron admitted that rum had history and specificity. "No other liquor has played such a terrific yet romantic role in history," he gushed. As he described in menus and cookbooks the varying tastes of Caribbean rum to an American public (that treated rum as the cheapest of booze), he mapped the Caribbean archipelago as a set of discrete cultures, cuisines, and rums. Jamaican rum was particularly "perfumy" because of the old pot still method and their unique yeast culture. Trinidadian rum was amber colored with an "apple-butterscotchy" taste (Bergeron 1974, 9–13; Nesbitt 2008; Kessler 2015; Foss 2012). However, he dissolved rum's colonial history into fictional stories of pirates. He might "like" rum's history, but he cast that history as progress from pirates to "beachcombers." In the age of beach tourism, rum "has become the favorite potion of millions of civilized people" (Bergeron 1946, 16).

Rum and its pirate fables helped Bergeron connect the Caribbean to the Pacific. Gin may have been the fortifying drink of empire, but rum was relaxing, the perfect potion, alongside soy-soaked diasporic Asian tastes, to reproduce the essence of Polynesia on the mainland. If Bergeron mapped the Caribbean in which specific island borders were reproduced in distinct tastes, the alcoholic effects of rum on mainland consumers remapped Pacific geographies from specific islands and cultures into a generalized Polynesian party in which the drinks were Caribbean and the foods were Chinese-American. Polynesian history (at least in Bergeron's telling) wasn't a fable of pirates, but a children's story of "little people." Taking older folk tales and turning them into a (rather clumsy) 1972 children's book, Bergeron located the origins of Polynesian peoples and hospitality in the "little people" called Menehunes. They arrived from a distant planet to a rocky Hawai'ian archipelago devoid of history, plants, or people. The first humans on the Hawai'ian beaches (from Tahiti) enjoyed its first feasts of fruits planted by the Menehunes from outer space. Trader Vic's would later feature the Menehunes in advertisements and the commentary on history was obvious: the Polynesian feast was the stuff of myth and magic, not real cultures or history. Bergeron applied the same kind of description of Menehunes to Polynesians and Hawai'ians in general: "They are jolly, happy little people and make other people happy too" (Trader Vic 1972).

Through the intrusion of rum, Bergeron's own constructed self-history as a Pacific island trader enjoying Polynesian hospitality merged with the fiction and biography of Robert Louis Stevenson. The European author had retreated to Polynesia, but wrote about Caribbean pirates. As well, Stevenson described dissolute island traders. In bringing rum to Polynesia, Bergeron followed in Stevenson's footsteps. Thus, he opened his cookbook *Trader Vic's Food and Drink* (1946), like Stevenson's *Treasure Island*, with the pirate chant: "Yo, ho, ho, and a bottle of rum." Polynesia, in the narration of the nineteenth-century Pacific tourist sailor like Stevenson or the twentieth-century armchair traveler and army bootlegger like Bergeron, was timeless and the specifics of its cultures and cuisines irrelevant.

Bergeron replaced cultural traditions and local histories with partying and lovemaking. One of the restaurant's menu covers showed rum on the table in the midst of a drunken Polynesian feast. The old-fashioned wooden keg, marked with the trader's "XXX" mark, seemed straight from a pirate ship's hold. If rum had its regional specificities and chronology for Bergeron, the Polynesian party was ancient but without a chronology or cuisine. This repudiation of history and (for the most part) culinary tradition crucially downplayed the effects of colonialism on Pacific Islanders. When the London Trader Vic's promoted its Tahitian feast (a standard package throughout the chain), it returned Tahiti to an imagined state where French colonialism simply never happened. In Bergeron's interpretation, the natives "still cook and live in the old ways." They may have—somehow—acquired "a few of the white man's luxuries and an odd piece of clothing now and then," but they lived much as did their primitive ancestors (Bergeron 1946, 135). For Bergeron, colonialism was merely administration, but "it sure as hell" did not affect the local population or their hospitality, simplicity, and love of a good party.

Polynesian food normalized American presence in the South Pacific, even as it obscured military imperialism and nationalist movements (in both the Pacific and in Asia). One menu cover connects the roly-poly Polynesian chief at the head of the table, the barely clothed native woman, and the tourist, recognizable only by his dress coat. Dark skin and large red lips place the Polynesians in a long history of racial othering. The tourist, though, at first glance doesn't even seem an outsider. Sitting with his back to the viewer (thereby hiding his racial differences), he serves first to reject older formulations of racial segregation and second to formulate relations of Americans and Islanders as one of hospitality taken and given willingly. The lasciviousness of the South Pacific body in this image as it relates to the abundant food and drink obscures the individuality of South Pacific cultures and cuisines at the same time that it reaffirms Polynesia as a vast oceanic space of noble savagery and timeless joy. "Native life and fun in the South Pacific is pretty much the same on all islands" (Bergeron 1946, 135–6).

The Polynesian party hosted for the tourists wasn't service demanded, but hospitality offered. In Tahiti, a good party doesn't need "R.S.V.P.s" and Bergeron felt welcome at a local feast (invited or not). The number of pigs to be cooked expanded from two to five. The host's sons caught fish and a relative sent canoe-loads of coconuts. Bergeron didn't stop to listen to the chief's "benediction" or even wonder at the reason for the feast. Assuming that he was an honored guest, Bergeron was entranced by the rum punch and the evening's "lovemaking." Whether he had ever attended a Tahitian feast or whether this was simply a fictional yarn is immaterial; he was recycling and updating for the modern tourist / restaurant patron an older myth of Polynesia: untouched, infinitely welcoming, unabashedly sensual, and abundant in its food and—here was Bergeron's touch—rum drinks (Bergeron 1946, 139–40).

A meal at Trader Vic's (or, for that matter, any of the Polynesian restaurants that graced hotel lobbies) was a tourist voyage and the product of frenetic movement of edible goods of mostly Asian origin, material objects, labor and management, and, naturally enough, tourists. A visitor to the Trader Vic's at the Statler Hilton in Washington, DC could buy a souvenir postcard, picturing the restaurant's entrance. More than an advertisement, a postcard was a letter home from a trip taken. The wooden shingled doorway that evoked a South Seas native hut joined the primitive tropics to the clean, white hotel, suggesting the easy joining of primitive paradise to American modernity. Two colossal tiki head sculptures, evocative of Easter Island, guarded the entrance. Broad-leafed plants flanked the doors while well-dressed white couples posed outside, waiting to step/travel from the American capital to the South Seas.[10]

Flip the postcard to read the caption explaining the two heads. The tiki gods—regardless of whether they meant anything to Pacific communities—embodied the "abundance, laughter, and joy" of the South Seas. In bringing the "mystery of the South Seas" to the American hotel, Polynesian hotel food turned a traditional meal like the *luau* into a tourist party, but the dishes themselves and the cooks that prepared them depended on older routes of Chinese migration to the United States.

The exotic windowless chamber

Trader Vic's evoked the tropical Pacific, but it was an open secret that the cuisine was Chinese-American. Stephen Crane, the designer and operator of Kon-Tiki, admitted that "the Polynesian restaurant is usually Cantonese in style." The water chestnuts, pea pods, or bean sprouts that characteristically garnished the dishes "didn't even grow on the islands." Servicemen "discovered" the South Seas during the Second World War but "Mainland Polynesia" restaurants—Crane estimated that there were around 200 such restaurants in 1965—adapted Chinese foods (Loring 1965). Bergeron similarly recalled closing Hinky Dink's and opening Trader Vic's "selling tropical drinks and Chinese food" (Trader Vic 1973, 46).

The nature of the labor and menu at Polynesian restaurants meant that Chinese-Americans were literally serving up the Pacific to (white) Americans. Trader Vic's ripped Chinese-American food from its diaspora, decoupled it from Asia, and excluded it from the United States. Polynesian restaurants relocated Asian foods into a mythical Pacific. As low-end Chinese-American food became expensive Polynesian, one Trader Vic's menu cover presented an image of a white traveler, relaxing in a hammock and served rum drinks by a smiling, nearly naked native woman (Trader Vic 1973, 44–5). That was the atmosphere Trader Vic's wanted: a touch of lasciviousness and a lot of rum, but the servers and the cooks had to be Chinese. A publicity photo for the Outrigger, for example, proudly showed their waiters in Orientalist uniforms. For Bergeron, Chinese labor was essential to the experience of Trader Vic's. In a miniature of the labor migrations to plantation economies like Hawai'i, the Pacific provided the atmosphere, but the Chinese provided the expertise, original recipes, and the labor. An advertisement for a "TRADER VIC'S luau," invited diners to the "relaxing world of the Polynesian." This was a "dreamy creation of fun and laughter" with a sound track of Hawai'ian music. "The sorcery of Ping Lee's range" provided the food.[11]

Here was a new geographic and racial division of labor: wealthy (mostly white) Americans played the role of tourists; Polynesians played the role of carefree primitive hosts; people from the Caribbean made the rum; and the Chinese (Americans) cooked and served the food, completing a circle of exoticism. The journalist and self-proclaimed gourmand Lucius Beebe admired Bergeron because "he has contrived to make Oriental food not only sound enchanting but also extremely edible." He recognized that Bergeron had updated Chinese-American "chop suey." Bergeron started with Chinese-American staples, added many jiggers of rum and some South Seas polish, and revealed the "Chop-suey barons" as simply "traffickers in baled ensilage and coolie fodders." In praising Bergeron's success and in measuring the distance between San Francisco's Chinatown and the (physically nearby) Trader Vic's, Beebe turned to common and racist representations of Chinese foods (Beebe 1946, 22–3). As long as Trader Vic's placed such foods in the tourist Pacific, they remained embedded in imperial histories of service and tourism.

Bergeron might have avoided Beebe's crass racism, but his debt to individual Chinese-American and East Asian cooks and servers was undeniable (Trader Vic 1973, 44). Captains and managers typically started from the very bottom and then advanced to higher positions in the chain. Everett Park had come to the United States from Korea to study biology. During his summers, he worked at Trader Vic's as a part-time waiter and soon advanced to captain. He anticipated that soon he would work as a manager in a new branch of the empire. King Wong also advanced with the spread of the chain and had caught the attention of other restaurateurs looking to enter the Polynesian restaurant business. Yet when he turned down a substantial raise from a competitor, he expressed his loyalty to Bergeron. "I still hold a strong feeling of gratitude and appreciation toward him personally."[12]

In parallel to the way Hilton proposed a "foreign policy of hotels" that rejected the pre–Second World War imperial racial hierarchies, Bergeron reframed the place of Chinese-Americans in the United States. He abhorred previous, explicitly racist exclusions of Chinese migrants and even helped fund a memorial to those who suffered in the Exclusion era in California. He insisted on Chinese cooks and waiters. In racially segregated Houston, for example, he bemoaned the low wages of wait staff (typically paid to African-American servers) because it made it hard to hire his signature Chinese-American servers at "a much higher wage scale."[13]

Still, a different exclusion persisted in the connection of Chinese-American cooking and Polynesian parties. Bergeron excluded Chinese-American foodways from American foodways, thus keeping the food exotic in a diasporic geography delinked from independent Asia, but not genuinely Pacific. Bergeron had a sinophilic approach in his working-class upbringing in Oakland. "I get one hell of a bang out of the Oriental people," he confessed in his autobiography (Trader Vic 1973, 76). He equally scoffed at those who cast aspersions at Chinese ingredients. Those who cast soy sauce as "bug juice" were "uninformed." Yet he insisted that Chinese food remained exotic. Bergeron recognized the irony that Chinese food was popular on the mainland, but, in a slippage of language, defined it as intrinsically foreign—no matter how long Chinese had been in America. "Everyone"—and here he meant white Americans, the audience for both his cookbook and the patrons of his restaurants—"has a pet Chinese restaurant" where they enjoyed fried rice, chop suey, and barbecued pork. Chinese ingredients, methods, and flavors affected "our American eating habits" not because the Chinese themselves were American, but because Americans had learned to love their foods (Bergeron 1946, 157–8).

The exclusion of Chinese-Americans from American cooking enabled Bergeron, the restaurant owner, first to turn cheap working-class food into high-end Pacific dining and, second to lay claim to Chinese techniques—especially utensils and ovens—as the key to Polynesian cooking (Bergeron 1946, 159). Bergeron's relationship with Chinese food was sinophilic and sympathetic, even as it denied Chinese-American diasporic connections. It was also extractive, acquiring dishes, methods, and ingredients, and marketing them—at a premium—as his own. "I've acquired, experimented with, and made my own," he boasted, "Chinese, Javanese, or Tahitian dishes." The Hawai'ians cooked food wrapped in *ti* leaves in underground *imu* ovens, but Trader Vic's could master the same flavors with their signature and proprietary ancient Chinese ovens so "far superior to any other." After all, it was "constructed by a Chinese." Bergeron placed himself in the role of the entrepreneur standing firmly between American customers, Asian cooks, and Pacific Islanders for reasons of profit and culture. American (that is, white) customers might like good food and plenty of drink, but "their taste buds aren't educated enough to take foreign dishes first hand" (Bergeron 1946, 17).

The substitution of immigration exclusion with culinary exoticism returned postwar tourism to a world of colonial-era service. In the culinary fusion of Trader Vic's, Polynesians were the imagined hosts (otherwise absent), but the actual servers and cooks were East Asian and Chinese-American. Trader Vic's capitalized on American fascination with tropical abundance, familiarity with Chinese-American restaurants, and expectations of Chinese servants. At Boston's Statler Hotel, "one of its main attractions is the staff" (Rice 1968).

Polynesian food demanded the symbols and products of non-national and archipelagic space (Caribbean rum and Polynesian tourist souvenirs) and performative bodies (Asian cooks and servers and Polynesians, represented on menus). Chinese waiters, insisted a manager of Trader Vic's, must be "willing to serve and humble enough to do anything for the guests." Customers "must be taken care of." Through unquestioned service, "the self-effacing style" delivered with the "inscrutable Oriental smile," the Trader Vic cast "its magic spell." Chinese service combined with Polynesian bric-a-brac to create what one observer called "the netherworldly feeling of the exotic windowless chamber"—a perfect definition of Polynesian jet-age foods (Rice 1968).

The blending of Chinese ingredients and service with a Pacific setting naturalized in the American mind the connections between Asia, the Chinese diaspora, and the militarized Pacific. Tourist foods could entice and seduce; they could never acknowledge diasporic or national cuisines. If the "island" cartographically provides a model for understanding the nation as a geographic entity with fixed and distinguishable (watery) boundaries, then the substitution of the party for the island as the defining characteristic of the Pacific removed the possibility of Pacific nationhood. If the Pacific was less a vast space of distinct islands connected by flows of people and goods and more a sprawling archipelago with a shared thirst for a good drink, then postwar nationalism made little sense. The Pacific, as it was served by Chinese cooks and servers to American diners by Trader Vic's, was a space without nation (but with plenty of rum and parties), but not precisely with colonies. The subsuming of Chinese-American foodways into Polynesian menus—thereby twice removing the food from a newly "Red" China—similarly severed diasporic connections between Chinese-American cooks and postwar Chinese and Asian nationalisms.

The dishwashers wore paper bags

With its fantasy cuisine of a militourist empire, Trader Vic's and the hotels where they were housed represented both resorts and bases of Cold War strategy and that made them targets, as both Hilton and Bergeron would soon realize in Cuba. The very dynamics of nationalism, war, revolution, and migration together forced Polynesian food back into history. "Aloha," advertised Trader Vic's restaurants in Chicago, San Francisco, Denver, and New York. New dishes like "Lotus Chicken, Cho Cho Chicken and Fuji Beef" were proving popular. In Havana, though, the Trader Vic's "hasn't been busy." Apart from "Mr. Castro and his army of 400," the new Hilton had few guests with money to spare on Polynesian food and drinks.[14]

From the start, Bergeron was nervous about opening a branch in Havana. For his Hilton partners the new hotel was key to tapping into the booming Caribbean tourist economy. Unfortunately for Hilton and for Bergeron, the hotel, constructed in partnership with the island's culinary workers' union, opened its doors just at the outbreak of the Cuban Revolution. Because Hilton had always lauded tourism as the antidote to communism, the modernist hotel and its Polynesian restaurant had an outsized political symbolism that matched its towering architecture. As Fidel Castro and his revolutionary followers claimed control over Havana, the Hilton became the unofficial new Cuban capital building. Revolutionary leaders became the hotel's principal guests, replacing tourists wary of traveling to the island.[15] At first the hotel's managers remained cautiously sympathetic. "Unfortunately, Dr. Fidel Castro received some bad press," reported the hotel's new manager to Conrad Hilton. Surely, the new Ministry of Labor and the emboldened unions wouldn't want to damage the hotels and the massive tourist business.[16]

What happens when tropical revolutions—real history—disrupt the timelessness of pirate tales? The manager of the Trader Vic's, Keith Hardman, soon reported that "Everyone still seems to be 'laying low'" instead of visiting Trader Vic's which hosted only about seventy-five guests a day. Even worse for Hardman, in a microcosm of the worsening relationship between the United States and Castro, someone (and he suspected it was a revolutionary) hotwired his car from the hotel's garage and Hilton refused to reimburse his loss.[17] For good reason: by early 1959, Hilton was losing $100,000 a month on his Cuban investment.[18]

The American hotel and its Pacific restaurant serving Chinese food had become a Caribbean revolution in miniature. Trader Vic's and Bergeron's vision of the tropics as the site of safe tourist leisure, not insurrection, was at stake. Hardman was growing frustrated. "I often feel the desire to bundle up the restaurant, strap on the Trader Vic sign, and shove off looking for a happy home somewhere else in a location ... where all the people are hungry millionaires," he confessed.[19] Sign or not, the company repatriated most of the Chinese-American employees. Inside the hotel, tensions were rising between the hotel and remaining restaurant workers, organized now into revolutionary unions, and the American managers. The hotel frantically sought ways of saving money. As Hilton contemplated closing the hotel's restaurants, the new government, prodded by the hotel workers union, refused to allow any redundancies. At a March 1959 meeting that lasted until the wee hours of the morning, the hotel workers' union insisted that the Trader Vic's continue its full lunch service to a mostly empty room (Merrill 2009; Skwiot 2010; Berger and Wood 2010; Thompson 2006).[20]

At Trader Vic's the revolutionary union struck at the very center of the postcolonial tourist economy. The union action aimed in sensory ways to disrupt illusions of Polynesian plenty, native hospitality, and service; it did not withdraw its labor. The revolutionary union ordered Trader Vic's waiters—now fully Cuban—not to wash or shave for three days. In place of the aroma of orchids or the wafting smoke of grilled meat, human sweat brought revolutionary politics into a make-believe South Pacific. Instead of Orientalist uniforms, workers wore "guayaberas," Cuban shirts associated politically with Castro and the revolutionary movement. "I know this all sounds like someone's D.T.'s but damn it, it's a fact," bemoaned the Trader Vic's managers. And the kitchen crew wore paper bags.[21]

The Hilton and Trader Vic's managers complained that the Cuban hotel had become a "breeding ground for communism" and tourism was suffering. Even the future of casinos was uncertain. The Trader Vic's manager even noted that "pornographic movies are outlawed."[22] In October 1960, the hotel and Trader Vic's were abruptly nationalized and Hilton and Bergeron were left to squabble about unpaid bills. Trader Vic's, the private outpost of an American tourist empire, became the state-owned El Polinesio restaurant and soon enough, a destination for Russian advisers eager (like Khrushchev before them) for a taste of tropical paradise.

The drama in the Havana Hilton did not derail either Hilton or Trader Vic's. However, it did reveal that if Polynesian food would spread alongside anti-communism, Trader Vic's could never be insulated from challenges to US expansion. Trader Vic's had become the catering wing of a foreign policy of hotels. Trader Vic's was just as implicated as Hilton in the expansion of the postwar American empire, requiring a real mobilization of people, skilled and racialized Asian labor, as well as exotic foodstuffs and drinks.

How Scorpions became Chinese . . . and American

Trader Vic's would continue to thrive for at least a few years after the capitalist branch in Cuba was nationalized. A few outposts still linger on in Hilton hotels. Within a decade the chain, though, had slowed its expansion. There are different explanations for how Polynesian food went from high-end dining to crass kitsch, a parody of Chinese cuisine. With growing acknowledgment of Chinese foodways that came with the American détente with the People's Republic, Trader Vic's could less easily place its menu in a mythical Polynesia. Practically, the chain expanded too quickly alongside a single hotel chain that slowly lost its position as a suave beacon of postwar American affluence and style. That hotel chain even became separated from Hilton himself, after the 1967 sale of Hilton International to TWA. Trader Vic's was a product of a particular Cold War moment. The myth of the tropics nurtured at Trader Vic's would persist, however, in all-inclusive resorts that appealed to the broader traveling public. After all, they continue to serve flower-garnished sweet rum drinks (Enloe 2000).

More people were also coming to the United States as part of a transformation in patterns of global mobility that began in the 1960s. New Chinese migrants arrived in the United States after the 1965 revision of American immigration policy and brought with them a refreshed version of Chinese cooking. Hotel restaurants increasingly seemed less like places to experience exotic tastes and more like refuges for the culturally timid. Bergeron's rejection of authenticity in favor of myth and atmosphere, once a signature, became a liability. By 1973 the restaurant reviewer Doris Tobias dismissed the chain's Polynesian artifacts as cheap kitsch. Unconvinced that the cuisine was somehow Polynesian exotic, she located particular dishes in specific, very real national cuisines. And she was not impressed. The Peking duck breast was as poorly cooked as the Chinese cabbage. For Tobias "authenticity" now seemed more important than an evening's virtual trip to tropical paradise. "[I]f you must take great aunt Lavinia to a . . . oriental restaurant," she recommended, head to Chinatown. At least the food there is "authentic" (Tobias 1973, 16).

Such a reading of the decline of Trader Vic's rooted in the reconfiguration of global mobilities challenges the otherwise simple notion that President Richard Nixon's rather touristic trip to China (and the subsequent "One China" policy) launched a new excitement for Chinese cuisine that privileged the genuine over the exotic. In fact, if the international lasting legacy of Trader Vic's was the tropical resort, the drinks and flavors of "Polynesia" also lived on in new kinds of Chinese-American restaurants. Trader Vic's had long sought a home in St. Louis (around the time I was growing up there), but never found the right Hilton host. By that time my family and I dined regularly at the China Garden and its sister restaurant, the Mandarin House. Both had begun to challenge the non-Chinese palate with new dishes and ingredients. Yet among the appetizers was Bergeron's signature Crab Rangoon. The crabmeat was long gone in everything but the name and replaced simply by molten cream cheese. The drinks menu served Scorpions and other sweet rum concoctions in ceramic bamboo, coconut shells, and tiki figures.

By then Nixon was also back from China and embroiled in the Watergate scandal. When he emerged from a White House that seemed like a bunker for an embattled president, reporters noted that he headed for Trader Vic's. (Spiro Agnew, Nixon's disgraced former vice-president, had already eaten his last meal before his resignation at Trader Vic's.) They wondered whether the president was seeking solace in his newfound taste for Chinese foods. Reading closely, this account reveals how the interweaving of Caribbean rum, Polynesian idylls, and Chinese cooking had unraveled. The disgraced president was dining on Chinese flavors and drinking rum. This was the same food also served to the Chinese diplomats who arrived in Washington, DC to set up their first embassy since the Revolution. Chef James C. Chen from the nearby Trader Vic's served as their personal cook (Smyth 1973a, 1973b).

But what were those diplomats really tasting? In its waning years of popularity Trader Vic's was serving China (and Chinese-American) back to the Chinese and simultaneously reminding these guests that the Pacific was part of the US militourist empire (Cho 2010). These Chinese diplomats, though, likely tasted only "American" food. Khrushchev had sought out an American tourist attraction that had whisked her off to the mythical South Pacific. Chinese diplomats were, according to the newspapers, satiated by American flavors (like sole and peach Melba). So, the White House sent them food from Trader Vic's, which was, by then, Chinese again. To Chinese diners, sweet soy grilled meats and "Imperial beef" must also have tasted distinctly American (Smyth 1973a).

Notes

1   Trader Vic's Menu, c. 1950, Randall H. Greenlee Menu Collection, Box 1, Kroch Library, Division of Rare & Manuscript Collections, Cornell University.
2   "Starting a Bergeron Dynasty," *San Francisco Examiner* (January 6, 1963) and "Salty Czar of Cosmo Place," *San Francisco Examiner* (January 6, 1963), both in Conrad N. Hilton Papers, Box 215, Folder Trader Vic.
3   "Ports O' Call" (menu, n.d.), Hilton Library and Archives, Conrad Hilton Papers; "War of Exotic Restaurant Chains Comes to a Head in Portland" (December 26, 1959), Conrad N. Hilton Papers, Box 159, Folder Trader Vic, 1959–62.
4   Conrad N. Hilton, "Toward a Foreign Policy for Hotels, an Address Before the Los Angeles Rotary Club" (July 27, 1956), Hilton Hotels International Papers, Box 6, Folder 1.

5   Bill Cunningham, "Hilton Spreading Foreign Aid," *Boston Sunday Herald* (June 24, 1956), Hilton Hotels International Papers, Box 7, Folder 8.

6   "Hilton Hotels Corporation, Statistics" (March, 1964), Hilton Hotels International Papers, Box 6, Folder 8.

7   "Confidential" (June 20, 1957), Conrad N. Hilton Papers, H RG1, Legal Series, Box 22; "Conrad Hilton to Robert Caverly" (February 22, 1961), Conrad N. Hilton Papers, Box 159, Folder Trader Vic, 1959–62.

8   "Gregory R. Dillon to Conrad N. Hilton" (January 17, 1959) and "Hilton Hotels Corporation—The Savory Hilton, Trader Vic's" (1960), Conrad N. Hilton Papers, Box 159, Folder Trader Vic, 1959–62.

9   "Conrad H. Hilton to Victor Bergeron" (May 11, 1959) and "Robert J. Caverly to Gregory R. Dillon" (May 1, 1959), both in Conrad N. Hilton Papers, Box 159, Folder Trader Vic, 1959–62.

10 "Trader Vic's" (Postcard, n.d.), Trader Vic's Menus, Hilton Library and Archives.

11 "Albert K. Gans to 'fellow Gourmand'" (March 15, 1965), Conrad N. Hilton Papers, Box 215, Folder Trader Vic.

12 "King Wong to William Irwin" (April 9, 1959), Conrad N. Hilton Papers, Box 159, Folder Trader Vic, 1959–62.

13 "Greg Dillon to Conrad Hilton" (n.d. 1960), Conrad N. Hilton Papers, Box 159, Folder Trader Vic, 1959–62.

14 "A Message from Trader Vic" (n.d., c. 1959), Conrad N. Hilton Papers, Box 159, Folder Trader Vic, 1959–62.

15 "Conrad Hilton to Bergeron" (January 21, 1959), Conrad N. Hilton Papers, Box 159, Folder Trader Vic, 1959–62.

16 "José A. Menendez to Conrad Hilton" (January 29, 1959), Conrad N. Hilton Papers, Box 159, Folder Trader Vic, 1959–62.

17 "Keith Hardman to Chan Wong" (January 16, 1959), Conrad N. Hilton Papers, Box 159, Folder Trader Vic, 1959–62.

18 "Conrad N. Hilton to Victor Bergeron" (March 10, 1959), Conrad N. Hilton Papers, Box 159, Folder Trader Vic, 1959–62.

19 "Hardman to Wong" (January 16, 1959).

20 "I. Keith Hardman to Chan Wong" (March 7, 1959), Conrad N. Hilton Papers, Box 159, Folder Trader Vic, 1959–62.

21 "Keith Hardman to Chan Wong" (May 4, 1959), Conrad N. Hilton Papers, Box 159, Folder Trader Vic, 1959–62.

22 "Keith Hardman to Chan Wong" (May 23, 1959), Conrad N. Hilton Papers, Box 159, Folder Trader Vic, 1959–62.

References

Archival sources

Hilton, Conrad N. Papers. Hilton Library and Archives, University of Houston, Houston, Texas.

Hilton Hotels International Papers. Hilton Library and Archives, University of Houston, Houston, Texas.

Randall H. Greenlee Menu Collection. Box 1. Kroch Library, Division of Rare & Manuscript Collections, Cornell University, Ithaca, New York.

Trader Vic's Menus. Hilton Library and Archives, University of Houston, Houston, Texas.

Works cited

Beebe, Lucius. 1946. "Introduction." In *Trader Vic's Book of Food and Drink*, by Victor J. Bergeron. Garden City: Doubleday.

Berger, Dina, and Andrew Grant Wood, eds. 2010. *Holiday in Mexico: Critical Reflections on Tourism and Tourist Encounters*. Durham, NC: Duke University Press.

Bergeron, Victor J. 1946. *Trader Vic's Book of Food and Drink*. Garden City: Doubleday.

Bergeron, Victor J. 1974. *Trader Vic's Rum Cookery and Drinkery*. Garden City: Doubleday.

Chicago Daily Tribune. 1959. "Nikita's Wife Spends Happy Day: Shopping." September 22, 1959, 4F.

Cho, Lily. 2010. *Eating Chinese: Culture on the Menu in Small Town Canada*. Toronto: University of Toronto Press.

Connell, John. 2003. "Island Dreaming: The Contemplation of Polynesian Paradise." *Journal of Historical Geography* 29, no. 4: 554–81.

Enloe, Cynthia. [1989, 1990] 2000. *Bananas, Beaches, and Bases: Making Feminist Sense of International Politics*. Berkeley: University of California Press.

Foss, Richard. 2012. *Rum: A Global History*. London: Reaktion.

Imada, Adria L. 2008. "The Army Learns to Luau: Imperial Hospitality and Military Photography in Hawai'i." *Contemporary Pacific* 20, no. 2: 329–61.

Kessler, Lawrence H. 2015. "A Plantation upon a Hill; Or, Sugar Without Rum: Hawai'i's Missionaries and the Founding of the Hawaiian Sugarcane Plantation System." *Pacific Historical Review* 84: 129–62.

Kirsten, Sven A. 2000. *The Book of Tiki: The Cult of Polynesian Pop in Fifties America*. Cologne: Taschen.

Klein, Christina. 2003. *Cold War Orientalism: Asia in the Middlebrow Imagination, 1945–1961*. Berkeley: University of California Press.

Laudan, Rachel. 1996. *The Foods of Paradise: Exploring Hawaii's Culinary Heritage*. Honolulu: University of Hawai'i Press.

Lepofsky, Dana. 1999. "Gardens of Eden? An Ethnohistoric Reconstruction of Maohi (Tahitian) Cultivation." *Ethnohistory* 46, no. 1: 1–29.

London Life. 1966. "TRADER VIC'S."

Loring, Kay. 1965. "Polynesian Restaurants: Exotic as Ham and Eggs." *Chicago Tribune*, August 15, 1965, F10.

Loring, Kay. 1968. "Like Fresh Papaya? You'll Find it at Trader Vic's." *Chicago Tribune*, March 3, 1968, 1.

Lovegren, Sylvia. 2005. *Fashionable Food: Seven Decades of Food Fads*. Chicago: University of Chicago Press.

Lowe, Lisa. 2015. *Intimacy of Four Continents*. Durham, NC: Duke University Press.

Matsuda, Matt K. 2012. *Pacific Worlds: A History of Seas, Peoples, and Cultures*. Cambridge: Cambridge University Press.

Mayland, Edward J. 1957. "Dine in Tropical Splendor at the Traders." *Cooking for Profit* 26: 9–11, 18.

Merrill, Dennis. 2009. *Negotiating Paradise: U.S. Tourism and Empire in Twentieth-Century Latin America*. Chapel Hill: University of North Carolina Press.

Nesbitt, Jennifer P. 2008. "Under the Influence: Thinking Through Rum." *ARIEL* 39, no. 3: 1–22.

O'Connor, Kaori. 2008. "The Hawaiian Luau: Food as Tradition, Transgression, Transformation and Travel." *Food, Culture & Society* 11, no. 2: 149–72.

Padoongpatt, Mark. 2013. "'Oriental Cookery': Devouring Asian and Pacific Cuisine during the Cold War." In *Eating Asian America: A Food Studies Reader*, edited by Robert Ji-Song Ku, Martin F. Manalansan IV, and Anita Mannur, 186–207. New York: New York University Press.

Perez, Craig Santos. 2015. "Transterritorial Currents and the Imperial Terripelago." *American Quarterly* 67, no. 3: 619–24.

Rennie, Neil. 2013. *Treasure Neverland: Real and Imaginary Pirates*. Oxford: Oxford University Press.

Rice, William. 1968. "Providing Good Service Is a Way of Life for Trader Vic's Well-Trained Staff." *Washington Post*, March 10, 1968, 1.

Roberts, Brian Russell, and Michelle Stephens. 2013. "Archipelagic American Studies and the Caribbean." *Journal of Transnational American Studies* 5, no. 1: 1–20.

Sherman, Daniel J. 2011. *French Primitivism and the Ends of Empire, 1945–1975*. Chicago: University of Chicago Press.

Skwiot, Christine. 2010. *The Purposes of Paradise: U.S. Tourism and Empire in Cuba and Hawai'i*. Philadelphia: University of Pennsylvania Press.

Smyth, Jeannette. 1973a. "The Guests Own Chef." *Washington Post*, April 25, 1973, B3.

Smyth, Jeannette. 1973b. "The Nixons Return to Trader Vic's." *Washington Post*, October 2, 1973, B1.

Teaiwa, Teresia. 1999. "Reading Paul Gauguin's *Noa Noa* with Epeli Hau'ofa's *Kisses in the Nederends*: Militourism, Feminism, and the 'Polynesian' Body." In *Inside Out: Literature, Cultural Politics, and Identity in the New Pacific*, edited by Vilsoni Hereniko and Rob Wilson, 249–64. Lanham, MD: Rowman & Littlefield.

Thompson, Krista. 2006. *An Eye for the Tropics: Tourism, Photography, and Framing the Caribbean Picturesque*. Durham, NC: Duke University Press.

Tobias, Doris. 1973. "At Table: Trader Vic's." *Women's Wear Daily*, July 11, 1973.

Trader Vic. 1972. *The Menehunes*. Garden City: Doubleday.

Trader Vic. 1973. *Frankly Speaking: Trader Vic's Own Story*. Garden City: Doubleday.

12

Laksa Nation: Tastes of "Asian" Belonging, Borrowed and Reimagined

Jean Duruz
University of South Australia

The city, its buildings and spaces, its tastes and sounds, all deposited in the physical and poignant languages of locality and place, is not merely a crypt conserving dead matter; it is also witness to the disquieting ambiguity of who we "are" and what we might become.

Chambers 2008, 91

I thought ... [Mom] must be out shopping ... [in Sydney's Chinatown] for the necessary ingredients—hot chillies, kaffir lime leaves, green peppercorns—that she needed to cook dinner that night; a dinner that would allow her and ... [my father] to pretend for a meal span that they were back home in Singapore. Nasi lemak. Laksa. Beef rendang...

Teo 2000, 169

This is the fourth in a suite of papers (the first three being Duruz 2007, 2011, 2016b), mapping a series of reflective journeys within the Southeast Asian region (Map 4). These journeys have their culinary origins in trade routes between China and the Strait of Melaka from the fourteenth century onward. More recently, such journeys have origins in nineteenth-century British colonialism in Malaysia, Singapore, and Australia, and its persistence in the twentieth century. At the heart of these journeys, according to my own cartographic inclinations, I have positioned the Peranakan people with their distinctive Nyonya dish, *laksa*. This is a spicy soup of Chinese and local ingredients, emerging from the "mixed" relationships of Chinese traders and local women, chiefly in the Port of Melaka (Map 4) during the seventeenth to nineteenth centuries, and embraced by Peranakan descendants in the Strait Settlements of Penang and Singapore throughout the nineteenth century and beyond (Brissenden 1995, 185–6; Hutton 2000, 22–4; Duruz and Khoo 2015, 125–6).

With my writing perpetually haunted by the lingering tastes of the "*laksa* trail," this chapter builds on moments of migration, place-making, and identity-making that I've described previously. However, having explored Singapore as a place of origins (Duruz

2011, 2016b), this chapter travels somewhat in the reverse direction back to Adelaide but also to other Australian cities, such as Sydney (Map 4). First of all though, from the vantage of the present, and from urban spaces ambivalently "in" and "out of" Asia (Johnson, Ahluwalia, and McCarthy 2010), briefly I want to reflect on resonances of these previous attempts to unravel *laksa* as an "entangled object" (Crang quoted in Law 2001, 276) for sensing cities as places of "tastes and sounds," and for "witnessing" rituals of eating and remembering as the material culture of the urban everyday (Chambers 2008, 91). For this task, *laksa* will continue to be my iconic dish.

As well, this present vantage poses a wealth of intriguing questions for the current cultural and gastronomic scene of global cities, whether "Asian" or "Western." In Adelaide, for example, amid the city's dominant planning discourse of "creative cities," "vibrancy" and "laneway" entrepreneurialism, together with media promotions of a stylish "hipsterism" (Duruz 2018), we might be tempted to ask: how does *laksa* now "sit" in this city's, or, indeed, in the Australian nation's, imaginary? Are inflections of its "localized" Chinese-ness and complex traveling history still apparent (Tan 2010, 37–8)? Does its ubiquitous acceptance by the nation's palate continue to resonate iconic significance or has this dish simply become a normalized presence on supermarket shelves and in menus of "pan-Asian" cafés? Is *laksa* indeed a sign of culinary nationalism for all Australians (Anglo-Celtic or otherwise) or does the concept of a bordered "nation" present a contradiction of terms for complex, multiethnic communities? And finally, is the 1970s dream of "*laksa* nation" fading fast despite both the previous Australian Labor government and the (now former) Liberal Prime Minister Malcolm Turnbull designating this as the "Asian Century" (Australian Government 2012; Turnbull 2015)?

There are too many issues here for a short chapter to do justice. So, while keeping to the spirit of these questions, I will focus on the first as the most critical: how does *laksa* now "sit" in Adelaide's, or, indeed, in the Australian nation's imaginary? This will enable meditation on *laksa* past and present in Australia, with intimations, possibly, for *laksa* futures (for a sense of that "disquieting ambiguity of who we 'are' and what we might become"; Chambers 2008, 91). The approach will involve drawing analytic threads from my previous papers and positioning these alongside close readings of selected appearances of *laksa* in Adelaide and Sydney foodscapes. To organize this disparate collection of conceptual threads and on the ground "sightings," the analysis will trace tropes of "belonging," "borrowing," and "reimagining," especially as these pertain to national imaginaries mediated by meanings of food, movement, and difference.

Knowing *laksa* as belonging?

In 1978, when Khut Chee Lan and her husband, Khut Kok Chin, arrived in Adelaide from Melaka, Malaysia, Khut Chee Lan carried precious cargo of remembrance. This included the recipe for *laksa lemak*, a version of *laksa* renowned for the richness of its coconut milk soup, the succulence of its chicken and noodles, and for the pungency of its spices and flavorings—chilies, shallots, lemongrass, galangal, turmeric, belacan . . . (Hutton 2000, 58). However, Chee Lan's particular skill in cooking Nyonya dishes was not an inherited one. (In fact, both Mr. and Mrs. Khut were not Peranakan, but Hakka, their respective parents from Guangdong Province, China.) Instead Chee Lan remembers the cooking of her early married years in Melaka as a process of learning through neighborly exchange: "I learnt to make *poh pia* first from … [my Nyonya] neighbor opposite … After *poh pia*, I learn curry, *laksa*, everything … [Then it's] practice, more practice … try and try. I cook my Chinese food for them, and we exchange, we learn."[1]

"[W]e exchange, we learn" might be considered a mantra for the Khuts' approach to business and the setting up of a small café, Malacca Corner (using the former English spelling of the name of the city now known as Melaka), in the early 1980s in Adelaide's Central Market. The rest, one might say, is history. The processes of learning and exchanging to which Mrs. Khut refers extend beyond neighborly reciprocity with tried and tested recipes for the purposes of household cooking to the gradual introduction of her own familiar, homey tastes made "strange" by the changed gastronomic landscape that migration tends to produce. It is a "strangeness" readily embraced by young people who recognize it as a form of "familiar-exotic" as a result of travels through Asia. For others, it may appear as the unexpected taste of "home" in an alien environment. For others still, the "strangeness" is overcome simply by membership in a budget-conscious generation not averse to trying the "new." All have contributed to Malacca Corner's iconic status in the Central Market's foodscapes and produced a certain amount of wistfulness. This mood is one that may be associated with a farewell to childhood and a gastronomic coming of age (an Asianized coming of age, perhaps, and an Asianized age?) (Duruz 2007, 195–6). "Do you remember your first taste of *laksa*?" my friends and I all ask each other, as if an age without *laksa* is scarcely able to be comprehended. Meanwhile, market cafés such as Malacca Corner and Asian Gourmet continue to feed this nostalgia through the everyday rituals associated with patronage of these businesses. Catherine Murphy, in her history of Adelaide Central Market, says, for example, "On Friday nights customers still queue for tables at these cafes where they first tasted authentic Asian food" (2003, 129–30) (Figure 12.1).

It would be easy to regard this learned enthusiasm for "authentic" Asian food simply as a form of gastroappropriation, and worthy of bell hooks' classic criticism of colonizing attempts, using ethnicity as "spice, seasoning that can liven up the dull dish that is mainstream white culture" (hooks quoted in Heldke 2003, 9). Meanwhile, Sherrie Inness (2001, 8) expresses the dilemma in these terms: "what happens when a food shifts from being a 'normal' staple of a region to being a 'gourmet' item or the newest food trend in a different region?"

I suspect my *laksa* story is far more ordinary than that. I am more interested in *laksa*'s normalizing properties in Australia than in any intimation of glamor or trendiness. Revisiting my account of the establishment of Malacca Corner (Duruz 2007, 190–3) and reflecting on the subsequent spread of the café's reputation, and of *laksa* itself throughout Adelaide—on the palate, by word of mouth, through proliferation of cafés and food courts, in print, and later, social media—it seems that the process of "normal" to "exotic" here takes the reverse direction. Instead the "strange" becomes ordinary, or, rather, through familiarization, its meanings manage to contain elements of both (Highmore 2002, 16; Duruz 2017). In Mrs. Khut's own words, her customers

Figure 12.1 The entrance to Malacca Corner in Adelaide's Central Market, an originary site for *laksa* in Australia (2018). Photograph by Jean Duruz.

were "mostly Australian[s] . . . [who] have been to Malaysia . . . They know what *laksa* is." Meanwhile, for those without this knowledge, the Khuts encourage customers to extend their culinary horizons. So a borrowed dish ceases simply to be one on temporary loan or a source of fashionable novelty. Instead, this dish becomes embedded—admittedly, differentially, and never equally—in everyday memories and practices of a community who, for a given time and place, "knows" the tastes of *laksa*, and savors these tastes.

Let me run with the thread of "knowing *laksa*" a little. I want to claim its significance not only for a generation learning to "eat Asian" (and more specifically Southeast Asian) in the 1970s and 1980s, but also, more generally and recently among Australians for whom *laksa* does not simply represent a welcome addition to the diverse flavors of Australia's multiethnic eating (Santich 2012, 300). Ann Oliver, the editor of a local food guide, traces the ubiquitous presence of *laksa*, particularly within Adelaide foodscapes. Reviewing Asian Gourmet (a café we remember as an originary site of *laksa*), Oliver comments: "For some reason laksa is peculiar to South Australia, evidenced by people returning home and heading straight for the nearest laksa shop lamenting that neither Sydney nor Melbourne have a decent laksa" (Oliver n.d.). Of course, other cities compete with Adelaide for honors in the *laksa* stakes. Ting, a Sydney journalist, for example, describes *laksa* as "comfort food for spice lovers" and one of "the most popular Asian dishes in Australia" (Ting 2013). Joanna Savill (2006, 6), while recommending Sydney food outlets, evocatively describes *laksa* as the taste and smell of Australian cities.

So much for *laksa*'s ubiquity and popularity, and the extent of *laksa* being borrowed and enthusiastically adopted by a nation with a continuing history of colonization—a nation, in terms of its indigenous citizens, still operating as a British colonial settler-society, and one with an uneasy positioning in the Asia-Pacific (Moreton-Robinson 2003, 37–8). However, despite a "mixed" and troubled past that inflects national debate and policy into the present, we might wonder whether, for Australians, *laksa* might be regarded as a marker of national belonging, of citizenship . . . of "who we 'are', and what we might become"? Might *laksa* be regarded, legitimately, as a collectively ingested symbol of such histories, such futures?

For glimpses of possibilities of "such histories, such futures"—geopolitical and gastronomic—I want to quote a few fragments, beginning with Paul Keating. After his retirement from the office of prime minister and from the Australian parliament in 1996, Keating declares his vision for "the New Australia":

> Australia cannot retreat behind a white picket fence . . . rather Australians must embrace the future and the Government must take the lead. This means adopting a positive outward-looking attitude to all parts of the world, including Asia, and encouraging an understanding of the benefits of immigration so that fear does not drive discussion of it. It means coming to terms with the various, and sometimes painful, histories of Australians and working towards creating a tolerant and inclusive society.
>
> Keating 1996

Here Keating urges citizens to abandon conservative white racism ("the white picket fence") that has contributed to a "painful" history (at this point he is possibly referencing a history of White Australia Policy restrictions on Asian immigration—restrictions persisting until the 1970s—as well as continuing discrimination against indigenous populations) (Huggins 2016). Instead, Australia is to value immigration and to look to, for example, Asia, in the spirit of multicultural "tolerance" and "inclusivity." *Laksa* as icon of this vision would not be incompatible with the spirit of

Keating's "working towards," or with his metaphor of Australian society as "the Chinese wok, in which all the ingredients retain their own distinct identity but become part of a harmonious and balanced whole," rather than the assimilationist "melting pot" (Keating 1995).

Of course, there are many contenders in the icon stakes—meat pies, roast lamb, Anzac biscuits, Vegemite on toast, and, more recently, salt and pepper squid. Usually the debate surfaces close to Australia Day (January 26) but continues throughout the year (Santich 2012, 24–6; Yeow n.d.). Increasingly, *laksa* is listed in the line-up as the "normal" in everyday Australian eating:

> It has been joked that "spag bog" (spaghetti bolognese) is now Australia's real national dish. If so, then Thai pad Thai and Malaysian laksas surely can't be that far behind. Australian food culture has been as influenced by *South East Asian cuisines as it has by Italian home cooking and American fast food.* . . .
>
> Modern Australian cuisine brings us the eclectic menus that can be found in pubs and clubs around the country; dishes such as pasta, laksa, bangers and mash [sausages and mashed potato] and crème caramel all sit side by side.
>
> SBS 2013; emphasis added

It seems that *laksa* has come full circle. Now its ingredients are listed as possible pantry staples by Adam Liaw of MasterChef Australia fame and its everyday ordinariness judged to rival that of solidly British/Italian dishes—sausages and mashed potato, meat pies, roast lamb, spaghetti bolognese (Hunter n.d.). From *laksa's* positioning within cultures of the mundane, it might appear somewhat fanciful then to cast this dish on the national stage as a shining symbol of reconciliation, of Keating's "tolerant and inclusive society." Let us take the argument down less predictable tracks toward the dark side of "creative cities." Following not so much the *laksa* trail but that of re-created ethnic neighborhoods and ethnic festivals, I want to ask: to what extent can the innocence and ordinariness of *laksa* survive tendencies to carnivalization that mark the twenty-first century city and its spaces?

Looking for "vibrancy": Urban planning's reimagined spaces

On a somewhat chilly spring evening, I am enticed by the following to a riverbank park in the center of Adelaide:

> Picture a hidden alleyway in the backstreets of Hong Kong that opens up to a festival of colours, aromas and sounds . . . .
>
> From today Elder Park will transform into a feast for the senses when the Good Fortune Market hits town . . . a kaleidoscope of the strongest influences of Asian culture, from India to Japan . . . .
>
> [According to the event director] "One thing that has heavily influenced Good Fortune Market from our travels is the overall look and feel of the event, with our theming and dressing. . . . We have more Asian food than you can stick a skewer at, more lanterns than you'll be able to count, more activities than you have time for,

more musicians than you can dance to and more creative design than you will have enough time to enjoy under the stars."

The Advertiser 2016

As promised, food stalls are set up around a green open space with strings of lanterns overhead. The stalls' menus include Vietnamese fusion and Sri Lankan dishes; wood oven pizza (with Asian-style roast duck with plum and hoisin sauce); Cambodian, Lao, and Vietnamese dishes (under the banner of "South-East Asian street food"); Japanese, Indian, Filipino, and Thai dishes. Ever in search of *laksa*, I arrive at the only Malaysian food stall in the market, set up by its parent restaurant, PappaRich, from Adelaide's Chinatown.

The publicity blurb for this food stall is instructive. PappaRich, we are told, "serves authentic Malaysian food" and at the riverbank Good Fortune Market "aims to provide something different" (different from other stalls, or different from the parent restaurant, we wonder?). Whatever "difference" constitutes, there is an emphasis on charcoal-grilled satays "in the traditional way," together with "authentic" freshly made *roti canai* [flatbread]. "Malaysian food is inspired by Malay, Chinese and Indian cuisine," the blurb continues, "so it is packed with flavour." Meanwhile "Malaysian *laksa*" is simply listed without comment—presumably so well-known, as not to need one (*The Advertiser* 2016)?

Seated at an outdoor table consuming a bowl of PappaRich's *laksa*, I reflect on the identity *laksa* adopts at a festival such as this. In fact, initially, I have trouble in finding any *laksa* at all. Is this a testament to the ordinariness of *laksa* in my home town, as, indeed, I have been arguing throughout this chapter? With *laksa* simply listed on the menus of various cafés that I patronize on an everyday basis (such as the stalls in the Central Market's Asian food halls or local mixed-menu Filipino and Vietnamese cafés), has *laksa* lost its elements of distinctiveness and novelty? Is it no longer "exotic"? In fact, does *laksa* even belong to "a veritable smorgasbord of *exotic* gastronomic delights showcasing Asian inventiveness" that a festival like the Good Fortune Market demands (*The Advertiser* 2016, emphasis added)?

Of course, this is not the first time that I have puzzled over *laksa*'s limited presence at staged events, despite those ritual Friday-night queues at the Central Market. Previously, researching mobile food trucks as part of the city of Adelaide's call for more "vibrancy" of approach to city planning and more creativity in fostering pop-up initiatives, I have been curious to discern the ways in which these "new" mobile food vans (think "gourmet") are to be distinguished from the "old" (for example, Adelaide's legendary piecart, now only to be seen at occasional football matches) (Duruz 2018). How does the predictability of *laksa*, its tastes familiar to non-Peranakan, non-Singaporean, and non-Malaysian communities to the point of assumed ownership, now fit with the "vibrancy" and "creativity" of urban "pop-up" economies and built environments?

The city council's instructions for establishing mobile food businesses provide us with some clues to worry at these questions. Drawing on the guidelines produced in 2013 (with the spirit of these echoed in later reports), we find the council insists that "A mobile food vending area should relate to its surroundings, to protect and enhance the urban heritage and streetscape appearance and character."² So, in the distribution of permits, priority will be accorded to those "applicants presenting a well-designed, creative, artistic setup." Curiously, however, there is little direction given about the actual food to be sold from these "well-designed . . . setups." Except for the insistence that community hygiene and safety should be observed, and that trucks should neither replicate the food products of fixed businesses nor be located too close to these, the only directive regarding food sold from mobile vans is that this simply should offer "an unique experience or product to customers." As well, where possible, in the interests of sustainability and support for the local, it seems that South Australian produce should feature significantly among product ingredients (Adelaide City Council 2013, 2–5).

There are two threads I wish to disentangle here. The first is the emphasis on trucks' visual aesthetics, together with an endorsement of the fashionably "green" and "local." Obviously, trucks are meant to produce, collectively, a qualitatively different kind of urban landscape from that inscribed by mobile vendors of the past. This emphasis on styling is also echoed in the Good Fortune Market's promotional discourse: "a feast for" . . . "a kaleidoscope of" . . . "overall look and feel of the event" . . . "more Asian food than" . . . "more lanterns" . . . "more creative design." The overall effect is of excess and spectacle, consciously created through "theming" and "dressing" the site. While a riverbank park in Adelaide in no way resembles any hidden alley in Hong Kong's back streets, through the magic of theatricality and imaginative reference, one can participate in the staging of its production. Furthermore, and this is the second thread, the trucks' gastronomic content should allow customers the purchase of "an unique experience or product"—food that is different, is distinctive. Application of "uniqueness" and "creativity" to the reinvention of urban sites is very much in accord with manifestos for "creative cities" appearing in twenty-first century city planning, such as Richard Florida's *The Rise of the Creative Class* (2003) and Charles Landry's *The Creative City* (2000).

But what of *laksa* and its low-key appearance in the Good Fortune Market or its almost total absence from the menus of Adelaide's food trucks? Is it simply a glimmer in the "kaleidoscope"—in the spectacle of a particular "Asian" public event—or does the ordinariness of *laksa* on which I'm insisting, disqualify it from urbanscapes of "vibrancy" and "uniqueness"? Pondering these questions, I have been following Adelaide's food trucks for several years and, interestingly, *laksa* has at last made an appearance within these. Simon Bryant, a well-known Adelaide chef, was reported to have set up a food truck for Fork on the Road, an established network of Adelaide trucks that gathers at festivals, charity events, and other public occasions. Listed on the menu of Bryant's truck was vegan *laksa* (Kristy C. 2014). Here, *laksa* had attained the badge of distinctiveness in ways the "ordinary" *laksa* had not. As *vegan laksa*, it signaled a particular niche market, different from the normalized food-court *laksa* yet "exotic," and recognizable for its connections with current "alternative" food fashions, such as vegetarianism and veganism.

Meanings of dishes, however, are not fixed. It is possible that *laksa* can fulfill the role of either "ordinary" or "spectacular," either "traditional" or "modern," according to the nature of its "entanglements"—to its cultural and political framing in place and time.

So, keeping in mind *laksa*'s mobility and plasticity—both the dish itself and its meanings (Wa 2011, 226), we'll now leave the staged performances of the Good Fortune Market and head toward Chinatown to pay a quick visit to the Malaysian restaurant, PappaRich. My assumption is that, like Malacca Corner and Asian Gourmet, PappaRich represents, for Adelaide's *laksa*, another originary site. However, it is not—well, at least, not in the sense of first tastes and epiphanies. PappaRich, a comparatively recent addition to the Adelaide culinary scene, is a form of casual eatery that elsewhere I call a yuppie coffee shop or "new" Kopitiam (Duruz and Khoo 2015, 57–61; Lai 2016, 129) (Figure 12.2). Yuppie coffee shops, like Toast Box in Singapore, are usually a part of a standardized snack food chain, distinguished by their serving traditional food and drinks but employing a modern aesthetic (based on Western cafés like Starbucks, with their plate-glass windows, air conditioning, artfully arranged food products, and cutely

Figure 12.2 PappaRich, a fashionable "yuppie" coffeeshop in Australia renowned for serving traditional Malaysian food in a modern setting. Chinatown, Adelaide, Australia (2018). Photograph by Jean Duruz.

uniformed wait staff). Originating in Malaysia and spreading rapidly through Southeast Asia, PappaRich strives for recognition as a global brand.

PappaRich describes its philosophy in the following terms:

> Our delicately crafted dishes never fail to deliver bursts of flavour and colour because we use only an authentic mix of herbs, spices and fresh produce, cooked according to traditional recipes. From the fiery sambal of the Nasi Lemak to the silky smooth Curry Laksa broth, from the savoury Satay to the unforgettable Char Koay Teow, our food reflects the balance and harmony of the different cultures in Malaysia that have combined to give us the distinctive, unique taste of Malaysian cuisine.
>
> PappaRich 2018

In this context, *laksa* becomes anything but mundane. Vociferously calling on the senses in its promotional discourse ("bursts of flavour" ... "fiery" ... "silky smooth" ... "savoury" ...), PappaRich performs, in a glamorous setting of gleaming glass, varnished timbers, and low-hanging lamps, an array of "authentic" flavors, "traditional" approaches, and "unforgettable" products. This reimagining of everyday hawker food, through a heightened sense of flavor, visual effect, and nostalgic meaning, has a specific political intention: to mirror the supposed "balance and harmony" of a modern, multiethnic nation, and to produce, as a reflection of its national cohesion, "a distinctive, unique taste." Hence *laksa* at PappaRich joins with other heritage dishes to represent the brand "Malaysian." Meanwhile, down on the river bank at the Good Fortune Market, it seems that *laksa* eschews a performance of the ordinary, after all, or even of a "borrowed" Australian identity. Instead, this dish, transported and reinvented, becomes something else—a consciously *Malaysian laksa*, offered in a gentrified "market" setting as symbolic of cosmopolitan and regional sensibilities. At this point we might remember, from Chapter 6 of this volume, Gaik Cheng Khoo's account of Malaysian chefs creatively referencing traditional food in their cooking. Nevertheless, while these chefs' culinary practices also contribute to "brand Malaysian" in an essentializing fashion, their cooking represents, perhaps, the opposite end of gentrification's spectrum—"Malaysian" haute cuisine rather than restyled tastes of "ordinary" *laksa*?[3]

Remaking downtown Sydney as "flavors of the Asian metropolis"

I leave Adelaide for Sydney, where friends urge me to visit the newly created Spice Alley (Figure 12.3), constructed within the site of a former brewery and its surrounding access streets in the center of the city. Inside the complex, there are living walls of greenery and a variety of restaurants and other retail spaces, such as high-fashion clothing stores and galleries. With soaring ceilings and mood lighting, the emphasis is on cosmopolitan luxuriousness and modern urban "lifestyle." Spice Alley, winding through peripheral buildings at ground level, deliberately presents a different ambiance, however:

Narrow paved streets with alley nooks are loud from the bustle of hungry locals. A beguiling aroma of pounded spices and wok fires fills the air, and in open kitchens chefs swing roti, boil stocks and cleave slabs of crisp pork belly. It sounds like a description of George Town, Penang or one of Singapore's hawker centres. But this is Spice Alley, an outdoor street-food market that's on Central Park's Kensington Street development.

Jordan 2015

And again, and speaking of the Kensington Street component of the overall development:

[T]he street paves the path to our city's future.... Industrial structures that were once vacant and hollow are now filled with life ... Cafes, bars and restaurants are open for old friends to rendezvous, and new friends to meet. Spice Alley's Kopi-Tiam weaves into our street's architectural fabric the flavours of an Asian metropolis.... Kensington Street is home to all.

Greencliff Agency 2015

However, I want to look beyond obvious examples of hyperbole ("path to our city's future"..."home to all") being attached to what is, after all, simply a collection of fancy apartments, galleries, restaurants, and shops beside a pleasant open space. Instead, in

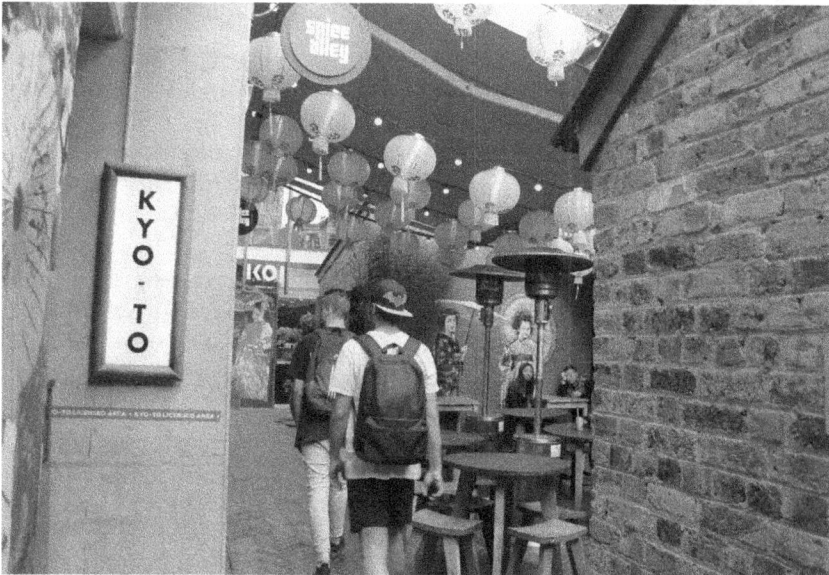

Figure 12.3 Spice Alley, an invented back alley of Asian food stalls in a new shopping/housing development in Sydney. Central Park, Sydney, Australia (2018). Photograph courtesy of Angela Giovanangeli.

these accounts I am more interested in the echoes of "creative city" discourse—of "vibrancy" and urban renewal through "theming" consumption spaces, and the significance of food and art in this "theming" (Davies 2016; City of Sydney 2011).

While debates centering on whose creative city is at stake here (debates of gentrification's apparent lack of inclusivity, for example, and of its marginalization of indigenous and homeless people) persist with some intensity (Atkinson and Easthope 2007), I want to leave these aside for the moment, and follow the wafting aromas of Spice Alley. Once again I'm seeking the taste of *laksa*, this time in the shadow of the newly constructed Kopi-Tiam. Following the laneways of Sydney's "first outdoor Singaporean-style hawker centre" (Jordan 2015), I head toward Old Jim Kee, one of the four permanent outlets in the Alley and where, I'm told the "food is the best thematic match for its surroundings" (Jordan 2015).

To my delight, *laksa* is on the menu and Katong *laksa* at that. I order, and prepare myself for a taste of that other "home." The broth is excellent—coconutty with spices beautifully balanced, resonant of months I've spent eating street food in Katong. The other ingredients, however, are a disappointment—simply rice-flour noodles and chunks of chicken. Where is the seafood I've always associated with "my" Katong *laksa*? Hastily I check my understanding of Katong *laksa* to be reassured: as well as "fish based gravy with dried shrimp and rich coconut milk . . . Katong laksa [is distinguished by] . . . fresh shrimp and sliced fish cake served with sambal chili and fresh daun kesom or laksa leaf as garnishings" (Wong 2011).

Perhaps my mistake has been to frame venturing into Spice Alley as that impossible search for "authentic" flavors of the "other," and for flavors of those "other" places that, tentatively, I think of as "home"? A website post regarding Old Jim Kee might serve a salutary reminder that this is a constructed neighborhood, after all: "Sitting and eating in the lane way made me feel like being in Asia on a hot muggy night . . . I love the simplicity of this up market pseudo hawker centre" (Zomato n.d. a). And again, another website contributor comments, though in regard to Spice Alley as a whole: "The vibe is amazing—you literally feel like you are eating street food in an alleyway somewhere in south-east Asia. The food is pretty mediocre to be honest, but I guess that's to be expected for fast takeaway style food. But the experience makes it worth it" (Zomato n.d. b). In both of the above, there is acknowledgment of Spice Alley's theme park ambiance—a sense of playfulness and performance in this "upmarket pseudo hawker centre" with its "amazing vibe." It is also a nostalgic "experience" for travelers with its sensory references to remembered "hot muggy nights" and "eating street food in an alley somewhere . . . in Asia."

At the same time, however, I wonder to what extent that Spice Alley demands, primarily, a touristic performance where even the name "Spice Alley" suggests a degree of orientalism—of consumers' exoticizing cuisines with complex spices from the perspective of familiar cuisines that don't. Even the "Alley" part to the street's name implies a frisson of danger, of adventurous exploration outside one's usual comfort zone. This is very much a stranger's eye view of the unfamiliar and taking pleasure from this. Given the diversity and complexity of spices in cuisines throughout Southeast Asia and the range of informal eating places in Singaporean and Malaysian cities, it seems ludicrous to imagine any urban street or laneway of these cities singled out as

"Spice Alley"! Does this mean that, perhaps like the Good Fortune Market, Spice Alley is an "outsider" attribution—an imagined landscape of the Asian "experience" . . . an instance of white Western dreaming?

On the other hand, as I eat my *laksa* and glance at other tables, the whiteness of this landscape is not so obvious. The tables are filled mainly with customers who appear to be international students, and this is hardly surprising as several universities and colleges are in close proximity. As well, there seem to be numerous office workers from adjacent high-rise buildings having lunch here, as well as people one would also expect to see in nearby Chinatown. The majority of these patrons appear to be "Asian" (as much as I can tell, and not wanting to be essentialist about this, either in relation to customers who might be overseas-born or Australians of Asian descent). Conversation with a colleague, who works for the state government and who eats lunch regularly in the neighborhood, confirms this impression. The cheapness of the food in Spice Alley with its obvious "homey" references draws a non-white crowd on a daily basis, she says. Of course, this is not to say that patrons themselves do not recognize the "faux" qualities of this development and do not actively engage in its playfulness. Nevertheless, I still suspect that, however "pseudo" the references, the pull of the *idea* of home cooking, and nostalgia for remembered home or street cuisine is strong, even if the taste of this is not always as "authentic" as it might be.

There is another point to consider if we want to be critical of urban developments like Spice Alley. There is a temptation to assume these "fabrications"—building constructions deliberately designed to form a "themed" landscape rather than ones organically growing, sometimes haphazardly, within urban spaces—are pure simulacra, and without referents (Baudrillard 1994). Do we treat these phenomena simply as "pseudo," and hence disengaged from the "real"? Does this mean that the stalls of Spice Alley's Kopi-Tiam have been created purely as a marketing exercise, their imagery plucked out of the air—or rather, out of a vaguely imagined gastronomic landscape of "Southeast Asian-ness," its flavors lacking rootedness in specific histories or places of belonging?

The history of Spice Alley, however, does not quite allow us to dismiss it as a superficial, commercially driven project of urban planning. Old Jim Kee is a case in point. The stall in Kopi-Tiam is certainly not devoid of "roots" as the following illustrates:

> Born and bred in George Town, Malaysia, Chef Jim Yong is fondly known in the industry as Uncle Jim. Specialising in Malaysian Nyonya cuisine, Jim Yong spent many years perfecting authentic Nyonya cooking techniques working with Nyonya communities in Penang and Melaka. He has accumulated over 30 years' experience cooking in both Malaysia and Australia, as owner and head chef of Mosman's popular eatery Uncle Jim's Malaysian Restaurant.
>
> Greencliff Agency 2018

The chefs of the other food stalls have similar lists of credentials to Jim Yong. As "veterans of Sydney's most popular South-East Asian restaurants," with their cooking claimed as "true to the hawker-centre tradition," they represent a group of highly successful entrepreneurs drawing on their ethnic capital to establish "Asian" food empires in the Sydney dining scene. Alan Lee, for example, is renowned for "making some of Sydney's best laksa, roti canai and satay at popular [Sydney] Singaporean restaurants Ginger and Spice and Temasek," while Tiw Rakarin of Bang Luck stall, "drawing on the food of his ancestry," has established his reputation as executive chef of an expanding group of Vietnamese bar-cum-restaurants in Sydney and Melbourne (Jordan 2015). With credentials like these, such chefs should *know* the taste of "home," and in Alan Lee and Uncle Jim's case, should specifically *know* the taste of *laksa*. Nevertheless, for the global city of Sydney, a city known to be an obsessively "foodie" one, it is probably the co-option of familiar names from the Australian restaurant industry that adds to the gloss of Spice Alley's performance. It is this second layer of culinary history, perhaps, that enhances this reinvented neighborhood's reputation as much as the details of its entrepreneurs' stories of origin. In this way, Spice Alley is not simply a place tied to memories of "a hot muggy night [in Southeast Asia]" or "an alleyway somewhere in … Asia." Instead, it has provenance in eating "Asian" in Australia—an immediate history and geography of everyday tastes to be brought to the table.

I worry, however, that I am too easily seduced by the charms of this structured space—by its consciously crafted landscapes, its promotional promises of conviviality and cosmopolitanism. I have encountered this dilemma before when walking the streets of Katong, Singapore, where the urban landscape is being remade as I write this—a favorite *laksa* stall becomes an upmarket restaurant and bed-and-breakfast, for example (Duruz 2016b, 143). Here too, I was reminded of Nora's (1989, 7) poignant pronouncement that "We speak so much of memory because there is so little of it left" and of his critical distinction between constructed efforts to memorialize the "past" [*lieux de mémoire*] to address a profound sense of loss, and the resonances of "real environments of memory" [*milieux de mémoire*]. Embodying the spirit of this distinction between the "fabricated" and the "real" in relation to the heritage industry in Singapore, with its "meticulous restoration of the physical fabric in historic districts," Yeoh and Kong (1999, 142) claim: "[P]lace is invoked as a concrete showcase of history rather than as an active process. Emphasis is given to the visual qualities, the facades and concrete forms which constitute place rather than the lifeworlds integral to the making of place."

Returning to Spice Alley, we might speculate in regard to how much of this development is concerned with monumentalism and pastiche—with glass, concrete, steel, and bricks, shaped in an image of the "past" intersecting with meanings of "present" and "future" … a postmodern Asianized cosmopolis. However, within these supposedly static monuments to postindustrial prosperity and global tourism, it is the possibility of Yeoh and Kong's "active process" that captures my attention. The crowds thronging Spice Alley suggest to me an intrusion of lifeworlds and diverse practices of place-making. These crowds simply may be using these spaces for their own purposes, over and above any appreciation for aesthetics or high-end consumption, as observations in any coffee shop will reveal. Eating, writing, reading, studying, meeting, chatting, watching, musing—all these activities and more become possible for the price of a dollar chicken wing in a congenial "public" space. Such daily rituals over time, secured by memories, together form "active process." And here, we should add the significance of food to the mix. After all, according to Wong (2007, 120, original emphasis), "It is the *sensorial* experience of food that endures in one's memory bank, long after the context in which it is consumed disappears or changes." Having a *laksa* at Uncle Jim's then may not be the best *laksa* one has eaten. As well, having a *laksa* in Spice Alley may not "feel" the same as in one's favorite *laksa* stall or café, in or out of Australia. Nevertheless, this *laksa* at Uncle Jim's, while criticized perhaps for its lack of "authenticity," is anchored in the accumulated experience of "knowing *laksa*," anchored in rituals of *laksa* eating as everyday "tactics" for questioning dominant prescriptions of national cuisine, and anchored in alternative collective "Asian" imaginaries of nation that *laksa* and other dishes of the region inscribe (de Certeau 1984, xviii–xx). Although Spice Alley invests much energy, materials, and financial resources into rendering *laksa* "exotic," at the end of the day it is the ordinary, sometimes, subversive practice of daily life that reconverts glamor in the direction of the mundane.

Looking back over the two moments of culinary history I have described here (the arrival of Southeast Asian "ethnic" entrepreneurs in Adelaide during the 1970s and 1980s and their establishment of traditional food businesses; the twenty-first century spectacularization of "Asian" cuisines through food fairs, ethnic neighborhoods, and upmarket restaurants, with the overall effect of "a kaleidoscope … of Asian culture, from India to Japan"), we might be tempted to construct either a narrative of progress or, alternatively, a lament for lost spaces and lost tastes. Adopting a mode of celebration, we might begin to trace a path from small-scale cultural capital of family cooking drawn from the immediate region to large-scale global capital invested in trade, tourism, and urban gentrification, underwritten by governments' desire to forge links with the Asian economic powerhouses, such as China and India (Australian Government 2012). Strolling around the "food streets" adjacent to Adelaide's Central Market, however, I am less convinced by this argument. While there is evidence of regional and global food chains, such as PappaRich, the small one-owner cafés such as Malacca Corner persist, alongside a plethora of new cafés and restaurants—Thai, Sichuanese, Japanese ramen, Hong Kong dumpling shops, for example. Certainly, this mélange of businesses reflects global food fashions and changing patterns of immigration. As well, these enterprises range from the basic food-court shop to the upmarket, glitzy café or restaurant. The impression is more one of adding layers to the existing foodscape rather than replacing or losing it. And here there is a reminder, of course, that the examples of urban development I have discussed—Good Fortune Market, PappaRich, Spice Alley—also retain some connection with their traditional roots. The question remains, however: where does *laksa* sit in this rather congested "ethnic" foodscape and does the tempo of the times (the "Asian Century") allow *laksa* a significance beyond sentimental attachment (Australian Government 2012)?

Laksa nation: Eating the Asian Century in Australia?

To celebrate the 2017 Chinese New Year (Lunar Year of the Fire Rooster), the *South Australian Business Journal* featured a special report on "Our Asian Century," proclaiming:

"The importance of Asian trade in South Australia cannot be underestimated. China is our single largest trading partner and the largest buyer of Australian wine globally. Asian tourists are flocking to our shores and the State is welcoming thousands of overseas students each year, with many choosing to stay on and make a life here" (*The Advertiser* 2017, 25).

Australia, however, has not always embraced interaction with its Asian region with such enthusiasm. In fact, historically, such relations have been marked with ambivalence—the contradictions of a British colonial past (with colonial settler relations with indigenous people continuing into the present and the White Australia Policy restrictions on Asian immigration persisting until the 1970s) (Jupp 1995) intersecting with Australia's ambiguous geographical position among non-Western nations of the Asia-Pacific. However, from the 1970s onward, increasing emphasis on orientation toward "Asia" especially from Australian left-wing political parties has resulted in significant shifts in rhetoric: "'Asia' was not just a region, or a collection of trading partners, it was a potent sign mobilized by Australian politicians for domestic political advantage" (Johnson, Ahluwalia, and McCarthy 2010, 71). Furthermore, "as belief in Western superiority, born of Western conceptions of modernity, is challenged by the rise of the 'Asian Century', Australia finds itself in a particularly interesting location, in particularly interesting times" (Johnson, Ahluwalia, and McCarthy 2010, 71).

So where does *laksa* fit in this reimagined Asian Century, in this "particularly interesting location, in particularly interesting times"—times which recent geopolitical events (for example, the escalation of Islamic State terror throughout the region and the West, Britain's foreshadowed departure from the European Union, and the rise of Trumpism in America) have made even more "interesting"? Is *laksa*, in its turn, "a potent sign" of Australian-ness? Is *laksa* a culinary emblem of national reorientation from a predominantly Anglo-Celtic past to a future of regional "Asian" belonging, a future of borrowed tastes, appropriated memories and culinary reinventions? Despite former Malaysian President Mahathir's scornful dismissal of Australia's "Asian" credentials, will Australians at last become "proper" Asians (*Sydney Morning Herald* 2004; Blackburn 2002)?

There is something that disturbs me in all this. The slippage from *laksa* to *Laksa Nation* is too easy, too neat. My fourth journey on the *laksa* trail is far messier than a simple equation of *laksa* with Australia. We have found too many fragments, too many loose ends to describe a discretely bounded nation and its single, iconic dish. Here I am reminded of a powerful call from Krishnendu Ray, in his discussion of hybrid colonial cuisines, to eschew conventional colonial-based conceptions of the modern nation-state. Instead, says Ray, we might draw on traces of food and the sensorium as alternative approaches to cartographies of globalization and cosmopolitanism: "Colonial dishes show us if we take taste and sensory memory seriously, then the geography can shift" (Ray 2016, 12).

Seeking an alternative to proclaiming *laksa* as, quintessentially, the taste of Australia, the modern "multicultural" dish (an act of restitution, perhaps, from the penitent, now inclusive, nation-state), I pause for reflection on Ray's taking "sensory memory seriously" and "that geography can shift." A different landscape of belonging presents itself, intimated in this chapter's opening quotations, whether a landscape inscribed with "tastes and sounds . . . the physical and poignant languages of locality and place" (Chambers 2008, 91) or with memory's palatal baggage of "hot chillies, kaffir lime leaves, green peppercorns . . . *Nasi lemak. Laksa.* Beef *rendang*" (Teo 2000, 169). So the imagined landscape this chapter sketches is less about conventional national imagery and boundaries—Singapore, Malaysia, Australia, and beyond—and more about loosely defined communities of "knowing *laksa*" and the points of connection this knowledge creates. At the same time, this is not to deny the differences and complexities of positioning of those who "know": the Anglo-Celtic traveler looking for Adelaide's best *laksa* is hardly comparable to the ethnic restaurateur whose long hours and hard work are needed to sustain a small business in the host country's difficult economic times. "Knowing *laksa*," nevertheless, even from different perspectives, becomes a modest way of challenging the fixity of boundaries and oddly enough leads back to conceptions of nation, though a different sort of nation than the one that the "rigid grids of national geographies" imply (Chambers 2008, 131).

What then is this different conception of nation? I suggest that if Australia is imagined as a hybrid nation with some flexibility of borders and with strong regional connections—both geopolitical and cultural—then it might be the case that Paul Keating's vision of "coming to terms with the various, and sometimes painful, histories of Australians and working toward creating a tolerant and inclusive society" has some purchase. At the same time, for such a nation of multiethnic eaters whose roots are entangled with multiple places, movements around the globe and catastrophic events (such as war and displacement), the designation of single dishes as iconic seems an impossible task and begs a collective imaginary—an "imagined community"—of nuance and complexity (Anderson 1991). Here, it is possible that points of connection between communities (that are not necessarily nationally based, or that have overlapping national borders) might create a basis for commensality and cultural empathy (Duruz 2016a, 26; see also Ferguson 2010, 106 on "culinary countries").

So, it seems logical that the taste of *laksa*, with its already-"mixed" histories and global geographies, would become a familiar taste as well in a "multicultural" Australia, located, as it is, adjacent to Southeast Asia. As a result, *laksa* is not only deeply embedded in the culinary heritage of diasporic Asians but also in the cultural memory of "borrowing" Australians. This might appear to be the case whether all these *laksa* eaters are nostalgically remembering or playfully inventing, or both. And for Anglo-Australians in particular, the appropriation of a "localized" Chinese dish becomes an acknowledgment of regional positioning by an already multicultural and hybrid nation.

Nevertheless, if we are tempted to dismiss these speculations as utopian ones, it simply remains to be seen how "knowing *laksa*" becomes significant, embodied, and, primarily, ordinary knowledge for negotiating the "Asian Century," in and out of Australia, and within Asia and beyond. At the same time, the hope remains that the taste of *laksa*, and others like it, might build collective cultural muscle and cosmopolitan sensibilities (might build, in Ferguson's words, a "culinary country") for meeting the everyday challenges of "eating together" in these tricky times (Duruz and Khoo 2015).

Notes

1   All quotations attributed to Khut Chee Lan are from the transcript of an extended interview I conducted with her and Khut Kok Chin in Adelaide 2003.
2   See also Adelaide City Council (2015).
3   It should be noted that, although *laksa* is regarded as a Peranakan Chinese or Straits Chinese dish, historically its origins in trade and colonial settlement have produced particular flavor combinations and place attachments throughout the Southeast Asian region. Its naming may be related to specific ingredients and flavors (e.g., *asam* [sour] *laksa*, *laksa lemak* [creamy]) or specific places (e.g., Johor *laksa*, Katong *laksa*) or to its contribution to national cuisines (e.g., Singapore *laksa*, Malaysian *laksa*). In the latter case, this usually relates to commodifying meanings of nation for nostalgic and touristic purposes.

References

Adelaide City Council. 2013. *Operating Guidelines: Mobile Food Vending Program. Adelaide: Adelaide City Council.* Adelaide: Adelaide City Council. Page discontinued. http://www.adelaidecitycouncil.com/assets/CURRENT_Mobile_Food_Vending_ Operating_Guidelines_approved_by_Council_7_Oct.pdf.

Adelaide City Council. 2015. *The Mobile Food Vending Program: Application Information and Operating Guidelines.* Adelaide: Adelaide City Council. http://www.cityofadelaide. com.au/assets/Mobile_Food_Vending_Program_Application_Information_and_ Operating_Guidelines-Approved_15_December_2015.pdf.

Advertiser, The. 2016. "Savour Tastes of Asia at OzAsia's Good Fortune Market." September 20, 2016. https://www.adelaidenow.com.au/news/south-australia/savour-tastes-of-asia- at-ozasias-good-fortune-market/news-story/19cfb1065bfc13c48c9b0f91f3cea2a9.

Advertiser, The. 2017. "Our Asian Century." *South Australian Business Journal* (supplement), January 31, 2017.

Anderson, Benedict. 1991. *Imagined Communities: Reflections on the Origin and Spread of Nationalism.* London: Verso.

Atkinson, Roland, and Hazel Easthope. 2007. "The Consequences of the Creative Class: The Pursuit of Creative Strategies in Australia's Cities." In *Proceedings of the State Of Australian Cities National Conference 2007*, 586–97. Adelaide: Causal Productions.

Australian Government. 2012. *Australia in the Asian Century.* White paper. Canberra ACT: Commonwealth of Australia. http://www.defence.gov.au/whitepaper/2013/docs/ australia_in_the_asian_century_white_paper.pdf.

Baudrillard, Jean. 1994. *Simulacra and Simulation.* Ann Arbor: University of Michigan Press.

Blackburn, Kevin. 2002. "Migration and Perceptions of Identity: The Case of Singapore and Malaysian Perceptions of the Australian Identity." In *Pacific Centuries: Pacific and Pacific Rim Economic History since the 16th Century*, edited by Lionel Frost, Dennis O. Flynn, and A. J. H. Latham, 224–49. London: Routledge.

Brissenden, Rosemary. 1996. *Southeast Asian Food.* Ringwood, Vic: Penguin.

Chambers, Iain. 2008. *Mediterranean Crossings: The Politics of an Interrupted Modernity.* Durham, NC: Duke University Press.

City of Sydney. 2011. "Future-Proofing Sydney with Imagination and Creativity." City of Sydney News. Page discontinued. http://www.sydneymedia.com.au/4758-future- proofing-sydney-with-imagination-and-creativity/.

Davies, Anne. 2016. "Mapping Sydney's Creative Clusters." *The Sydney Morning Herald*, April 8, 2016. http://www.smh.com.au/nsw/boho-sydney-mapping-our-creative-clusters-20160407-go1dbo.html.

de Certeau, Michel. 1984. *The Practice of Everyday Life*. Berkeley: University of California Press.

Duruz, Jean. 2007. "From Malacca to Adelaide . . .: Fragments Towards a Biography of Cooking, Yearning and Laksa." In *Food and Foodways in Asia: Resource, Tradition and Cooking*, edited by Sidney C. H. Cheung and Tan Chee-Beng, 183–200. Abingdon: Routledge.

Duruz, Jean. 2011. "Tastes of Hybrid Belonging: Following the Laksa Trail in Katong, Singapore." *Continuum* 25, no. 5: 605–18.

Duruz, Jean. 2016a. "Love in a Hot Climate: Foodscapes of Trade, Travel, War and Intimacy." *Gastronomica* 16, no. 1: 16–27.

Duruz, Jean. 2016b. "The Taste of Retro: Nostalgia, Sensory Landscapes and Cosmopolitanism in Singapore." In *Food, Foodways and Foodscapes: Culture, Community and Consumption in Post-Colonial Singapore*, edited by Lily Kong and Vineeta Sinha, 133–58. Singapore: World Scientific.

Duruz, Jean. 2017. "Global Travels Haunted by the Taste of Laksa: Eating 'Asia' in Australia and Canada." Paper presented at the Asian Diasporas: Transnational and Regional Cultural Heritage(s) Conference. National Heritage Board and Asian Civilisations Museum, Singapore.

Duruz, Jean. 2018. "Trucking in Tastes and Smells: Adelaide's Street Food and the Politics of Urban 'Vibrancy.'" In *Senses in Cities: Experiences in Urban Settings*, edited by Kelvin E. Y. Low and Devorah Kalekin Fishman, 169–84. Abingdon: Routledge.

Duruz, Jean, and Gaik Cheng Khoo. 2015. *Eating Together: Food, Space, and Identity in Malaysia and Singapore*. Lanham, MD: Rowman and Littlefield.

Ferguson, Priscilla Parkhurst. 2010. "Culinary Nationalism." *Gastronomica* 10, no. 1: 102–9.

Florida, Richard. 2003. *The Rise of the Creative Class*. North Melbourne: Pluto.

Greencliff Agency. 2015. "Welcome to Kensington Street." Kensington Street. http://www.kensingtonstreet.com.au/.

Greencliff Agency. 2018. "Old Jim Kee." Kensington Street. https://www.kensingtonstreet.com.au/vendor/old-jim-kee/.

Heldke, Lisa. 2003. *Exotic Appetites: Ruminations of a Food Adventurer*. New York: Routledge.

Highmore, Ben. 2002. *Everyday Life and Cultural Theory: An Introduction*. London: Routledge.

Huggins, Jackie. 2016. "Government Has Not Met Its International Human Rights Standards." NITV. http://www.sbs.com.au/nitv/nitv-news/article/2016/05/20/jackie-huggins-un-government-has-not-met-its-international-human-rights-standards.

Hunter, Brooke. n.d. "Adam Liaw: Malaysia Kitchen Interview." https://www.femail.com.au/adam-liaw-malaysia-kitchen-interview.htm.

Hutton, Wendy. 2000. *The Food of Malaysia: Authentic Recipes from the Crossroads of Asia*. Singapore: Periplus.

Inness, Sherrie A. 2001. "Introduction: Eating Ethnic," In *Pilaf, Pozole, and Pad Thai: American Woman and Ethnic Food*, edited by Sherrie A. Inness, 1–13. Amherst: University of Massachusetts.

Johnson, Carol, Pal Ahluwalia, and Greg McCarthy. 2010. "Australia's Ambivalent Re-imagining of Asia." *Australian Journal of Political Science* 45, no. 1: 59–74.

Jordan, Nicholas. 2015. "Central Park's New Spice Alley: The Kensington Street Development Brings Sydney Its First Outdoor Singaporean-Style Hawker Centre." Broadsheet: Sydney. Last modified January 24, 2018. https://www.broadsheet.com.au/sydney/food-and-drink/article/central-parks-new-spice-alley.

Jupp, James. 1995. "From 'White Australia' to 'Part of Asia': Recent Shifts in Australian Immigration Policy Towards the Region." *International Migration Review* 29, no. 1: 207–28.

Keating, Paul. 1995. "Address by the Prime Minister, the Hon. P. J. Keating MP to the Chinese Chamber of Commerce—'Australia and Asia: The Next Steps,' Perth, Wednesday 15 February 1995." Australian Government. https://pmtranscripts.pmc.gov.au/release/transcript-9481.

Keating, Paul. 1996. "For the New Australia: 11 November 1996." Paul Keating. http://www.keating.org.au/shop/item/for-the-new-australia---11-november-1996.

Kristy C. 2014. "Fork on the Road" (review). Yelp, August 27, 2014. https://www.yelp.com.au/biz/fork-on-the-road-adelaide.

Lai Ah Eng. 2016. "The Kopitiam in Singapore: An Evolving Story of Cultural Diversity and Cultural Politics." In *Food, Foodways and Foodscapes: Culture, Community and Consumption in Post-Colonial Singapore*, edited by Lily Kong and Vineeta Sinha, 103–32. Singapore: World Scientific.

Landry, Charles. 2000. *The Creative City: A Toolkit for Urban Innovators*. Stroud: Commedia.

Law, Lisa. 2001. "Home Cooking: Filipino Women and Geographies of the Senses in Hong Kong." *Ecumene* 8, no. 3: 264–83.

Moreton-Robinson, Aileen. 2003. "I Still Call Australia Home: Indigenous Belonging and Place in a White Colonizing Society." In *Uprootings/Regroundings: Questions of Home and Migration*, edited by Sara Ahmed, Claudia Castañeda, Anne-Marie Fortier, and Mimi Sheller, 23–40. Oxford: Berg.

Murphy, Catherine. 2003. *The Market: Stories, History and Recipes from the Adelaide Central Market*, Kent Town: Wakefield Press.

Nora, Pierre. 1989. "Between History and Memory: Les Lieux de Mémoire." *Representations* 26: 7–24.

Oliver, Ann. n.d. "Australia's Best Laksa: Asian Gourmet." Galaxy Guides. http://www.galaxyguides.com/australia/sa/$20/asian_gourmet.php.

PappaRich. 2018. "About Papparich." Our Story. https://www.papparich.net.au/pages/our-story/about.

Ray, Krishnendu. 2016. *The Ethnic Restaurateur*. London: Bloomsbury.

Santich, Barbara. 2012. *Bold Palates: Australia's Gastronomic Heritage*. Kent Town, SA: Wakefield Press.

Savill, Joanna. 2006. "Three of a Kind: Laksa." *The Sydney Morning Herald*, July 25, Good Living section.

SBS. 2013. "About Modern Australian Food." Food. Posted July 1, 2008; last modified September 16, 2013. http://www.sbs.com.au/food/article/2008/07/01/about-modern-australian-food.

Sydney Morning Herald. 2004. "Mahathir: Australia Can't be Part of East Asian Group." December 8, 2004. http://www.smh.com.au/news/World/Mahathir-Australia-cant-be-part-of-East-Asian-group/2004/12/06/1102182222051.html.

Tan, Chee-Beng. 2010. "Intermarriage and the Chinese Peranakan in Southeast Asia." In *Peranakan Chinese in a Globalizing Southeast Asia*, edited by Leo Suryadinata, 27–40. Singapore: Chinese Heritage Centre and Baba House.

Teo, Hsu-Ming. 2000. *Love and Vertigo*. Crows Nest: Allen and Unwin.

Ting, Inga. 2013. "Hot and Hearty: Sydney's Top Spots for a Laksa." Good Food, July 30, 2013. https://www.goodfood.com.au/eat-out/hot-and-hearty-sydneys-top-spots-for-a-laksa-20130730-2qwh2.

Turnbull, Malcolm. 2015. "Interview with David Koch, Sunrise, September 21, 2015." Transcripts. https://www.malcolmturnbull.com.au/media/transcript-sunrise-21-september-2015.

Wa, Veronica Mac Sau. 2011. "Southeast Asian Chinese Food in Tea Café and Noodle Shops in Hong Kong." In *Chinese Food and Foodways in Southeast Asia and Beyond*, edited by Tan Chee-Beng, 218–35. Singapore: NUS Press.

Wong, Hong Suen. 2007. "A Taste of the Past: Historically Themed Restaurants and Social Memory in Singapore." In *Food and Foodways in Asia: Resource, Tradition and Cooking*, edited by Sidney C. H. Cheung and Tan Chee-Beng, 115–28. Abingdon: Routledge.

Wong, Russel. 2011. "Which is the Real 'Katong' Laksa?" *The Wong List* (blog). December 17, 2011. http://thewonglist.blogspot.com.au/2011/12/which-is-real-katong-laksa.html.

Yeoh, Brenda S. A., and Lily Kong. 1999. "The Notion of Place in the Construction of History, Nostalgia and Heritage." In *Our Place in Time; Exploring Heritage and Memory in Singapore*, edited by Kian Woon Kwok, Chong Guan Kwa, Lily Kong, and Brenda S. A. Yeoh, 132–51. Singapore: Singapore Heritage Society.

Yeow, Poh Ling. n.d. "What Is Australia's National Dish?" *Taste Magazine* http://www.taste.com.au/articles/what-is-australias-national-dish/nRdTzF9U.

Zomato. n.d. a. "Old Jim Kee—Spice Alley." Reviews. https://www.zomato.com/sydney/old-jim-kee-1-chippendale/reviews; quotation taken from: https://www.zomato.com/review/pAPGQE.

Zomato. n.d. b. "Kopi-Tiam Spice Alley." Reviews. Formerly available at: https://www.zomato.com/sydney/kopi-tiam-spice-alley-chippendale/reviews.

Afterword: Feasting and the Pursuit of National Unity—American Thanksgiving and Cantonese Common-Pot Dining

James L. Watson
Harvard University

It is not surprising that culinary nationalism has become a central feature of social life in the early twenty-first century. Nationalism in all of its many forms is emerging (and, alas, reemerging) throughout the world. The 2016 American presidential election, together with the UK Brexit vote and the simultaneous rise of anti-immigrant sentiments in Europe, has dashed hopes for a new era of global tolerance. Meanwhile, China's inexorable rise as a global superpower has shattered twentieth-century notions of a bipolar, capitalist-versus-socialist world. Who among today's youth understands the symbolism of the Berlin Wall? And what, if anything, does the Cultural Revolution mean to young people in 2019 China?

The essays in this volume make it clear that consumers in Asia are refashioning their cultural worlds, and that food is a central feature of these movements. Culinary nationalism, as Michelle King notes in the Introduction to this volume, takes many forms. Is it the content, the taste, or the style of presentation that matters most? Who determines what is, or what is not, "Chinese," or "Indian," or "Thai" food? One ethnographic example from a region I know well illustrates the complexity of this question: on the main streets of several small towns in western Illinois are diners that serve versions of Chinese food. Among the patrons who regularly eat lunch in these restaurants are veterans of the Vietnam War who claim to know how "real" Asian food should taste. But what, other than the chopped vegetables and the heavy soy sauce, makes this cuisine Chinese? For local consumers, at least, it is the *idea* of Chinese food that matters most, not the content (which would puzzle my friends who live in Hong Kong or Beijing).

Ethnic or national labels attaching to food are the result of agreements between consumers and providers. There is nothing inherently foundational about what constitutes a national cuisine.

Inventing a national culinary tradition: American Thanksgiving

One of the best examples of harnessing culinary traditions to serve the needs of national identity—a central theme of this volume—is President Abraham Lincoln's appropriation and promotion of a parochial feast that first emerged among English settlers on the American east coast. Later known as "Thanksgiving," this annual celebration is believed to have emerged in the 1690s among Protestants as a means of expressing gratitude for divine intervention that made it possible to survive in the "New World" (Linton and Linton 1949). The original feast included Native American neighbors as guests, but—as more European immigrants began to arrive—the annual event became exclusively Protestant. Not surprisingly, for the next century Catholic priests denounced the event as a "Protestant heretic feast." The religious controversy finally ended in the early nineteenth century when the Cardinal of Baltimore encouraged his priests to celebrate Thanksgiving masses in local churches (Fischer 1991).

By the mid-nineteenth century the annual feast had become intertwined with the political question of slavery and the North–South division which led to the American Civil War (1861–5). Due largely to the organizational genius and dynamism of Sarah Hale, the editor of a mass-circulation women's magazine (*Godey's Lady's Book*), every northern state in the American union began celebrating Thanksgiving on the last Thursday of November (Baker 2007). Southern, slave-holding states either ignored Thanksgiving or observed a local harvest festival on a variety of dates—avoiding the last Thursday in November. The menus excluded foods deemed to be "northern" (Moss 2014).

In 1863, during the worst days of the Civil War, President Lincoln proclaimed that, henceforth, Thanksgiving would be observed in all states of the American Union on the last Thursday of November. The celebration thus became a *consciously designed symbol* of national unity and has been celebrated, as such, since that date. Diana Appelbaum (1984) tracks this complex development and shows how this "Yankee abolitionist feast" was eventually accepted by residents of the defeated southern states and is, today, embraced by a majority of Americans as an annual event celebrating family unity.[1]

For most Americans of my generation, born in the 1940s and 1950s, Thanksgiving festivities often included a reenactment of cooperation among European settler-immigrants and Native American peoples during the early, precarious phase of expansion into the "New World." Public schools in Iowa, for instance, held annual Thanksgiving skits with students (like me) dressing in homemade costumes, half as "Indian" and half as "Pilgrims." Nobody in my class ever wanted to be a Pilgrim, so the positions were assigned by lot. Celebrations of this nature have long since disappeared from most American schools, but the sentiments of close cooperation among ethnic groups constitutes an important foundational myth for many citizens.

By the 1980s and 1990s, Native American groups began to observe the day as an occasion for mourning, rather than celebration. For instance, on Thanksgiving morning in 1991 representatives of the Mashpee Wampanoag Tribe gathered in Plymouth Harbor for a day of fasting rather than feasting (Hart 1998). The Mashpee Wampanoag are indigenous to the territory that became Massachusetts. In 1995 several activists poured sand over Plymouth Rock, a national shrine celebrating the arrival of English settlers; the act symbolized "burying racism," according to demonstrators who referred to the occasion as "Unthanksgiving" (Lepore 1998; Mehren 1997).

An interesting dimension of Thanksgiving is the purposeful promotion of an "American" menu, featuring food items that are indigenous to the New World (Mann 2012; Stavely and Fitzgerald 2011, 195–205). The centerpiece is *Meleagris gallopavo*, the common American turkey; support dishes almost always include some combination of pumpkin pie, cranberry sauce, maize/corn pudding, sweet potatoes, squash, and other "native" food species that the original European settlers had not encountered prior to arrival. Highlighting the turkey was an act of pure genius: it allows people of (almost) all religious traditions to partake in the feast. Turkey is considered *kosher* (proper, clean) by the overwhelming majority of American rabbis (Davis 2005; Heller 2003), and the Fiqh Council of North America, a Muslim scholarly organization, has ruled that the bird is *halal*, "permissible."[2] Brahmanic Hindus, Jains, Seventh-Day Adventists, and non-religious vegetarians are challenged by the turkey, but alternatives—including bean curd or vegetable substitutes—have always been acceptable. The turkey may be the centerpiece for most American celebrants, but it has never been mandatory. The other items on the standard Thanksgiving menu are acceptable to (almost) all diners and are often considered to be hyper-American. Pumpkin pie, for instance, is common fare in the United States but my British friends—when confronted with it—always considered it to be bizarre.[3]

During my twenty years of teaching an undergraduate course on food and society in the Harvard core curriculum, I always asked students to prepare brief essays on their Thanksgiving holiday dining experiences. The following list provides a window on American ethnicity and immigrant adaptations:

- black-bean stuffed turkey (Cuban)
- red-pepper rubbed, deep-fried turkey (New Orleans Cajun)
- stewed turkey with fish sauce and vegetables (Vietnamese)
- roast turkey stuffed with nutmeg and cracked pepper dressing (Greek Orthodox)
- curried turkey (Jamaican)
- roast turkey in hot mole sauce (Mexican)
- ground turkey in fried filo dough with spicy yogurt (Yemeni)
- herb-wrapped, stewed turkey (Puerto Rican)
- ground turkey with cumin, mint, and cilantro (Jewish, "Jerusalem-style")
- turkey scaloppini (Italian)
- hot-pepper roast turkey (Sichuan-style Chinese)
- shredded roast turkey with pasta (Italian)
- bean-curd molded turkey (Hindu Indian)
- almond-stuffed turkey with lingonberry sauce (Swedish)
- halal-tandoori roast turkey (Pakistani Muslim)
- roast turkey with tourshee spicy sauce and crusty rice (Iranian)
- marinated turkey with bok choy, shrimp, and bean curd (Cantonese)
- mushroom and prosciutto-stuffed turkey (French)

The turkey clearly stands for something greater than its status as a bird, or a menu item. It has become a highly charged symbol of assimilation and Americanization. The fact that the American military always serves roast turkey and "all the trimmings" to soldiers and sailors serving abroad (or on ships)—even in forward combat stations—reinforces the association between food and country. As Cwiertka (2012) and Marx de Salcedo (2015) have argued, one should never underestimate the unifying role of military cuisine in the creation of national cultures.

Inventing a culinary tradition: Cantonese common-pot dining and regional autonomy

In 1969 I began what has turned out to be a life-long ethnographic study of Cantonese villages in the Hong Kong New Territories (Map 2).[4] Soon after arriving in the village of San Tin my neighbor and patron, Mr. Man Tso-chuen, invited me to accompany him to a banquet celebrating the birth of male offspring. We stood at the entrance to the banquet hall and waited until six other invitees—all male—had arrived. We were presented with chopsticks and a large wooden bowl of mixed foods (Figure A.1). Together our group of eight squatted on the floor and proceeded to dig in, each of us searching for something identifiable to eat. No one spoke and there were no speeches, religious performances, or ceremonies of any kind. Guests ate quickly and left as soon as they could to make way for other diners queuing at the entrance. Save for the local rice-shop owner, I was the only guest who was not a member of the local patrilineage, a kinship group that had dominated San Tin for the past eight centuries.

Thus was my introduction to the Cantonese custom known as *sihk-puhn* (食盤), best translated as "to eat from the common pot" (Watson 1987). I learned later that my group of eight included one of the wealthiest emigrant entrepreneurs in the New Territories, as well as a penniless ploughman who survived with the help of his aging

Figure A.1 *Puhn-choi* bowls, ready for the banquet. San Tin, Hong Kong New Territories (1969). Photograph by James Watson.

water buffalo. By eating from the common pot each attendee signaled his recognition of the "new male" (新丁) as a legitimate member of the lineage.

Village banquets in the 1960s consisted of seven items cooked separately and later mixed together in a common pot: boiled fat-back pork, dried salt fish, fish balls, dried (reconstituted) pig skin, dried bean-curd skin, white turnips, and dried (reconstituted) squid. This is peasant food, reminiscent of life in coastal south China prior to the modern era of transnational markets and plentiful, fresh food supplies. My village friends were steadfast—even defiant—in their acceptance of this local style of banquet cuisine. They knew, of course, that there were better alternatives in nearby towns but they clung to the rustic, seven-item menu[5] when celebrating local weddings, births, and housewarmings (Watson 1985, 118–26).

The primary attraction of common-pot dining was the opportunity to eat meat (pork)—other ingredients, such as fish and squid, were consumed after the meat was gone. Older guests, the majority of whom had lost most of their teeth, chewed as best they could on cubes of fat rather than pieces of muscle fiber. During hard times villagers craved fat more than any other food, and many remembered going for years without eating any meat at all (Watson 2014). Rubie Watson and I learned to eat (with a smile) pieces of glistening fat-back presented to us by banquet hosts (Figure A.2).[6]

When I told my urban Hong Kong friends about *puhn-choi* (盤菜, or alternatively 盆菜, "pot food") in 1969 they were—quite frankly—horrified. Although many prided themselves in their knowledge of Chinese history and folklore, they had never heard of this style of dining—even though many had grandparents who originated in villages located in the Cantonese-speaking regions of Guangdong Province. "Those people out there must be ethnic minorities (少數民族), not Han Chinese (漢) like us. We Chinese don't eat like that," a Professor of Chinese at Hong Kong University told me after I showed him photographs of the San Tin banquet. Other friends warned that *puhn-choi* was, in their view, obviously unsanitary and advised against attending village banquets.[7]

Contrary to the interpretations of many urban observers, literate villagers claimed that *puhn-choi* originated as a survival mechanism among their ethnic Han ancestors

Figure A.2 Fat-back pork for the *puhn-choi* banquet. San Tin, Hong Kong New Territories (1969). Photograph by James Watson.

who first settled along the south China coast in two waves during the Tang and Song dynastic eras (ninth and thirteenth centuries). Mixing locally available foods together in a common pot was, in their retelling of history, the only way for hardy settlers to prevail; no one had time or energy to cook and serve everything separately. The local foundation myths I collected all featured *puhn-choi* as a means of surviving in what was then a hostile environment (Watson 1987; see also Cheung 2002, 108–9; Leung 2009). The parallels to American myths regarding the Pilgrims, and their encounters with the New England coastal frontier, are striking. In both cases settlers had to struggle with unfamiliar foods before turning them into iconic symbols of determination and triumph.[8]

Changing notions of identity in Hong Kong

As the 1997 date for Hong Kong's "return" (回歸) to Chinese sovereignty approached, people in the soon-to-be former colony began a search for local customs that did *not* reflect their status as subjects of the British Empire. They wanted their homeland to be perceived as a legitimate, but yet unique, part of China. After 155 years of British rule it proved difficult to find cultural forms that were not, in some sense, "colonial."

To my utter astonishment (I must confess) *puhn-choi* was embraced by urban elites, political officials, and community activists as a symbol of "authentic" Hong Kong culture (see, e.g., *South China Morning Post* 1997). Upmarket versions of common-pot dining became a regular feature of repatriation celebrations all over Hong Kong—not just in the New Territories. *Puhn-choi* cooks were transformed into celebrity "chefs" who were interviewed on television; restaurants specializing in "Village Cuisine" opened in high-rent districts throughout Hong Kong.[9]

In 1997, just prior to "Repatriation Day" (July 1), Rubie Watson and I were invited to attend an elaborate *puhn-choi* banquet hosted by the Hong Kong Tourist Association. Chinese officials from Beijing and Shanghai were the primary guests, along with various Hong Kong politicians and business tycoons. As a speaker of (very rusty) Mandarin[10] I was seated at a table with Communist Party bureaucrats who had never been in Hong Kong. My role was to "explain" the history and meaning of *puhn-choi* (happily for me, they were only interested in eating).

The food was a far cry from the New Territories banquets of the 1960s. The wooden *puhn* (bowls) had been replaced with a sanitized aluminum pans and the chopsticks were plastic throwaways—not the battered, wooden implements of the past. Roast chicken, fresh-caught sea bass, shrimp, lobster (airfreighted from Maine), and exotic mushrooms were piled high in the pans. Rather than digging in and eating directly from the *puhn*, as I had learned decades earlier, waiters used large serving chopsticks to move selected pieces of food to diners' plates. Guests listened politely to speeches delivered (in Cantonese with Mandarin translations) by Hong Kong politicians and a handful of New Territories leaders in suits and ties. Ordinary villagers were not invited and none were present. A professional catering firm provided the servers, chef's assistants, and clean-up crew. In effect, the community-based *puhn-choi* banquets of the past had been appropriated, sanitized (in a quite literal sense), and repackaged as a symbol of Hong Kong's unique status as a "Special Administrative Region" (SAR) of the People's Republic of China.[11]

The irony of this situation did not escape my village friends in the New Territories, who roared with laughter when I showed them photographs of the event. Several recalled picking pig's bristles out of 1960s and 1970s *puhn* as they searched for edible bits of pork and reconstituted fish. For men now in their seventies and eighties, those memories were bittersweet and hearkened to a time when village life involved a constant round of community rituals and banquets. (And I confess to having similar, very fond memories of those events. Anthropologists are not alone in suffering the afflictions of nostalgia.)

Puhn-choi in transition

But the story of *puhn-choi*'s transformation did not end here: In 2017 large banquets based on versions of *puhn-choi* were featured in celebrations to mark the twentieth anniversary of Hong Kong's return to China. Today there is a widely recognized connection between common-pot dining and loyalty to the People's Republic,[12] in opposition to various protest movements that support the political and cultural autonomy of Hong Kong. One organization in the New Territories held a *puhn-choi* banquet for 13,000 people to mark the anniversary; a large poster displayed at this event encouraged people to "Celebrate the Return [to Chinese sovereignty], Support Economic Reform, Oppose Occupy Central."[13] The final part of this slogan refers to the 2014 Umbrella Movement (and subsequent events) that involved closing highways and government offices in what is commonly known as "Central," the core of Hong Kong Island's business district (see, e.g., Bosco 2016; Veg 2016). Although students and workers who participated in these protests enjoy occasional restaurant meals that include a version *puhn-choi*, they have not embraced it as an organizing symbol.[14]

In recent years, common-pot banqueting has also become a symbol of Hong Kong's cultural distinctiveness within the broader context of Chinese society. In 2017 it was selected as one of Hong Kong's contributions to the Chinese government's national "Intangible Cultural Heritage List" (ICHO 2018). The identification of *puhn-choi* with Hong Kong's postcolonial development is now firmly established: for instance, on July 2, 2017, the London Chinatown Association—in conjunction with the Hong Kong Government's Economic and Trade Office—organized a *puhn-choi* banquet for a thousand people in London's Gerrard Street, the original heart of Britain's overseas Chinese community (Ng 1968; Watson 1975, 116–31). Among the 800 guests were the mayors of several London Boroughs and Lord Bates, the Minister of State for International Development (Government of Hong Kong Special Administrative Region 2017).

Meanwhile, across the Hong Kong border in rural districts throughout Guangdong Province, *puhn-choi* has begun to appear (or reappear?) as a feature of local village celebrations (Map 2).[15] The ethnographic forms, and the symbolic meanings attached to these celebrations, are not yet clear but it cannot be a coincidence that these banquets are celebrated in Cantonese-speaking areas that were subject to decades of cultural obliteration campaigns organized by Communist Party activists during the 1950s, 1960s, and 1970s (see, e.g., Chan, Madsen, and Unger 1992).[16] Red Guard and party activists were particularly vigilant in their attacks on traditional rites associated with ancestor worship, marriage, and funerals. Banquets, other than those sponsored by the local party, were banned (Watson 2016).

Could it be that *puhn-choi* has become an acceptable (and politically safe) way for many Guangdong villagers to express a sense of exclusiveness and "specialness" in south China's rapidly changing social system?[17] It is interesting in this regard that Chinese Central Television (CCTV) has included *puhn-choi* in two episodes of its blockbuster series, "A Bite of China." One episode from 2014 features common-pot banqueting in a Cantonese village located in the Shenzhen Special Economic Zone, five miles north of the Hong Kong–SEZ border. Another episode highlights a Hakka version of *puhn-choi* in the district of Meizhou, northern Guangdong Province.[18]

Although more ethnographic research needs to be done on this topic, it appears that common-pot dining—as a cultural form—is now thoroughly immersed in the rapidly changing politics of south China. We have seen this pattern before. Since its inception, Thanksgiving has been entangled with the ever-changing politics of American identity. The Cantonese practice of *puhn-choi* has morphed through a comparable series of symbolic representations during the half-century I have worked in the Hong Kong region. There is no reason to think that either of these culinary sagas will ever end.

Acknowledgments

I am grateful to Chan Kwok-shing, Selena Chan, Sidney Cheung, Robert Eng, Michelle King, Liu Tik-sang, and Gonçalo Santos for their help in tracking the recent history of *puhn-choi* in Hong Kong and Guangdong Province.

Notes

1   In my own extended family, Thanksgiving is the only occasion when cousins, their children, and grandchildren, make serious efforts to gather and eat together, once each year. See Siskind (1992) on the role that Thanksgiving plays in the maintenance of American kinship groups.

2   Although the turkey, as a food, is deemed *halal* among most American Muslims, there is still some debate regarding the practice of Thanksgiving in certain Islamic circles (Bandler 2001).

3   During our eleven years in London (1972–83), Rubie Watson and I often invited neighbors and colleagues to a Thanksgiving meal. It was always a challenge to find a genuine turkey and the ingredients for pumpkin pie. Years later, one of our friends confessed that he hated the pumpkin pie and always wondered if we had served it to him as a form of punishment.

4   The "New Territories" constitutes a 365 square mile section of Guangdong's Xin'an District that was leased to the British Crown Colony of Hong Kong in 1898—for a ninety-nine-year period. It contains approximately 600 original villages inhabited by speakers of Cantonese and Hakka. Rubie Watson and I lived in two of these Cantonese villages (San Tin and Ha Tsuen) during the late 1960s and 1970s, and we have returned to the New Territories for many follow-up studies during the past five decades (Watson and Watson 2004).

5 Formal Chinese banqueting procedures, as practiced in restaurants and urban homes, also call for seven items—delivered to the table *in sequence*, one after the other (Cooper 1986). *Puhn-choi* hosts deliberately defy this convention. The seven original ingredients of *puhn-choi* have changed since I first encountered the practice in the late 1960s. For instance, boiled fat-back pork has been replaced by roast pork and dried squid has disappeared in favor of fresh fish and/or shrimp.

6 Fat of this type was sometimes dangerous for older villagers who suffered from gallbladder complications.

7 Rubie Watson and I attended dozens of village *puhn-choi* banquets during our years of fieldwork in the New Territories. We never fell ill from any of these experiences, although we did suffer from numerous intestinal episodes after eating in Kowloon restaurants.

8 Pilgrims had difficulty eating local foods when they first arrived, including the plentiful eel and shellfish available in the nearby waters (Prosek 2010). Han pioneers in South China's Pearl River Delta no doubt had similar problems with many of the foods they encountered, such as dried squid, snake, and local root crops.

9 These developments are discussed in Chan (2011), Chan (1998), and Cheung (2005). *Puhn-choi* has even appeared on the menu of at least one Chinese restaurant in Calgary, Canada (Josephine Smart, email to author, February 6, 2001).

10 I started learning Mandarin as an undergraduate at the University of Iowa in 1963 and continued with this language as a graduate student at the University of California, Berkeley. Immediately upon arrival in Hong Kong in 1969, it was obvious that Mandarin was all but useless for research among local people. Rubie Watson and I studied basic Cantonese at New Asia College (Kowloon) and moved into San Tin a few months later—only to discover that villagers in the New Territories spoke a rural dialect that was radically different from the urban Cantonese spoken in Kowloon and Hong Kong Island. Thus began a linguistic saga that has continued for nearly half a century—and the story is by no means finished, given recent dialect changes in Hong Kong and Guangdong (Watson and Watson 2004, 12–13).

11 As one example, a 100-table *puhn-choi* banquet was provided for Chinese soldiers who had recently taken up residence in a New Territories barracks (formerly occupied by British forces). The banquet's host institution was the Heung Yee Kuk, an association of New Territories political leaders (Wong 1997).

12 This political connection does *not* apply to the small-scale, kinship-based banquets still being held in New Territories villages. *Puhn-choi* celebrations are still a requirement for the legitimation of marriage for many of the "original" (本地) inhabitants of the region (Chan 2007; Chan 2010).

13 Email correspondence with Robert Eng, June 17, 2018; for a description of events see Guteng (2017).

14 Verified by emails and conversations with Hong Kong friends and colleagues (and their children—some of whom participated in the Umbrella Movement and related protests).

15 Colleagues who work in Guangdong rural districts report the appearance of *puhn-choi*, and *puhn-choi*-like banquets in many parts of the province. It is unclear at this point whether these events are inspired by Hong Kong examples or reinventions (revivals?) of pre-1950s cultural forms (emails to author from Carsten Herrmann-Pillah, Sidney Cheung, Liu Tik-sang, and Gonçalo Santos). Of interest in this regard is the fact that many elders from New Territories lineage communities (such as Ha Tsuen and San Tin) have visited their agnatic kinsmen in Guangdong regions where ancestor

worship and lineage rites had disappeared during the heyday of Maoism. These men have served as cultural instructors (of a sort), teaching people how to worship ancestors, how to kowtow at ancestral tombs, and how to design ancestral halls. The introduction (reintroduction?) of *puhn-choi* banquets has been a central feature of these cultural exchanges.

16 Cantonese was systematically suppressed in Guangdong public schools during the 1960s and 1970s. Today, Mandarin is the primary medium of exchange outside the home—where Cantonese still dominates (Eng 2010).

17 Selina Chan's (1998) account of similar developments among New Territories villagers during the run-up to 1997 may be instructive in this regard.

18 For *puhn-choi* recipes, see Cook King Room (2017). For the Hakka village *puhn-choi* banquet clip from *A Bite of China*, see CCTV (2018). I am grateful to Michelle King for drawing my attention to these sites.

References

Appelbaum, Diana. 1984. *Thanksgiving: An American Holiday, An American History*. New York: Facts On File.

Baker, Peggy M. 2007. *The Godmother of Thanksgiving: The Story of Sarah Josepha Hale*. Plymouth: Pilgrim Hall Museum.

Bandler, James. 2001 "U.S. Muslims, Long Split Over Thanksgiving, Find Debate Has New Gravity After Sept. 11." *Wall Street Journal*, November 20, 2001. https://www.wsj.com/articles/SB1006207507957947000#CORRECT.

Bosco, Joseph. 2016. "The Sacred in Urban Political Protests in Hong Kong." *International Sociology* 31, no. 4: 375–95.

CCTV. 2018. "[舌尖上的中国3] 客家盆菜 Shejianshang de Zhongguo 3: Kejia pencai" ["A Bite of China, Season 3: Hakka *puhn-choi*"]. YouTube video, 3:23. March 2, 2018. https://www.youtube.com/watch?v=vuEfZ-DrvVo.

Chan, Anita, Richard Madsen, and Jonathan Unger. 1992. *Chen Village Under Mao and Deng*. Berkeley: University of California Press.

Chan, Kwok Shing. 2007. "*Poonchoi*: The Production and Popularity of a Rural Festive Cuisine in Urban and Modern Hong Kong." In *Food and Foodways in Asia*, edited by Sidney C. H. Cheung and Tan Chee-Beng, 53–66. Abingdon: Routledge.

Chan, Kwok Shing. 2011. "Traditionality and Hybridity: A Village Cuisine in Metropolitan Hong Kong." *Visual Anthropology* 24, no. 1: 171–88.

Chan, Selina C. 1998. "Politicizing Tradition: The Identity of Indigenous Inhabitants in Hong Kong." *Ethnology* 37, no. 1: 39–54.

Chan, Selina C. 2010. "Food, Memories, and Identities in Hong Kong." *Identities* 17: 204–27.

Cheung, Sidney C. H. 2002. "Food and Cuisine in a Changing Society." In *The Globalization of Chinese Food*, edited by David Y. H. Wu and Sidney C. H. Cheung, 100–17. Honolulu: University of Hawai'i Press.

Cheung, Sidney C. H. 2005. "Consuming 'Low' Cuisine after Hong Kong's Handover: Village Banquets and Private Kitchens." *Asian Studies Review* 29: 259–72.

Cook King Room. 2017. " 【盆菜】簡易自家版 中秋 冬至 新年 過節都啱使！ 'Pencai' jianyi zijiaban zhongqiu dongzhi xinnian guojie douyanshi" ["*Puhn-choi*: Easy DIY Version, Good for Mid-Autumn Festival, Winter Solstice, Chinese New Year, and

Other Festivals"]. YouTube video, 14:37. December 20, 2017. https://www.youtube.com/watch?v=BaGcNDQzF6Y.

Cooper, Eugene. 1986. "Chinese Table Manners: You Are How You Eat." *Human Organization* 45, no. 2: 179–84.

Cwiertka, Katarzyna J. 2012. *Cuisine, Colonialism and Cold War: Food in Twentieth-Century Korea*. London: Reaktion Books.

Davis, Joseph. 2005. *Yom-Tov Lipman Heller: Portrait of a Seventeenth-Century Rabbi*. Oxford: Littman Library of Jewish Civilization.

Eng, Robert Y. 2010. "Is Cantonese in Danger of Extinction? The Politics and Culture of Language Policy in China." *China Notes: Superfluous Musings of A Chinese Historian* (blog). August 20, 2010. http://chinamusictech.blogspot.com/2010/08/is-cantonese-in-danger-of-extinction.html.

Fischer, David H. 1991. "Multicultural Fowl." *New York Times*, November 28, 1991. https://www.nytimes.com/1991/11/28/opinion/multicultural-fowl.html.

Government of Hong Kong Special Administrative Region. 2017. "Hundreds Celebrate 20th Anniversary of Establishment of Hong Kong Special Administrative Region at Poon Choi Festival in London." Press Releases. July 3, 2017. http://www.info.gov.hk/gia/general/201707/03/P2017070301173.htm?fontSize=1%3E.

Guteng Changlin. 2017. "万人盆菜宴：香港风情 Wanren pencai yan: Xianggang fengqing" ["'Ten-thousand' person *puhn-choi* banquet: Hong Kong local custom"]. 360doc. October 21, 2017. http://www.360doc.com/content/17/1021/20/19830080_696975608.shtml.

Hart, Jordana. "In Plymouth, Peaceful Protest." *Boston Globe*, November 27, 1998.

Heller, Joshua. 2003. "Turkey's Kosher Journey." JTS (Jewish Theological Seminary) Torah Online. August 23, 2003. www.jtsa.edu/turkeys-kosher-journey.

ICHO (Intangible Cultural Heritage Office). 2018. "*Sek Pun* (Basin Feast)." The Representative List of the Intangible Cultural Heritage of Hong Kong. Last modified October 2, 2018. https://www.lcsd.gov.hk/CE/Museum/ICHO/en_US/web/icho/representative_list_sek_pun.html.

Lepore, Jill. 1998. "Revenge of the Wampanoags." *New York Times*, November 25, 1998. https://www.nytimes.com/1998/11/25/opinion/revenge-of-the-wampanoags.html.

Leung, Ping-kwan. 2009. "Pun Choi is Pure Hong Kong." *Wall Street Journal* (Hong Kong edition), March 27, 2009.

Linton, Ralph, and Adelin Linton. 1949. *We Gather Together: The Story of Thanksgiving*. New York: Schuman.

Mann, Charles C. 2012. *1493: Uncovering the New World Columbus Created*. New York: Vintage.

Marx de Salcedo, Anastacia. 2015. *Combat-Ready Kitchen: How the U.S. Military Shapes the Way You Eat*. New York: Current.

Mehren, Elizabeth. 1997. "Arrests During 'Day of Mourning' March in Plymouth." *Los Angeles Times*, December 3, 1997.

Moss, Robert. 2014. "How Thanksgiving, the 'Yankee Abolitionist Holiday,' Won Over the South." *Serious Eats*, November [13], 2014. https://www.seriouseats.com/2014/11/history-southern-thanksgiving.html.

Ng, Kwee Choo. 1968. *The Chinese in London*. London: Institute of Race Relations.

Prosek, James. 2010. "Give Thanks for . . . Eel?" *New York Times*, November 24, 2010. https://www.nytimes.com/2010/11/25/opinion/25prosek.html.

Siskind, Janet. 1992. "The Invention of Thanksgiving: A Ritual of American Nationality." *Critique of Anthropology* 12, no. 2: 167–91.

South China Morning Post. 1997. "Early Start to Handover Parties." March 17, 1997.

Stavely, Keith, and Kathleen Fitzgerald. 2001. *Northern Hospitality: Cooking by the Book in New England*. Amherst: University of Massachusetts Press.

Veg, Sebastian. 2016. "Creating a Textual Public Space: Slogans and Texts from Hong Kong's Umbrella Movement." *Journal of Asian Studies* 75, no. 3: 673–702.

Watson, James L. 1975. *Emigration and the Chinese Lineage: The Mans in Hong Kong and London*. Berkeley: University of California Press.

Watson, James L. 1987. "From the Common Pot: Feasting with Equals in Chinese Society." *Anthropos* 82: 389–401.

Watson, James L. 2014. "Meat: A Cultural Biography (in South China)." In *Food Consumption in Global Perspective: Essays in the Anthropology of Food in Honour of Jack Goody*, edited by Jakob A. Klein and Anne Murcott, 25–44. London: Palgrave Macmillan.

Watson, James L. 2016. "Feeding the Revolution: Public Mess Halls and Coercive Commensality in Maoist China." In *Handbook of Food and Anthropology*, edited by Jakob A. Klein and James L. Watson, 308–20. London: Bloomsbury.

Watson, James L., and Rubie S. Watson. 2004. "Fieldwork in the Hong Kong New Territories (1969–1997)." In *Village Life in Hong Kong: Politics, Gender, and Ritual in the New Territories*, edited by James L. Watson and Rubie S. Watson, 3–16. Hong Kong: Chinese University Press.

Watson, Rubie S. 1985. *Inequality Among Brothers: Class and Kinship in South China*. Cambridge: Cambridge University Press.

Wong, Billy W.-Y. 1997. "Song and Dance for PLA." *South China Morning Post*, July 16, 1997.

Contributors

Daniel E. Bender is the Canada Research Chair in Cultural History and Analysis, Professor of History in the Department of Historical and Cultural Studies at the University of Toronto Scarborough and is the director of the University of Toronto's Culinaria Research Centre. He is currently working on a project about empire and culinary tourism. He is the author most recently of *Making the Empire Work: Labor and United States Imperialism* (ed., 2015) and *The Animal Game: Searching for Wildness at the American Zoo* (2016).

Rachel Berger is an associate professor of History at Concordia University, Montreal and a fellow of the Simone De Beauvoir Institute. Her work primarily revolves around concepts of Ayurveda and biopolitics in colonial South Asia, and the study of reproductive medicine, diet, health, and consumption in the late-colonial period. She is the author of *Ayurveda Made Modern: Political Histories of Indigenous Medicine in North India, 1900–1955* (2013).

Michelle E. Bloom is a professor of French and Comparative Literature at the University of California, Riverside. She explores the interplay between the Francophone world and the Sinophone world, most recently in her book, *Contemporary Sino-French Cinema: Absent Fathers, Banned Books, and Red Balloons* (2015). She aims to go beyond the polarities of orientalism, instead considering contemporary cinema through the optics of métissage, translation, intertextuality, and imitation. Related articles address Sino-French films by directors Dai Sijie, Hou Hsiao-hsien, Jia Zhangke, Emily Tang Xiaobai and Tsai Ming-liang.

Michaël Bruckert is a researcher at CIRAD (French Agricultural Research Centre for International Development) in France. He has been trained as a geographer and as a cook in Paris. His research explores how global cities and mobilities reshape the production, distribution, preparation, and consumption of food (and particularly meat) and, in turn, how food circuits produce artifacts, meanings, norms, environments, and spaces. His book, *La chair, les hommes et les dieux: La viande en Inde* (CNRS Editions, 2018) offers a systemic approach to the production and consumption of meat in contemporary India, in particular in the city of Chennai.

Katarzyna J. Cwiertka is Chair of Modern Japan Studies at Leiden University. Her books include *Modern Japanese Cuisine: Food, Power and National Identity* (2006), *Cuisine, Colonialism and Cold War: Food in Twentieth Century Korea* (2012), *Too Pretty to Throw Away: Packaging Design from Japan* (2016; co-author), and *Branding Japanese Food: From* Meibutsu *to* Washoku (Forthcoming; co-author). She edited *Asian Food:*

The Global and the Local (2002), *Critical Readings on Food in East Asia* (2012), *Food and War in Mid-Twentieth-Century East Asia* (2013), and *Consuming Post-Bubble Japan* (2018). She is the founding editor of *Global Food History* and editor-in-chief of *Worldwide Waste: Journal of Interdisciplinary Studies.*

Jean Duruz is an adjunct senior research fellow at the School of Creative Industries at the University of South Australia. For a number of years her research has focused on food as a medium of interethnic exchange in global cities, such as Singapore, Mexico City, and Sydney. Her recent publications include (with Gaik Cheng Khoo) *Eating Together: Food, Space, and Identity in Malaysia and Singapore* (2015) and chapters in edited collections such as Kong and Sinha's *Food, Foodways and Foodscapes* (2016) and Banerjee-Dube's *Cooking Cultures* (2016).

James Farrer is Professor of Sociology and Global Studies at Sophia University in Tokyo, specializing in urban sociology in East Asia, researching sexuality, nightlife expatriate communities, and food cultures. His publications include *Opening Up: Youth Sex Culture and Market Reform in Shanghai* (2002), *Shanghai Nightscapes: A Nocturnal Biography of a Global City* (with Andrew Field, 2015), *The Globalization of Asian Cuisines: Transnational Networks and Contact Zones* (ed., 2015), and *International Migrants in China's Global City: The New Shanghailanders* (2019). He has also published more than fifty book chapters and articles and written for general media, including *Newsweek Japan, Asian Wall Street Journal,* and *Global Asia.*

Satoko Kakihara is Assistant Professor of Japanese at California State University, Fullerton. Her research areas include modern Japanese literature, gender, and imperialism. She is currently working on a monograph that analyzes literary productions by female writers throughout the Japanese empire.

Gaik Cheng Khoo is an associate professor of Media and Cultural Studies at the University of Nottingham Malaysia. Co-author (with Jean Duruz) of *Eating Together: Food, Space, and Identity in Malaysia and Singapore* (2014), her other food publications include "The Cheapskate Highbrow and the Dilemma of Sustaining Penang Hawker Food as Intangible Cultural Heritage" (SOJOURN, March 2017) and the book chapter "Penang Hawker Food: Preserving Taste, Affirming Local 'Distinction'?" in *Space, Taste and Affect* (forthcoming). She has also written about vegetarian restaurants as possible third places in Malaysia and on Korean restaurants in Malaysia.

Michelle T. King is an associate professor of History at the University of North Carolina at Chapel Hill. Her latest research project focuses on the career of Fu Pei-mei, Taiwan's noted cookbook author and television celebrity, as a way to understand changes in postwar society, including the development of foodways as a critical national political project, shifting gender roles, and the transnational construction of identity through successive generations. She also teaches about the cultural history of Chinese food. Her prior publications on Chinese gender history include *Between Birth and Death: Female Infanticide in Nineteenth-Century China* (2014).

Tatsuya Mitsuda is Assistant Professor, Faculty of Economics, Keio University, Japan. He was educated at Keio, Bonn, and Cambridge universities. His teaching and research interests are in the histories of food and animals, with particular reference to Germany and Japan. His recent publications include the book chapter, "'Sweets Reimagined': The Construction of Confectionary Identities, 1890–1930," in *Feeding Japan* (2017) and "Trichinosis Revisited: Scientific Interventions in the Assessment of Meat and Animals in Imperial Germany" (*Food and Foodways*, forthcoming).

Eric C. Rath is Professor of Premodern Japanese History at the University of Kansas and a specialist in Japanese dietary cultures. His publications include *Japan's Cuisines: Food, Place and Identity* (2016), *Food and Fantasy in Early Modern Japan* (2010), and *Japanese Foodways, Past and Present* (2010), co-edited with Stephanie Assmann. At Kansas he teaches the courses "History of Sushi" and "Beer, Sake, and Tea: Beverages in Japanese History."

Krishnendu Ray is Chair of the Department of Nutrition and Food Studies at New York University. Prior to joining NYU, he was a faculty member and an Associate Dean for Curriculum Development at The Culinary Institute of America. A food studies scholar with interest in the role of immigrants in American food culture, he is the author of *The Migrant's Table* (2004), the co-editor of *Curried Cultures: Globalization, Food and South Asia* (2012), and the author of *The Ethnic Restaurateur* (2016).

James L. Watson is Fairbank Professor of Chinese Society and Professor of Anthropology Emeritus at Harvard University. He is an ethnographer who specializes in southern Chinese rural society. Watson has authored two books and edited nine more on Chinese emigration, ancestor worship and popular religion, family life and village organization, food systems, and post-socialist culture in the People's Republic of China. His food-related volumes include *The Handbook of Food and Anthropology* (ed., 2016); *The Cultural Politics of Food and Eating* (ed., 2005); and *Golden Arches East: McDonald's in East Asia* (ed., 1997), as well as numerous book chapters and articles.

Index

www.ingramcontent.com/pod-product-compliance
Lightning Source LLC
Chambersburg PA
CBHW060150280326
41932CB00012B/1704